ROMANTICISM AND T[

CW00587117

There has recently been a resurgence of interest in the importance of the emotions in Romantic literature and thought. This collection, the first to stress the centrality of the emotions to Romanticism, addresses a complex range of issues including the relation of affect to figuration and knowing, emotions and the discipline of knowledge, the motivational powers of emotion, and emotions as a shared ground of meaning. Contributors offer significant new insights into the ways in which a wide range of Romantic writers, including Jane Austen, William Wordsworth, Immanuel Kant, Lord Byron, Mary and Percy Bysshe Shelley, Thomas De Quincey, and Adam Smith, worried about the emotions as a register of human experience. Though varied in scope, the essays are united by the argument that the current affective and emotional turn in the humanities benefits from a Romantic skepticism about the relations between language, emotion, and agency.

JOEL FAFLAK is Professor of English and Theory, and Director of the School for Advanced Studies in the Arts and Humanities at Western University. He is author of *Romantic Psychoanalysis: The Burden of the Mystery* (2008) and co-editor of *A Handbook to Romanticism Studies* (2012).

RICHARD C. SHA is Professor of Literature and Affiliate Professor of Philosophy at American University in Washington, DC. He is author of *Perverse Romanticism: Aesthetics and Sexuality in Britain, 1750–1832* (2009) and editor of *Historicizing Romantic Sexuality* (2006).

ROMANTICISM AND THE EMOTIONS

EDITED BY

JOEL FAFLAK AND RICHARD C. SHA

CAMBRIDGE
UNIVERSITY PRESS

CAMBRIDGE
UNIVERSITY PRESS

University Printing House, Cambridge CB2 8BS, United Kingdom

Cambridge University Press is part of the University of Cambridge.

It furthers the University's mission by disseminating knowledge in the pursuit of education, learning and research at the highest international levels of excellence.

www.cambridge.org
Information on this title: www.cambridge.org/9781107637283

© Cambridge University Press 2014

First published 2014
First paperback edition 2016

A catalogue record for this publication is available from the British Library

Library of Congress Cataloguing in Publication data
Romanticism and the Emotions / edited by Joel Faflak and Richard C. Sha.
pages   cm
Includes bibliographical references and index.
ISBN 978-1-107-05239-0 (Hardback)
1. Romanticism–Great Britain.   2. Emotions in literature.   3. English literature–18th century–History and criticism.   I. Faflak, Joel, editor of compilation.   II. Sha, Richard C., editor of compilation.
PR448.E46R66 2014
820.9′353–dc23   2013031191

ISBN 978-1-107-05239-0 Hardback
ISBN 978-1-107-63728-3 Paperback

Contents

Notes on contributors

JULIE CARLSON, Professor of English at the University of California, Santa Barbara, is the author of *In the Theatre of Romanticism: Coleridge, Nationalism, Women* (Cambridge University Press, 1994) and *England's First Family of Writers: Mary Wollstonecraft, William Godwin, Mary Shelley* (2004), is guest editor of *Domestic/Tragedy* (1997), and co-editor (with Elisabeth Weber) of *Speaking about Torture* (2012). She is currently writing about books and friends in post-1790s British Romantic-era literary culture.

DAVID COLLINGS, Professor of English at Bowdoin College, is the author of *Wordsworthian Errancies: The Poetics of Cultural Dismemberment* (1994) and *Monstrous Society: Reciprocity, Discipline, and the Political Uncanny, c. 1780–1848* (2009), as well as co-editor, with Michael O'Rourke, of *Queer Romanticisms* (2004–5) and with Jacques Khalip, of *Romanticism and Disaster* (2012). His articles touch on authors such as Godwin and Thelwall, Coleridge and Malthus, and Bentham and Mary Shelley. He has completed a book for a general educated readership, *Stolen Future, Broken Present: The Human Significance of Climate Change*, and his work in progress is tentatively entitled *Disastrous Subjectivities: Romanticism, Catastrophe, and the Real.*

JOEL FAFLAK, Professor of English and Theory and Director of the School for Advanced Studies in the Arts and Humanities at Western University, is author of *Romantic Psychoanalysis: The Burden of the Mystery* (2008); co-author of *Revelation and Knowledge: Romanticism and Religious Faith* (2011); editor of Thomas De Quincey's *Confessions of an English Opium-Eater* (2009); and editor or co-editor of seven volumes, most recently *The Romanticism Handbook* (2011) and *The Handbook to Romanticism Studies* (2012). He is currently finishing a book on Romantic psychiatry, and working on two further monographs, one on Romanticism and the psychopathology of happiness and the other on utopianism in American film musicals.

MARY A. FAVRET is Professor of English and Affiliate Faculty in Gender Studies at Indiana University-Bloomington. Her recent work has taken up questions of affect and history, especially the feeling of wartime, developed in *War at a Distance: Romanticism and the Making of Modern Wartime* (2010). Earlier works include *Romantic Correspondence: Women, Politics and the Fiction of Letters* (Cambridge University Press, 1993) and, with Nicky Watson, the collection *At the Limits of Romanticism* (1994). Two new projects now occupy her: one concerning the relationship between numbers and moral feeling, the other a history of the pains of reading.

JACQUES KHALIP, Associate Professor of English at Brown University, is the author of *Anonymous Life: Romanticism and Dispossession* (2009), as well as the co-editor of *Releasing The Image: From Literature to New Media* (2011) and *Romanticism and Disaster*, a special issue of *Romantic Circles Praxis*. He is also the editor of *Future Foucault: Afterlives of Bodies and Pleasures* (2012). Currently, he is co-editing, with Forest Pyle, a volume of essays on Romanticism and theories of the contemporary, as well as completing a book entitled *Dwelling in Disaster*, a study of Romantic reflections on extinction and wasted life.

THOMAS PFAU is Alice Mary Baldwin Professor of English and Professor of German at Duke University, with a secondary appointment in the Duke Divinity School. A native of Germany, he gained his PhD from SUNY-Buffalo in 1989 with a dissertation on self-consciousness in Romantic poetry and theory (Wordsworth, Shelley, et al.). Since then, his interests have broadened to include topics in eighteenth- and nineteenth-century literature, philosophy, and intellectual history. Besides translating and editing two volumes of theoretical writings by Hölderlin and Schelling, he has edited two essay collections on English Romanticism, two special issues of *European Romantic Review* (2010), and a special issue of *Modernist Cultures* (2005). He is the author of *Wordsworth's Profession* (1997) and *Romantic Moods: Paranoia, Trauma, and Melancholy, 1794–1840* (2005). He has published some thirty essays in numerous essay collections and scholarly journals. His latest study, *Minding the Modern: Human Agency, Intellectual Traditions, and Responsible Knowledge*, has just been published.

TILOTTAMA RAJAN is Canada Research Chair, Distinguished University Professor, and Director of the Centre for Theory and Criticism at Western University. In addition to over seventy articles on Romantic literature, Idealist and Romantic philosophy, and contemporary theory, she is the author of four books, among them: *Dark Interpreter: The Discourse of Romanticism* (1980), *The Supplement of Reading: Figures of Understanding in Romantic Theory and Practice* (1990), and *Romantic Narrative: Shelley, Hays, Godwin, Wollstonecraft* (2010). She has also edited or co-edited six books, including *Idealism without Absolutes* (2004). She is currently working on two books related to the present essay: *Zones of Entanglement: Encyclopedics, Theory, and the University from Hegel and Schelling to Foucault*, and *Reading between Hegel and Schelling*.

RICHARD C. SHA, Professor of Literature and Affiliate Professor of Philosophy at American University in Washington, DC, is working on *Imagining the Imagination: Science and British Romanticism*, for which he has received a National Endowment for the Humanities 2012–13 Fellowship and 2008 American Philosophical Society Benjamin Franklin Research Grant. His previous books and edited volumes are: *Perverse Romanticism: Aesthetics and Sexuality in Britain, 1750–1850* (2009), *Historicizing Romantic Sexuality* (2006), *Romanticism and Sexuality* (2001), and *The Visual and Verbal Sketch in British Romanticism* (1998). In 2014, he plans to team-teach a course on "Thinking Emotion: From Physiology to Ethics" with a neuro-psychologist and an historian.

REI TERADA, Professor of Comparative Literature at University of California, Irvine, is the author of *Looking Away: Phenomenality and Dissatisfaction, Kant to Adorno* (2009) and *Feeling in Theory: Emotion after the "Death of the Subject"* (2001). Her recent essays on various topics (Pasolini, Arendt, impasse, expropriation, student protest) have appeared in journals such as *New Formations, Qui Parle, South Atlantic Quarterly*, and *Studies in Romanticism*.

Acknowledgments

The editors first thank our contributors, whose generous and collegial feeling for, not to mention brilliant thought about the topic have made this an even greater success than we could have imagined. At Cambridge University Press we wish to thank Anna Bond and Vania Cunha for their always patient, punctual, and professional shepherding of the manuscript through to completion. We are indebted, too, to our copy-editor, Rebecca du Plessis. We especially thank our editor, Linda Bree, for recognizing and championing this project's timely and unique approach to its subject matter, and to finding this material a worthy home. We were very happy that external readers for the Press shared this view, and we thank them for invaluable feedback, which was crucial to helping us re-shape the volume's contextualization and representation of the field, all for the better. Joel Faflak wishes to thank the Social Sciences and Humanities Research Council of Canada for funding research time related to the editing of this volume. Richard Sha wishes to thank American University for providing the sabbatical that enabled the editing of the volume, Deans Peter Starr and U. J. Sofia for providing indexing funds, Dianne Hosmer for the index, Trevor Levere for his encouragement, and Joel for endless good cheer and camaraderie. And Joel returns the thanks, in kind.

Introduction
Feeling Romanticism
Joel Faflak and Richard C. Sha

I. Once more with feeling

Recently, economic theory has had to deal with the growing recognition that rational choice theory is impotent because, as it turns out, investors make choices based on emotion. The results are no surprise, although an increasingly interconnected, global economy makes us feel the effects in unanticipated ways. The decisions of a stockbroker battling depression, having fought with his kids while dropping them off to school en route to his downtown office to advise clients on billion-dollar transactions, can trickle down onto markets and populations around the world. Sadly, sometimes a hunch is just a hunch, and, like it or not, emotions are an essential part of human experience: difficult to manage, impossible to ignore. Once a toxic chemical, emotion now fuels the affective turn in humanities and social science research, propelled by a return to the body in feminist and queer theory and the transformation of emotion into a scientific object. From historians like Ute Frevert on the gendered history of emotion and Barbara Rosenwein on the relation between emotion and community; to political theorist Michael Hardt on affective labor; to philosopher and cultural theorist Brian Massumi on affect's virtual environment; to the discovery of mirror neurons in humans as a potential basis for empathy – a renewed interest in the emotions is transforming how we view history, culture, and science. This shift is especially powerful for how it re-thinks the transfer between mind and body in ways that are transforming how we view the "ontology of the human," even at times rendering the "human" suspect. This causality allows us to "illuminate ... both our power to affect the world around us and our power to be affected by it, along with the relationship between these two powers."[1]

Severally global, emotion is the matrix through which the world is brought to our sensoria; it registers our response to this world; it worlds our world and thus makes sense of sense, but *as sense* (as opposed to intellect, to reason, to "common sense") it impresses upon this world a passionate attachment that can be at once compassionate and violent, creative and destructive, energizing and enervating, utopian and dystopian. At its most magical and disturbing, emotion is profoundly anticipatory and prehensive, materializing worlds before we know or even desire their being. To ask how we feel about the world or how it or others feel about us is to register at once the most human and inhuman of responses – care, *ressentiment*, disregard. To feel is also to mark the autonomy of an existence beyond regard. Like Heidegger's *Stimmung* or Schopenhauer's *Wille*, emotion is, one might say, the air we breathe: our very mode of ontological sustenance, but for this reason completely beyond our sight or comprehension except via witnessing and, ironically, *feeling* its effects. It is a knowing beyond thought that requires no knowing, but that makes all knowledge possible. Or to tread into psychoanalytical waters, it is like the unconscious in which we swim: empty the ocean and we're nothing. To put a specifically Lacanian spin on this Jungian formulation: emotions are the not-being-said within the said of human experience.

Perhaps our current fascination with emotion, then, is *because* of its unavoidably paradoxical nature. As one of the most ambient ways of gauging and understanding human sentience, it is at once vital or fundamental and primordial or inchoate, mind and body, material and virtual. But ours is not the first era to have its attention grabbed by emotion. Rousseau's, Byron's, or Hazlitt's erotic confessions; Blake's or Hölderlin's tears; Smith's dark ruminations on historical decline, Hemans's fervent patriotism, More's ardent evangelicism; Goethe's "sorrows," Coleridge's dejection; the passionately melancholic yearnings of Austen's, Wollstonecraft's, Mary Shelley's, Mary Robinson's, or Hays's feminist protagonists; Clare's or Burns's or Wordsworth's pastoral enthusiasms; Baillie's or Beddoes's passionate dramatic forms; Equiano's pleas against the barbarisms of slavery; the Della Cruscans' rhetorical excesses; gothic (in)sensation – all speak to an age compelled by affect's intimate and extimate (re)cognition. Most essays herein take up Romantic literature as the most powerful register of the period's gravitational pull toward feeling. In his 1800 Preface to *Lyrical Ballads* Wordsworth calls poetry a "spontaneous overflow of powerful feeling."[2] Blunted by reiteration, the statement now asks us to resist its earnest effusion. As a sentient gauge of (its) time and place, however, it still has affective immediacy as one of the epochal and epoch-making statements about feeling's nature and status. Calling for poetry's rule-bound idiom to be more, well, idiomatic, Wordsworth marks the reciprocity between aesthetic pursuit and affective reality, but also something out of joint within this transport. Invoking Aristotle's *katharsis ton pathematon*, he speaks of "emotion recollected in tranquility,"[3] which by summoning memory to regulate impulse exposes within the purgation of emotion a temporal delay. The poetry of common life yields to an unmediated force (not yet expression) of human experience that evades our grasp even or precisely as it is tried upon the pulses. This feeling (for there seems no more choate way of saying what "it" is) marks how bodies mark and leave their mark within environments, not just with the body in mind, but as part of a whole sensorium attuned to the transports and shocks of lived experience. It is to this thrown nature of Romantic emotion, to emotional nature itself, that the chapters in this book address themselves.

Not so long ago this issue was dead, or worse, a critical liability. How else to explain why, even after Adela Pinch's *Strange Fits of Passion* or Jerome McGann's *The Poetics of Sensibility*, both from 1996, this volume is the first collection of essays on Romantic emotion?[4] To generalize, early on Romanticism was pegged in two ways: a secular religion of elevated, imaginative (masculine) passion; or a (feminine, often racially other) excess that enervated the pulse[5] of everyday life. Even the period saw itself as a stereotype (think of Austen's *Northanger Abbey* or Coleridge's *Christabel*). Arnold's "premature" view of Romantic creativity, Browning's wish for Shelley's Christianity, George Eliot's imprudent Romantic radicals, or Carlyle's call to forego Byron for Goethe all seem anxious that Romantic feeling passive-aggressively forebodes anarchy. Robert Buchanan disparaged the "fleshly" pre-Raphaelites, whose morbid model was Tennyson's *Maud* (1855), itself symptomatic of Romantic dis-ease (though reviews of Tennyson's 1830 *Poems, Chiefly Lyrical* praised its tempered emotion), or Browning's corpus for devolving from classic Wordsworth reflectiveness to grotesque Keatsianism. All sense, no common sense; all body, no brain; a recessive, effete beauty – the threat of degenerate, animalistic sensation plagued Romanticism's unfit survival, its maladaptiveness, into the twentieth century. Like Freud dealing with "woman," liberal humanism – Eliot's or Leavis's (great) tradition – didn't know what to do with Romanticism's split religion (Hulme) or multiple personality (Lovejoy). To paraphrase Mary Favret, subsequent criticism followed Wimsatt and Beardsley's 1949 attack on affective criticism as sheer (Romantic) subjectivism.[6] Not until feminist theory urged us to reclaim writing minoritized as the "woman's work" of "mere" feeling, especially in a period when women as well as men were taking up the profession of author, was it OK to consider feelings betrayed by an earlier critical "objectivity."[7] Isobel Armstrong has even chided critics for notions of close reading that pay no attention to

the affective elements of a text.[8] The traditional, simple view of Romanticism as a hyper-affective reaction against Enlightenment rationalism did
not survive attempts by M. H. Abrams, Thomas McFarland, and James
Engell to stress both the philosophical robustness of Romanticism and its
intellectual debts to the Enlightenment.

We might say that emotion's current notice is the recurrence of
a Romantic passion for and curiosity about understanding, testing, and
acclimatizing to the very pulses of life – a Romantic response to a modern
problem. For Patricia Clough, the return to "bodily matter" in critical
theory and cultural criticism in order to move past the "constructionisms
under the influence of post-structuralism and deconstruction" marks
"a dynamism immanent to bodily matter and matter generally – matter's
capacity for self-organization in being informational."[9] But this concern
with the "biomediated body" of our "postbiological" age as a "historically
specific mode of organization of material forces" overlooks how Romantic
emotion got there first, exploring itself as (post)human cognition and
experience. *This* return, more than mere historical precedent, foregrounds
Romanticism's contribution to our growing awareness of the centrality of
the emotions by deploying recent critical work on the history of emotions
to reassess Romanticism's ongoing role in writing this history. The essays
in this volume confront us with Romanticism's still unexpected affective
resonance. Julie Carlson on Shelley's similes as political affect, David
Collings or Jacques Khalip on Wordsworth's un-passionate attachment
to being, Richard Sha on Romantic emotion as physiochemical force, Joel
Faflak on the price of happiness, Rei Terada on De Quincey's impassioned
life of ruin – all make us feel Romanticism's profound difference. To wit,
this collection offers fresh directions for the study of Romantic emotion,
including some focus on emotions yet to receive their due, like happiness,
humiliation, and various states of peaceful apatheia or affectlessness. Yet it
also includes a return to old standards like trauma and melancholy – but in
ways that subtly re-think or reconfigure these categories along the trajectory between the pleasure principle and its beyond, known as trauma.

Never idle dabbling nor airy idealism, Romantic experiments with
emotion form the laboratory for current research on the interconnections
between emotion and cognition, as Sha's or Favret's essays remind us.
Recently Antonio Damasio argued that without the emotions moving the
subject out of homeostasis to provide the content of consciousness, there
would be nothing to think about – there would be no thought.[10] Against
Damasio's universalizing of emotion as the constitutive form of consciousness, Daniel Gross implicates emotions within social circumstances,

insisting upon their rhetoricity.[11] This struggle between emotional content and form, between bodily consciousness and (its) history, reminds us that emotions have a temporality as well as ontology, a non-linear, non-causal but also *intentional* and contingent relationality. Mapping this emotional terrain without origin reflects a Romantic idealism that is also Romanticism's crucible, as it has become ours. The currents and undercurrents between and among individuals, groups, and their environments are calling us to account with some urgency. If, as Adorno and Horkheimer say, the human ascendancy of enlightenment "radiates disaster triumphant,"[12] it seems clear we have moved past the religious question "What do we believe?" to the scientific question "What do we think or know?" to ask what might be the vital question of our time: "What and how do we feel?" In a world too much with and upon us, the Romantic desire to distill essence from accumulation calls for us to respond with measured urgency to the shock and awe of a history in flux. Romanticism confronts historical experience *as* flux, a traumatic and traumatizing sense of history that locates affect beyond the pleasure principle. In short, if feeling is the barometer of Romanticism's temperament, Romantic writers in turn asked not only why it was a time *of* feeling but also whose feelings and which feelings counted. The danger of rendering history as trauma is the trivialization of both.

Begging the question stymies solutions but offers possibilities. What often troubles the affective turn in Romantic studies, Favret suggests, is the attempt to categorize what by definition at once sustains and eludes both thought and language. Favret cites Brian Massumi, for whom affect is a "system" of "autonomic responses" that the cognition of emotions "may seize upon ... [in order to] ... 'qualify' or name them, but in doing so it 'dampens' their force or 'resonance.'" Massumi distinguishes affect from emotion, which "is too easily named; it is affect 'owned and recognized'; it translates affect into 'conventional, consensual' form, where it can be given 'function and meaning.'"[13] Terada elaborates further:

> *Emotion* is a psychologically, at least minimally interpretive experience whose physiological aspect is *affect*. *Feeling* is a capacious term that connotes both physiological sensations (affects) and psychological states (emotions). Although philosophers reserve "feeling" for bodily conditions, I use it when it seems fruitful to emphasize the common ground of the physiological and the psychological. *Passion* highlights an interesting phenomenon, the difficulty of classifying emotion as passive or active ... Of course passion's very force makes it seem compulsive. Thus passion drives intentional subjectivity to its self-undoing in senseless vigor – an undoing that does

not have to be figured as decadent excess, but can be conceived as an interior limit of volition. Passion, therefore, characterizes the nonsubjectivity within the very concept of the subject. Finally, *pathos* conveys the explicitly representational, vicarious, and supplementary dimensions of emotion. Scenes are not played for passion, but for pathos; debates about pathos come to be about the relation between representation and intensity.[14]

Keep such designations in mind when reading through the following essays, but bear in mind their contemporary heuristic. Clough tracks emotion's affective valence as what Massumi, addressing the affect of threat, calls a "zone of indistinction," which reminds us how thinking the transfer between affect and emotion – at once constitutive, irreducible, and incompossible – forms the ground zero of affect theory both current and Romantic.[15] This paradoxical transfer informs Terada's sense of passion's "undoing" of "intentional subjectivity" to register the "nonsubjectivity within the very concept of the subject," the non-human within the human. And we can see how *pathos*, indicating emotion's historical or sociopolitical dimension, at once performs and encrypts within itself a kind of primordial condition of theater to which the emotions give dramaturgical shape, a Dionysian energy within their Apollonian form that indicates affect's drive toward emotional effect – the affective resonance or feeling *of* emotion.

Put another way, in Romantic feeling experience and the aesthetic become intimately, irrevocably, unassimilably imbricated. Nietzsche reminds us that, as form's expression of an ineffable content, the aesthetic works by a profound forgetting of its primordial being in sense. To (re)capture this (in)tangible source is to mark the political and ethical dimension of language's mediation *as*, as well as *of*, life. This means that emotion bears the force of tropes and is in fact, as Pinch and Terada remind us, constituted by them. Emotion tropes experience, just as language turns, directs, alters emotion, a transfer that is transferential. In her essay for this volume, Julie Carlson explores Percy Shelley's use of simile as the embodied affect of thought and its "capacity for alterity." Simile registers language's affective pull as the feeling relationality among selves as others. Rather than subordinate or dominate the reality they speak (as in metaphor), similes entrench, temporalize, and defer to the difference they mark from reality. Enacting this difference *of* language as their very constitutive possibility, similes offer a non-defensive, non-coercive relationship to the very antagonisms they stage in turn – simile as a kind of poetic UN, albeit a perhaps more effective political and ethical instrument. Carlson's account of Shelley's language shows how Romantic statements *of* feeling, blunted by reiteration and overdetermined by aesthetic, social, political, and economic forces, arrest and detain us precisely by their continued *in*ability to ring true or clearly.

This volume thus addresses within Romantic thought and writing on emotion a complex range of issues: the relation of affect to figuration and knowing (associationism, empirical psychology, the psychosomatic, imagination, the aesthetic, idealism); emotions and the discipline of knowledge (natural philosophy, moral philosophy, political economy, ideology, science, psychiatry, philosophy); the motivational powers of emotion (volition and the will, the existence of the soul); emotions as a shared ground of meaning (community, nationalism, radicalism, reformation, religion); and the problems of historicizing emotion (gender, sexuality, class, race, ethnicity). Imbricated within a broader matrix of scientific, medical, political, and philosophical explorations of connections between minds and bodies, Romantic writing evolved a robust lexicon for thinking about emotion: feeling(s), passion(s), sentiment, sensibility, sympathy, vitality, volition, fascination, curiosity, magnetism, mesmerism, galvanism, nerves, nervousness, the reflex arc, excitability, irritability. Both consciously and unconsciously this rubric shaped subsequent cognitive discourse – neuroscientists are fond of quoting Adam Smith – and reflects the historical, critical, and theoretical implications of a concern with the emotions in recent humanities and social science research. This affective turn is forging among these fields an interdisciplinarity directly traceable to Romantic thought and speculation on the emotions; which is also to say this new venture continues a Romantic history of the emotions we are only beginning to understand. And yet as trace, Romantic emotions acquire the scars of writing, a fact that Romantic writers could not evade even as they turn to the emotions as a kind of compensatory phenomenality. It is our collective view that the current affective and emotional turn would profit from a Romantic skepticism about the relations between language, emotion, and agency.[16] However much Romantic writers might have wanted to believe that emotions are, in the current evolutionary idiom, actions in the rough, or even to think that it is possible to get in touch with one's emotions, they also insistently registered, as the following essays show, their awareness of the gaps between desire, subject, and action.

II. More than a feeling

Wordsworthian "overflow" signals affect's automatic political, ecological, and ethical power to galvanize others, the ineluctable if overwhelming transfer between bodies and the body politic. Touting the language of common man, Wordsworth distinguishes poetry from prosaic expressions of historical experience and from the deadening scientific or pragmatic impulse to make rational or mundane sense of things as they are, or the vulgarizing impulse of an increasingly mediated society prone to spectacle and sensation, degraded and entropied by its own unrestrained nature. Wordsworth sought what Jeremy Bentham called the "springs of human action." With managerial precision, Bentham groups affects and motives according to two main springs, pain and pleasure, thus forming a delicate balance in which the former, like Brunonian excitability, agitates the latter into action, a "felicific calculus" designed to maximize pleasure for the greater good.[17] Here "spring" suggests at once "source," "agency," "mechanism," or "vehicle" – energy and volition as well as the individual hardwire and social relay by which they are conducted, delivered, disseminated, act and are acted upon in turn. Yet Bentham's efficiency belies what was for most Romantic writers a rather more heterogeneous, complex, and often bewildering experiential range. This may have been Bentham's spur: the impulse to enlighten what resisted scientific or philosophical perception, or to curb social and political menace. At first the impulse is aspiring and inspiring. Wordsworth galvanizes for future audiences the renovating and ameliorative emotional afflatus of what in 1820 William Hazlitt calls the spirit of the age. As Shelley wrote the next year, "the literature of England, an energetic development of which has ever preceded or accompanied a great and free development of the national will, has arisen as it were from a new birth."[18] Thomas De Quincey later elevates the literature of power above the literature of knowledge that is, like Coleridge's fancy, the mere reproduction of data.

Yet various fears trouble these statements: a blunted and entropied inspiration and discernment; emotions outside of discipline; stupefaction by the welter of a burgeoning information age; literature's inability to arrest and galvanize public attention in order to inform, enlighten, and ennoble public taste. All speak to a deeper anxiety about the "springs" of bodily affect. Just as sensation fiction was to remind the realist novel about its autonomous psychosomatic body, Wordsworth saw in gothic writing an affect that can't be controlled, obviated, put to rest. As Joanna Baillie suggests in her 1798 "Introductory Discourse," the dramatization of passion stages its properly social deployment, discharge, and communication. The times became increasingly proto-Victorian (Bentham gives utilitarianism to the Romantics first), calling for the moral hygiene of a body capable of restraining and disciplining its impulses toward the greater good of an industrial, civil, and civilized sphere bent on global advance and moral edification. Romantic surfeits of feeling could be happily spontaneous and potently transformational, but also seemed recklessly progressive, demanding Burkean restraint (or worse) to curb their dangerous enthusiasm. For the Romantics, memory's contemplative authority rallies a restricted economy that processes – "qualifies" or "dampens" – the general economy of affect's powerfully inchoate surplus. Feeling should be reflective as well as expressive. Yet memory also collapses an aesthetic or scientific distance haunted by a virtual affect that elides and confuses epistemological, ontological, and ethical categories, making it hard to tell where subjects and their meanings reside. The hubris behind Bentham's project of emotional calculation should perhaps serve as a shot across the bow of evolutionary theorists of emotion, bent on reducing the emotions to predispositions to action and accomplishing such reduction in large part by labeling emotions that do not lead to action as forms of maladaptiveness that are the deadly exception to evolution's rule.[19] Emotion has become scientific at the expense of what Claudia Johnson called its "egregious affectivity."[20] How much Romantic literature, we wonder, would evolution thereby consign to the dustbin of history? How many Romantic writers would thereby become the evolutionary equivalent of lunch?

The question "What or how do I feel?" invokes the genesis of eighteenth-century discourses on the passions, sentiment, or sympathy in slightly earlier natural rights and social contract theories. More selfless than self-ish, refined attention to one's environment epitomized personal sovereignty as the linchpin of civil society: sensitivity, thoughtfulness, and self-cultivation, the capacity to think and feel about others and thus assume the duty and responsibility of citizen. Yet the excessive qualities of sentiment or later sensibility were also symptomatic of narcissism, introversion, nervousness, doubt, ambition, and a host of enlightenment deadly sins – a sovereignty vexed by its own autonomous functioning. Events before and after 1798 materialized this radical (in)operativeness, despite Hume's contention that reason was inert and only the passions had the power to motivate us. We might say, to paraphrase Chantal Mouffe's point in *The Democratic Paradox*, that feeling signals the failure of democracy's concern for collective sovereignty in favor of liberalism's fetishization of individual rights.[21] Contributor Thomas Pfau argues this shift differently. For Pfau, Adam Smith's *Theory of Moral Sentiments* (1759), whose model of sympathy underwrote the classical political liberalism of eighteenth-century moral philosophy and political economy, constructs a virtual model of sentiment, a "dramaturgy of emotion . . . actualized in . . . social spaces" that makes affective reality "inseparable from its social phenomen-ology, that is, from its mode of appearance as 'behavior.'" Voiding emotion of content, Smith "renders the inner life moral ... precisely [for] its susceptibility to being transformed from mute and inchoate desire into socially expedient sentiment," a precursor of behaviorism. Put another way, sympathy's virtual logic of sentiment stages Bentham's utilitarianism as a specular form that tropes, maps, and regulates emotions as "socially and objectively classifiable phenomena." Democracy's man-agerial success is thus Romanticism's emotional failure as transport, trans-formation, or transgression. Joel Faflak similarly argues that Romanticism's post-moral philosophy trains, administers, and manufactures feelings as manageable behavior within civil society. For Faflak, Jane Austen's fic-tions, particularly her final *Persuasion*, puts this behavior into the cultural practice of a cheerful readerly acquiescence whose harmlessly felicitous payoff is the last influence of a happiness quotient, whose felicific calculus computes our current solution to dread.

Yet there is more than one way to view "failure." As a "zone of indistinction," emotions register the alterity of being within everyday experience, for which we have little regard except when we are nervously compelled by *being* nervously compelled.[22] Like disease in Hegel or like the event for Badiou, emotions are the rupture of a material happening whose break calls forth truth's reality out of truth's non-existence, reminding us of our bodily matter precisely where and when we are embodied as virtual presence. Richard Sha's essay addresses this issue as the motion or *force* of emotion. This "metalepsis" of the human and non-human (mechanical/divine) force constitutes an unstable but productive matrix of relationality through which subjectivity materializes as a non-quantifiable entity that nonetheless has the allure of quantifiability (force = mass × acceleration). In Sha's words, "Emotions ... literally matter because of the force they contain." Exploring elective affinities between Romantic science and literature, Sha sees force as the "mechanism by which the mental becomes somatic and emotion is communicated." Yet force also suggests automaticity, an "agency without an agent." Or rather, emotions lack agency, but not intentionality. In Goethe's *Elective Affinities* and Wordsworth's "A Slumber did my Spirit Seal," Sha reads emotional force as a moving inertia resistant to knowledge, yet one that redefines agency "as the ability to accept and not thwart this unknowing."

For Sha emotions confuse the "border between matter and sociality," so that "affinities are necessarily multiple, and by implication, transient," leaving the borders of and between subjects "fungible." Emotions thus suspend us between solitude and sociality, where the subject is a (no)one or (no)body, what Tilottama Rajan, after (Žižek's) Schelling, calls the "abyss of emotion." For Rajan, taking up Mary Shelley's later fiction as a journey back to Romanticism's *un*Victorian future, this no-zone figures emotional force as something like Hegel's restlessness of the negative, which turns the negative into emotion itself. After Žižek, Rajan calls Romantic emotion "the insistent showing of a missed encounter" that stages how "'the breakdown (failure) of symbolization, which cannot be signified, *shows itself.*'" This failure marks emotion as a "crisis of [Kantian] judgment," one of Romanticism's legacies to a history of affect. At this perverse core of how desire (de)materializes reality we catch a mood of a Romantic futurity "at once traumatic and promissory." Shelley's fictions thus model a Romantic belonging that is neither Lee Edelman's "absolute negation of reproductive futurism" nor the instrumentation of the family unit, but something akin to Nancy's sense of community as an incommensurable status quo among individuals.

Like many of the essays in this book, Rajan's exemplifies recent attempts to gauge the temper or mood rather than delineate the character of Romantic experience. This locates the subject as feeling's effect rather than the other way around and thus takes Romanticism's pulse after the death of the subject.[23] In *Romantic Moods* Pfau argues that Romantic aesthetics "affect" three overarching moods – (revolutionary) paranoia, (post-revolutionary) trauma, (post-Napoleonic) melancholy – that in turn shape and are shaped by the period's historical and political unconscious.[24] That is, Romantic mood already recognizes itself as an aesthetic phenomenon, a virtual or figural construction that marks our perilous connection to and within history. Examining the General Fasts of the late eighteenth and early nineteenth centuries, Mary Favret reads the social aesthetics of a different mood: humiliation. Working from theories of the ideology of affect (especially Silvan Tomkins), Favret explores how humiliation at once galvanizes, alchemizes, and mortifies society. If Coleridge argues for the *Bildungstreib* epitomized and mobilized by the Cleric who models how citizens internalize the psychological idea(l)s of church and state, the General Fast was this process's penitential form. Humiliation forms the fellow feeling of an internalized shame made extimate by statewide deployment, a stain felt on the pulses and bred in the bone of a body politic thus made at once vigilant of and virtually distant from the horrors of war.

David Collings reads Romantic mood at a more ontological and existential level. Asking of Pfau's model how "one mood might modulate into another or encrypt another within itself," Collings, turning to

Wordsworth's verse, addresses the "affective and discursive mobility," the quasi-cognitive nature of emotion that he calls the "mood *of* mood" or "primary affect," the matrix of emotion's possibility. "Primary affect" delineates the transitional space between emotion coming into being *ex nihilo*, as it were, and the world and its history that, in response to it, emotion brings into being. In this way emotion is before *Dasein* as the ground of being: it is a kind of givenness that itself enables the disclosure of being. Emotion isn't quite quasi-cognitive, but neither is it entirely quasi-. Rather, emotion is what Wordsworth calls the "sentiment of being." Again Collings's essay takes us forward to Nietzsche's eternal return to the sentience of the aesthetic as the *Ungrund* of feeling's always already figural quality. This also takes us back to Carlson's or Sha's sense of emotion's agential motion, what Collings calls the "very movement of trope" as "the most adequate language for evoking *Dasein*'s perilous, ultimately unknowable condition."

Collings's, Favret's, or Rajan's essays typify a recent concern with the limits of (Romantic) experience (and limit experiences or affects) previously neglected in the field – war, disaster, ruin, decline, volatility, melancholy, catastrophe, anonymity, disinterestedness – in order to read the precipitous archive of Romantic emotional life as an allegory for our own times.[25] This critical body is animated by a theoretical spirit that, like the mark on Mandeville's face in Godwin's novel or incest in Shelley's *Matilda*, makes trauma at once unavoidable and the constitutive possibility *of* existence, the both irrevocable and unassimilable sign of how we got here.[26] This is once again to invoke Adorno and Horkheimer. As Jacques Khalip suggests in his contribution on Kant (on peace) and Wordsworth (on slumber), however, to pose enlightenment's failure is somehow to encrypt a desire for its recuperation on behalf of the subject whose very legitimacy the failure of enlightenment calls into question. Beyond such illusions Khalip imagines an at once unsettling and comforting sense of living beyond boredom and despair as a way of "thinking and feeling peace" that resists or exists past enlightenment's lure precisely to avoid its implicitly violent nature. This "habituation and acclimatization" to dolorous or inert affects demands neither reparation nor mobilization; it insists upon destitution precisely to do, because it does, *nothing*. Radicalizing Freud's account of trauma and melancholy, Rei Terada makes a similar case for Thomas De Quincey's *Suspiria de Profundis*, whose "account of ruin offers transformation without recovery," an acceptance of trauma without any desire for reparation that constitutes a "nonpathological response to ruin that is not working-through." For Khalip or Terada,

Romanticism offers a productively non-productive design for living a life *of* and *by* the emotions, a stay so utterly against the models of liberal progress, usefulness, and efficacy informing the Romantic and post-Romantic deployment of feeling that it agitates our own liberal conditioning.

Perhaps that is this book's most salient point: Romanticism rarely "felt right" about itself and the paradigms by which it was shaped and that it helped to shape in turn, because feeling right was to ask the wrong question. Among the following essays we witness, like the specter of Brocken in De Quincey, the *umbras* and *penumbras* of an unfolding Heideggerian horizon of emotion between Romanticism and our own time – at once insistent, informative, (self-)reflective, elusive, disruptive, constitutive, and above all moving. This responds implicitly yet incisively to the kind of Habermasian positivism that informs our ongoing mapping of the Romantic public sphere in all its intricacies (one imagines the giddy result of this cultural topography as a cross between the Human Genome Project and Borges). Productively spurred by Feminism and later New Historicism in Romantic Studies, this effort offers a striated, nuanced, thick description of what, apart from stymieing earlier critical approaches, renders Romanticism's cultural apogee at once heterogeneous and incoherent (this might make Lovejoy happy). If the play of Victorian literature and culture caught the resolute conscience of its singular monarch (setting aside her vast stretches of grief), Romanticism was dramatized in one whose mercurial symbolic power was vexed, not by the emotional lethargy of melancholy, which at least sustains a kind of affective status quo, but the schizophrenic result of sheer endurance in madness, a borderline for a state anxious to define its own political, national, economic, social, cultural, and psychological borders. Perhaps this makes George III a rather more prescient and productive bellwether of Romantic emotion than we had anticipated. The Romantic *dramatis personae* explored herein are (dis) passionately (un)attached to their own time, for they begin to understand emotion as the fundamental way in which we are always out of joint with (in) history, a necessary strategy for surviving the times, if not time itself. Together, these essays argue for unacknowledged forms of Romantic emotional productivity especially when they interrupt the possibility of productivity, and in so doing, hope to encourage disruptions of current neuroscientific accounts of emotion that insist upon the automaticity of the emotions at the expense of their intentionality.[27] To the extent that they share goals, the essays question whether emotions are predispositions to action, as scientists are fond of claiming, or whether it is action that makes otherwise excessive emotion intelligible.

We offer our reader one invitation and impose one restriction. However much we and our contributors are implicated with one another in this venture, sparked and challenged by each other's work and shared allegiances, a reader should expect more than variations on a theme. The restriction: do not look among the shared and cumulative knowledge comprised by this volume's essays for a single or coherent theory of affect, or even the desire for one. We take our cue from Melissa Gregg and Gregory J. Seigworth: "[t]here is no single, generalizable theory of affect: not yet, and (thankfully) there never will be. If anything, it is more tempting to imagine that there can only ever be infinitely multiple iterations of affect and theories of affect: theories as diverse and singularly delineated as their own highly particular encounters with bodies, affects, worlds."[28] The invitation: to exploit emotion's resistance to rational categories – indeed, Thomas Dixon questions whether emotion as a singular category has any historical value – to pollinate further the following arguments.

If anything, the essays herein deploy contemporary terminologies to mark the inchoate and inaccessible affective terrain of emotion that Romanticism feels in coming to terms with feeling, and that we are made to feel in turn. The affects they track in Romanticism contribute to a history of emotion, but also thereby read our current fascination with emotion as a form of history. Romanticism's particular job is to reflect this history to us as the shadows its futurity casts upon our present: a profound, and profoundly Romantic, re-thinking and re-feeling of the "ontology of the human" and of human knowledge, along with its costs. The florid elaboration of Romantic culture that is ongoing in criticism is perhaps a symptom of ever-increasing anxiety about the continued viability and authority of the humanities which, by so scrupulously, nakedly, and affectively exposing themselves to self-critique and thus confessing their faults, have exhausted their cultural capital, sold themselves down the river – pick your cliché (maybe this was Monroe and Beardsley's fear). Yet here is the telling catch-22 of this scenario: while some might decry the recent ethico-political turn in Romantic Studies as a diminution of its formal or analytical precision and thus a dulling of its critical focus (which would make Monroe and Beardsley happy), the field has never been more vital, more alive to its own inner resources, and thus to its times' own connection to a Romantic past. We hope in reading the following essays you feel some shivering, shimmering sense of the past's uncanny pull on your affective reality as a world not quite your own, yet all the more precious for that reason.

NOTES

1 Michael Hardt, "Foreword: What Affects Are Good For," *The Affective Turn: Theorizing the Social*, ed. Patricia T. Clough with Jean Halley (Durham, NC: Duke University Press, 2007), xi.

2 William Wordsworth, "Preface to *Lyrical Ballads*," *Poetical Works*, ed. Thomas Hutchinson; rev. edn. Ernest de Selincourt (Oxford: Oxford University Press, 1988), 740.

3 Ibid.

4 See Adela Pinch, *Strange Fits of Passion: Epistemologies of Emotion, Hume to Austen* (Stanford, CA: Stanford University Press, 1996); and Jerome McGann, *The Poetics of Sensibility: A Revolution in Poetic Style* (Oxford: Clarendon, 1996).

5 See Steven Goldsmith, "William Blake and the Future of Enthusiasm," *Nineteenth-Century Literature* 63, no. 4 (2009): 439–60.

6 Mary A. Favret, "The Study of Affect and Romanticism," *Literature Compass* 6, no. 6 (2009): 1161.

7 For instance, the turn to emotion *per se* can be traced to studies of sensibility, such as Janet Todd, *Sensibility: An Introduction* (New York: Methuen, 1986); G. J. Barker-Benfield, *The Culture of Sensibility: Sex and Society in Eighteenth-Century England* (Chicago: University of Chicago Press, 1992); Julie Ellison, *Cato's Tears: The Making of Anglo-American Emotion* (Chicago: University of Chicago Press, 1999); McGann, *The Poetics of Sensibility*; Noel Jackson, *Science and Sensation in Romantic Poetry* (Cambridge: Cambridge University Press, 2008); Christopher Nagle, *Sexuality and the Culture of Sensibility in the British Romantic Era* (New York: Palgrave Macmillan, 2007); or Alan Richardson, *British Romanticism and the Science of the Mind* (Cambridge: Cambridge University Press, 2001); studies of nervousness such as: Peter Melville Logan, *Nerves and Narratives: A Cultural History of Hysteria in Nineteenth-Century British Prose* (Berkeley: University of California Press, 1997); studies of radical culture and emotion such as: Jon Mee, *Dangerous Enthusiasm: William Blake and the Culture of Radicalism in the 1790s* (Oxford: Clarendon, 1992); studies of how emotional regimes acquire resonance and power such as: William Reddy, *The Navigation of Feeling: A Framework for the History of Emotions* (Cambridge: Cambridge University Press, 2001); Saree Makdisi, *William Blake and the Impossible History of the 1790s* (Chicago: University of Chicago Press, 2002); Andrew Stauffer, *Anger, Revolution, and Romanticism* (Cambridge: Cambridge University Press, 2005); Lauren Berlant, *Cruel Optimism* (Durham, NC: Duke University Press, 2011); or via the broad influence of Feminism and queer theory on Romantic Studies.

8 Isobel Armstrong, "Textual Harassment: The Ideology of Close Reading, or How Close is Close?" *Textual Practice* 9, no. 3 (1995): 401–20.

9 Patricia T. Clough, "The Affective Turn: Political Economy, Biomedia, and Bodies," *The Affect Theory Reader*, ed. Melissa Gregg and Gregory J. Seigworth (Durham, NC: Duke University Press, 2010), 206–7. Clough argues that the turn to the "openness, emergence, and creativity" of affect is a way of thinking

otherwise the political economy of what she calls the biomediated body poised
at the "postbiological threshold" of our own times – to think this body's
potentialities and resistances to the "devastating potential of biopolitical racism"
(224). As Clough writes, "a threshold is indeterminate, . . . the limit beyond
which there will have been change irreducible to causes." She begins by invoking
one of this volume's contributors, Rei Terada, who speaks to the role of affect
after the supposed "death of the subject" announced by post-structuralism and
deconstruction. See Rei Terada, *Feeling in Theory: Emotion after the "Death of the
Subject"* (Cambridge, MA: Harvard University Press, 2001).

10 Antonio Damasio, *The Feeling of What Happens: Body and Emotion in the
Making of Consciousness* (New York: Harcourt Brace, 1999), 26.

11 See Daniel M. Gross, *The Secret History of Emotion: From Aristotle's Rhetoric to
Modern Brain Science* (Chicago: University of Chicago Press, 2006).

12 Theodor W. Adorno and Max Horkheimer, *Dialectic of Enlightenment*
(London: Verso, 1997), 3. The full quotation is the opening sentence of the
opening essay of *Dialectic of Enlightenment*, "The Concept of Enlightenment":
"In the most general sense of progressive thought, the enlightenment has
always aimed at liberating men from fear and establishing their sovereignty.
Yet the fully enlightened earth radiates disaster triumphant" (3).

13 Favret, "Study," 1159.

14 Terada, *Feeling in Theory*, 4–5.

15 Brian Massumi, "The Future Birth of the Affective Fact: The Political Ontol-
ogy of Threat," *The Affect Theory Reader*, ed. Melissa Gregg and Gregory
J. Seigworth (Durham, NC: Duke University Press, 2010), 65. We use
Massumi's phrase about emotion less in the exclusive way he attaches it
to threat and as a more general marker of what Melissa Gregg and Gregory
J. Seigworth evocatively refer to as "the affective bloom-space of an
ever-processual materiality" ("An Inventory of Shimmers," *The Affect Theory
Reader*, 9). Here they cite Barthes's idea of the "neutral," not as "ready
acquiescence" or "political neutrality, a lapse into grayness," but as offering a
"neutrally inflected, immanent *pathos* or 'patho-logy' that would be an 'inventory of shimmers. . .' as they gather into 'affectivity, sensibility, sentiment,' and
come to serve as 'the passion for difference'" (11).

16 Thomas Dixon reminds us that the emotions have only been with us for a few
centuries, and that the period between 1800 and 1850 was crucial to the
secularization of the emotions as a psychological category. See Dixon, *From
Passions to Emotions: The Creation of a Secular Psychological Category*
(Cambridge: Cambridge University Press, 2003).

17 Bentham outlines his felicific calculus in Chapter 4 of *An Introduction to the
Principles or Morals and Legislation* (1789), entitled "Value of a Lot of Pleasure
or Pain, How to be Measured." See Bentham, *An Introduction to the Principles
of Morals and Legislation*, ed. J. H. Burns and H. L. A. Hart, intro. R. Rosen
(Oxford: Clarendon, 1996). Bentham measures either pain or pleasure
according to four circumstances: intensity, duration, certainty/uncertainty,
propinquity/remoteness. When estimating the acts produced by pain or

pleasure, Bentham adds two further factors: fecundity and purity. He also provides a table of the springs of human action in his 1815 book of the same name. See Bentham, *Deontology, together with A Table of the Springs of Action and The Article on Utilitarianism*, ed. Amnon Goldsmith (Oxford: Clarendon, 1983).

18 Percy Shelley, "A Defence of Poetry," *Shelley's Poetry and Prose*, ed. Donald H. Reiman and Neil Fraistat, 2nd edn. (New York: Norton, 2002), 535.

19 Damasio writes, "But the fact that the deployment of some emotions in current human circumstances may be maladaptive does not deny their evolutionary role in advantageous life regulation" (*Looking for Spinoza: Joy, Sorrow, and the Feeling Brain* [Orlando: Harcourt, 2003], 39).

20 Claudia Johnson, *Equivocal Beings: Politics, Gender, and Sentimentality in the 1790s* (Chicago: University of Chicago Press, 1995), 1.

21 Chantal Mouffe, *The Democratic Paradox* (London: Verso, 2000), 1.

22 This paraphrases more broadly Massumi's specific point about the impact of threat as what C. S. Pierce calls a "dynamical object," "'something forced upon the mind in perception, but including more than a perception reveals.'" Massumi here argues for the effect of affect more broadly: "At that instant, nothing but this transitional break exists. *Its* feeling, the sudden bustle, fills the still dreamily reawakening world of experience" (Massumi, "Future Birth," 64). As Melissa Gregg and Gregory J. Seigworth, editors of a recently published compendium of current scholarship in affect theory which includes the essay from which we cite Massumi, argue, "Affect arises in the midst of *in-between-ness*: in the capacities to act and be acted upon ... Affect is in many ways synonymous with *force* or *forces of encounter*... At once intimate and impersonal, affect *accumulates* across both relatedness and interruptions in relatedness, becoming a palimpsest of force-encounters traversing the ebbs and swells of intensities that pass between 'bodies' (bodies defined not only by an outer skin-envelope or other surface boundary but by their potential to reciprocate or co-participate in the passages of affect)" ("Shimmer," 1–2). The language here is Deleuzian.

23 This is to cite Terada's point that "theories of emotion are always poststructuralist theories" (*Feeling in Theory*, 3).

24 Thomas Pfau, *Romantic Moods: Paranoia, Trauma, and Melancholy, 1790–1840* (Baltimore, MD: Johns Hopkins University Press, 2005).

25 We are thinking, but not only or exclusively, of Mary Favret, *War at a Distance: Romanticism and the Making of Modern Wartime* (Princeton, NJ: Princeton University Press, 2010); Jacques Khalip, *Anonymous Life: Romanticism and Dispossession* (Stanford, CA: Stanford University Press, 2009); Tilottama Rajan, *Romantic Narrative: Shelley, Hays, Godwin, Wollstonecraft* (Baltimore, MD: Johns Hopkins University Press, 2011), which collects some of her recent writings on what she calls the political economy of melancholy; Rei Terada, *Feeling in Theory*; Thomas Pfau, *Romantic Moods*.

26 But even the visionary or apocalyptic seductions of an earlier criticism (Harold Bloom, Northrop Frye, Ross Woodman), whatever its resolve (one thinks of

the magisterial hermeneutic completion of Wasserman's sublime formalism) and whatever its post-World War II idealism, bore the feeling that it, like the Romanticism it reflected, was never at one with itself (i.e., the ambivalence of Hartman's Wordsworth, a vital correlate to de Man's Romanticism and its lurid specters). Indeed, whatever imaginative and quotidian post-Enlightenment capacities were mobilized in the name of a subject who might transcend historical contingency, the victorious moment was always, well, momentary. We can recall that Lovejoy's anxious psychology informed something like Mario Praz's *The Romantic Agony* (1933), and one conjures in turn their inter-war historical context.

27 See Ruth Leys, "The Turn to Affect: A Critique," *Critical Inquiry* 37, no.3 (2011): 434–72; and Sianne Ngai, *Ugly Feelings* (Cambridge, MA: Harvard University Press, 2005). Ngai seeks to recuperate ugly feelings for critical productivity, even as she turns to them to disrupt both their reduction to mere ressentiment and valorization as "therapeutic solutions" (3). Neuroscientist Joseph Ledoux goes so far as to label conscious feelings that we know and love (or hate) our emotions by [as] red herrings … in the scientific study of emotions, because for him fear is "the system that detects the danger in the first place" (*The Emotional Brain* [New York: Simon and Schuster, 1996], 18).

28 Gregg and Seigworth, "Shimmer," 4.

CHAPTER I

The motion behind Romantic emotion
Towards a chemistry and physics of feeling

Richard C. Sha

This essay considers what it means to think of the emotions in terms of physical force and chemical affinity and the role that Romantic science played in making the emotions manageable. Emotion of course is etymologically connected to motion, and is derived from the Latin "to move" and "to move out." I turn to physics and chemistry, the two disciplines that had the most to say about movement, to challenge the popular view that emotions embody subjectivity, and consequently to resist the narrow framing of emotions as a site of psychological intensity. I also highlight the sustained use of "force" within current and Romantic period affect and emotion theory; if we are still invoking a term from physics and chemistry to think about the emotions, then these disciplines must be doing more than freezing being.[1] Indeed, because Kant thought of matter as being constituted by attractive and repulsive forces, force carries with it a curious materiality that makes the emotions seemingly graspable yet dynamic and hardly simply mechanistic.[2] Not only does matter now have its essence in force, but objects take on a dynamism, which grants them a phenomenality that approaches the psychological. Even within physics, force begins as an analogy to human willpower.[3] Force furthermore gives emotion a generalizable material impact upon the world. Far from severing emotions from a social world as critics ranging from Merleau-Ponty to Daniel Gross contend, chemistry and physics provide ways of thinking about sociality itself insofar as these disciplines attempt to understand in human terms why entities seek association to begin with, and develop concepts that underwrite the language of emotion.[4] The fact that scientists like Humphry Davy and Michael Faraday could turn to "force" to reconcile

I thank Joel Faflak, Jonathan Loesberg, Steve Goldsmith, and Trevor Levere for insightful comments. Trevor Levere gave generously his expertise. The Centre for the History of Emotions at Queen Mary, London, provided a stimulating audience for this essay, and I thank Rhodri Hayward and Allan Young for their encouragement. Helle Slutz helped convert this essay to Cambridge University Press style.

their physics with spirituality underscores the nuanced but neglected possibilities within these sciences.

Force endowed emotion with a vital mechanicity[5] and even spirituality that belies both the traditional Romantic declared disdain of mechanism, and the cordoning off of physics and chemistry from the emotions. Such mechanicity proffered the idea of an integration of person and environment because force permeates all matter. Percy Shelley in *Prometheus Unbound* thought of love, for instance, as a physical force in the universe (that "powerful attraction towards all ... beyond ourselves"), and in his *Lyrical Drama* he compares it to gravity, planetary attraction (Venus), rain, light, electricity, and magnetism.[6] In his "Speculations on Metaphysics," he essentializes differences between "thoughts, or ideas, or notions" in terms of "Force," and thus the term bridges mind and body, thought and emotion.[7] Shelley claims that since we are surrounded by these forces, the absence of love within any particular society (Jupiter's, and even initially Prometheus's own) perverts nature. The key is to embrace and direct them, and by directing them, adopt them as one's own. Force thereby takes on the psychological state associated with emotion.

Mechanics also offered intelligibility, a way of understanding the body as machine and the universe in terms of laws, and mechanics even within the period was crucial to understanding the physiology of the heart, circulation, and nervous and glandular systems. Indeed, it offered an undifferentiated understanding of agency: philosopher Matthew Ratcliffe suggests that agency begins as undifferentiated from others and thus the problem is not the need to bridge a gap between two different mental lives but rather to distinguish human force from surrounding forces.[8] When linked to emotion such mechanical motion skirted the problem of intentionality. Was emotion a physiological movement (understood in part through mechanics as a reaction) or an act of will, as Coleridge insisted love was, or something in between? He comments that "love, however sudden, as when we fall in love at first sight ..., is yet an act of the will."[9]

Coleridge's "yet" hints that mechanism and will are hardly mutually exclusive and love remains willed so long as we identify with love and want it to move us.[10] To harness the intelligibility that came with understanding the body as mechanism without the alleged soul and spirit sapping that came with man as machine, thinkers such as Joseph Priestley, physiologist John Hunter, and Erasmus Darwin developed a vital mechanicity through an electrical body, one that avoided strict mechanism, often by conflating electricity and spirit. Indeed, "motion" and "action" are the very bases of Darwin's ideas about the nervous system.[11] Such vital mechanicity had its origins in a long history of the emotions being both connected to perception and understood as essentially passive (passion and passive are etymologically related), and, paradoxically, in the idea of the emotions as having a direction or motives of their own.[12] Identifying with the force and making it a part of the self allows force to become agency. Allison Muri warns that many have "mistakenly diminished the image of the man-machine to a philosophy that seems to oppose thought, reason, free will, sensibility, orthodox Christianity, or human spirituality," and she demonstrates how mechanicity and vitality were "complementary."[13] Although John Hunter insisted that the body was a machine, he rendered the source of its power as the vital living principle.[14] These thinkers converted spirit into substance with the power to produce motion,[15] and this meant that some strands of vitalism could harmonize physico-chemical forces with vital energy. Hegel, for example, thought that matter was not dead, and that electrical charge was an upsurge of anger in it,[16] and he turns to force to oscillate between pure perception and the nuances of self-consciousness.[17] He thus situates anger on the cusp between perception and consciousness, making it a potential ground of synthesis. While this vital mechanicity conceded the power of emotions to move a person, this did not mean that every emotional movement results in human action. Between emotion, motion, and action, then, could be found a "productive opacity" of force, otherwise known as the space of human will.[18] Articulating the will, in fact, entails distinguishing between the forces that passively move us and the forces through which we allow ourselves to be moved. Crucially, by highlighting the fact of movement and by making movement the sign of visible action, both alternatives allow for the preservation of the ideal of human will, even though movement may amount to merely being moved – passivity – and not with any intended action.[19]

Both physics and chemistry, of course, had a huge impact on Romantic physiology, largely through John Brown's theories of excitability, which listed the emotions and passions as internal exciting powers. The Oxford-shire surgeon Francis Penrose sought to connect recent work in chemistry by Lavoisier and Fourcroy with an understanding of the passions, and he argued in true Brunonian fashion that "the high force of passions that produces indirect debility, must be avoided."[20] If "force" converts other-wise passive passions into actions, it risks debility, making lack of action an action. Commenting on Erasmus Darwin's *Zoonomia*, philosopher and medical practitioner Thomas Brown explained sympathy: "The mental affection, thus excited, induces the motion, by which it is expressed, and is, hence, communicated, with increasing force; till, at length, the general emotion overcomes all, that is private, in the heart, and the burst of enthusiasm resounds, from the whole assembly."[21] Mechanical motion must be excited through vitality. Vitality produces motion. Motion is the mechanism by which the mental becomes somatic, psychological, and communicated; increasing force almost guarantees that sympathy will have not only impact but the right impact. Such automaticity, of course, hinges entirely upon the excitation of the mental affections, and here is where personality, habit, and the individual shape such outcomes.

Alexander Crichton's *An Inquiry into the Causes of Mental Derangement* (1798), a seminal work on the physiology of the passions that influenced Pinel and Esquirol (*Dictionary of National Biography*), solidifies the links between force, physiology, and emotion.[22] Many of Crichton's uses of "force" connect it to the power of the heart to drive the circulation of blood. Crichton suggested that emotions follow passions not in terms of the principles of psychological association but rather it "resembles the motion of a body when impelled by another."[23] Two things are of interest here. One, motion replaces associationism, and physics has something to offer that one of the then most important tools of psychology does not.[24] In a larger view, since so much was understood about the mechanics of blood circulation, nerves were imagined as circulating nervous fluid or force so that science could analogize nervous force from circulation. Two, the bodies he describes are self-impelled, and this raises the question of who or what is in charge. This invests emotion with machine-like automaticity. Crichton's mathematicization of emotional forces – think here of Bentham's felicific calculus – made the emotions and passions seem manipulable, controllable, and subject to logic. At the same time, insofar as forces endow matter with a kind of subjectivity – Levere argues that matter was thought to have emotions[25] – this vital subjectivity within mechanicity throws a wrench into the logic of emotion, but bridges the gap between humans and machines.

But there is more to the productive opacity of vital mechanicity. As we shall see, since force is sometimes understood as a cause whose effect is motion, metonymy – the figure for substitution – shades into a metalepsis that links two things, human force and mechanical force, in such a way that it is not clear which has priority over the other.[26] This absence of ontological and temporal priority opens the identification of cause and effect to interpretation; claims of causality are thus symbolic and metaphorical idealizations[27] and therefore open to contest. Metalepsis (motion replaces force which brings emotion into being) thus disperses human, natural, and divine forces since the origin of "force" is sometimes under natural philosophy, God. "Force," that is, provides agency without an agent because the agent is essentially unlocatable in both time and space, rendering human beings at best nuanced emotional machines and at worst passive objects or forces of God. Briefly, as "cause of the change in the state of the body when being at rest it begins to move," force is visible only as motion.[28] This unlocatability is exacerbated by the fact that force's links with causality make it both internal and external to materialization, further granting it the power to slide between cause and effect. Under Newtonianism, which insisted that things are prior to action, force as thing was incoherent. Hence dynamists like Leibniz and Kant redefined things in terms of action/force – "things exist only so long as they act" – making force a form and cause of materiality and the very essence of thingness.[29] Emotions therefore literally matter because of the force they contain.

"Force," I argue, thus offers emotion studies a moving conceptual place-holder, one which provides to the emotions the aura of effectivity and materiality, because emotions themselves are rendered into dispositions for automatic action without clear actors: at times, the disposition sufficed as action. The ability of force to slide between cause and effect confers upon it a vitality that allows when convenient the illusion of human control, and, in times of skepticism, the sense that we are helpless bystanders to the forces which move us. Isabelle Stengers argues that under dynamism, "cause is what is exhausted in producing the effect, while effect, in exhausting itself, will in turn reproduce the cause," and the upshot of the relationship of conservation that cause "shares with that effect" is that nothing has been allowed to escape scientific measurement and description, even as cause has miraculously become effect.[30]

As both vital and mechanistic, "force" in Romanticism anticipates today's emphasis on the vitality of otherwise automatic affects, which worked then to attenuate the downsides of automaticity, and which now "allow the vitality affects to escape from the strictures of hard-wired fixity."[31] Automaticity and autonomy have always been at odds since automaticity is a mindless mechanical causality that seems inhuman because it lacks purposive activity, and yet given the tenacious historical linkages of automaticity and emotion, especially with regard to the passions, can purposive activity be made intelligible without recourse to mechanical comparisons?[32] Recognizing where the self stands with regard to the forces around it is the start of something like meaningful intentionality: assessing the motivating forces by which we are impelled is the very ground of autonomy.[33]

Force and current affect theory

Because force now is divested of any animistic associations, and because it has become purely relational and describes an interaction between two things,[34] affect as force disrupts subjectivity and notions of the human.

Force thereby helps either to ontologize post-structuralism's death of the subject, or to ontologize queerness (sometimes these alternatives amount to the same thing).[35] By rendering suspect the already constituted subject since constitution is thought inimical to change, force replaces that subject with relationality and potentiality. Patricia Clough puts money on those affect theorists who "conceptualize affect as pre-individual bodily *forces* augmenting or diminishing a body's capacity to act."[36] Here is Sara Ahmed: "we need to consider how emotions operate to 'make' or 'shape' bodies as forms of action, which also involve orientations towards others" and thus she studies "how they 'stick' as well as move." Though she does not use the term "force," her sense is that emotions circulate between the internal and the external, cause and effect, and thus circumscribe a mere relationality.[37] She thereby makes emotions virtual forces that shape the very borders of subject and object.[38] Brian Massumi links affects with "transduction, ... the transmission of a force of potential that cannot but be felt."[39] And here is Eve Sedgwick: "if that sprawling body offered testimony [Sedgwick's own after she collapsed during a protest], it was less to a triumphal purposiveness than to a certain magnetic queerness (by magnetic I mean productive of deviance)."[40] Clough, Massumi, and Ahmed further profit from the ability of "force" to move between cause (it impels movement) and effect (motion is the effect of such movement), and this temporal depth where cause is mapped onto effect grants the emotions the status of event that leads, miraculously, to nothing less than the formation of the subject or to the ontology of change (a transmission that cannot but be felt) or queerness.[41] Sedgwick too profits from "magnetism" as deviance, which queers one of the earth's basic forces at the expense of giving it an intentionality it cannot have. If force currently enables an agency without a human subject, what distinguishes emotion from physics? No wonder a recent critic of the turn to emotions and affect argues that "it ... suppl[ies] the evidence for change when no other evidence presents itself." He concludes, "when do the emotions stand in for jeopardized or attenuated agency?"[42] We are still, like the Romantics, harnessing the elasticity of force either to grant ourselves agency at the expense of a mechanistic materiality, or to emphasize the vitality of matter in hopes that the mechanical automaticity of our emotions will not disallow the possibility of choice or will.

For the Romantics, however, force was oft aligned with animism and vitality, and this meant that if force conferred on the emotions the possibility of rational understanding, as in Newton's second law of force $=$ mass $\times$ acceleration, the ambiguous ontology of force threatened to undermine such control. The difference between emotion and motion is a real problem for the Romantics (hence their declared hatred of mechanism), even as they seek to elide the two. For Newton, there was innate force, inertia, and external "impressed" force that is external to bodies, and this begs the question of where external force originated.[43] Newton himself hypothesized in Query 31 of the *Opticks* that God's agents preside over those forces.[44] This uncertain origin of force meant that it could be harnessed by whatever theory of agency was needed, but that theory of agency at least presents the missing subject as something to be mourned.

Even within physics the concept of force was borrowed from an analogy to human willpower or muscular effort and became projected into physical objects as the power of inanimate things.[45] David Hume understands the emotions in terms of Newtonian force yet he modifies Newton to think of force as the quality of the mind's attention to its own ideas.[46] Since physicists based the concept of force upon human power, thinking about emotions as forces did not entail their autonomy from personhood.[47] That is, emotions are not necessarily extravagant and beyond the individual in the ways that Adela Pinch insists upon because force maps human will onto the world, and makes matter sympathetic, rather than indifferent to human beings.[48] At issue, then, is the metalepsis between the human and the mechanical/divine within the term force, itself a metonymy for emotion, and this metalepsis confers upon the emotions a curious yet capacious form of materiality and agency, one whose ground is on the move from the outside to the inside and back again. While materiality offers the laws of physics as a lever for control over emotion, this dynamic materiality complicates human agency insofar as it resists the determinism of Newtonian mechanics.[49] Nonetheless it makes human agency a mediation between subjects and objects that at times obey the laws of force but at other times assert vitality not merely subject to physics and chemistry. Put in its most positive terms, force suggested a somewhat seamless interaction between inside and outside, and if one could control it, one might manipulate both the self and its environment.

Hence, for Byron, thinking about human beings as subjects of multiple, quantifiable, and conflicting forces like emotions helped him to understand why human history so often repeated itself. The motion behind emotion further enabled him to see human beings as victims of circumstance; this is after all the poet who thought of the human body at present as contained: "a sad jar of atoms."[50] Part of the attraction of force is that it connects the outside to the inside. Hence in the fourth of his orientalist tales, *Lara*, Byron bemoans the "oft-repeated tale of strife," war. Notably,

Byron here levels distinctions between East and West, Turks and non-Turks, by making universalizing claims about human vulnerability to the emotions through the language of force. Byron comments,

> In this the struggle was the same with all;
> Save that distempered passions lent their force
> In bitterness that banished all remorse.[51]

Byron frames the emotions here as almost having an intrinsic force of their own: "distempered passions lent their force." Much in the way that physicists used force to equivocate between cause and effect, Byron situates the emotions somewhere between them. On the one hand, *distempered* passions are an effect because the passions were originally tempered; on the other hand, they also play the role of a cause since they then *lend* their force. Byron's choice of "lending" as opposed to giving bears comment. Lending implies something like the overall conservation of force in that forces do not have the power to give; any force they have is borrowed from somewhere else. The fact that "remorse" has been banished implies that remorse is the baseline emotion, but that it has been displaced by distempering, which in turn allows bitterness to take the place of remorse. As the names for a set of interchangeable emotions – remorse and bitterness – Byron thinks of emotions as metonyms for the forces that make human beings beholden to circumstance. To wit, Byron refers to Lara early on as "Lord of himself; – that heritage of woe,"[52] rendering autonomy as the accretion of past woes. The subject as cause becomes the net effect of the forces of emotion, and the poet's 4/6 split in syllable count overwhelms the cause (autonomy) into effect (woe). Byron recognizes that emotion nonetheless may lead to intentionality once one distinguishes the psyche from the forces surrounding it, as his semi-colon ("himself;") attempts to do.

Romantic chemistry: affinity and emotion

In Romantic-period chemistry, "force" is a term borrowed from physics but one also wrapped up in the concept of affinity, first developed by Albertus Magnus in 1250. Eighteenth-century chemists began to understand affinity as a property-bearing principle: by 1770, for most chemists, principles were material, with modes of action.[53] The language of force equivocated between idea and thing, enabling traffic between propositions and things, and therefore the disciplining of things into objects. Where objects necessarily bear the trace of the subject looking at them, things resist the subject position, and, in the process, become subjects. Even worse, although Lavoisier tried to mathematicize the field primarily through measuring weight and the matter of heat, the concept of affinity – the attractive force of one entity for another – remained qualitative, approaching qualia, the subjective sense of something. The solution was to create tables of affinity so that the occult nature of force did not have to be dealt with: tables of affinity regularized the interactions of metals and salts to laws and sets of numbers that had some predictive value. Numbers promised some order over chemical "rapports," and these tables were elaborated over the eighteenth century. This promise was strengthened when Lavoisier noticed that chemical reactions were always accompanied by changes in heat, and thus the calorimeter could provide a reliable measure of chemical attraction.[54] Keats's "pleasure thermometer" associated with *Endymion* works precisely on this principle: heat indexed pleasure insofar as it showed a chemical reaction and therefore the work of affinity.[55] In his 1779 "General Consideration on the Nature of Acids" paper, Lavoisier looked forward to the day when "one arrives at determining the degree of affinity ... with all the substances with which it is susceptible of being combined."[56] Insofar as Lavoisier made heat and affinities part of the constitution of chemical bodies, he strengthened the causal connections between force and substance, and helped chemists to "characterize composition as the result of affinities, rather than encompassing affinities as a facet of composition."[57] Once again substance is imbedded in causality, and the force of emotion was thereby materialized into elements with desires that have palpable designs upon us.

On a deeper level, distinguishing between theory and practice gave chemists two lenses through which to view the force of attraction, as well as offering the possibility of thinking about affinity as a concept that made chemical combinations intelligible without committing any one necessarily to claims about ontology. Caught between ontology and epistemology, affinity and its dynamism could temporarily suture the two. The ambiguous status of chemistry as science, along with its need to purify nature into commodities,[58] made such sutures more necessary since the vulgarity of trade could be offset by the promise of intelligibility of substances. In chemistry, the relationship between practice/ontology/experimentation and theory/intelligibility was complicated, due to the fact that chemistry was a practical science, tied to commerce, but the field cried out for the intellectual cachet that theory might provide. We should also not lose sight of the possibility that mechanics was a useful form of explanation but entailed no necessary ontological claims. To wit, about 1800, "dynamical" "implied a view of the world in which the phenomena were to be described in terms of forces."[59] Note the scrupulous avoidance of ontology.

Like Lavoisier, the meteorologist John Dalton took comfort in the fact that "the force of a mass of elastic fluid is directly [sic] as the density;"[60] he proposed that the structure of compounds could be expressed in whole number weight ratios and thus mathematicized and mechanized what had been understood under the rubric of affinity and made it picturable into chemical atoms. He quite literally believed that atoms were solid and spherical, and that they combined in "accord with simple mechanistic considerations."[61] For Dalton, mechanical processes were sharply differentiated from those of affinity,[62] and thus he makes every effort to split mechanicity and vitalism, physics and chemistry. He accomplishes this by converting anything smacking of vitality like force into a property of matter, a transition finessed by force's ability to hover between causality and materiality. Although he admitted that "we remain ignorant of the attractive force," his December 1803 Royal Institution lectures listed "extension, Motion – forces" as "properties of matter."[63] Ultimately, his ability to produce physical pictures of chemical atoms and their combinations satisfied his version of intelligibility,[64] and Dalton's wooden models of chemical atoms combining inadvertently helped to leave the basis for attraction vague while popularizing and concretizing his chemical theory.

Yet affinity meant that matter too had emotions since substances had attractions and repulsions for one another.[65] Not only does this imply that the study of matter is central to the history of the emotions, but also that the metalepsis between human and natural force helped to make matter far from indifferent to the human, and even more human. At the same time, the idea of emotion as force allowed the short-circuiting of emotion and action into movement, defending in advance the emotions from fecklessness. If emotion is movement, the price for emotional efficacy is that human beings become more like living automata whose automaticity is paradoxically attenuated by the emotions within matter.[66] Emotional efficacy had the further benefit of leveling the hierarchy between subjects and objects. The famous chemist and friend of Byron, Coleridge, and the Shelleys, Humphry Davy, wrote in 1796, "far from being conscious of the existence of matter, we are only conscious of the active powers of some being."[67] The Romantic ability to see objects as living things – recall Wordsworth's demand that we "see into the life of things" – defuses the subject/object binary into that of being and being, a maneuver, pace Kant and his noumena, that both enhances the ability of humans to make claims about the natural world because they are not necessarily apart from it, and allows mechanism to become suffused with vitality. Human agency, thus, must be situated in an environmental context since there are no absolute distinctions between subjects and objects. In his early years, Davy conceived of matter in terms of "actual central corpuscles whence forces radiate,"[68] and this theory enabled him to unify matter under the umbrella of force as well as to allow chemistry to remain compatible with natural theology. Trevor Levere argues that religion played an important role in Davy's and Faraday's selection of scientific theories;[69] their demonstration of the unity of chemical and electrical forces allowed them to show the divine wisdom of the cosmos. Physics and chemistry were thus ultimately compatible with spirituality, and vital mechanicity was hardly necessarily bereft of the human.[70]

Seeking to discover the source of love's and beauty's power, John Keats turned to chemistry in *Endymion* as if it could explain why human beings are moved. In the poet's *Anatomical and Physiological Notebooks*, he captures the age's prevailing mechanical understanding of how the passions, raw emotions, interact with the endocrine system: "The Passions of the Mind have great influence on the Secretions, Fear produces increase [of] bile and urine, Sorrow increases Tears … Fluids when agitated in a particular Manner will change their nature and that the gland performs an operation similar to Churning in which Cream is changed into Butter and Butter milk."[71] The poet describes the glands' power to agitate the fluids along with the capacity to convey force and thus transform substances much in the same way milk becomes butter or buttermilk; emotions like fear increase the fluids which in turn puts pressure on the glands. Endymion implores, "what is there in thee, Moon! That thou shouldst move / My heart so potently."[72] As the science of substances, chemistry promised to pierce the internal matter of things, and the two chemistry courses Keats took at Guy's Hospital[73] prepared him to think about affinity and force and their curious relation to matter. Affinity inhered in matter, but could affinity explain matter? Keats pointedly asks what is *in* the moon that moves his heart. The ability of force to elide substance and movement at once grants an incipient emotion materiality and effectivity.

When Endymion listens to Glaucus' tale of having been seduced by Scylla, he comes closer to an answer. Glaucus describes Scylla's "urn of tears" and promise that she will "pour / From these devoted eyes their silver store, / Until exhausted of the latest drop, / So it will pleasure thee, and force thee stop / Here, that I too may live."[74] Keats here creates a metonymic chain of signifiers – tears, pleasure, force, language – and by reforming pleasure from a noun into a verb, he signals awareness of how force can be noun and verb, substance and action. That Keats highlights the "dew of her [Scylla's] rich speech"[75] links the first term in the chain, tears, with the last, and thus condenses pleasure and force into the poet's language. The implicit logic here is that if understood as a force, pleasure has the inertial power to arrest Glaucus in the same way that Keats hopes his language will still readers. Indeed, the poet's insistent and violent caesuras – one occurring in the first foot of the final line quoted just after the enjambment only to be followed by a second medial caesura – do stop readers in their tracks. Given that Humphry Davy had noted both that silver was a good conductor and that it has "considerable tenacity,"[76] Keats's specification of silver tears may have also attempted a material explanation for the power of those tears. After all, silver had known medical uses in the caring of wounds, preventing what would later be known as infections, and in the treatment of venereal diseases. The *Edinburgh New Dispensatory* (1789) even listed it frequently in its "Tables of Attractions" and "Affinities,"[77] documenting its ample attractive powers, and therefore its capacity for dynamic interaction. Notwithstanding these powers, and in spite of her ambrosial breath, "Scylla [was] quite forgot," which reminds us that any emotional force relies on the frail powers of human attention. Any material basis of such force is further ironized by the fact that Glaucus' arrest serves as an allegory for Endymion's, and by the poet's proliferating and wayward quest romance that externalizes the emotions onto the landscape, giving them whatever momentum the poem has.

Romantic-period chemists acquired the power to break affinity, and this indeed promised further mastery over the natural world and over the emotions. Indeed, unbeknownst to Keats's Glaucus, Humphry Davy had noted that "silver is easily separated from solutions in which it exists by muriatic acid."[78] Volta's invention of the battery in 1800 further enabled Davy to overcome affinity through the decomposition of compounds into elements. In Davy's 1807 essay "On the Chemical Agency of Electricity," he argued that the "attractive and repulsive forces are sufficiently energetic to destroy or suspend the usual operation of elective affinity," rendering affinity more firmly within man's grasp. He speculated that chemical affinity and electrical affinity were "identical" and "an essential property of matter."[79] Electrical affinity also could be measured with a Voltaic apparatus,[80] and with the quantification of force, rational understanding of the emotions seemed possible.

Given advances in the scientific ability to break chemical affinity, it is especially curious that in Goethe's 1809 *Wahlverwandtschaften*, commonly translated as *Elective Affinities*, the chemical analogy to human emotion provides so little mastery.[81] The German refers to the tendency of chemical entities to combine or reject combinations, largely for reasons unknown. More specifically, *Wahl* means both choice and implies a qualitative selection; *Wahl* itself is on the cusp between the psychological and chemical, for what would it mean for chemicals to make qualitative relationships (*Verwandtschaften*)? Even as Ottilie stops eating because she cannot marry Eduard, who is already married to Charlotte, the power of attraction between Ottilie and Eduard does not dissipate. The narrator comments, "now as before they exerted an indescribable, almost magical power of attraction over one another."[82] If "magic" and "indescribable" threaten to situate *Wahlverwandtschaften* outside of science and language, so too do these forces seem uncannily outside of Eduard and Ottilie, thus recalling Charlotte's claim that violent passion extends "outwards from ourselves." In the original German, the sentence reads: "Nach wie vor übten sie eine unbeschreibliche, fast magische Anziehungskraft gegen einander aus" (*EA*, 248). The German syntax makes Eduard and Ottilie float between subjects and objects because the force is *gegen einander* or *between* them and therefore not *in* them, and the *sie* pronoun (meaning "they") is literally separated from the force by a comma, much like the verb is dispersed (*übten . . . aus*) between the two sides of the sentence (the verb is *ausüben*, to exert). The paragraph in which this description occurs, moreover, only refers to Eduard and Ottilie as pronouns that within that paragraph actually lack a specific referent. These attractions occur without them "exactly thinking of one another" (*EA*, 229). Together, the externality of the emotions heighten the power of them over us, and Goethe underscores this because *Anziehungskraft* also means magnetism, or gravity, or the forces that allow different compounds to cling together.

Charlotte claims that the use of affinity to speak of human beings is "playing with analogies" (*EA*, 33), but this is to ignore the play within the title itself. Goethe's title announces difficulty rather than illumination: as force veils its origin – who or what is choosing? – the only certainty is that affinities are necessarily multiple, and by implication transient. This plurality suggests that marriage is ill equipped to deal with emotion, especially since emotion is a force that extends well beyond the human. Walter Benjamin put it thus: "At the height of [the characters'] cultivation, they are subject to the forces that cultivation claims to have mastered, even if it may forever prove impotent to curb them."[83] Goethe, commenting on *Werther*, phrased it better: "I found myself therefore in the position where any attraction, as long as it appears in a semblance of disguise, succeeds in creeping up upon one unawares and can thwart all one's best intentions."[84] Here, the very effectivity of the "attractions" is contingent upon their triple cloakedness: they appear in the semblance of disguise (why does Goethe need both semblance and disguise?) and they thwart intention by becoming intentionality without intention. This insistence upon appearance implies that chemical affinity can only be gauged through visible effects whose meanings cannot be known in advance. Indeed, unbeknownst to the Architect, he is in love with Ottilie.[85] To the extent that chemistry provides an essence, that essence is shrouded in mystery. Benjamin further argued that "emotion is precisely that transition in which the semblance – the semblance of beauty as the semblance of reconciliation – once again dawns sweetest before its vanishing,"[86] and this captures well the lived intensity Goethe accorded the emotions; his sense that the emotions embodied transition, not telos, because new affinities are always possible; and the essential status of the emotions as appearances, semblances. The gap between the appearance and the emotion ironizes any knowledge claims about them.

What mastery over emotion can be had, thus, comes with the realization that emotion has a paradoxically moving inertia, an implacable resistance of emotion to external force – namely, morality, architecture, mediation (*Mittler*), aesthetics, knowledge, and even intentionality – that would bend them to any particular narrative. No longer inert, this inertia functions as a problematic figure of autonomy itself, problematic because it is a property of matter that is passive. Goethe redefines agency as the ability to accept and not thwart this unknowing. Although Charlotte deals with her love of the Captain and the threat this poses to her marriage with Eduard by invoking "courage to alter our situation, since it is not within our power to alter our feelings" (*EA*, 84), even this quite limited form of mastery – the mere power to change the situation – proves unhelpful. Charlotte warns Ottilie at the novel's end to "beware" of seeing Eduard again after having renounced him (*EA*, 219). Charlotte continues,

> Away from the person we love, the intenser our feelings are, the more we seem to gain mastery over ourselves, because we turn inwards the whole violence of our passion, which formerly extended outwards from ourselves; but how soon, how rapidly we are undeceived when the person we thought ourselves able to do without suddenly stands before us again, and doing without him is impossible. (*EA*, 219)

Here, mastery is illusory, and although Goethe seems to grant the agent's power to shift the direction of the force from outwards to inwards, whatever agency is gained proves detrimental to his or her health. Likewise, Eduard interprets Ottilie's renunciation of him as a ruse, "only so that a man may seem to have a will of his own and to be free to choose" (*EA*, 228). Formally, Goethe proliferates characters, each threatening possible new combinations, and potentially destabilizing old ones. Likewise, he proliferates heterogeneous predigested narratives – Ottilie's diary, the story of "Strange Neighbors," and Eduard's letter to Ottilie – as if to suggest aesthetic form is itself the product of chemical affinity.

Despite the enormous influence that the force of emotion and beauty has upon us – Charlotte claims to have been "forced" by her feelings (*EA*, 228) – Goethe nonetheless insists that human nature is far less changeable than we think it is. Part of the reason is that he posits "every attraction is mutual" (*EA*, 166), a theory no doubt therapeutic to the male ego. Goethe elaborates:

> There is more repetition in a person's life than we suppose. His own nature is the immediate cause of it. Character, individuality, disposition, bent, locality, surrounding, and habits make up an entirety in which a person lives, as in an element, an atmosphere, and only in that element does he feel himself contented and at ease. And so we find human beings, about whose changeability there is so much complaint, after many years, to our amazement, not changed at all, and after an infinite number of inner and outer stimuli in fact unchangeable. (*EA*, 21)

The concept of affinity allows Goethe generally to understand the emotions metaleptically as both cause and effect, and thus the very essence of being to the extent that emotions become habitual. Think of all his characters who name the passions as the cause of their decisions. In the passage above, although human beings are beset by "an infinite number of inner and outer stimuli," our very nature causes repetition, not change. The fact that humans are "at ease" within a certain element or atmosphere means that change is actively discouraged, and that the laws of inertia partly apply to humanity. Humans are like chemical elements, and their character ensues from their essence. Indeed, what should redound to the subject's control or self – the resistance to stimuli – is actually framed as the result of essence. On the one hand, we can resist both inner and outer stimuli. On the other hand, such resistance is really the pursuit of our very nature, an elemental nature that is most content within a particular environment. If Goethe widens the scope of agency to include one's environment, then, the price of such broadened powers is a kind of passive but moving inertia or automaticity or homeostasis.

At the same time, he has helped to make emotions both cause and effect: in short, our very, if figural essence.

And yet this essence is expansive. Affinity remains external to materiality and nonetheless finds its way inside it, and all this serves to break down the borders between people and their environments. This curious immaterial materiality makes affinity so slippery and thus so useful; it is at times material, and at other times merely proximate to materiality; at times cause, and at other times effect. Goethe illustrates how the very slipperiness of force makes it useful: "In general a family's usual mode of life, engendered by the given persons and necessary circumstances, will take even an extraordinary new affection, a developing passion, into itself as into a new vessel, and quite some time may elapse before this new ingredient causes any noticeable fermentation and rises foaming over the brim" (*EA*, 49). Persons and circumstances "engender" (*EA*, 53), allowing a metalepsis between personhood and the environment, one underscored by the modifier *gegebenen* for persons, which means "given," but which echoes with *Umständen*, the word for circumstances. Persons and circumstances furthermore function as the compound subject doing the engendering in this phrase. The metaphor of chemical reactions changes the family from one vessel into another even as the developing new affection has no immediate perceptible effects, but undergoes the work of fermentation, which, in turn, eventually demands a new vessel as containment. Here, Goethe frames the developing passion as external to the family yet incorporated within it, and in the process, changing the family itself. While "developing" indicates ontology in process because materiality has become materialization, the reaction interacts with the vessel itself. Goethe understands both identity and sociality here as processes of chemical materialization, with the end result that all are constantly open to the possibility of change but nonetheless remain surprisingly constant. Chemistry thus provides the explanatory mechanism for how the internal forces interact, stitching together the unseen with the seen.

So too is the border between matter and sociality confused: Goethe insists that "the Captain was already beginning to feel that a process of irresistible habituation was threatening to bind him to Charlotte" (*EA*, 56). Goethe's choice of "habituation" to describe affinity locates the event on the very border between nature and culture, the material and the social, and this disperses intentionality into an environmental field. Emotion, thus, is the materializing nodal point between such binary oppositions as nature/culture, individual/social, chemistry/subjectivity, self/environment, and mind/body that either extends the reach of agency or diminishes it to passivity so that arguments about blame or lack of responsibility can be made, which, in turn, makes agency rhetorical.

Romantic physics and the force of emotion

Force in Romantic physics also moves from being a metaphysical concept to a measurable, calculable, empirical entity, and this movement likewise tames emotion into a dynamic object of knowledge. Because physics then increasingly emphasized the dynamism of matter, physicists thus are hardly necessarily engaged in the process of freezing being, as Merleau-Ponty charged.[87] The elasticity of the concept "force" helped align being with becoming. Newton defined force as both internal and external: inertia and the external force necessary to move an object. Newton's definitions of force are problematic in that they are immaterial concepts and causes, not subject to empirical investigation, and in that matter is endowed with an internal force that resists demonstration. In this view, force is a metaphysical concept whose effect is motion. In 1803, French politician and mathematician, Lazare Carnot, proposed a way around metaphysics by identifying force with the quantity of motion that a force caused in a body.[88] Carnot must translate force as cause to effect as motion. When explaining forces to children in one of his Christmas lectures, Michael Faraday pulled a piece of paper over with an attached string, and then proceeded to equate the power of his hand with "force."[89] Force is best understood in relation to human power, and only later does it become a property of things. The ability of force and emotion to connect the human and the non-human, then, promised some agency that extended into the environment, so long as the connections could be understood.

Within Romantic period physics, force is important because of its "unique position among all possible basic concepts in physical science since it may be regarded as having a direct relation to the concept of cause." Not only does the "concept of substance derive from the empirical applications of the principle of causality," but also "causality, thus attached to substance, is called 'force' and the substance to which the actions of this force are referred is regarded as the 'carrier' of this force."[90] In a similar vein, emotion as force enables each to carry the other, with the immateriality of the one reinforcing the materiality of the other, and the upshot of all of this is a unity between inner and outer worlds, mind and body. For instance, in an essay on matter and its relation to force, Michael Faraday built upon a British tradition of force atoms, which regarded the atomic center as being surrounded by spheres of attraction, and he argued that we can only know matter by the properties it exhibits. Faraday continues, "these properties belong to it by virtue of the forces which belong to it and in no other way; for, by consent of all natural philosophers, the word force or forces is used to express that which gives to them their properties or powers." He summed up the relation between matter and force by conflating them: "the force is an essential property or part of the matter and, to speak absurdly, the matter without the force would not be matter."[91] By making matter and force interchangeable, Faraday rendered matter dynamic, force substantial, and force essentially active and not merely mechanical. Historian of science David Gooding comments: forces "are the active bases of physical reality."[92] Materiality thereby shades into materialization – the thing has become a process while the agent has become a thing. As the name for the relationship between cause and thing, force then helped to make emotion substantive and impactful.

In 1818, Faraday would give a lecture for the City Philosophical Society on "Observations on the Inertia of the Mind" that would explicitly connect physics with emotion. Like Goethe, he claimed, "Whatever is in motion is by it retained in motion; and whatever is at rest, remains at rest under its sway. It opposes every new influence, strengthens every old one." Beginning with the idea that man is "an improving animal," he grants humanity a forward momentum that moves through inertia towards progress.[93] He elaborates:

> The centripetal force, the centrifugal force, the force resulting from chemical action and that which originates in muscular exertion are at all times active in changing and varying the states induced by inertia, sometimes aiding, sometimes counteracting its effect. – These are represented among intellectual beings by the sensations, perceptions, passions, and other mental influences which interfere, (frequently so much to our inconvenience) in the dictates of our reason.[94]

Several features here demand comment. Note Faraday's implicit faith in the unity of disparate forces – force is so useful as a concept because it enables him to bring together chemical action, muscular action, inertia, sensations and perceptions, and passions, and such unity was in part underwritten by Faraday's conflation of the potential capacity and actual effect of force.[95] Indeed the unifying and simplifying powers of force to explain such disparate actions were in keeping with Faraday's devout Sandemanianism, a Christian sect that based faith on the simple assent to divine testimony, and thus allowed Faraday to harmonize his physics and theology without denigrating the human. And yet this unity founders upon both the ability to impute causality and the problem of representation: are sensation and passion representations of forces? Is chemical action the cause of force or the result of it? Is muscular exertion properly the origin, or would that be something like the will? Can one count potential force as an actual one? The emphasis on potential makes time the arbiter between cause and effect since in time cause appears as effect. While Faraday recognizes that the passions can interfere with reason, they do not necessarily have to work to the detriment of reason. He adds that "vanity, ambition, pride, interest, and a thousand other influences tend to make men redouble their efforts; and the effect is such, that what appeared at first an impassable barrier easily gives way before the increasing power opposed to it."[96] Thus framed, human beings need the emotions to summon the effort to overcome counter forces: emotions are the psyche manifesting itself through the effort (force) of overcoming external forces.

Hence when William Blake equates the "force of Los's hammer" with "eternal forgiveness," he reorients its force from the violent "blow" of "Justice" and "swing" of hypocritical "Mercy" into a "force" of never-ending virtue. In the next line, Blake then substitutes that hammer for "his rage or his mildness," and metonymy confers upon the emotions an equal and opposite force to that of Los's hammer even as rage is transformed into a "vain" mildness.[97] The Christ-like Los, Blake's figure for the poet, thereby enacts a kind of self-annihilation, one underscored by the cancellation of one form of force, violence, for another, forgiveness, and these forces are in turn cancelled by Enitharmon's love. By moving force from its initial empirical visible manifestations – its blow and swing – to the thing behind it, Blake maps Christ-like love on top of Urizenic or Old Testament law, allowing love literally to overcome its other. Seeing forgiveness as having an equal and counter force to violence enables Blake to prepare readers for the eventuality of Jerusalem, and violent oneness with Christ.

Read in the light of the physics of force, Wordsworth's "A Slumber Did my Spirit Seal," becomes a poem less about an individual subjective response to death and loss, or about the poet's appropriation of a feminine subjectivity as his own, or about intentionality, and more about the ways in which the emotions are a synecdoche of larger cosmic forces.[98] Indeed, I challenge the tendency in Wordsworth criticism to read the Lucy poems as "euphemistic" or "abortive elegies."[99] Seen as part of larger cosmic forces, the emotions participate in an ongoing and dynamic world of force interactions; within this larger economy there is no loss because of the law of conservation of force, and therefore the issue is not so much failure to console but whether one is willing to pay the price for the doing away with

the need for consolation. Although this law was not fully articulated until
Hermann von Helmholtz did so in 1847, Helmholtz himself acknowledged
Newton, Davy, and Franklin as having previously enunciated this law,[100]
and in his *Principles of Philosophy*, Descartes had argued that the quantity
of motion in the world remains constant. Indeed, the concept of the
conservation of force underwrote eighteenth-century electrical science;
electricians like Franklin posited the conservation of electric charge (force),
and Franklin conclusively showed that positive and negative electricity
were equal and opposite in character,[101] a demonstration that significantly
advanced electrical science because a loss of charge had to be offset by an
equal gain of charge elsewhere. To the extent that something like force
continues after death, and to the extent that force is not lost, physics
provides a way of reading these poems beyond abortion, but it can do so
only so long as subjectivity is seen as a microscopic lens:

> A slumber did my spirit seal;
>   I had no human fears:
> She seem'd a thing that could not feel
>   The touch of earthly years.
>
> No motion has she now, no force;
>   She neither hears nor sees;
> Rolled round in earth's diurnal course,
>   With rocks, and stones, and trees.[102]

Wordsworth initially separates emotion from motion, giving each a stanza
of its own, and thus invites a reading that dwells on subjectivity and its
loss.[103] The first stanza defines its female subject as that which "seem'd a
thing that could not feel / The touch of earthly years." The appearance of
the absence of feeling belies the actual presence of the emotion of apathy,
underscores that appearance makes no necessary claims about substance,
and prepares the ground for the poet's end to substance dualism and
replacement of that dualism with "sensible 'aspect' dualism" because
emotion is a kind of motion.[104] Force and emotion appear differently
but are really symptoms of the same substance, and the poet's turn to
"seem'd" gives him the power to unify a world that is only split in
appearance. Synchronicity replaces causality[105] and frames the past-tense
verbs of the first stanza also as appearance. Such synchronicity further
enables the poet to imply that no human loss is truly loss since the forces
behind emotion (fears) are essentially conserved.

   Wordsworth's second stanza therefore highlights the absence of a "she"
that can be connected to motion and force, only then to describe a rolling

around in "earth's diurnal course": the "she" has been replaced by earth's motion and force, perhaps the inhuman fears of the first stanza. That Wordsworth specifies her disconnect from both motion and force hints that he is aware that motion is the external sign of force, and that force is its own internal cause. The mere presence of an internal point of view de-emphasizes the subjective, since the inside looks out. More importantly, when Wordsworth refers to the earth's "diurnal course," he acknowledges that although the stars appear to revolve diurnally around the earth, it is the earth that rotates, and once again the view of the subject is mere appearance, now trivialized in relation to cosmic force. The seemingly absent emotion of the first stanza has become the motion of the second, and both stanzas allegorize a force within the universe, which nonetheless unifies the two stanzas and what they symbolize. The collapse of force and substance thus materializes the ineffable emotion/motion whose name was Lucy, and this dynamic materiality gives Wordsworth the ability to see emotion as continuous with larger cosmic forces and thus deny from the bird's-eye view the very need for consolation since nothing is actually lost. Nonetheless, the symmetry of the poem, its balance of alliteration and contrasting sounds, speaks to the balance of cosmic forces, and to the need for aesthetic consolation.[106] To wit, if motion and emotion are in essence the same force, causality itself is suspended, and in a Humean move, rendered merely subjective when compared with a cosmic view. The difference in verb tenses between the stanzas – the first in the past, the second in the present – also belongs to appearance, and recalls Hume's argument that what we call causality is really merely temporal proximity. In an important sense, then, death has died. Wordsworth thereby sets emotion into motion, and mobilizes emotion from motion, enacting a phenomenology of emotion that replaces death.

By thinking about the emotions as something like force, Wordsworth, moreover, renders materiality into a dynamic process that encompasses all matter, and thus endows materiality with psychological complexity (agency) and unity instead of determinism. At the same time, since Lavoisier had demonstrated the essential conservation of mass in chemical reactions, this materiality changes form but also does not yield loss. If physics and chemistry highlight some genuine consolations in Wordsworth's poem, they remind us that consolation's price is the rendering of the subject into matter that has potential to re-emerge as living. His meter captures the costs of such consolation with the absence of deviation from the iambic tetrameter in the final line; unlike his penultimate line which deviates in the first foot with the spondee, "Rolled round," the final line is flatly iambic. Wordsworth's consonance thereby posits a synthesis of the human and the environment, but one attained at the expense of the agent, whose borders have become fungible.

I conclude by suggesting some larger implications of Romantic force for current interest in the science of emotions. What does it mean that the current science of emotions has largely left behind chemistry and physics, the very sciences that have the most to say about the motion behind emotion? Our selective use of science hints that we are actively subjectivizing and humanizing the emotions, if only in current affect theory to make the desubjectivizing powers of the emotions post-Romantic and post-human. The Romantic debates about force and affinity, however, raise the question of what is actually new in the turn to affect in the humanities and social sciences, since it unknowingly echoes the Romantic interest in both the mechanicity and vitality of force, rendering that mechanicity the backdrop against which to measure intentionality.

Attention to chemistry and physics and their contributions to Romantic emotion, moreover, undermines the alleged poverty of a mechanistic view of the emotions, especially since mechanism hardly precluded vitality or spirituality. Nonetheless by linking emotion to motion that could stop short of and be distinguished from action, Romantic writers like Hazlitt in *Liber Amoris* or Mary Robinson in *Lyrical Tales* are skeptical of accounts of emotions that render them into dispositions to action. Antonio Damasio, to cite only the most prominent current exemplar of this theory, links the emotions to "homeostatic processes" rendering the mind and emotions into machinery that is capable of evaluating information. He writes, "the apparatus of the emotions naturally evaluates, and the apparatus of the conscious mind thinkingly evaluates."[107] To render that thinking evaluation more amenable to evolutionary accounts of the emotions that demand quick processing for survival, Damasio speculates that we create neural maps so that processing time – the apparatus – is quicker. This choice of the language of machinery and the computational brain, however, returns us to the surprisingly Romantic interest in the mechanicity of force, with the caveat that unlike those Romantic theories which risk the subject by equivocating on who is doing what to whom through a vitalist and animist language, current automaticity of the emotions comes at the considerable price of denying the very possibility of intentionality behind affects. Indeed, Damasio is really talking about physiological affects, not emotions as psychological states. Brian Massumi, for instance, collapses affect with vitality, defined as "potential for interaction," granting the affects autonomy without an intentional agent and without even a body because he is wary of thinking in terms of the already constituted, because that allegedly renders change impotent.[108] Romantic interest in the animism behind force and elasticity of force, by contrast, makes animism/elasticity a space of automaticity but one that does not banish intent. Romantic scientific debates about the ontology of force, paradoxically, then proffer a useful caution to the emotional science of today bent on understanding the affects and emotions as automatic and without intentionality,[109] but without a sense of how that very automaticity underwrites the psychic space of intentionality.

NOTES

1 Physics and chemistry have long been enemies to the emotions. In *The Phe-nomenology of Perception* (New York: Routledge, 2002), Merleau-Ponty rejects empiricism because it reduces sensation to physical and chemical processes. He refers to "this freezing of being which appeared to be the task of physics" (54). Daniel Gross takes for granted that physics has nothing to say about the social (*The Secret History of Emotion*, 34). To the extent that physicists think about the forces behind collectivity, and to the extent that they map human will onto the world through force, physics does have the potential to say something meaning-ful about the social. Brian Massumi argues that attention to movement within affect has been deflected by fears of a "'naïve realism,' a reductive empiricism that would dissolve ... the cultural domain ... into the 'presence' of dumb matter" (*Parables for the Virtual: Movement, Affect, Sensation* [Durham, NC: Duke University Press, 2002], 1). Humanist hostility to chemistry and physics has now been challenged by current affect theory's and post-humanism's turn to quantum physics and even quantum biology, because these "name the inherent dynamism and mutability of matter" (Constantina Papoulias and Felicity Callard, "Biology's Gift: Interrogating the Turn to Affect," *Body and Society* 16, no. 29 [2010]: 33–4, 47).

2 Immanuel Kant, *Philosophy of Material Nature*, trans. James Ellington (Indian-apolis: Hackett, 1985), 18. In his *Metaphysical Foundations of Natural Science*, published in *Philosophy of Material Nature*, Kant stipulated, "no other property than movability is here attributed to the subject of motion, namely matter" (480).

3 Max Jammer, *Concepts of Force* (Cambridge, MA: Harvard University Press, 1957), 7.

4 For many Romantic scientists, force is elided with the human. Since then physicists have sought to make force rigorously mathematical, restricting it to a change in motion.

5 Arnold Thackray comments on the "emotional hold" Newton's quantification of the macrocosm had on eighteenth-century chemists (*Atoms and Powers: An Essay on Newtonian Matter-Theory and the Development of Chemistry* [Cambridge, MA: Harvard University Press, 1970], 3).

6 Percy Shelley, "On Love," in *Shelley's Poetry and Prose*, ed. Donald Reiman and Neil Fraistat, 2nd edn. (New York: Norton, 2002), 503.

7 Percy Shelley, "Speculations on Metaphysics," in *The Complete Works of Percy Bysshe Shelley*, 10 vols., ed. Roger Ingpen and Walter Peck, vol. 5 (New York: Gordian Press, 1965), 59.

8 Matthew Ratcliffe, *Rethinking Commonsense Psychology* (Basingstoke: Palgrave Macmillan, 2007), 135. Thomas Dixon aptly notes that "mechanical design-theology metaphors" were conducive to a psychology in which agency was ascribed to the intelligence of the Maker (*From Passions to Emotions*, 92).

9 Robert Southey and Samuel Taylor Coleridge, "Love an act of the will," in *Omniana* (Fontwell: Centaur Press, 1969), 339. In a computer analysis of Coleridge's use of "emotion" in his *Notebooks*, David S. Miall shows that emotion in 1805 is often coupled with "bodily" ("Estimating Changes in Collocations of Key Words across a Large Text: A Case Study of Coleridge's *Notebooks*," *Computers and the Humanities* 26, no. 1 [1992]: 6). From 1806 to 1819, consciousness and thought take precedence.

10 Harry Frankfurt insists that love's demands on us do not preempt our will ("Autonomy, Necessity, and Love," in *Necessity, Volition, and Love* [Cambridge: Cambridge University Press, 1999], 137).

11 Erasmus Darwin, *Zoonomia* (London: 1794–6), vol. 1: 5–6.

12 Amy M. Schmitter, "Seventeenth- and Eighteenth-Century Theories of Emotions," *Stanford Encyclopedia of Philosophy*, http://plato.stanford.edu/entries/emotions-17th18th, last accessed 29 August 2013.

13 Allison Muri, *The Enlightenment Cyborg* (Toronto: University of Toronto Press, 2007), 59, 49.

14 Muri, *Enlightenment*, 50.

15 Ibid., 161.

16 D. M. Knight, *Science and Spirituality: The Volatile Connection* (London: Routledge, 2004), 70.

17 G. W. F. Hegel, *Phenomenology of Spirit*, trans. A. V. Miller (Oxford: Oxford University Press, 1979), 79–103. On Hegel's use of "force," see Charles Altieri, "The Concept of Force as Modernist Response to the Authority of Science," *Modernism/Modernity* 5, no. 2 (1998): 77–93.

18 Eve Sedgwick, *Touching Feeling: Affect, Pedagogy, Performativity* (Durham, NC: Duke University Press, 2003), 107. Frankfurt argues that personhood equates to a differently structured will from animals.

19 Emotional movement then only becomes agency at the moment of willed action. "When a person acts, the desire by which he is moved is either the will he wants or a will he wants to be without" (Frankfurt, "Autonomy," 134).

20 Francis Penrose, *Essays, Physiological and Practical; Founded on the Modern Chemistry of Lavoisier* (London: Fourcroy, &c., 1794), 119.

21 Thomas Brown, *Observations on the Zoonomia of Erasmus Darwin, MD* (Edinburgh, 1798), 9.

22 On vitalism and the use of "force" and "motion" to explain the emotions and passions, see Philippe Huneman, "Montpelier Vitalism and the Emergence of

Alienism in France (1750–1850): The Case of the Passions," *Science in Context* 21, no. 4 (2008): 619–22. As the passions move from moral philosophy to the physician in the eighteenth century, they are increasingly physicalized in terms of motion.

23 Alexander Crichton, *An Inquiry into the Causes of Mental Derangement* (London: T. Cadell, 1798), 345.

24 Dora Weiner reminds me in a personal communication that French physicians around 1800 were all trained in "medical physics," a category devoted to understanding movement in the body.

25 Trevor Levere, *Affinity and Matter: Elements of Chemistry 1800–1865* (Oxford: Clarendon, 1971), 3.

26 "Hunter, Keats, and Shelley understood the 'being of sensation' not as a mirroring of the world by the organism but as the 'compound of nonhuman forces of the cosmos'" (Robert Mitchell, "Suspended Animation, Slow Time, and the Poetics of Trance," *PMLA* 126, no. 1 [2011]: 118). "Force" in the seventeenth and eighteenth centuries "can refer either to the momentum or energy of a moving body" (Thomas L. Hankins, "Eighteenth-Century Attempts to Resolve the *Vis Viva* Controversy," *Isis* 56, no. 3 [1965]: 281). On emotion as "disaggregated selves," see Reddy, *The Navigation of Feeling*, 95–8. Kevin Chang argues that, "ironically, the mechanists sometimes put principles of vitalism back into matter" (Ku-Ming [Kevin] Chang, "Alchemy as Studies of Life and Matter," *Isis* 102, no. 2 [2011]: 328).

27 Arkady Plotnitsky, "All Shapes of Light: The Quantum Mechanical Shelley," in *Shelley: Poet and Legislator of the World*, ed. Betty Bennett and Stuart Curran (Baltimore, MD: Johns Hopkins University Press, 1996), 262–73.

28 Definition of force from the *Encyclopaedia Britannica* (Edinburgh, 1771), s.v. "force."

29 Charis Anastopoulos, *Particle or Wave: The Evolution of the Concept of Matter in Modern Physics* (Princeton, NJ: Princeton University Press, 2008), 60.

30 Isabelle Stengers, *Cosmopolitics I*, trans. Robert Bononno (Minneapolis: University of Minnesota Press, 2003), 106.

31 Papoulias and Callard, "Biology's Gift." For Mark Hansen, protention is a form of vitality in that it has "an openness that is capable of self-movement" ("The Time of Affect, or Bearing Witness to Life," *Critical Inquiry* 30 [2004]: 608–9. Mitchell highlights the Romantic interest in the suspension of time in part to "'delay' otherwise automatic relations of action and reaction" (Mitchell, "Suspended Animation," 118).

32 See Pheng Cheah on automatism and autonomy in "Non-dialectical Materialism," *Diacritics* 38, nos. 1/2 (2008): 147. Reddy argues that as voluntary action has acquired multiple pathways and multiple types of activation, the distinction between thought and affect has become increasingly muddled (Reddy, *Navigation*, 31). Dixon credits Thomas Brown with the invention of emotions as passive non-intellectual feelings or states (Dixon, *Passions*, 124).

33 Harry Frankfurt, *The Reasons of Love* (Princeton, NJ: Princeton University Press, 2004), 18.

34 Jammer, *Concepts*, 7.

35 Ruth Leys critiques much current affect program theory on the grounds of its insistent anti-intentionality, and the granting of autotelism to affect (*From Guilt to Shame: Auschwitz and After* [Princeton, NJ: Princeton University Press, 2007], 133–7) at the expense of intention. Much of this anti-intentionality is frankly unreflective, but historically, according to Dixon, the emotions were initially more passive than intentional (*Passions*, 25–6). More recently, she has argued that this anti-intentionality insulates affect from ideology ("Turn to Affect," 435–6) along with meaning from the body. Neuroscientist David Eagleman (*Incognito* [New York: Pantheon, 2011], 55–74), who emphasizes the automaticity and anti-intentionality of consciousness, suggests that mind work itself may be most effective when we are not conscious of it. Because intentionality is at the core of humanistic study, and the emotions navigate somewhere in between intentionality and the lack thereof (Reddy), emotions can only be valuable to humanists in so far as they carry intent.

36 Clough, "The Affective Turn," 207. Elsewhere, Clough claims that the "affective turn ... expresses a new configuration of bodies, technology" (Patricia T. Clough, "Introduction," *The Affective Turn: Theorizing the Social*, ed. Patricia Clough [Durham, NC: Duke University Press, 2007], 3).

37 Sara Ahmed, *The Cultural Politics of Emotion* (New York: Routledge, 2004), 4, 8.

38 Michael Hardt ignores the complex Romantic genealogy of this affective shift. Helpfully, he argues, "Affects require us to enter the realm of causality because the affects belong simultaneously to both sides of the causal relationship" ("Foreword: What Affects Are Good For," in *The Affective Turn: Theorizing the Social*, ed. Patricia Clough [Durham, NC: Duke University Press, 2007], ix).

39 Massumi, *Parables for the Virtual*, 42.

40 Sedgwick, *Touching Feeling*, 33.

41 Ahmed claims, "emotions are crucial to the very constitution of the psychic and the social as objects, a process which suggests that the 'objectivity' of the psychic and the social is an effect rather than a cause" (*Cultural Politics*, 10); she thereby reverses cause and effect. Sedgwick's *Touching Feeling* is littered with physics: to cite just a few examples, "primary narcissism ... throws itself dangerously into the gravitational field of the other" (36); "Henry James' ass ... generates a list of other 'repeated, magnetic' signifiers" (54); and "the peri-performative necessarily represent a diminution in force" (78). See also Sedgwick, *Touching Feeling*, 114.

42 Goldsmith, "William Blake and the Future of Enthusiasm," 446, 456.

43 Ricardo Lopes Coelho, "On the Concept of Force: How Understanding its History Can Improve Physics Teaching," *Science and Education* 19 (2010): 92.

44 By the 1690s Newton was more willing to publicly accept an atomistic philosophy, and he developed "belief in forces as 'God's Guarantee'" (Thackray, *Atoms and Powers*, 15).

45 Jammer, *Concepts of Force*, 7. "To understand force, one needs to refer to metaphor and intuition" (Anastopoulos, *Particle or Wave*, 52).

46 Pinch, *Strange Fits of Passion*, 36.
47 Michael Frazer defends sympathy on the grounds that it "see[s] such forces as emotion and imagination as part of the process of moral and political reflection itself" (*The Enlightenment of Sympathy* [Oxford: Oxford University Press, 2010], 14).
48 Jessica Riskin, *Science in the Age of Sensibility* (Chicago: University of Chicago Press, 2002), 70.
49 Newtonian theory implies "that the initial conditions of the Universe – its state at the moment of creation – allow an absolute determination of every single event that has happened or will ever happen" (Anastapolous, *Particle or Wave*, 56).
50 George Gordon Byron, *Byron's Letters and Journals*, 13 vols., ed. Leslie Marchand, vol. 9 (London: John Murray, 1973–94), 46.
51 George Gordon Byron, *The Complete Poetical Works*, 7 vols., ed. Jerome J. McGann (Oxford: Oxford University Press, 1980–93), vol. 3, lines 269–71.
52 Byron, *Complete Poetical Works*, vol. 3, line 244.
53 Mi-Gyung Kim, *Affinity, That Elusive Dream: A Genealogy of the Chemical Revolution* (Cambridge, MA: MIT Press, 2003), 11.
54 Ibid., 15.
55 Keats uses "pleasure thermometer" in his 30 January 1818 letter to John Taylor (*The Letters of John Keats*, 2 vols., ed. Hyder Rollins, vol. 1 [Cambridge, MA: Harvard University Press, 1958], 218–19). Stuart Sperry misses the degree to which thermometers get to the essence of chemical constitution (*Keats, the Poet* [Princeton, NJ: Princeton University Press, 1973], 49).
56 Cited in Kim, *Affinity*, 135.
57 Ibid., 45 and 15.
58 Ursula Klein and Wolfgang Lefevre, *Materials in Eighteenth-Century Science* (Cambridge, MA: MIT Press, 2007), 14.
59 Knight, *Science and Spirituality*, 60.
60 John Dalton, *A New System of Chemical Philosophy* (1808) (New York: Philosophical Library, 1967), 117.
61 Thackray, *Atoms and Powers*, 264.
62 Ibid., 262.
63 Dalton, *A New System*, 117; Thackray, *Atoms and Powers*, 271.
64 Peter Dear, *The Intelligibility of Nature* (Chicago: University of Chicago Press, 2006), 89.
65 Levere, *Affinity and Matter*, 3.
66 Marvin Minsky thinks of emotions in terms of machinery that turns certain resources off and others on (*The Emotional Machine* [New York: Simon and Schuster, 2006], 4). Silvan Tomkins defined the "affect system" as the "motivational system in human beings" and linked his study of affect with automata (*Shame and Its Sisters*, ed. Eve Kosofsky Sedgwick and Adam Frank [Durham, NC: Duke University Press, 1995], 34), and indeed correlated freedom with complexity of the machine (35). Tomkins' theorizing of aims independent of affects (44) provides an important corrective to evolutionary theories of the emotions.

67 Cited in Levere, *Affinity and Matter*, 26.
68 Ibid., 29.
69 Ibid., 105.
70 On this, see especially Knight, *Science and Spirituality*.
71 John Keats, *John Keats's Anatomical and Physiological Note Book*, ed. Hyder Rollins (New York: Haskell House, 1970), 64.
72 John Keats, *Endymion*, *The Poems of John Keats*, Book 3, lines 142–3.
73 Sperry, *Keats, the Poet*, 36.
74 Keats, *Endymion*, Book 3, lines 432–7.
75 Ibid., line 429.
76 Humphry Davy, *Elements of Chemical Philosophy*, Part 1, vol. 1 (Philadelphia, 1812), 252; see also p. 188.
77 William Lewis, *The Edinburgh New Dispensatory* (London, 1789), 70, 72, 76, 69.
78 Davy, *Elements*, 285.
79 Ibid., 25, 39.
80 Ibid., 42.
81 For help with the German translations, I thank David Bratt Pfotenhauer. Jeremy Adler argues that Eduard thinks in terms of simple single affinity rather than double affinity ("Goethe and Chemical Theory in Elective Affinities," in *Romanticism and the Sciences*, ed. Andrew Cunningham and Nicholas Jardine [Cambridge: Cambridge University Press, 1990], 272).
82 Johann Wolfgang von Goethe, *Elective Affinities*, trans. David Constantine (Oxford: Oxford University Press, 1994), 229. Hereafter cited as *EA*.
83 Walter Benjamin, "Goethe's *Elective Affinities*," in *Walter Benjamin: Selected Writings*, vol. 1, *1913–1926*, ed. Marcus Bullock and Michael W. Jennings (Cambridge, MA: Harvard University Press, 1996), 303.
84 Johann Wolfgang von Goethe, *The Sorrows of Young Werther and Selected Writings*, ed. Marcelle Clements, trans. Catherine Hutter (New York: Signet Books, 1962), 133.
85 Goethe, *Sorrows of Young Werther*, 156.
86 Benjamin, "Goethe's *Elective Affinities*," 348.
87 For a powerful critique of Descartes's physics, see Diana Coole, "The Inertia of Matter," in *New Materialisms: Ontology, Agency, and Politics*, ed. Diana Coole and Samantha Frost (Durham, NC: Duke University Press, 2010), 92–115.
88 Coelho, "On the Concept of Force," 97. Isabelle Stengers credits Euler and Lagrange for defining force by acceleration, its measureable effect (*Cosmopolitics I*, 117).
89 Michael Faraday, *The Forces of Matter* (Mineola, NY: Dover Books, 2010), 8.
90 Jammer, *Concepts of Force*, 14–15.
91 Cited in Levere, *Affinity and Matter*, 105.
92 David Gooding, "Metaphysics versus Measurement: The Conversion and Conservation of Force in Faraday's Physics," *Annals of Science* 37 (1980): 8. See also p. 26.
93 Alice Jenkins, ed., *Michael Faraday's Mental Exercises: An Artisan Essay-Circle in Regency London* (Liverpool: Liverpool University Press, 2008), 190.

94 Michael Faraday, "Observations on the Inertia of the Mind," IET Manuscript
   SC MSS 002/1/4, London, p. 350. I thank the Institute for Engineering and
   Technology for permission to quote from this manuscript. At the end of his
   Christmas lectures to children, Michael Faraday announced that he "might
   show you many other experiments whereby [he] could obtain electricity and
   chemical action, heat and light from a magnet" (*Forces of Matter*, 87).
95 Gooding, "Metaphysics versus Measurement," 10–11.
96 Jenkins, *Faraday's Mental Exercises*, 192.
97 William Blake, *Jerusalem*, ed. Morton D. Paley (Princeton, NJ: William
   Blake Trust and Princeton University Press, 1991), 88, lines 49–50.
   Goldsmith analyzes how in *Milton* a prior change in emotion sets a change
   of motion into motion ("William Blake," 457). I suggest that the traffic
   between motion and emotion goes multiple ways.
98 See G. Kim Blank, *Wordsworth and Feeling* (Madison, WI: Fairleigh Dickinson University Press, 1995), 147–56. Because "there is no such thing as the
   absence of emotion," Rei Terada traces how feelings recirculate in an "economy of pathos" (*Feeling in Theory*, 13).
99 Geoffrey Hartman, *Easy Pieces* (New York: Columbia University Press, 1985),
   149; Susan Eilenberg, *Strange Power of Speech: Wordsworth, Coleridge, and
   Literary Possession* (New York: Oxford University Press, 1992), 117.
100 See Alan Weber, *Nineteenth-Century Science: A Selection of Original Texts*
   (Peterborough, ON: Broadview, 2000), 279. Davy's work on the unity and
   convertibility of light, heat, and electricity established interconnections
   between forces. Anastopoulos details Lavoisier's development of the concept
   of the conservation of matter. As matter is understood in terms of force, it
   stands to reason that forces are also conserved (*Particle or Wave*, 64–5).
101 J. L. Heilbron, *Electricity in the Seventeenth and Eighteenth Centuries* (Berkeley: University of California Press, 1979), 330–3.
102 William Wordsworth, "A Slumber Did My Spirit Seal," *Shorter Poems,
   1807–1820*, ed. Carl H. Ketchum (Ithaca, NY: Cornell University Press, 1989).
103 See Marjorie Levinson, "A Motion and a Spirit: Romancing Spinoza," *Studies
   in Romanticism* 47, no. 4 (2007): 366–408, 390–1. She suggests that Spinoza
   allows Lucy to be a part of the continuum of motion.
104 Damasio, *Looking for Spinoza*, 209.
105 Mark Lussier, *Romantic Dynamics: The Poetics of Physicality* (Basingstoke:
   Macmillan, 2000), 9.
106 I am indebted to Steve Goldsmith for this insight.
107 Damasio, *Looking for Spinoza*, 54.
108 Massumi, *Parables for the Virtual*, 35–6. See also pp. 70–1.
109 Leys, "Turn to Affect," 434–72.

CHAPTER 2

A certain mediocrity
Adam Smith's moral behaviorism

Thomas Pfau

A distinguishing feature of Smith's *Theory of Moral Sentiments* is its striking reversal of emphasis, away from the Humean drama of volatile and non-cognitive passions and toward reaffirming the continuity of a more settled kind of affect. In an attempt at retreating from the dead-end of Hume's epistemological skepticism, Smith's proposes to re-describe the passions by correlating them with a firmly empirical, at times actuarial understanding of reason manifested in established customs, prevailing manners, average forms of behavior, and a mimetic conception of virtue. Viewing his arguments as post-metaphysical, yet also wishing to move beyond the rationalist, emotivist, and skeptical critiques of metaphysics that had dominated since the Restoration, Adam Smith seeks to overcome the antagonism of will and intellect – a dilemma that, unbeknownst to him, modernity had not so much discovered as created. To David Marshall, Smith "seems less concerned about the constitution of the self" and indeed "presupposes a certain instability of the self; it depends upon an eclipsing of identity, a transfer of persons."[1] Marshall's compact formula risks obscuring, however, that to construe sociality as a product of continued imaginative substitution constitutes something of a logical paradox. For "how can one become another person without suffering the dramatic change that is self-liquidation?" Furthermore, "if my identity is caught up with yours, and yours with another's, and so in a perpetually spawning web of affiliations, how can I ever know that your approving glance is *your* glance, rather than the effect of an unreadable palimpsest of selves?" After all, any such knowledge hinges on "entering into another experience while retaining enough rational capacity of one's own to assess what one finds there. The cognitive distance which such judgments require cuts against the grain of an imaginary ethics."[2]

Arguably, none of these logical paradoxes can be resolved in the terms in which they are here being stated – that is, in a vocabulary still committed to knowledge as propositional in nature and originating in a solitary and self-aware epistemological agent. Though far from meaning to present an apologia for Smith's transferential conception of moral agency, the reading here undertaken suggests that it is precisely this mentalist idea of knowledge – viz., as a type of intentionality issuing in a distinct representation – which Smith means to leave behind. In fact, his solution to the epistemological dilemma rests on distilling how the inherently non-cognitive conduct of individuals will yield rational, systemic effects that could never be secured if social meaning were to depend on subjective intention. To this end, Smith comprehensively re-describes passion as "sentiment" and, in turn, sentiment as a social transaction or "behavior." As I have argued elsewhere, Smith's sweeping account of sociality as the circulation and mimetic appraisal of sentiments bears more than a passing affinity to modern behaviorism.[3]

In recasting truth as a product of epistemological *method*, seventeenth-century thought (from Bacon to Hobbes and Locke) had effectively repudiated the idea of knowledge as a result of active contemplation (*theoria*) for which the cosmos had once furnished the ontological source and ethical *telos*. Instead, modern inquiry radicalizes tenets of theological nominalism by insisting that to know means to isolate singular entities as the only viable locus of meaning. The resulting paradigm of knowledge as "information" gradually creates the fact/value divide that Hume eventually sets forth as an axiom of modern rational inquiry, the result being that knowledge as an intellectual commodity has become terminally estranged from the broader ideal of wisdom and human flourishing. After 1750, epistemology and ethics are fundamentally conceived as distinct and, increasingly, as unrelated pursuits, and it is in Adam Smith that this bifurcation is completed as the project of moral philosophy migrates from a theological to a sociological, and from a normative to a descriptive endeavor. His *Theory of Moral Sentiments* offers prima facie evidence of how some key terms (e.g., passion, sentiment, sympathy) traditionally associated with introspective accounts of moral judgment and human flourishing are for the first time being systematically reinterpreted as objectively classifiable, social phenomena.

To be sure, Smith's own project rests on a few distinguished precursors, including the Stoics, Shaftesbury, Hutcheson (Smith's teacher), and Hume. Preferring a meliorist, conversational tone to Hume's sharp-edged analytical idiom, Smith in 1759 locates the "selfish passions" as occupying "a sort of middle place" between "the social and the unsocial."[4] Long before Kant's late utopian musings advanced "the most extreme counter-position to the [Hobbesian] principle *auctoritas non veritas facit legem*," Scottish political economists had already begun to shift from a voluntarist command ethic toward a narrative model that conceives the will or, at least, its empirical heirs – the passions – as susceptible of "improvement."[5] The trajectory in question typically proceeds from the mindless force of mute desire, advancing to an expressive but inadequately socialized "passion," and culminating in the eventual lucidity of a stable set of "interests" or, in Hutcheson's phrase, "secondary desires" responsive to the systemic cues of modern commerce.[6] Even for the skeptical Hume, the project's logic is quite irresistible. Acknowledging that it simply is not feasible to "infuse into each breast … a passion for the public good," Hume instead suggests that it is "requisite to govern men by other passions, and animate them with a spirit of avarice and industry."[7]

Albert O. Hirshman has called this the "marvelous metamorphosis of destructive 'passions' into 'virtues'" through the new paradigm of "interest."[8] Anticipating Hirshman's thesis, John Pocock had previously qualified this view in one important respect; for even as credit was being "translated into virtue," this "restoration of virtue was subject to a single sharp limitation." Thus, insofar as "virtue was now the cognition of social, moral and commercial reality, … imagination … is replaced in the Whig literature of 1710–11 by nothing more than opinion" and "rationality is only that of opinion and experience."[9] More than any of his contemporaries, Smith bears out this insight by systematically disabling the Augustinian conception of virtue as predicated on sustained introspection and standing counterfactually vis-à-vis a fallen world. In its place, Smith ventures a mimetic conception of the good bound up with the vicarious transfer of prevailing, socially sanctioned sentiments, an approach that "made it possible to dismiss the egoistic motivational theory underpinning Mandeville's paradoxes."[10] While Smith's focus on the passions is a familiar feature of eighteenth-century moral philosophy, his objectives differ markedly from those of Hutcheson and Hume. For underlying his concern with the passions, and their potential commutation into durable sentiments, is no longer Locke's or Hume's epistemological quest for a viable and verifiable successor to the metaphysical notion of the will. Rather, Smith seeks to disengage moral reflection from the stranglehold of Hume's radical skepticism, which had pushed Lockean nominalism to such extremes as to render basic humanistic key concepts (e.g., will, action, consciousness, self, introspection, judgment) all but meaningless. Retreating from this philosophical dead-end, Smith finds Stoicism to be of particular value to his objectives, in part because the Stoics, even as they had acknowledged the intrinsic deficiency of human intelligence (moral and otherwise), had also sought to remedy that predicament dialectically by arguing for the complementarity of finite and imperfect human perspectives. From Smith's neo-Stoic viewpoint, this fortuitous alignment of blind volition and systemic rationality reflects a divinely ordained arrangement: "Nature, accordingly, has endowed [man], not only with a desire of being approved of, but with a desire of being what ought to be approved of; or of being what he himself approves of in other men." Moral and economic self-improvement thus follow the same behavioral template, viz., a quest for "self-approbation" whose pursuit constitutes "the principal object, about which [a wise man] can or ought to be anxious. The love of it, is the love of virtue" (*TMS*, 117). This neo-Stoic project is echoed time and again in *The Wealth of Nations*, as in Smith's familiar assurance that "the desire of bettering our condition, a desire which, though *generally calm and dispassionate*, comes with us from the womb and never leaves us till we go into the grave."[11]

At first glance, this new credit-based and self-interested, entrepreneurial self promises to offer "a countervailing strategy" to the Hobbesian, all-consuming will "on a continuing day-to-day basis" rather than demanding for its containment the Leviathan's ad-hoc projection of overwhelming force.[12] For Smith, it is above all sympathy that counterbalances the specter of a radically particularist and pluralist nation where "every individual is . . . attached to his own particular order, . . . his own interest, [and] his own vanity." In the innumerable encounters of which quotidian sociality is composed, the practice of sympathy gradually effects an enduring, if imaginary model of community. Smith calls it "that more gentle public spirit" (*TMS*, 230–2). Yet in postulating that "every man is . . . by nature, first and principally recommended to his own care" (82), Smith makes clear that voluntarism remains very much the default model of agency. Indeed, far from remedying Hobbes's and Hume's anti-rationalism, the Whig conception of commercial society proved in its own ways just as "fantastic and nonrational" and threatened "to submerge the world in a flood of fantasy."[13] Parallel to this transformation of the will into potentially rational, predictable, and manageable "interests" run various cultural narratives about the rise of modern "refinement," "manners," and "taste," as well as a host of new institutions dedicated to their advancement. To the Scottish political economists of the mid-century, governmental authority and individual will were increasingly mediated by the impersonal rationality of complex networks and expert languages, rather than by a sovereign and centralized power. As Adam Smith puts it, "in the great chess-board of human society, every single piece has a principle of motion of its own, altogether different from that which the legislature might chuse to impress upon it" (*TMS*, 234).

Though differing widely in their critical stance vis-à-vis the story they wish to tell, Norbert Elias, John Brewer, J. G. A. Pocock, Linda Colley, and Michel Foucault (to name but a few), all converge in interpreting this "rise of disciplinary society" (as Charles Taylor most recently labeled it) as a process that increasingly disperses and so obscures the force of hedonism that had loomed so conspicuous and ominous in Hobbes's *Leviathan* and Mandeville's *Fable*. Hutcheson's *Essay* (1728) had pointed the way here, arguing that it was "foolish" to infer "from the universal Prevalence of these Desires [of Wealth and Power] that human Nature is wholly selfish, or that each one is only studious of his *own Advantages*; since Wealth or Power are as naturally fit to gratify our *Publick Desires*, or to serve *virtuous Purposes*, as the *selfish* ones."[14] With the opportunities for economic and social mobility largely cordoned off by the mercantilist system of his native France, Montesquieu's theory concerning the separation of powers pursues a cognate objective within the field of constitutional philosophy. Thus he also posits a systemic balancing of interests as the most auspicious strategy for containing a will that, like Locke and Mandeville, he also regards as inherently volatile, blind, and irremediably selfish. This shift from an *auratic* to a *technocratic* and from a *personal* to a *systemic* understanding of power would, of course, continue and in time spawn often brilliant analyses of modern constitutional, political, and economic thought (from Montesquieu to the *Federalist Papers* to Hegel's *Philosophy of Right* to Marx's critique of political economy and even Max Weber's sociological account of institutionalized politics, science, and culture).

Their highly diverse ideological commitments notwithstanding, however, the mid-eighteenth-century works of political, economic, and moral theory converge on this one point: they all regard the will as essentially opaque, unfree, and irrational. Such is the case wherever the individual will is subject to the impersonal and remedial discipline of the law and to institutions of education and cultural literacy broadly speaking – all of which are gradually being aligned with the instrumental rationality said to govern economic behavior. Smith's account of the "impartial spectator" perfectly embodies this meliorist logic by positing moral development as a complex process of transference: just as the other's "sympathy makes them look at [suffering], in some measure, with his eyes, so his sympathy makes him look at it, in some measure with theirs, especially when in their presence and under their observation" (*TMS*, 72). A new, notably transactional conception of sociality thus takes shape, one that pivots on reconciled customs and manners of mid-eighteenth-century polite and commercial culture, fueled by a rhetoric of "improvement" that oscillates between the obliquely moral and the emphatically sentimental. Under this new dispensation, the containment of the (Hobbesian) will and the restoration of a certain kind of rationality is conceived as a *procedural* question, a matter of the right *technique* being brought to bear on the passions. In classical Stoic fashion, Smith thus views his own philosophical enterprise as therapeutic in nature and, in particular, as a quest for incentives such as will effectively and efficiently regulate *behavior*. No longer considered are Aristotelian and Thomistic conceptions of the will as susceptible of *internal* clarification and as an integral part of moral cognition. Hobbes's view of the will as a strictly appetitive, volatile, and opaque *pathos* devoid of intellectual potential and impervious to introspective remediation thus is not so much opposed by his Enlightenment heirs as it is turned into a bleak premise for their meliorist view of politics, culture, and economics as the most auspicious venues for recovering a socially responsible model of human agency.

In fundamental if not entirely obvious ways, Smith accepts Locke's and Hume's account of a self driven by hedonistic pleasures and all but bereft of personal identity due to the discontinuity and incommensurability of all sensation. The self as an inner agent, while perhaps real, is ultimately deemed inaccessible to philosophical speculation; it is constitutively opaque and, to judge by such evidence of the inner life as still reaches us, it lacks any coherent and sustained sense of its reality *as a person*. Hence, Smith's strategic investment in the notion of sympathy arises from his deep-seated conviction "that others' states of mind are naturally inaccessible to us, concealed as they are by the fleshly encasements of their bodies." Moreover, Smith "was not convinced that sympathy could, on its own, maintain social order" and, where the limits of sympathetic sociality arose, was quite willing to maintain such order "through the fear of death operating in conjunction with a sovereign power."[15]

It is not merely a breakdown of inter-subjective discourse, then, but the underlying, radically nominalist view of a self dissolved into heterogeneous impressions, sensations, states, desires, and affections that prompts Smith to concede from the outset that "we have no immediate experience of what other men feel" (*TMS*, 9). The apparent tension between Locke's epistemology of the self and his political theory of rational agents electively and deliberatively entering into social relations by means of propositional, quasi-contractual arrangements had been thrown into disarray by Hume's dispersal of personal identity, his atomistic view of the passions, and his disjunction of fact from value. Smith's *Theory of Moral Sentiments* thus attempts to re-think the very project of moral philosophy following the

massive onslaught of post-Hobbesian skepticism on the self's epistemological coherence and moral integrity. Crucially, passion in Smith's *Theory*
is no longer viewed as a purely impulsive, hedonistic, and self-consuming
mental event. Rather its seemingly irrational thrust is being attenuated,
even reversed, in that the inter-subjective phenomenon of "sentiment"
constitutes less an expressive act than a behavioral norm designed and
displayed so as to maximize prospects of "approval" by others.

While the Stoic project of overcoming the emotions (as de facto
misjudgments) remains a central feature of Smith's argument, it is
deployed here for very different strategic purposes. For the objective
is no longer a quest for inner balance and wisdom (*apatheia*), but rather
the smooth operation of social life as an end in its own right. In anticipating and accommodating itself to projected conditions of reception, Smith's
individual will "conceiv[e] some degree of that coolness about his own
fortune, with which he is sensible that they will view it" (*TMS*, 22). In
sharp contrast to classical Stoicism, then, self-possession and self-mastery
(*autarkeia*) are at most incidental to the decidedly un-Stoic project of an
affect-based and strictly "imagined" community. Indeed, the meaning,
value, and significance of the inner life will only disclose themselves insofar
as passion has been successfully converted into the social currency of
behavior, a term that will occupy us shortly. If a primal passion still
furnishes the raw material for this transformation, it signifies and is
credited with reality only to the extent that it has been successfully
transposed into "sentiment" – that is, a type of behavior sanctioned
by the social grammar that undergirds Smith's sympathetic community.
The imagined sphere of discursive sociality at once *recovers* passion from
the netherworld of mute and unfocused animal desire and in so doing
redeems it for purposive human life: "Society and conversation, therefore,
are the most powerful remedies for restoring the mind to its tranquillity"
(23). Conversely, an inner life that refuses to accommodate the sociality of
sentiments is at best value-neutral, though more likely of a pathological or
criminal nature – a vagrant, opaque, and intractable symptom on the order
of Nietzsche's "extra-moral" (*aussermoralisch*) sense.

Just this conversion shows Smith's use of Stoic philosophy to be rather
peculiar and selective and also reveals the acute modernity of his *Theory of
Moral Sentiments*. For the Stoics, who follow Aristotle rather than Plato,
lack of self-command or irresoluteness of will (*akrasia*) is not a result of
hedonistic and compulsive appetition but of a flawed judgment, which is
to say, of precipitous or ill-conceived "assent" to some desire or other.
Inasmuch as Stoicism views the mind as substantially one and not to be

partitioned in the spirit of modern faculty psychology, the emotions cannot be understood as physiologically conditioned surges intruding on the otherwise distinct and separate superagency of reason. "There is," Nussbaum argues, "in Greek thought about the emotions, from Plato and Aristotle straight on through Epicurus, an agreement that the emotions are not simply blind surges of affect, stirrings or sensations that are unidentified, and distinguished from one another, by their felt quality alone." Indeed, "it was not an item of unargued dogma for the Stoics that the soul has just one part ... was a conclusion, and a conclusion of arguments in moral psychology."[16] Seneca remarks that "if any one supposes that pallor, falling tears, prurient itching or deep-drawn sigh, a sudden brightening of the eyes, and the like, are an evidence of passion and a manifestation of the mind, he is mistaken and fails to understand that these are disturbances of the body." It is not that the mind is victimized by quasi-physical passions (*pathē*) but, rather, that it "suffers" them to acquire excessive or distorted epistemic and moral force. An emotion thus "does not consist in being moved by the impressions that are presented to the mind, but in the surrendering to these." It is an act of precipitous and misguided "assent," which is to say, an intellectual operation that has eluded the kind of scrupulous supervision that the Stoics mean to instill in their disciples. Speaking of the paradigmatic emotion of anger, Seneca thus notes that it "must not only be aroused, but it must rush forth, for it is an active impulse; but an active impulse never comes without the consent of the will [*numquam autem impetus sine adsensu mentis est*]."[17] While a fuller exploration of this complex and still contested issue of the Stoics' concept of emotion is not feasible here, a number of points can be extracted that will reveal the very different thrust of Smith's seemingly neo-Stoic argument.

First, the Stoics understand all acts of mind – including the passions – as propositional in nature. Second, to the extent that a passion has any hold on the mind it does so solely in consequence of the intellect's assent to the (oblique) proposition with which it is presented. Passion, then, is not a distinct antagonist of reason but evidence of the latter's as yet incomplete cultivation. To the extent that passion holds sway over someone's mind, it points to one's failure to apprehend and appraise the propositional nature of "impressions" with the requisite care. Third, just this type of failure gives rise to a disorder of judgment and, ultimately, to ill-conceived action, a syndrome for which the Stoics adopt the Aristotelian concept of *akrasia*. Here again, it is important not to misidentify *akrasia* as some isolated failure to act on a good clearly perceived; neither is it some deficient act of mind or "opinion" randomly insinuating itself into the otherwise rational and responsible narrative of a life. Far from some contingent psychological mishap obtruded from without, akratic "weakness of will" is integral to human psychology. For Aristotle, *akrasia* thus involves a specific kind of desire (*orexis*), one that is not determinative like the craving for food or sex but, rather, something unpredictable and self-fuelling. Unsurprisingly, the Stoics, and Seneca in particular, identify "anger" (*ira*) as the very embodiment of *akrasia* – viz., a pointedly *a*-social passion that can be either prospective (e.g., revenge) or retrospective (e.g., resentment). In the first case, there is no determinate causal link between the akratic disposition and a specific course of action, for as we well realize, Hamlet may or may not act to avenge his father's murder. Conversely, in the case of looking back in anger it is even more obvious that *akrasia* does not compel a specific action since the past cannot be changed. Crucially, the Stoic objective of heading off misjudgment – that is, the precipitous assent to an emotionally colored and distorted perception – was to be realized by methodical and sustained introspection.

Not so in the *Theory of Moral Sentiments*; for while Smith appears to echo the Stoic quest for isolating and disabling the sources of a disordered inner life, his solution is precisely *not* one of introspection but, rather, to declare all passion akratic until and unless it has been socialized as a benevolent sentiment. The result is a marked shift in emphasis, which in turn yields a distinctively modern conception of moral agency. To begin with, Smith no longer views the passions as propositional in nature. Both in its primitive state and once converted into a socially recognized "sentiment," emotion in Smith's *Theory* proves to be altogether extrarational and non-propositional. The *telos* of Smith's account is thus neither knowledge nor the self's ability to form logical and critical judgments on the quasi-propositional character of the emotions. Rather, Smith seeks to effect a mimetic alignment of the self's emotively charged impressions with what are hypostatized to be the cognate affective experiences of other individuals. Simply put, the modern objective is emulation, not cognition. From this a second point follows; for contrary to views that the Enlightenment came to hold, classical Stoicism's methodical quest for inward composure and rational self-governance had always served the final objective of building up the self's capacity for active and selfless citizenship. Its structured regimen of self-mastery was aimed at furnishing certain and unbiased representations (not sentiments) such as would prove conducive to political "action." Indeed, it is just this framework of a *vita contemplativa* integrated with, rather than opposed to, the *vita activa* that was also shared by Augustine and Aquinas (the latter taking his cue directly from Aristotle rather than the Stoics). By contrast, Smith's critique of Stoicism as expiring in the languor of "sublime contemplation" and after-the-fact "consolation" is not only misleading but also obscures his own theory's far more equivocal outlook on action. In Smith's rather one-sided portrayal, Stoicism limits the self to a cultivation of "apathy" and to a concerted attempt at "eradicat[ing] all our private, partial, and selfish affections, by suffering us to feel ... not even the sympathetic and reduced passions of the impartial spectator." The result, we are told, is to have removed the self from "every thing which Nature has prescribed to us as the proper business and occupation of our lives" (*TMS*, 292–3).

Notably, Smith's critique of Stoicism in his survey of moral philosophy (added as Part VII to the 1790 edition of his *Theory of Moral Sentiments*) also departs from the neo-Stoic thrust of his book's earlier sections, written some three decades earlier. There Smith had firmly aligned himself with the Stoic ideal of affective self-governance: "to restrain our selfish, and to indulge our benevolent affections, constitutes the perfection of human nature; and can alone produce among mankind that harmony of sentiments and passions in which consists their whole grace and propriety" (*TMS*, 25). Echoing Joseph Addison's *Cato* and anticipating similar claims in Gotthold Ephraim Lessing's *Laokoon*, Smith expresses admiration for "the man who has lost his leg by a cannon shot, and who, the moment after, speaks and acts with his usual coolness and tranquillity." What is put on theatrical display here is the ostensibly anti-theatrical Stoic virtue of "self-command." Yet there is something decidedly equivocal about Smith's claim that "in proportion to the degree of self-command which is necessary in order to conquer our natural sensibility, the pleasure and pride of the conquest are so much the greater" (147). For just this ostensibly Stoic conquest of the passions, in Smith's account, has to be put on display inasmuch as its success remains in epistemological limbo until and unless it has been confirmed by outside spectators. Elsewhere in *Theory of Moral Sentiments*, Smith thus extols

> that reserved, that silent and majestic sorrow, which discovers itself only in the swelling of the eyes, in the quivering of the lips and cheeks, and in the distant, but affecting coldness of the whole behaviour. It imposes the like silence upon us. We regard it with respectful attention, and watch with anxious concern over our whole behaviour, lest by any impropriety we should disturb that concerted tranquility, which it requires so great an effort to support. (24)

This is a fine instance of *faux* apathy, a modern, theatrical simulation of the Stoic ideal whose original purposes, however, substantially elude Smith. What stands out is not its professed extirpation of passion, but rather the manner in which its seeming conquest is put on display. The conspicuous theatricality with which the raw and unfiltered psychic data of passion are shown to have been commuted into the artifact of a "concerted tranquility" is lauded as a worthy achievement precisely because it enables the spectator to admire the "effort" expended in that very transformation. What accounts for the pivotal role of both behavior and sympathy here is that, being socially intimated with such "propriety," they call for no action whatsoever on the part of the spectator. Following Rousseau, Smith consistently holds "that sympathy be something that one feels rather than something that one does," and as Nancy Armstrong has argued it is this very premise "that our most compelling feelings might have a source external to ourselves [that] becomes especially apparent in writing associated with 'sensibility.'"[18]

As in Smith's later economic arguments in the *Wealth of Nations* – a book now understood to have grown out of his moral philosophy – sympathy gives rise to a distinctly modern conception of sociality as an imagined, indeed simulated lateral bond between anonymous, hermetic, and substantially unrelated individuals. The compact that defines the modern economic and social order is strictly virtual; sympathy here functions as the moral equivalent of the speculative commodity of modern stock. Its value pivots on the shrewd management of how it is socially perceived, that is, on the accommodating and confident "behavior" (an important word used twice in the above passage) with which it is introduced into social space. Notably, the following rhetorical question (whose closing exclamation mark suggests that it only admits of an affirmative reply) shows Smith entirely blinded to the possibility of deception – collectively felt and reinforced – about the import and value of moral sentiments: "How amiable does he appear to be, whose sympathetic heart seems to re-echo all the sentiments of those with whom he converses, who grieves for their calamities, who resents their injuries, and who rejoices at their good fortune!" (*TMS*, 24). To embrace this stance is to delegate one's moral judgment and orientation to others, to make it dependent on behavioral cues furnished by others, and to collapse the good and the true into the contingent (and possibly opportunistic) affirmation that some particular view is perceived to have been accorded by others. Few models could be farther removed from the Stoic ideal of *autarkeia* than this transferential and manifestly heteronomous cultivation of moral agency.

For a canonical counterexample, one might look at Augustine's suspicious probing of theatrically induced "sympathy" (*misericordia*) in Book 3 (Chapter 2) of the *Confessions*. Sheer spectatorship, in Augustine's view, does not constitute but merely simulates moral meanings: "What compassion is to be shown at those feigned and scenical passions? For the auditors here are not provoked to help the sufferer [*sed qualis tandem misericordia in rebus fictis et scenicis? Non enim ad subveniendum provocatur auditor*]."[19] Spectatorship by itself is corrosive of action and agency in that it shifts the focus from the practical realization of the good to a narcissistic delight in the very failure of it. If staged suffering elicits sympathy, an increase of it will augment the sympathetic emotion and the spectators' gratification in its experience: "they so much the more love the author of these fictions, by how much the more he can move passion in them [*et auctori earum imaginum amplius favet, cum amplius dolet*]." Indeed, not only do theatrical simulations of suffering beget in the spectator an analogous, virtual attachment to "sympathy" ("Are tears therefore loved, and passions? [*lacrimae ergo amantur et dolores*]"), but they thereby also create an incentive to desist from practical action. The attenuation of moral agency, Augustine contends, stems from the spectator's attachment to the gratifying emotion of sympathy, over and against envisioning himself or herself as capable of achieving the good. To do the latter, in fact, is to conjure the logically absurd scenario of wishing for both the flourishing and the suffering of others at the same time:

> For if there be a good will that is ill-willed (which can never be), then only may he, who is truly and sincerely compassionate, wish there might still be some men miserable, that he might still be compassionate [*si enim est malevola benevolentia, quod fieri non potest, potest et ille, qui veraciter sinceriterque miseretur, cupere esse miseros, ut misereatur*].

As embodied by the stage and the hedonistic model of spectatorship to which it gives rise, Augustine's view of sympathy (*misericordia*) is that of a false good, a "joy that enchains" (*vinculum fruendi*), as he puts it with deliberate emphasis on the sexual connotations of *vinculum* (fetters, bondage). For Augustine, emotion is legitimate only inasmuch as it is a source of action, not a self-consuming, narcissistic experience; it enjoins the self "to relieve" (*ad subveniendum*) genuine "suffering" (*miseria*). The antitheatrical passage that opens Book 3 thus becomes a template for similar scenes in subsequent books, such as Augustine's deeply suspicious hermeneutic of his own grief at the death of a young friend in the book following (*Confessions* 4: 4–7); and it only finds its completion when, mourning the death of his mother in Book 9, Augustine appears at last to have achieved the proper ratio of grief, sympathy, and purposive action.

Fifteen hundred years later, the *Theory of Moral Sentiments* offers a starkly different picture by construing sympathy as a type of virtual action, rather than the inner condition to be complemented by an active quest for providing material relief to suffering. For Smith, both the spectator and "the sufferer long less for relief from pain than for the relief that is afforded only by sympathy," and the latter necessarily requires some material suffering (or theatrical simulation of it) as its precondition.[20] Discussing sympathy under the heading of the "social passions" (*TMS*, 38–40), Smith is at pains to conceive moral sentiments as the implicit approval of a prevailing social consensus. Having all but lost the hortatory and potentially transformative function as *source* that it held in Augustine, sympathy instead names (and affirms as valid) an existing and manifestly self-certifying social *outcome*: "Generosity, humanity, kindness, compassion, mutual friendship and esteem, all the social and benevolent affections, when expressed in the countenance or behavior, even towards those who are not peculiarly connected with ourselves, please the indifferent spectator … We have always, therefore, the strongest disposition to sympathize with the benevolent affections" (38–9). What facilitates this lateral, albeit inarticulate comradeship where "these affects, that harmony, this commerce, are felt" (39) is the virtual agency of the impartial spectator, a heuristic fiction that effectively collapses the distinction between self and other, thereby suspending the individual's self-awareness as a responsible being.

A coded answer to Hume's dystopia of a world where empirical fact and normative meaning have become terminally estranged, Smith's moral sentiment goes to the other extreme. By its very nature, he repeatedly argues, sympathy is a psychological fact that implies its own value – something suggested by the equivalent position of "countenance and behaviour" or "sentiments and behaviour" (*TMS*, 162). The moral significance of emotion is thus confined to its inter-subjective realization qua sentiment, a "fellow-feeling" whose meaning and value expire in the narcissistic dramaturgy of sentiments displayed and approved, respectively. David Marshall's well-known account of Smith's theatrical aesthetic seems rather oblivious to the question of just what kind of theater it is that the *Theory of Moral Sentiments* stages. On his account, Smith's "self is theatricalized [sic] in its relation to others and in its self-conscious relation to itself," even as it "must be an actor who can dramatize or represent to himself the spectacle of self-division in which the self personates two different persons who try to play each other's part, change positions, and identify with each other." Quoting Hume on how "the minds of men are mirrors to one another," Terry Eagleton likewise remarks on the narcissistic logic underpinning both Hume's and Smith's social theories: here "the [Lacanian] imaginary ... is a sort of mutual admiration society, in which in a kind of *mise-en-abyme* each act of reflection gives birth to another," thus revealing to us "the cyclical time of the imaginary rather than the linear evolution of the symbolic."[21] In so orchestrating a kind of *égoïsme à deux*, sympathy no longer furnishes the occasion for focused deliberation and judgment as to what action a given situation calls for. Rather, Smith's sociality is theatrical to its very core; here all the world is indeed a stage, albeit with this peculiar qualification that everyone is always on stage, but takes himself or herself to be a mere spectator.

At the same time, action and plot have been all but supplanted by an invariant display of epistemological narcissism inasmuch as every individual's performance is mimetically enslaved to the same role and script. We are much closer to the realm of Pirandello and Beckett than to that of Joseph Addison or even Shakespeare. The result is a system based on "substitution as a foundational principle [*eine Art fundamentaler Stellvertretung*]" where the "spectator is above all spectator of himself [*dieser Zuschauer ist vor allem auch Zuschauer seiner selbst*]"; subjective experience and meaning thus unfold within a hypothetical, indeed, virtual matrix of "as if" relations that render "truth values inseparable from role-playing, illusion, semblance, and stage dynamics."[22] This structural ambiguity of Smith's "moral sentiment" prompts Vivasvan Soni to speak of a persistent "double meaning of ... sympathy as affective identification and sympathy as pity" and, hence, to read Smith's *Theory* as inaugurating "an epochal shift ... from an ethical to an epistemological and identificatory structure of reading." According to the latter model, for the first time fully realized in Smith's account, "the purpose of a narrative is to allow one to reproduce imaginatively the world and the experiences of the protagonist, instead of producing an ethical relation to the narrative situation of the other." [23] In Smith's post-teleological world, action has been supplanted by the merely transactional, and rational deliberation by a cascade of minute transferences. No longer is human flourishing conceived as a dialectical (and potentially tragic) narrative composed of introspection, (mis-)judgment, and purposive action, however imperfect. Instead, by shifting focus to the socialization of potentially isomorphous selves – types rather than persons – Smith's project pivots on the mimetic acquisition and circulation of virtual sentiments in the guise of approved forms of "behavior." No longer understood as the teleological fulfillment of rational personhood (as in Aristotelian and Thomistic thought), action has instead been all but absorbed into this "sentiment of approbation" wherein, as Smith tells us, "there are two things to be taken notice of; first, the sympathetic passion of the spectator; and, secondly, the emotion which arises from his *observing the perfect coincidence* between this sympathetic passion in himself and the original passion in the person principally concerned" (*TMS*, 46; italics mine).

More pointedly yet, a later section probes the "difference between the approbation of propriety and that of merit or beneficence," with Smith concluding that "'till I perceive the harmony between his emotions and mine, I cannot be said to approve the sentiments which influence his behaviour" (*TMS*, 78). In both cases, Smith is responding to Hume's astute query whether it is reasonable to suppose that "all kinds of Sympathy are necessarily Agreeable," considering that "the Sympathetic Passion is a reflex image of the principal, [and hence] it must partake of its Qualities, and be painful where it is so."[24] In the event, Hume's question reflects something of a misunderstanding of Smith's argument, which is no longer premised on some garden-variety intersubjective relation between otherwise autonomous agents, but on the contrary understands moral agency as something transferentially constituted. In this regard, the word "sentiment" in Smith's eponymous moral theory is rather misleading in that it seemingly posits an interior and authentic emotional certitude as the epistemological point of departure for its argument.

Yet there are multiple indications that this is not the case. For one thing, the concept of the will has now definitively vanished from the vocabulary of moral theory, a development only intelligible when seen in the broader context of Smith's overall retreat from an interiorist, *res cogitans* model of subjectivity. To understand the nature and significance of that shift, it helps to interrogate the work's central concept: what does Smith mean by "sentiment," and what can that word signify in a philosophical context that has rendered the notion of a unified and autonomous self substantially inoperative? In Part VII of the *Theory of Moral Sentiments*, added to the sixth edition (1790), a short but incisive critique of Hutcheson's "moral sense" signals what Smith had taken to be his overall retreat from an internalist account of human agency. As Smith points out, Hutcheson's hypothesis of a moral sense operating wholly unconditioned by external contingency or interest actually breaks down when certain qualities are introduced that, "belong[ing] to the objects of any sense, cannot, without the greatest absurdity, be ascribed to the sense itself" (*TMS*, 323). What

Smith objects to is the very supposition that vice and virtue could ever be established by an inner sense operating independent of any contextual awareness or feedback; and his fictitious scenario of a "man shouting with admiration and applause at a barbarous and unmerited execution, which some insolent tyrant had ordered," is meant to illustrate the way that moral judgment is fully enmeshed with some ambient, social dynamic. Characteristically, Smith thus flags the susceptibility of Hutcheson's "moral sense" to possible misjudgments by depicting how the surrounding spectators should "feel nothing but horror and detestation" at such an inappropriate response, and how they are likely to "abominate him even more than the tyrant" who had ordered the execution. As he sees it, absent a reciprocally constituting social awareness, Hutcheson's moral sense lacks all criteria. For Smith, then, there can be no such thing as *synderesis*, for to hypothesize a purely inward source of moral orientation is to hazard a "perversion of sentiment" that may rise to "the very last and most dreadful stage of moral depravity" (*TMS*, 323).

Yet Smith's alternative of moral sentiments bound up with a spectatorial infrastructure that supplants judgment with "wonder and applause" is not without problems of its own. Above all, it is not easy to conceive of "sentiment," as Smith repeatedly insists we must, as socially conditioned and only arising from "mutual regard" (*TMS*, 39). Would not such sentiment be but a more genteel term for a prolonged bout of Freudian "transference" (*Übertragung*) or "projection"? As Vivasvan Soni notes, "affective communion does not occur simply on the evidence of the other's affect; a narrative is required to engender analogous affects in us." Yet if "a narrative understanding of sentiments is already built into [Smith's] theory," the self-certifying nature of affect allows us to take that narrative for granted and allows us to "focus our attention on the emotional state of the other without regard for narrative."[25] To this one might add that a "narrative" that tacitly regulates the specific dynamics of affect, both as it is expressed and received, should perhaps be thought of as an underlying "grammar" rather than narrative. In what is to follow, we shall think of it under the heading of "behavior."

Moreover, how is a spectator to "admire the delicate precision of [someone else's] moral sentiments" if not by autonomously interpreting the symbolic and gestural language ostensibly "expressing" such sentiments? If sentiment is inter-subjectively constituted, would this not preclude any critical or counterintuitive perspective on it? Does the *Theory of Moral Sentiments* recognize the need for a genuine hermeneutic of sentiment? To judge by contemporary responses to Smith's, the answer is "no." Characteristic of early reactions to the *Theory* is a peculiar blend of the enthusiastic and the unreflexive; reporting to the author that his *Theory of Moral Sentiments* "is in the hands of all persons of the best fashion," William Robertson notes "that it meets with great approbation both on account of the matter and stile" and that it is "impossible for any book on so serious a subject to be received in a more gracious manner."[26] A notice published in the *Monthly Review* echoes this appraisal and singles out the author's "agreeable manner of illustrating his argument, by the frequent appeals he makes to fact and experience." While declining to endorse Smith's account of sympathy outright, the reviewer depicts the book's argument as "extremely ingenious and plausible."[27] Finally making good on a promise (to Hume) that he would write to the author of the *Theory of Moral Sentiments*, Edmund Burke is quick to zero in on the favorable ratio between intellectual gain (large) and intellectual effort (small) involved in the perusal of Smith's work: "I do not know that it ever cost me less trouble to admit to so many things to which I had been a stranger before." Like so many other readers, Burke also dwells on "those easy and happy illustrations from common Life and manners in which your works abounds more than any other that I know by far," and he echoes similar praise by referring to Smith's "lively and elegant" style.

Writing for his *Annual Register*, Burke extends the latter comment in particularly revealing manner by remarking how Smith's "language is easy and spirited ... it is rather painting than writing."[28] Smith's stylistic accomplishments are well received on the Continent, too, with an early French review approving "par la beauté et la noblesse des sentiments." More surprising might be the same review's affirmation that "religion is respected throughout the work [*que la Religion y est par-tout respectée*]," considering that the same had been affirmed in the *Monthly Review* – viz., that "the strictest regard [is] preserved, throughout, to the principles of religion."[29] That both Anglo-Protestant and Catholic readers should reach such uniform (if notably vague) conclusions on the lingering question of Smith's attitude to religion brings us to the one point observable throughout virtually all of the responses to Smith's book: none of them actually identify, let alone engage, its thesis. Bearing a striking resemblance to Thomas Gray's contemporaneous "Elegy Written in an Country Churchyard," Smith's book draws responses that prove both sympathetic and non-cognitive. Working by accretion, the *Theory* sets forth "a system of moral philosophy able to propagate itself by accommodating ever more examples of its central claims. Where Hume had sought, through his

Treatise, to regulate social systems by means of systematic reflection on sympathy, Smith opted for a form of regulation that denied the appearance of systematicity."[30] The peculiar appeal of the *Theory of Moral Sentiments* stems from its having so successfully harnessed the power of the moral commonplace as both medium and message. Conspicuous for the low interpretive demands it imposes on the reader, Smith's *Theory* truly embodies its implicit conception of virtue, morality, and the good as so many behaviorally instantiated sentiments.

Yet another set of questions concerns the traditions of inquiry, ancient and modern, that are being linked by Smith's unprecedented emphasis on the sociality of the emotions. The two conceptual traditions that intersect in his work are classical (and early modern) Stoicism and, from what we may call the "future-past," the twentieth-century project of "behaviorism," whose conceptual roots have often been traced back to Locke's and Hume's epistemology, yet whose conceptual intent is uniquely anticipated in the *Theory of Moral Sentiments*. Though ostensibly consumed with psychological discriminations of all sorts, Smith's argument undertakes a comprehensive de-psychologizing of human agency. Hints to this effect come early, and they typically take the form of shifting focus from the (seemingly inscrutable) inner phenomenology of passion toward an analysis of its social, mediated character: "Sympathy ... does not arise so much from the view of the passion, as from that of the situation which excites it." By choosing emotions such as only ever occur in social settings (flustering, awkwardness, embarrassment, wit, etc.) rather than those liable to crystallize by way of sustained introspection (doubt, despair, hope), Smith draws attention to sociality as positively constitutive of the meaning of "passion" – a term that throughout the *Theory of Moral Sentiments* is all but synonymous with "emotion" yet categorically distinct from "sentiment." Smith's passing observation that "we blush *for* the impudence and rudeness of another" (*TMS*, 12) emphasizes how emotion involves an element of imagination, projection, and transference. Its semantics are conditioned not by an inner certitude, but rather by an agent's appraisal of a social situation as it is (probabilistically) taken to be perceived by multiple individuals. Moreover, Smith contends that this sublation of individual emotions into socially constituted sentiments is not some adventitious occurrence but is teleologically inscribed into the passions themselves. For intrinsic to every emotion there is a distinctive "motion," a gravitational force or tropism oriented toward the other person, much like Jacques Lacan's account of the "symptom" as something both real and intelligible only insofar as it is directed at an addressee.

Yet for Smith, inasmuch as that other is conjectured to be experiencing the same inner state, she or he is not simply the recipient of some seemingly interior, private feeling. Rather, she mimetically confers reality on that emotion as a socially viable sentiment: "Whatever may be the cause of sympathy, or however it may be excited, nothing pleases us more than to observe in other men a fellow-feeling with all the emotions in our own breast" (*TMS*, 13). If the first part of this sentence discounts the Platonic and Christian conception of emotion as an inner "source," it is not so much that Smith means to reject that view outright but that it no longer holds a central role within his overall philosophical project. Instead, an emotion in his *Theory* acquires distinctness, significance, and prima facie reality only if and inasmuch as it is reflected back by another self. What Smith calls "fellow-feeling" furnishes, if not the material ground (*ratio essendi*), then certainly the ground whereby an emotion becomes positively intelligible and significant (*ratio cognoscendi*). To the extent that "our approbation is ultimately founded upon a sympathy or correspondence [of sentiments]" (17), emotions can be credited with epistemological standing and moral significance only insofar as they reflect and reaffirm an underlying social consensus.

Central to the *Theory of Moral Sentiments*, and widely recognized as the book's main contribution to modern thought, is Smith's spectatorial model of moral cognition. Arguing that every sentiment encrypts an instance of approbation or disapprobation, Smith suggests that any judgment ventured about the merits or demerits of one's own (proposed) action is achieved by imagining whether the motive underlying it would meet with someone else's approval. Merely to put the question in that way is to have already migrated from an introspective to a transferential account of moral value. Sentiments in Smith do not identify but constitute their objects; social "facts" do not precede, let alone exist independent of, but are only realized *by* the interpretive and evaluative process of social exchange. Having famously enjoined his readers that "we must become the impartial spectators of our own character and conduct," Smith notes how any instance of subjective "approbation necessarily confirms our own self-approbation." The praise of others "necessarily strengthens our own sense of our praiseworthiness," an interesting update on the problem of Aristotelian *megalopsychia*, which had vexed virtue ethics for more than two millennia. For Smith, praiseworthiness is not inwardly felt, let alone unilaterally asserted by a moral agent about herself or himself. Rather, it is an inference compelled by how others have assessed one's own conduct: "So far is the love of praise-worthiness being derived altogether from that of praise; that the love of praise seems, at least in a great measure, to be derived from that of praise-worthiness" (*TMS*, 114).

Smith's claim that a spectatorial type of moral judgment performatively *creates* the very values to which individuals take themselves to be responding tends to come in two preferred metaphors, the theatrical and the optical. In one of his programmatic accounts of the impartial spectator (*TMS* 109–13), Smith thus insists that this virtual agent "is the only looking-glass by which we can, in some measure, with the eyes of other people, scrutinize the propriety of our own conduct" (112). That all moral judgment thus rests on, and is conditioned by, the a priori sociality of human beings becomes, according to Smith, evident if one entertains the counterfactual scenario. For a completely isolated self such as the noble savage of Rousseau's second *Discourse* "is provided with no mirror which can present . . . to his view" the "beauty or deformity of his mind" any more than that of his body. Yet "bring him into society, and he is immediately provided with the mirror which he wanted before. It is placed in the countenance and *behavior* of those he lives with, which always mark when they enter into, and when they disapprove of his sentiments; and it is here that he first views the propriety and impropriety of his own passions" (112). A fuller reading than can here be offered would have to take account of the peculiar conjunction of a regime of vision ("countenances" looking out, and being looked into, like looking glasses) with a term suddenly rising to prominence in post-metaphysical social theory: "behavior."

Striking about both is the absence of any deliberative, discursively reasoning component. Indeed, behavior and vision alike are valued precisely on account of their supposedly seamless, transparent, and effortless operation. At least for Smith – herein markedly differing from the forensic and evolving concept of vision that we find in Wordsworth, Goethe, Darwin, Ruskin, and Hopkins – neither sight nor behavior involve any sustained cognitive effort. Furthermore, both the concept of vision and of behavior can only signify on the basis of an already established (and likely complex) matrix of socio-cultural values. To derive moral approval or disapproval from the gaze of the other, like the kind of implicit social orientation denoted by the concept of "behavior," requires that a grammar of social propriety and order has already been internalized and thus has enabled the self to *look for* specific meanings rather than gazing outward without either purpose or comprehension. Yet to premise moral orientation on a specular and performative model of sociality comes at a price. At the very least, it means that moral cognition and judgment have been demoted from inner reflection to a mere reflex gesture, and that the counterfactual or creative potential of thought has yielded to the mimetic affirmation of some already established, albeit inarticulate notion of social propriety.

To develop a clearer sense of Smith's overarching objectives in the *Theory of Moral Sentiments*, and its overall implications for subsequent accounts of practical reason and ethics, one must scrutinize precisely this transposition of passion into sentiment. What prompts Smith's sweeping re-description of the inner life is a desire to restore to the self the epistemological coherence and moral authority that it had lost in Locke's *Essay*, Mandeville's *Fable*, and, especially, in Hume's *Treatise* and second *Enquiry*. As a result, stress is no longer placed on the ideational content of emotion, a point on which Smith appears cannily agnostic. Rather, scrutiny is brought to bear on the dramaturgy of emotion as it is "actualized" (in the Hegelian sense of *Verwirklichung*) in social exchange. The reality of emotion, Smith suggests, proves altogether inseparable from its social phenomenology, that is, from its mode of appearance as "behavior." For passion to be commensurate with (rather than disruptive of) social relations, it must take the form of a recognized symbolic practice (as opposed to subjective "expression"). Such practice, Smith shows, is likely to take the form of subtly evaluative discriminations whose referent is no longer some separate object "out there" but, rather, a set of circumstances socially shared and acknowledged as pertinent to the present situation. Insofar as it has been successfully transmuted into outward symbolic practice – viz., has been enacted as a specific "sentiment" *for* others – and only then, does passion acquire meaning and social value. Its true significance resides not in the moral value that it ostensibly "expresses" about some particular issue or fact. Rather, sentiment by its very nature accredits and reinforces a shared understanding of social relations as they are presently taken to be constituted.

The language of Smith's sentiment ultimately functions as a meta-language in Roman Jakobson's sense of appraising a prevailing "code" rather than denoting a distinct "referent."[31] As Smith puts it: "to approve of the passions of another . . . as suitable to their objects, is the same thing as to observe that we entirely sympathize with them" (*TMS*, 16); and again: "we approve of another man's judgment, not as something useful, but as right, as accurate, as agreeable to truth and reality: and it is evident we attribute those qualities to it for no other reason but because we find that it agrees with our own" (*TMS*, 20). Moral sentiments, then, are not stand-alone units of subjective experience. On the contrary, they constitute prima facie acts of "assent" or value judgments about a social situation, and as such they do not signify an inner (mental) action but a social transaction. By its very nature, such a type of "agreement may produce peace but it cannot produce truth."[32] Anticipating Kant's judgment of taste, which "imputes" (*ansinnen*) universal agreement to those for whom it is voiced, Smith here is able to recover from the extreme nominalism of Hobbes, Locke, and Hume whose strictly epistemological focus had led them to characterize passion as a hermetic, ineffable, and altogether transient phenomenon.

While there is an obvious and significant Stoic dimension to Smith's view of moral sentiments as quasi-judgments, his *Theory* no longer furnishes any frame of reference for such evaluation independent of (or anterior to) the social interaction whose success or failure such judgments ratify. In this regard, Smith's appeal to "the great machine of the universe" and the "secret wheels and springs which produce" its countless appearances (*TMS*, 19), or his later affirmation that "in every part of the universe we observe means adjusted with the nicest artifice to the ends which they are intended to produce" (87), is less a nod to Stoic physics than an echo of the pervasive deism and the commonplace, "just-so" story endlessly recycled by eighteenth-century natural theology, a subject on which Smith repeatedly lectured between 1752 and 1764 as professor of moral philosophy at the University of Glasgow. Particularly revealing in this regard are the uninspired, token references that Smith inserted into the sixth edition (1790) of the *Theory of Moral Sentiments*, such as his tribute to "the great Director of the universe" and to "the idea of that divine Being, whose benevolence and wisdom have, from all eternity, contrived and conducted the immense machine of the universe, so as at all times to produce the greatest possible quantity of happiness." There is a strong deist tendency in this notion of a God who makes sure the cosmic train runs on time but who has delegated day-to-day operations of the material world to "his viceregent upon earth," including the task of "superintend[ing] the behaviour of his brethren" (130). While affirming that "the administration of the great system of the universe . . . is the business of God and not of man," Smith's quick shift of focus strongly suggests that his God remains de facto invisible and, lacking credible revelation, has become all but irrelevant to moral thought: "To man is allotted a much humbler department, but one more suitable to the weakness of his power and to the narrowness of his comprehension; the care of his own happiness, and that of his family, his friends, and his country" (236–7).

The focus on ethics, which for the ancient Stoics was altogether inseparable from their physics, has here been compartmentalized as a separate province governed by finite, fallible, and self-determining human agents. There is no vertical connection between the judgments and appraisals ventured by the latter and the divine *logos* as disclosed in a cosmological system. Indeed, precisely because judgment appears terminally estranged from any transcendent, metaphysical source, its present-day incarnation as "moral sentiment" can only be focused on, and is exclusively licensed by, endlessly shifting social circumstances. It is just this definitive separation of judgment from ontology that attests to the modernity of Smith's entire project. Additionally, it bears recalling that whatever "social reality" happens to be contingently at issue in a case of moral sentiment does not pre-exist the specific judgment in question – say as a Platonic idea or Aristotelian/Thomist "substantial form." On the contrary, such reality is only instantiated by a vast number of affective micro-judgments and acts of transference.

In this regard, Smith's choice of laughter as an example is both revealing and shrewd inasmuch as it vividly displays the non-propositional and quintessentially social nature of moral cognition:

> He who laughs at the same joke, and laughs along with me, cannot well deny the propriety of my laughter ... If I laugh loud and heartily when he only smiles, or, on the contrary, only smile when he laughs loud and heartily; in all these cases, as soon as he comes from considering the object, to observe how I am affected by it, according as there is more or less disproportion between his sentiments and mine, I must incur a greater or less degree of his disapprobation: and upon all occasions his own sentiments are the standards and measures by which he judges of mine. (*TMS*, 16–17)

In ways that Keats would later explore to rich aesthetic effect, Smith identifies the misalignment of emotion as prima facie evidence for the way that all moral values are social in essence. That is, embarrassment of the kind here described shows Smith to understand moral interaction to be no longer about inner certitudes or metaphysical norms and aspirations. Rather, the objective at hand is the success (or failure) of social interaction itself.[33] Erving Goffman thus notes that contrary to a "breach" of some moral norm, which is likely to "give rise to resolute moral indignation," embarrassment amounts to a constitutively social emotion. For even as

> the expectations relevant to embarrassment are moral ... we should look to those moral obligations which surround the individual in only one of his capacities, that of someone who carries on social encounters. The individual, of course, is obliged to remain composed, but this tells us that things are going well, not why. And things go well or badly because of what is perceived about the social identities of those present.[34]

It is no accident that Smith and Goffman should both have happened upon the seeming benefits of embarrassment. Long before there was to be a discipline called sociology and a subsidiary specialization known as behaviorism, Smith offers a sophisticated (if deeply problematic) "account of the formation of groups"; and it is this account's structural reliance on the specter of embarrassment that prompts us to wonder "what sort of unity" sympathy could possibly generate.[35] As it turns out, the psychological constellation known as embarrassment operates at all times, and not merely when it is manifestly unfolding – along with all the outward symptoms of blushing, flustering, sweaty palms, and stammering speech so prominent in John Keats's canny fusion of depth-psychology and class-consciousness. In a remarkable passage, Smith thus contends that both the outward conduct and inner constitution of the self are at all times circumscribed by the specter of embarrassment. Even at its most introspective, the individual is intelligible to itself only as a socially constituted reality. However free from embarrassment at moments of introspection, it is precisely the constant possibility of some performative misadventure in public that furnishes the motivational prompt for how to cultivate one's persona:

> The man of real constancy and firmness, the wise and just man who has been thoroughly bred in the great school of self-command ... has never dared to forget for one moment the judgment which the impartial spectator would pass upon his sentiments and conduct. He has never dared to suffer the man within the breast to be absent one moment from his attention. With the eyes of this great inmate he has always been accustomed to regard whatever relates to himself. This habit has become perfectly familiar to him. He has been in the constant practice, and, indeed, under the constant necessity, of modeling, or of endeavouring to model, not only his outward conduct and behaviour, but, as much as he can, even his inward sentiments and feelings, according to those of this awful and respectable judge. He does not merely affect the sentiments of the impartial spectator. He really adopts them. He almost identifies himself with, he almost becomes himself that impartial spectator, and scarce feels but as that great arbiter of his conduct directs him to feel. (*TMS*, 146–7)

This is about as vivid and palpable an account of the concept of "introjection" (a term first coined by Sándor Ferenczi in 1909) as one could ask for. Unlike Ferenczi's and Freud's subject, however, Smith's impartial spectator is stripped of all magical or fantasy-like elements and, thus, appears much closer to Lacan's model according to which "introjection is always the introjection of the speech of the other."[36] Introjection thus attests to the incomplete and seemingly illegitimate nature of the individual understood in strictly inward, mentalist terms. Smith thus insists how the virtual superego of the impartial spectator is not merely to be accommodated in "outward conduct and behaviour," but that it is to be internalized as the real substance of moral agency. The "great inmate" or "man within the breast" is not merely some occasional complement of the self, nor is he to be construed as some didactic allegory of righteousness or virtue.

At first glance, the above passage appears to present us with a genuinely (neo-)Stoic model of self-cultivation. Still, the emphasis on "self-satisfaction" stands out as discordant, if for no other reason than that it revives the dilemma that Aristotelian *megalopsychia* had bequeathed Christian virtue ethics, which obviously looks upon pride with acute misgiving. Moreover, Smith here tells essentially a story of emancipation *from* a debilitating inner life. Stoic habituation – whose *telos* was wisdom – yields to modern, neo-Stoic self-discipline, whose *telos* is approval; and it is only for the sake of such approval (and the successful socialization it betokens) that the self embraces the surrogate or virtual interiority of the "man within the breast." The person qua unique, spiritual self is expunged, much in the way that seventeenth-century Calvinist and Jesuit thought had appropriated the neo-Stoic language of self-discipline. With the virtual agency of the impartial spectator having supplanted the metaphysical idea of the person, Smith's *Theory of Moral Sentiments* no longer grants epistemological legitimacy to the idea of the person – understood as a unique, unclassifiable, and "incommunicable" being (as Boethius had defined it). Concurrently, the emotions enjoy epistemic standing only insofar as they can be converted into socially sanctioned sentiments. At the same time, the inner life has reality and legitimacy solely as a socially constituted and accredited performance, a process for which Smith does not (indeed, cannot) identify any *telos* or *terminus ad quem*. Echoing Smith's position, Goffman's closing discussion of the "social function of embarrassment" stresses the extent to which this particular affect is properly *generative of the self*, rather than being the inward property of an already constituted individual:

> By showing embarrassment when he can be neither of two people, the individual leaves open the possibility that in the future he may effectively be either. His role in the current interaction may be sacrificed, and even the encounter itself, but he demonstrates that while he cannot present a sustainable and coherent self on this occasion, he is at least disturbed by the fact and may prove worthy at another time.[37]

Both Smith's account of the impartial spectator (a behavioral template to be introjected) and Goffman's embarrassment as a quintessentially "social" emotion betray an eagerness to abandon mentalistic and psychologizing conceptions of moral meaning and agency. Crucial to understanding Smith is that "sentiments" are not, properly speaking, *inner* states but arise from our unwitting negotiation of a complex grammar of social values and behavioral patterns or averages. A fuller account of this dynamic would further develop the revealing, indeed symptomatic assimilation of rational habits to a non-cognitive model of "behavior."[38]

NOTES

1 David Marshall, *The Figure of Theater: Shaftesbury, Defoe, Adam Smith, and George Eliot* (New York: Columbia University Press, 1986), 177.

2 Terry Eagleton, *The Trouble with Strangers: A Study of Ethics* (Oxford: Wiley-Blackwell, 2009), 71, 75.

3 Thomas Pfau, *Minding the Modern* (Notre Dame, IN: Notre Dame University Press, 2013), 356–61.

4 Adam Smith, *The Theory of Moral Sentiments*, ed. D. D. Raphael and A. L. Macfie (Indianapolis: Liberty Fund, 1984), 40; henceforth quoted parenthetically as *TMS*.

5 Jürgen Habermas, *Structural Transformation of the Public Sphere*, trans. Thomas Burger (Cambridge, MA: MIT Press, 1991), 103; on Smith's political and economic theory, see also Robert Mitchell, *Sympathy and the State in the Romantic Era* (New York: Routledge, 2007), 76–93.

6 Francis Hutcheson, *An Essay on the Conduct of the Passions and Affections, with Illustrations on the Moral Sense*, ed. Aaron Garrett (Indianapolis: Liberty Fund, 2002), 19.

7 David Hume, *Essays Moral, Political, and Literary*, ed. Eugene F. Miller (Indianapolis: Liberty Fund, 1985), 262–3.

8 Albert O. Hirshman, *The Passions and the Interests: Political Arguments for Capitalism before its Triumph* (Princeton, NJ: Princeton University Press, 1977), 17; on the emergence of financial and industrial capitalism, see also Karl Polanyi, *The Great Transformation* (Boston, MA: Beacon, 1957), 33–42 and 56–76; J. G. A. Pocock, *Virtue, Commerce, and History* (New York: Cambridge University Press, 2009), 103–24, and Pocock, *The Machiavellian Moment* (Princeton, NJ: Princeton University Press, 1975), 462–505; Linda Colley, *Britons: Forging the Nation, 1707–1837* (New Haven, CT: Yale University Press, 1992), 55–100; for basic statistical information on this shift, see Roy Porter, *English Society in the Eighteenth Century* (Harmondsworth: Penguin, 1982), 185–213.

9 Pocock, *Machiavellian Moment*, 456–7.

10 Jerome Schneewind, *The Invention of Autonomy* (Cambridge: Cambridge University Press, 1998), 380.

11 Adam Smith, *The Wealth of Nations*, ed. James Cannan (Chicago: University of Chicago Press, 1976), 28; italics mine.

12 Pocock, *Machiavellian Moment*, 456–7; Hirshman, *Passions*, 32.

13 Pocock, *Machiavellian Moment*, 457.

14 Hutcheson, *Essay*, 19.

15 Eagleton, *Trouble*, 43; Mitchell, *Sympathy*, 82, 87.

16 Martha Nussbaum, *The Therapy of Desire* (Princeton, NJ: Princeton University Press, 1996), 369, 373.

17 Seneca, *De Ira* ["On Anger"], trans. Jeffrey Henderson (Cambridge, MA: Harvard University Press, 2003), 2, 3.

18 Nancy B. Armstrong, *How Novels Think: The Limits of Individualism, 1719–1900* (New York: Columbia University Press, 2005), 14–15.

19 St. Augustine of Hippo, *The Confessions*, trans. William Watts (Cambridge, MA: Harvard University Press, 2006); all citations are from Book 3, Chapter 2 of *Confessions*, 100–5.

20 Marshall, *Figure of Theater*, 173.

21 Ibid., 176; Eagleton, *Trouble*, 48.

22 Joseph Vogl, *Kalkül und Leidenschaft: Poetik des ökonomischen Menschen* (Zurich: Diaphanes, 2008), 80. Sympathy, which "promised to serve as a bridge between self and other, betrays its promise and leaves the self embroiled with its own emotions, which it imagines to have come from the other." Vivasvan Soni, *Mourning Happiness: Narrative and the Politics of Modernity* (Ithaca, NY: Cornell University Press, 2010), 309.

23 Soni, *Mourning*, 305, 311.

24 Hume to Smith (28 July 1759), in *The Letters of David Hume*, 2 vols., ed. John Young Thomson Greig, vol. 2 (Oxford: Clarendon, 1932), 313.

25 Soni, *Mourning*, 300–1.

26 Letter to Smith (14 June 1759), qtd. in *TMS*, 26.

27 July 1759 (no. xxi); the unsigned review is attributed to William Rose; qtd. in *TMS*, 27.

28 Burke, letter and review as quoted in *TMS*, 28–9.

29 *Journal encyclopédique* (October 1760), qtd. in *TMS*, 29.

30 Mitchell, *Sympathy*, 89. Similarly, Eagleton notes that in Smith's Lacanian framework, "there is no Other of the Other – no meta-language which would allow us to investigate our intersubjective meanings from a vantage-point beyond them, . . . rather as for Adam Smith there is no ground to our world beyond 'the concurring sentiments of mankind'" (*Trouble*, 75–6).

31 See Roman Jakobson, "Linguistics and Poetics," esp. his distinction between conative, emotive, referential, and meta-lingual functions, in *Language in Literature*, ed. Krystyna Pomorska (Cambridge, MA: Harvard University Press, 1987), 69–73.

32 Leo Strauss, *Natural Right and History* (Chicago: University of Chicago Press, 1953), 11.

33 On the sociality of emotion in Keats, see Christopher Ricks, *Keats and Embarrassment* (Oxford: Clarendon, 1984), 1–49; and Pfau, *Romantic Moods*, 309–39.

34 Erving Goffman, "Embarrassment and Social Organization," *American Journal of Sociology* 62, no. 3 (1956): 268.

35 Mitchell, *Sympathy*, 82–3.

36 Jacques Lacan, *The Seminar. Book I. Freud's Papers on Technique, 1953–54*, trans. John Forrester (New York: Cambridge University Press, 1988), 83. Terry Eagleton notes that "for Smith, as for Lacan, our actions are always at some level a message directed to the Other. It is just that in Lacan's view this dialogue can never be reduced to the imaginary reciprocities of a Smith, for whom each of us thrives under the benignant eye of a collective other" (*Trouble*, 75).

37 Goffman, "Embarrassment," 270–1.

38 See Pfau, *Minding the Modern*, 361–71.

CHAPTER 3

Like love
The feel of Shelley's similes

Julie Carlson

> Love is like understanding, that grows bright
> Gazing on many truths; 'tis like thy light,
> Imagination![1]

A major impediment to adopting a Shelleyan practice of love is the difficulty of seeing what he is talking about.[2] This involves trouble visualizing the features of Shelleyan love and concern that his love is irresponsible in its opportunistic modes of thinking and behaving. Emphasizing that indistinctness *is* Shelley's style and that this manner of depicting reality is central to his revolutionary vision and purpose has gone a way toward clarifying the practically utopian nature of his thought.[3] Person, place, thought, thing: all must be perceived as in no place permanently and as no place in particular if they are working to facilitate the vision of reform that Shelley's writing seeks to effect. But such multiplication and immaterializing of objects is often the ethical objection leveled against Shelleyan love, that can seem so cavalier or indifferent to the reality of others as domestic partners or subjugated communities.[4] The combination of these difficulties tends to exclude Shelley's voice from renewed critical interest in love as a political, pedagogical, or ethical force.[5] Yet Shelley's *A Defence of Poetry* (1821) maps out this path by linking poetry to general humanistic inquiry and both to imagination as the faculty by which we learn to love across difference.[6]

This essay, then, reconsiders the attractions of Shelleyan love by foregrounding simile as Shelley's most basic device for forging connection. It argues that the comparative simplicity of simile as a poetic figure and the overtness of its analogical worldview are vital to Shelley's theories of mind and his emphasis on the cognitive dimension of love. Usually folded into discussions of his practices of figuration and analogical

I thank Aranye Fradenburg, Christine Lewis, Vera Tobin, Joel Faflak, and Richard Sha for assistance in writing this essay.

processes generally, Shelley's use of simile warrants attention as central to his epistemology as well as poetry.

> What thou art we know not;
> What is most like thee?
> ("To a Skylark," 31–2)

My argument is that Shelley's well-analyzed growing ambivalence toward metaphor does not apply to simile and that his uses of it work against the ideological and thus deadening operations of metaphor, in part because they seek to relink thought to embodied affect.[7] At the same time, unlike the post-structuralist privileging of metonymy over metaphor as a way of countering metaphor's white mythologizing, Shelley favors the connection-makings of both simile and metaphor for their cultivation of both/and thinking.[8] But like the trope itself, this process does not occur in a vacuum, so a second argument concerns the primacy of simile to Shelley's habits, theories, and expressions of mind, especially his contention that essence is a being-like-thee. Like his better elaborated poetic figures, Shelley's similes work against entrenchment in linguistic and ethical realms, perpetually un-building the object world, including its putative opposition to the internal life of the subject, by showing objects to be as ethereal and ever-changing as subjects and the so-called subjective.[9] The specific affective achievement of simile is to *mobilize* subjects by allowing otherwise disparate energies to cohere for a time and directing the energy released in such new-found alliances toward legal, political, and literary reform.

My brief for Shelley's similes rests on the interrelated claims that Shelley's conception of the world is analogical, that simile's connection-forging features work by linking cognitive to affective processes, that both the achievement and reform of love depend on coordinating these levels and processes, and that the distinctiveness of Shelley's similes is their counter-intuitive aims. My thinking is greatly enhanced by Mark Bruhn's recent cognitive accounts of Shelley's theory of mind and poetics of analogy as well as by specific focus on simile advocated by cognitive linguists Michael Israel, Jennifer Riddle Harding, and Vera Tobin.[10] The chief difference between Bruhn's and my approach, besides the restrictiveness of my focus on simile, is the audience whose "mind" each of us seeks most to affect through reconsideration of Shelley. Bruhn aims to bring Shelley into dialogue with cognitive studies scholars, finding in Shelley's analogical poetics a challenge to contemporary cognitive-scientific models of blending theory and their overly restrictive view of poetry. I wish to bring Shelley's similes into an activist practice that recognizes literature as a partner in intersubjective and interpersonal relations.

I can sharpen the stakes of my focus by calling to mind one of the most objectionable similes in Shelley's entire arsenal: his advice to the disenfranchised to "Shake your chains to earth like dew / Which in sleep has fallen on you" (*The Mask of Anarchy*, 154–5). His seeming indifference to the crushing weight of material conditions is matched by over-sensitivity to the burden of being attached, for example in deeming life partnership as inhabitation with "one chained friend" (*Epipsychidion*, 158–9, 162–4). To a large degree, my reading of simile means to reconsider the functioning of chains in Shelley's worldview and epistemological-political analysis, his developing recognition that histories of enslavement are intimately linked to habits of mind, that the latter must become conscious before they and the histories that they perpetuate can be changed, and that a long history of disregarding the minds of the oppressed is what contemporary poets and poetry must redress: what he is coming to mean in 1819 by a philosophical view of reform that is trained on poets as the world's unacknowledged legislators. My claim is that simile is his primary tool for forging a notion of causality that is less driven by necessity. It can be seen as the most basic workout routine of Shelleyan imagination.[11]

Minding what is most like thee

Bruhn's most basic point in "Shelley's Theory of Mind: From Radical Empiricism to Cognitive Romanticism" is that Shelley adopts from empirical philosophers the view that analogizing is the foundational cognitive operation through which humans arrive at the concept as well as experience of mindedness but that, by also grounding morality in this elemental operation, Shelley aims to "rescue" moral thinking from the "*accidental logic*" of association. To do this, Shelley "installs" analogy "at the root of human epistemology and therefore of human sociality and morality" and also "*motivates* it developmentally." In terms germane to my investigation, the "force" that Bruhn sees as driving Shelley's developmental cognitive hierarchies is called "*analogy* in its operational dimension and *love* in its teleological dimension."[12]

Demonstrating the interconnections between these twin aspects of Shelley's thinking also proceeds by analogy, as Bruhn highlights in explicating Shelley's well-known assertion in *A Defence of Poetry* that "to be a poet is to apprehend the true and the beautiful, in a word the good which exists in the relation, subsisting, first between existence and perception, and secondly between perception and expression" (512). The "explanatory logic is not only chronological (or developmental) but explicitly *relational*, which is to say *analogical*: existence is to perception as perception is to expression, or in other words, there is a 'permanent analogy of things,' a sort of essential 'similitudes or relations' that constitute 'all knowledge' ('perception') and 'human intercourse' ('expression')."[13] This analogical framework is shown to underlie Shelley's various accounts of development that all depart from the striking claim made in "On Love" that "[w]e are born into the world and there is something within us which from the instant that we live and move thirsts after its likeness." This thirst for resemblance, Bruhn shows, underlies the "deep structural connections between such cognitive phenomena as analogy, imitation, language, representation, and theory of mind" that the second paragraph of the *Defence* maps out precisely as the "scaffolded evolution" of "symbolic representation systems" experienced by the infant and the savage in their joint acquisitions of culture.[14] Crucial in Bruhn's account is how the "ontology and teleology" of analogy as an elemental force of attraction not only "cause those effects of pattern recognition and social imitation that are instinctively deployed by the developing child" but also themselves are driven by "innate 'social sympathies,' the 'laws from which, as from its elements, society results'" – those "laws" being "equality, diversity, unity, contrast, mutual dependence." In Shelley's terms, social interaction installs "a being within our being," and it is this "one mind" that underlies both self- and other representation and thus "mind reading" and sociomoral reflection.[15]

The adequacy of Bruhn's linking this "being within our being" with social interaction merits further comment. A related concern is the degree to which Bruhn's exposition obscures the *feel* of Shelley's epistemological orientation and practice, geared as each is also to modeling how to continually unlearn and unsay what little we have come to think about existence, including our own.[16] This over-drive to coherence is mitigated by Bruhn's subsequent attention to Shelley's "Harmonious Madness: The Poetics of Analogy at the Limits of Blending Theory." As a general corrective to cognitive grammar and conceptual metaphor theory, the essay highlights how "Romantic theory and practice," especially Coleridge's and Shelley's, considers poetry's primary ambition and recommendation to be its capacity to surpass "horizons of consistent conceptualization" and to make visible in poems the "*activity* of imagination."[17] As a specific challenge to blending theory, it offers a sustained account of the analogies in "To a Skylark" to show that the avowed bafflement over them expressed in the poem's reception history is a success of its analogical workings, which cognitive theorists of poetry would do well to consider.

Bruhn's exposition of the analogies that go into composing a "bird thou never wert" reveals how consistently they "flout" the "directionality constraints" operative in metaphoric projections on the scores both of abstraction and saliency. Whereas most poetic metaphors proceed in their comparisons from concrete to abstract and from more salient to less salient, those in "To A Skylark" evince "exceptionally high frequencies of deviance" when measured against Yeshayahu Shen's statistical analysis of metaphors in a wide sampling of poems. "On the abstractness scale, one-third (33.3 percent) of the poem's first six metaphors involve second-order violations, as opposed to an average of 8.5 percent in Shen's corpus, while fully one-half (50.0 percent) of the six involve second-order violations on the saliency scale, as opposed to an average of 15.0 percent in" Shen's corpus. Shen delineates in a subsequent essay the cognitive costs of such deviance: these kinds of analogy take longer to interpret, evoke a "greater variety of interpretations," are "more difficult to recall, and are judged as less natural and meaningful than canonical similes." Precisely these costs are benefits in Shelley's mind and to the reformist appeal of his poetry. As a challenge to blending theorists, the cognitive process "coded in and primed by" his poem is better described as "conceptual *composition*, in which the elements 'positioned together'" do not "resolve into a unitary concept or representation."[18] Or, as critics like John Wright, William Keach, and Jerrold Hogle have demonstrated, Shelley's figures privilege mental processes and processing in order to enhance what Hogle calls human "sensitivity to activity in conceptual space."[19]

Cognitive theorists who disarticulate simile from metaphor identify the features that make simile less prone to join metaphor in becoming a tool of ideology. Interestingly, Shelley's critique mirrors George Lakoff and Mark Johnson's conceptual metaphor theory. Whereas for Shelley the evolution of vital metaphors into concepts makes language "dead to all the nobler purposes of human intercourse" (*A Defence*, 512), for Lakoff and Johnson this evolution is precisely what "we live by"; the "most fundamental values in a culture will be coherent with the metaphorical structure of the most fundamental concepts in the culture."[20] By contrast, the most "striking" feature of simile to Michael Israel, Jennifer Riddle Harding, and Vera Tobin is its explicitness as a comparison, one that requires the maker to hold in mind "both of the things [that] one is comparing." Unlike literal comparisons, simile requires that one *search* for a connection among otherwise unlike objects and their domain matrices and, unlike metaphor, similes do not project structure from a source that often remains "backgrounded and effectively transparent" and therefore determinative.[21] Instead, similes "match structures that are construed as simultaneously present in both domains," work by "description" that is highly "evocative" and associational, and, because similes often denote the respect in which the source and target are being compared through a *tertium*, they can feature "very fanciful and unexpected juxtapositions."[22] Like an unbodied joy whose race is just begun.

These cognitive features of simile appeal to Shelley also in confronting the reality that life *is* constrained, a reality that simile aims both to display as provisional and to reform by showcasing reality as a perception that can be changed through altering how humans, especially poets, express it. The difficulty here is that what constrains are not only the concepts, institutions, and systems that inform a human being but also the process of attachment through which a being emerges as a person and a potential human. Re-cognizing the determinations of this process is the most difficult aspect of the difficult education that Shelley's poetics offer as a means of countering the "education of error" that, according to "On Life," comprises life for most people, which Shelley views simultaneously as the challenge of human development and to conventional notions of development as progress (507).[23] The unlearning that Shelley perceives as the precondition to personal and cultural advances leads him to privilege states of infancy as harboring the cognitive (i.e., affective) stage which the current generation would do well to re-access, a state that in the infancy either of a person or a culture Shelley associates with poetry. But here too, Shelley recognizes that the proffered solution, the vitally metaphorical nature of poetic language, over time becomes the problem of desensitization through the successes of metaphor, a subset of the paradox that "[a]lmost all our familiar objects" over time come to index the percipient's subjectivity rather than their objectivity as things (507). I wish to apply Shelley's historicist thinking, then, to his notions of infancy and the being within one's being in relation to which subjects encounter and then have the opportunity to learn and change what they desire and might grow to love. Shelley's de-familiarizing of the trope that normally conceives the unfamiliar through resemblance to the familiar is essential to this project.

Vitalizing conception: simile's working potential

Like a child from the womb, like a ghost from the tomb,
   I arise, and unbuild it again.

("The Cloud," 83–4)

The topic of infants and infancy in Shelley is a minefield, especially around 1819 and even if one leaves aside the explosive issue of Shelley's parenting.[24] In part, this is because his version of infancy intensifies two cognitive challenges of his philosophical view of reform: underscoring that any solution becomes the problem if it is viewed in only one way or in the same way over time; that deepening the capacity for attachment entails lessening its entrenchment into normative social positions like parent/child, husband/wife, dominant/oppressed. In their depictions of potential new lives, the paired lyrical and tragic dramas of 1819, *Prometheus Unbound* and *The Cenci*, push to extremes and hold at extremes the ontological situation of the infant as sheer potentiality and as doomed by its conception. This dramatic polarity highlights what Shelleyan poetics otherwise confronts less schematically, the provisionally sad reality that "there is something within us which from the instant that we live and move thirsts after its likeness" and that there is so little that surrounds a newborn in the human sphere to which it should become attached ("On Love," 504). Indeed, the avidity of the newborn's desire for connection, whereby "the infant *drains* milk from the bosom of its mother" "probably in correspondence with this law," heightens the potential lyricism and tragedy ("On Love," 504; italics mine). In explicating Shelley's theory of mind, Bruhn shows how, through the (m)other–infant relation, the infant moves from a state of one-mindedness, where "*I, you, they*" exist neither as grammatical categories nor perceptual realities, and "learns to symbolically distribute an originally unassigned phenomenon (mental experience) for the purpose of shared representation," which the second paragraph of *A Defence of Poetry* delineates as a sequence of analogy-making developments evident in a child's forms of play ("On Love," 504). But not only is the end goal of human development for Shelley attainment of a similarly undifferentiated cognitive and moral state but also poetry is the means through which so-called developed minds intuit, re-experience, and learn to desire to regain this lack of differentiation. This is why I believe that the being within our being, that Bruhn correctly associates with the (m)other–infant dynamic and characterizes as installing a "*social* being within our *natural* being,"[25] must be thought also in relation to the function articulated for it in *A Defence of Poetry*, as what "defeats the curse which binds us to be subjected to the accident of surrounding impressions," especially those composing our parents (533). Until such time as more parents start behaving like poets – imaginative, playful, visionary, free – it falls to the "tragedies of the Athenian poets" to mirror "that ideal perfection and energy which every one feels to be the internal type of all that he loves, admires, and would become" (520). That is, the poetic holds open the social while new lives are formed in relation to it.

As Ann Rowland argues, Shelley's linkage of poetry and infancy in *A Defence of Poetry* draws on a rich tradition of late-eighteenth-century thought about the origins of language but in order to reverse standard conceptions of development.[26] The linkages that Shelley stresses highlight infancy's and poetry's shared pre-cognitions and how each is instrumental in keeping the other fresh, full of the potential each embodies. Wonder is the most familiar of their joint sensations, which "the babe / In the dim newness of its being feels" toward all creation and which poetry recaptures by "lift[ing] the veil from the hidden beauty of the world" and "purg[ing] from our inward sight the film of familiarity which obscures from us the wonder of our being" (*Queen Mab*, 7.152–3; *A Defence*, 517, 533). A second is vacancy, a lack of distinctness that characterizes the infant's "unpractised sense" and is characteristic of reverie in "persons who in this respect are always children" (*Queen Mab*, 7.155; "On Life," 507). "Let us recollect our sensations as children. What a distinct and intense apprehension had we of the world and of ourselves" *as* undifferentiated. "We less habitually distinguished all that we saw and felt from ourselves," instead experiencing things as "one mass," as if one's "nature were dissolved into the surrounding universe, or as if the surrounding universe were absorbed into their being" ("On Life," 507). Sensing wonder and vacancy together helps to keep the draining nature of the Shelleyan infant from being simply a drain on others or wholly self-negating. The inability to erect clear boundaries is met *and* fed by the hunger for ever-new connections – again, like the replenishments of poetry, whose thoughts attract and assimilate "all other thoughts, and which form new intervals and interstices whose void for ever craves fresh food" (*A Defence*, 517).

Viewed in this light, the delight of the infant playing in the second paragraph of the *Defence* expresses what play inaugurates: a *fort/da* mastery of (maternal) absence that is not pitched between the all-or-nothingness of presence as a concept. Drawing on infant observations, Aranye Fradenburg recasts the Freudian significance of the baby's play with a spool of thread as expressing "not so much alternating oppositions" (present/absent; here/there) as "particularities linked by this thread." "If the symbol substitutes for an absence, it does so only because a trail has been followed. Babies get what is meant by *fort* and *da* by following the clues that lead from here to there."[27] Shadowing forth this re-cognition, the Shelleyan child strings together particularities that are themselves insubstantial, already rendered as elemental, as if to facilitate ever-fresh connection-making and a conceptualization of the object-world as mutable, ever-changing, not there simply for the taking. For Shelley's infant to actualize the promise that it embodies, it must retain *as* its mental state that in which "we are born into the world" – where the not-one thirsts for attachment *and* is yet unattached to specific objects and habits of being.

This is not as regressive as it sounds, and it underlies two further projects that twine infancy to poetry, one on the level of representation, one of affect. The spacy features of Shelleyan children, the most ideal of whom have wings, are existentially space-clearing: of conventional habits of being-human; of the familial ties that bind; of anchorage in the familiarity that impedes delight in alterity, including fostering perceived resemblances among species. Portraying children as like the elements (cloud, mist, spark, seed), often being conveyed in highly fanciful vehicles (boats, cars, chariots), and lacking in standard human sentiments situates the value of a child less in singularity than elemental potentiality, which means mutability and attraction to alterity – at once desiring and being other to what coheres as "self" by means of language and social convention.

On the level of representation, Shelley's poetry also tries to simulate what a perennially newborn perspective takes in. As opposed to those "puling babes / Who, nursed in ease and luxury, make men / The playthings of their babyhood" and assume their destiny as once and future kings, promising infants arise "from the womb" eager to unbuild and rebuild (*Queen Mab*, 3.209–14). "Wild, yet gentle," their eyes are "gamesome," "laughing," "joyful," "darting," eager for connection and just as eager to detach and look elsewhere (*Julian and Maddalo*, 145).[28] Even in sleep, they are busy processing, their "little lips ... moving / Amid the changing light of their own smiles / Like one who talks of what he loves in dream" (*Prometheus Unbound*, 4.266–8). This activity of receptivity is nourished through a freedom linked to their rejection of constraints. Though the poem is split over why Alastor does not realize his potential, he is off to a good start, nursed as he is on "bright silver dream" as well as nature, with "thirsting lips" that drink also from the "fountains of divine philosophy" and the "truth" of "fable" (*Alastor*, 67–75). Nor is his fierce rejection of conformity portrayed as blameworthy. Children in other poems are similarly averse to the clod- and herd-like quality of the masses but, less dispirited by the discovery, begin un/building anew. In contrast to the "insensate mob," Ianthe alone weeps over the fate of the condemned man when, as "an infant," her mother took her to "see an atheist burned" (*Queen Mab*, 7.1–2, 10–11). Another "babe" shares "his morning's meal" with "the green and golden basilisk / That comes to lick his feet," while, "fearless and free," "ruddy children" play "within the massive prison's mouldering courts," their "notes" of "merriment" drowning out "the shuddering voice of hoarse despair," thereby "mock[ing] the dungeon's unavailing gloom" (*The Daemon of the World*, 3. 371, 375). Repeatedly, the beauty that these "wild but gentle" children perceive leads to harmony with other persons and species.

Sometimes Shelley portrays these features of infancy through simile. But conveying to grown persons the desirable sensation of infancy is what outpourings of simile in poems like "Hymn to Intellectual Beauty" and "To a Skylark" accomplish, no matter the target. According to Erik Gray, any poetic list is "to some extent self-defeating" in that it provides "too much sensory information in quick succession for a reader to be able to picture clearly the individual species." Listings of simile are "still more paradoxical – not just asymptotic, but essentially self-destructive."[29] For Shelley, this self-destructiveness is positive as long as it is a phase in a larger process. A profusion of source objects dissolves, diffuses and dissipates the solidity of any depicted target, physical or mental, at the same time that it mimes a breathless hunger and reaching out for experience. This use of simile achieves on the pulse what it cannot achieve in the mind or through the use of words alone: clearly holding in mind two or more things at once; experiencing as simultaneity what language can only portray as a series. In a word, "beauty" as "love" as "truth" as "freedom."

Exercising imagination

Rise like lions after slumber.

The paired topical poems, *The Mask of Anarchy* and *Peter Bell the Third*, demonstrate how this poetic re/vision of infancy aids in reforming grown persons and historically subordinated peoples. Linked through their inquiry into the Peterloo Massacre and composed within a month of each other in the fall of 1819, these poems confront how thoroughly hope has grounds for despair but enjoin readers against giving into the impulse. While it is tempting to deem the "seemingly effortless victory" of Hope over Anarchy at the beginning of *The Mask of Anarchy* as an instance of Shelley's magical thinking, especially on the score of class and gender politics, the verdict occludes the specificity of Shelley's philosophical view of reform as it is worked out in both of these poems.[30] Different as they are in tone, genre, and target, both envision a future of reform by giving a detailed presentation of *how* concepts and thus mental possibilities are changed, or precluded, in persons and peoples, and both stage this process through the interplay they choreograph between metaphor and simile.[31]

It is not as if nothing happens in the lines where hope vanquishes anarchy off-stage. What the passage literally observes is how thoughts emerge out of the anarchic substance of their inception and get set into action. "Small at first," this mist, light, or image – no matter which as long as its matter is depicted as visibly evanescent – is shown to grow increasingly powerful while remaining an undifferentiated "Shape" (104, 110). The eventual subject–verb completion ("mist . . . grew") is suspended over five intervening lines that chart mist's progress by comparing it to increasingly powerful forms of non-substance. Frail "[l]ike the vapour of a vale: / Till as clouds grow on the blast, / Like tower-crowned giants" who "speak in thunder to the sky, / It grew" (105–10). A mirroring series concludes the description of this shape's development into a force that provokes the springing up of "Thoughts." Here too arrival at thought is suspended over five lines that depict various processes that such an arrival resembles.

> As flowers beneath May's footstep waken
> As stars from Night's loose hair are shaken
> As waves arise when loud winds call
> Thoughts sprung where'er that step did fall.
> (122–6)

An important indication that thoughts do not spring up out of nowhere even if pinpointing from where they spring is impossible, this depiction naturalizes their emergence and suggests the contingency of causality. Equally important is how the depiction interweaves simile (as flowers, as stars, as waves) and metaphor (May's footstep, night's loose hair, and winds calling), an interweaving that enacts what "On Life" affirms about the similarity between thought and thing, mind and matter. It also heralds the defining strategy of the poem through which thoughts become actualized as Freedom. That section (156–261) begins by defining the concept of Freedom as what it is not – which is Slavery, characterized as what the people "know" experientially – and then shifts at line 209 to defining Freedom as a positivity, emphatically not "A shadow soon to pass away." The ensuing delineation (216–61) falls into three stages whose content but also method models the de/conceptualizing and actualization of freedom. At first enacting that a concept like Freedom is not all things to all people by presenting a series of homely scenarios ascribed to particular groups ("for the labourer," "to the rich"), it then shifts at line 230 to equating

Freedom with equally weighty concepts ("Thou art Justice," "Thou art Wisdom," "Thou art Peace"), ensuing descriptions of which stress their categorical and categorizing impulses – "never" being the term that connects the three. This set of assertions, rendered categorical also through their end-stoppings, cease at the point (246) where Freedom is said to be "Love," when the passage then shifts to a series of enjambed lines that name the means (Science, Poetry, Thought) through which a bedimmed, but not extinguished, Liberty rekindles its flame and posits the features of what Freedom "art": Spirit, Patience, Gentleness.

This defining strategy then generates ensuing directives on how the people can solidify their grasp on freedom through combined practices of coalition-building, free speech, and non-violence, each means being crucially dependent on the ontology and mechanics of simile: the capacity to perceive resemblances between unlike persons, to eschew even species-specific categories of identity, and to rise like lions after slumber. But it also simulates the mental preconditions to achieving these reforms by bringing home to oppressed persons what a concept of freedom feels like. What the definitions in their varying degrees of categorical thinking suggest is that, because freedom is still *only* a concept to persons systematically oppressed by power, it lacks the affective drawing power that might mobilize them to envision or claim freedom as a possible lived reality. At the same time, retrieving this birth-right involves keeping their concept of freedom as dynamic as possible and adaptable to changing circumstances. Portraying this conceptual dynamic may be why the entire passage (213–62) eschews simile but also depicts Freedom as a concept linked by metaphor to other concepts in various stages of de-conceptualization.[32] But the passage also enlists differences in the entailments of these metaphors to foreground how interactions between categorical and site-specific notions of freedom are part of the process through which a concept like freedom is felt and then actualized.

In my view, this is the point of concluding the definitional series with the disarmingly passive equation of Freedom to "Spirit, Patience, Gentleness" (258). Given that the poem's categorical imperative is physical non-violence, cultivating these pacific traits is crucial, the specified means of which ("Science, Poetry and Thought") take a long time to come into effect (254). At the same time, like its companion prose text, the poem acknowledges the unfair burden that the injunction against violence places on the disenfranchised. But whereas *A Philosophical View of Reform* treats sympathetically the people's episodic recourse to violence as provisionally necessary, given how frequently the powerful are out for their blood, *The Mask of Anarchy* places the responsibility for violence – both recourse to it and outlawing of it – on class privilege in its definitional explication of Love (246–53). The surprising positive linkage of love with "the rich" anticipates their inclusion in the call to join the people's Assembly so long as they meet the only criterion for inclusion: response-ability to the "moans" of the miserable and thus affiliation with an anti-identitarian coalitional politics (282–90). And it specifies the precondition for that response-ability: refusal to underwrite violence, however "noble" the cause – a condition that, for opposite reasons, rich and poor have a hard time visualizing.

This unusual address of "love" to the rich specifies how Shelley sees *The Mask of Anarchy* working to "awaken & direct the imagination of reformers" like himself – an analysis of personal responsibility that is also operative in *Peter Bell the Third*.[33] The poem's rousing refrain is directed to the oppressed, whose right to claim it must first be brought to their attention before they can direct it. "Rise like lions" articulates a strength within the multitude that has gone unapprehended even by them, and that, once apprehended as strength in number, starts the process of rendering their chains less weighty. The assertion that these chains fell on them while they were sleeping and because they were asleep only blames the victim if one does not register the implicit counter-assertions of the people's inherent strength when conscious and the inadequacy of their sleep since it is devoid of dreams. Expressing the latter as a failure, not an impossibility, is achieved through the "like dew" of sleep that voices the poem's alliance with the oppressed through two different processes. Semantically, "like dew" typically is linked in Shelley's poetry to dream, infancy, and renewal, not to a dampening of the senses, which suggests that the "like dew / Which in sleep has fallen on you" is the *means* by and through which chains can begin to be shaken off – that is, through a renewal of the people's dreams.[34] Syntactically, the positioning of "like dew" at the end of a line that is not end-stopped and that needs to be read through to its different conclusion mirrors the regressive-progressive method that underlies Shelley's philosophical view of reform.[35] Meaning-making, and the connections which inform it, require further reading. Reading through the enjambment corrects an initial misimpression (chains are like dew) to reveal that their shaking off occurs to the extent that the renewing properties of dew accompany a person's or people's sleep. Plus, the passage mandates that these words be heard "again – again – again" *so that* the possibility that they augur stands a chance of emerging as a possibility by first drowning out the "thundered doom" of "oppression" that has been "Ringing through each heart and brain" for eons (365–6).

This is how poetry holds open, and sometimes has to pry open, spaces of reform through forging ever-new alliances and possibilities. And this is why Peter Bell's selling out of his renovating verses is held responsible for maiming the people ("Slash them at Manchester, / Glasgow, Leeds and Chester"). Silencing these verses keeps oppression's doom thundering by means of the literary canon. In fact, the dullness attributed to apostate verse is even deadlier than the violence it incites because it is so invasive and pervasive.

> The woods and lakes, so beautiful,
> . . .
> All grew dull as Peter's self
> . . .
> Love's work was left unwrought: – no brood
> Near Peter's house took wing.
> (740, 742, 750–1)

Nor is Wordsworth the extent of the problem, as James Chandler indicates in underscoring the poem's expressed sympathy for early Wordsworth, its diagnosis of the problem of imagination as widespread, not particular (besides, Peter is "three in one"), and its rebuke of Popean satire for mistaking its target and critique: "as if a poet's character were simply his or her own affair" and not a complex amalgam of who s/he has read and how s/he has been read.[36] On the one hand, the problem is a literary establishment that serves concept and commodification rather than poetic vitality and thus is of the devil's party; on the other, a diagnosed imbalance in imagination that cuts extremely close to the composing poet's bone. Shelley risks identification with the imagination anatomized in *Peter Bell the Third* because the subject is indeed important: both true about the formation of his mind and key to maintaining his in the cause of freedom.

The odd chronology of the poem's sections, where "Grace" follows "Sin" but actually precedes it in Peter's development, resembles the time-warping of Hope's victory in *The Mask of Anarchy*. For "Grace" is an origin-story of Peter's receptivity to poetry that portrays the process as a being-in-relation that accesses and activates the being within his being, here described as a Nature in league with poetry. In the Devil's service but not fully awake at his party, Peter receives "divine" transmissions emitted from "a mighty poet" to whom Peter listens "like a man asleep." That poet speaks of what the divinity of "Poetry" is like: "wind" that blows as it likes;

dew that "rains down," whose power ("from God") "comes and goes like dream" (390–3). Once actually (near-) asleep, Peter begins composing songs that feature favored "spots" of his past life that he now visits "in his thought" but without knowing "whence the thoughts were fed" which fill his "fancy" (413–17). Said to "start and wake / Like a lover," sleeping Peter composes "in a wild measure" that keeps to the beat of his formerly "wayward" course (403–5, 415). "[O]bscure remembrances" of "the wide earth's bosom green" stir the "harmony in Peter" that is expressed in "metre" and that "augurs" to this cold age the "diviner flame" that Poetry keeps alive by "announcing" its untameability through enlistment of simile ("Like gentle rains," "Or like the sudden moon," "like day" (443–4, 438–42).

Unfortunately, Peter's "accustomed flame" goes out when he is "born anew" as a "formal Puritan," deferring the people's awakening indefinitely (562, 581, 551). But the "Sin" that precedes "Grace" already diagnoses a weakness in Peter's imagination on which the literary establishment capitalizes. Peter's "drift" only heads in one direction. "[A]ll things that [he] saw and felt / ... seemed to melt / Like cloud to cloud, into him," but "Nothing went ever out" – including enacted responsiveness to Nature's eroticism (273, 276–7, 296–7). "Sin" offers a loving corrective in the voice of a female Nature, who states her preference for errant poets like Burns, who "knew my joy / More, learned friend, than you," and Boccacio, "whose sweet words might cure a / Male prude like you from" this "low-tide in soul" that is "like a stagnant laguna" (327–8, 330–2). Of all possible "sweet words" Nature favors these in Italian:

> A mouth that's been kissed does not lose its charm;
> Rather, it renews itself as does the moon.
> (326–7, 330–2n3)

Such advice is left hanging in terms of Peter's fate, but it is taken up – and how – in Shelley's poetic production. For better and worse, *Epipsychidion* makes a platform out of the prescription, announcing an overhaul of the "code / Of modern morals" that intentionally constricts the "heart" and "brain" so that a lover remains blind to the wonder of fresh possibilities (153–4, 170). As counter to this concept of love, it offers a love that is "like understanding, that grows bright, / Gazing on many truths" and "like" the "light" of imagination which "fills / The Universe with glorious beams" and "kills / Error, the worm, with many a sun-like arrow / Of its reverberated lightning" (162–9). Much has been said against the male privilege apparent in this model of love and the self-absorption evident in Shelley's enactments of it.[37] Even sympathetic readers of the poem, who rightly construe its figurations as indicating the "insufficient void" that informs love rather than as a secret coding for his series of lovers, protest too much in their denial of the poem's autobiographical resonances.[38] Admitting multeity, seriality, and third parties into views and practices of sexual love *is* essential to re-cognizing the oneness that love in Shelley expresses, which is part and parcel of perceiving humans as im/personal and intertextual. The admission is phenomenally risky. That Shelley takes it, however, measures his difference from his mentors in liberation: Godwin, whose rejection of their lived fidelity to his strictures against marriage stunned both Percy and Mary; Wordsworth, whose championing of nature's freedom stopped at embrace of its sensuality and waywardness; and Coleridge, whose embrace of both was so weighted with denial. Put more positively, his relaying of love as like understanding and like imagination offers a theory and practice of simile.

Part of what a love that is like understanding and imagination offers is a method for bringing to consciousness the rhythms and patterns that comprise the being within one's being in order ultimately to make them more expansive. Since "neither the eye nor the mind can see itself, unless reflected upon that which it resembles," and since neither organ can perceive in advance what might resemble the "assemblage of the minutest particulars of which [its] nature is composed" ("On Love," 504), Shelleyan personae venture out into the "rough world" thirsting for what Christopher Bollas terms an "aesthetic moment" that signals a promising re-encounter with the "first human aesthetic" that composes the mother–infant environ.[39] Experiencing one's unexpected resonance with another indicates that the being within one's being has met its antitype and that the conscious being would do well to look into it – that is, gaze on the reflection in the other of what from the (m)other is producing this accord.

> Lift up thine eyes
> And let me read thy dream.
> (*Prometheus Unbound*, 2.1.55–6)

This necessarily experimental process of gazing on as "many truths" with as few preconceptions as possible suggests a provisional phenomenological value of chains. The clang of accord signals recovery of important data regarding to what one is pulled and presents one's unconscious modes of relating and for analysis. This may be why ideal Shelleyan couples, once they are through vibrating and dissolving into each other's beauty, usually (plan to) talk or read widely in an effort to narrativize their accord.[40] This may also be why ideal community members dedicate themselves to the re-writing of history, including of poetry, so that it bespeaks before-unapprehended experiences. For conscious analysis of the laws of attraction, especially magnetism, is even more important for altering the phenomenology *of* chains: their felt indissolubility, the inevitability and permanence of their linkages. Re-cognition of chains as soluble in turn affects conscious experiences of them: making, for example, marriages more sustainable or social, racial, and economic imprisonment less all-confining because not definitive of one's senses of possibility.

The most tangible way to exercise this hope of expansiveness is through simile, the linguistic tool of affective re-cognition. Similes enact and thus help to achieve a love that is like understanding and imagination by strengthening thirst for connection and forging connections among all manners of person, idea, and thing. As a trope, similes are unabashedly promiscuous, delighting in the most fanciful hook-ups. Moreover, learning to apprehend "this" as like "that" but also "this" as like "not-that" acknowledges the negativity in the coherence of objects and leaves room for their becoming something other over time and as a property of time. Because the something other which simile's mode of cognizing envisions does not congeal as concept or stereotype, simile keeps language alive to the "nobler purposes of human intercourse" (*A Defence*, 512). As opposed to metaphors, they do not have to be taken up by the speech community for them to be perceived as meaningful, do not have to be repeated often, even more than once, for them to have a discernible effect. Plus, they announce their like-minding intentions explicitly, rather than coercing harmony through covert power plays and overt appropriations of the other's reality, akin to what Gayatri Spivak perceives training in the humanities as effecting: the "*uncoercive* rearrangement of desires" that is fundamental to ending cycles of terror and violence.[41] One could even call them good-natured, as when the set of similes listed to envision the pig-queen's proposed angelic ascent in *Swellfoot the Tyrant* pokes fun at the "aught" of intellectual beauty by descending into "*anything*."[42] Such allowance for differences in perspective, even reversal of one's former perspective, frees knowledge from authority and makes the process of learning less likely to mobilize one's defenses. In this, similes help "kil[l] / Error, the worm" by valuing errancy as empirical method. This shift intensifies the willingness to try since making a mistake is no longer such a catastrophe.

That simile has at least two ways of being one is vital to the being-in-relation that its ontology supports: both that there is no "identity" prior to

attachment and that venturing out depends on feeling attached to someone or something somewhere. Shelley never wholly breaks free from the
metaphors by which humans live, as recourse to love and life as a journey
implies.[43] But by radically destabilizing where either can be said to begin,
end, or head, he makes the journey more of an adventure – also because no
one can start out if existentially detached. As "On Life" recognizes, a
phenomenological experience of the *concept* of life is so overwhelming –
both so astonishing and so unfathomable – that "it is well that we are thus
shielded" from it by the "familiarity" of living. If we were conscious every
moment of "[l]ife, and the world, or whatever we call that which we are
and feel," it would "absorb and overawe the functions of that which is [its]
object" ("On Life," 505). This is the one familiarizing aspect of conventional simile's modes of cognition that Shelley endorses. Since there is no
"identity" prior to attachment, "one" can only venture out to the degree
that one is and feels related. Simile manifests this twinning by having at
least two ways of being one – "like" and "as."[44]

  The doubling inherent *in* the "as" form of simile, its ability to compare
(like "like") and mark temporal duration (like "while"), accentuates the
both/and style of thinking inherent in its like-form and assists achievement
of it. Often denominated epic or Homeric simile, the as-form employs a
mini-narrative to depict its source object, a practice that de-materializes the
object world in an expressly narratological way. *This* resemblance-creating
tactic through narrative requires what the other grammatical function of
"as" specifies: duration, holding off conclusiveness while the story
unwinds. Moreover, not knowing, when an "as" clause begins, whether
it will be making a connection or marking a space of time intensifies the
suspension of mind that Shelleyan un/learning requires.[45] Both processes
aid the dwelling in uncertainty that a love like understanding and imagination requires and help "kil[l] / Error, the worm" by reconceiving errancy
as life's working method – a re-valuation that fosters willingness to try,
because making a mistake is a source more of pride than shame.

  The combination of these two forms of simile and the differing affective
registers that they activate and coordinate are underscored in *The Triumph
of Life* as the potential triumph of living. A phenomenal instantiation of
how the search for definitive answers enchains persons to life rather than
attaches them to living, the poem attempts to demolish "thought's empire
over thought" through staging as answers to life's pressing questions the
deferral of an answer, though precisely not avoidance either of questioning
or exchanges (211). Moreover, felt alienation from life's conventional
triumphs and the absence of questioning that joy in those triumphs

registers (45–9) not only characterizes both the narrator and the shade of Rousseau who emerges in response to his first voiced questions (177) but also is the founding condition for envisioning new forms of thought: that is, that the alienation is not existentially isolating but is processed through a being-in-relation, here relayed also as and in simile.

> Not wanted here the just similitude
> Of a triumphal pageant, for where'er
> The chariot rolled a captive multitude
> Was driven.
>
> (117–20)

The precondition to not being swept up by life's forward march is narrated by the shade of Rousseau, who depicts the "shape all light" trampling out his thoughts in a passage whose play of simile also induces the mental condition that its temporary conclusion articulates (367–95). That is, the passage not only specifies the state of mind most conducive to being shown "whence I came, and where I am, and why" "as one between desire and shame / Suspended" but also enacts this suspension through the interplay between "as" and "like" forms of simile: "as one enamoured is upborne in dream," "as if the gazer's mind was strewn beneath / Her feet like embers" (367, 385–6). Moreover, the interplay between the affective workings of each form, whereby "thirst for knowledge" involves a deferral of conclusion, ensures that avidity for life does not drain one's life force, that it remains a valued impulse in the degree to which it is not simply impulsive.

Learning this is what the shade of Rousseau hopes to be taught by his pupil-mentor, how not to "plung[e] into the 'thickest billows of the living storm'" to his enervation (466–7). This entails making a space of time (as) in which truly transformational connections (like/as) can be made – whereby the shape all light, in trampling out thought, is depicted "[a]s Day" treading "out the lamps of night" and then arriving "like day" (389–93). Something like Bollas's "aesthetic *moment*" as measuring momentousness rather than time. For errancy to flourish as a state of mind conducive to love, it thirsts after connections as a prophylactic against rushing to judgment or into prematurely permanent attachments. Otherwise, magnetic attraction is fateful, not freeing, where "[l]ike moths by light attracted and repelled," maidens and youth "[o]ft to new bright destruction come and go" (152–4). The doubling in the "as," its suspension of conclusion while it unfolds possibilities, like the outpouring of "like" clauses, is a grammatically ingenuous way to model an approach to life's questions: as a rush that suspends. *The Triumph of Life* need not conclude as a poem in order for its similes to advance a practice of life and love.

NOTES

1 Percy Shelley, *Epipsychidion*, in *Shelley's Poetry and Prose*, ll. 162–4. Unless otherwise noted, all citations hereafter are from this edition, cited parenthetically in the essay by title; book, canto, act, and/or scene and line numbers for poetry; and title and page numbers for prose.
2 For the theory, see Tedi Chichester Bonca, *Shelley's Mirrors of Love: Narcissism, Sacrifice, and Sorority* (Albany: State University Press of New York, 1999); Nathaniel Brown, *Sexuality and Feminism in Shelley* (Cambridge, MA: Harvard University Press, 1979); Samuel Lyndon Gladden, *Shelley's Textual Seductions: Plotting Utopia in the Erotic and Political Works* (New York: Routledge, 2002); William Ulmer, *Shelleyan Eros: The Rhetoric of Love* (Princeton, NJ: Princeton University Press, 1990).
3 Book-length examples include Oscar W. Firkins, *Power and Elusiveness in Shelley* (Minneapolis: University of Minnesota Press, 1937); William Keach, *Shelley's Style* (New York: Methuen, 1986); Karen A. Weisman, *Imageless Truths: Shelley's Poetic Fictions* (Philadelphia: University of Pennsylvania Press, 1994); Stuart Peterfreund, *Shelley among Others: The Play of the Intertext and the Idea of Language* (Baltimore, MD: Johns Hopkins University Press, 2002); and Stuart Sperry, *Shelley's Major Verse: The Narrative and Dramatic Poetry* (Cambridge, MA: Harvard University Press, 1988).
4 See Anne Mellor, *Mary Shelley: Her Life, Her Fiction, Her Monsters* (New York and London: Routledge, 1989); and Janet M. Todd, *Death and the Maidens: Fanny Wollstonecraft and the Shelley Circle* (Berkeley, CA: Counterpoint, 2007).
5 See Martha Nussbaum, *Political Emotions: Why Love Matters for Justice* (Cambridge, MA: Belknap, forthcoming); Eric Gregory, *Politics and the Order of Love: An Augustinian Ethic of Democratic Citizenship* (Chicago: University of Chicago Press, 2008); bell hooks, *All About Love: New Visions* (New York: William Morrow, 2001); and Adrian Blackwell, "Love is a force that acts as the productive motor of every emancipatory politics," an exhibition on urban space, JMB Gallery, University of Toronto, 2010. In terms of pedagogy, see especially Eve Kosofsky Sedgwick's concept of reparative criticism, "another name for which is love," in *Touching Feeling*, 123–52; and Pablo Ouziel, "Love-Force as Educator," Political Thoughts website, www.pabloouziel.com/academic-essays, last accessed 29 August 2013.
6 See Julie A. Carlson, "Romantic Poet Legislators: An End of Torture," in *Speaking about Torture*, ed. Julie A. Carlson and Elisabeth Weber (New York: Fordham University Press, 2012), 221–46.
7 On the inadequacies of metaphor, see Richard Cronin, *Shelley's Poetic Thoughts* (New York: St. Martin's Press, 1981), 5–8; and Ulmer, *Shelleyan Eros*, 78–109.
8 For classic formulations, see Jacques Derrida, "White Mythology: Metaphor in the Text of Philosophy," *New Literary History* 6, no. 1 (1974): 5–74; Jacques

Lacan, "Agency of the Letter in the Unconscious," *Ecrits: A Selection*, trans.
Alan Sheridan (New York: Norton, 1977), 146–78; Paul de Man, "The
Rhetoric of Temporality," in *Blindness and Insight*, 2nd rev. edn. (Minneapolis:
University of Minnesota Press, 1983), 187–228. On the inadequacies of meta-
phor, see Stuart Curran, *Shelley's Annus Mirabilis: The Maturing of an Epic
Vision* (San Marino, CA: Huntington Library, 1975).

9 On linguistic entrenchment, see Joan Bybee and Paul J. Hopper, eds., *Frequency
and the Emergence of Linguistic Structure* (Amsterdam: John Benjamins, 2001).

10 Mark J. Bruhn, "Shelley's Theory of Mind: From Radical Empiricism to
Cognitive Romanticism," *Poetics Today* 30, no. 3 (2009): 373–422; Bruhn,
"Harmonious Madness: The Poetics of Analogy at the Limits of Blending
Theory," *Poetics Today* 32, no. 4 (2011): 619–62; and Michael Israel, Jennifer
Riddle Harding, and Vera Tobin, "On Simile," *Language, Culture, and Mind*,
ed. Michel Achard and Suzanne Kemmer (Stanford, CA: CSLI Publications,
2004): 123–35.

11 I posit simile as the most instrumental aspect of the techne of the aesthetic. As
Marc Redfield elucidates Samuel Weber's definition: "'as something that *goes
on*,' technics moves *away* from itself in being what it is'" (*The Politics of
Aesthetics: Nationalism, Gender, Romanticism* [Stanford, CA: Stanford University Press, 2003], 19).

12 Bruhn, "Shelley's Theory," 374, 382, 417; all original emphasis.

13 Ibid., 382.

14 Ibid., 402, citing "On Love," 504.

15 Ibid., 406, 411.

16 Bruhn's concluding praise for Shelley's resemblance to Daniel Dennett, one of
whose "dangerous ideas" Bruhn sees Shelley's work anticipating and
deepening, depends on under-estimating Shelley's poetic resistance to it, i.e.,
Dennett's claim that "the memes for normative concepts – for *ought* and *good*
and *truth* and *beauty* – are among the most entrenched denizens of our minds"
("Shelley's Theory," 418).

17 Bruhn, "Harmonious Madness," 627.

18 Ibid., 656–7.

19 Ibid., 657–8.

20 George Lakoff and Mark Johnson, *Metaphors We Live By*, 2nd edn. (Chicago:
University of Chicago Press, 2003), 22.

21 Israel, Harding, and Tobin, "On Simile," 129, 130.

22 Ibid., 132, 126, 130.

23 See Joel Faflak, "The Difficult Education of Shelley's 'Triumph of Life',"
Keats–Shelley Journal 58 (2009): 53–78.

24 For his notoriety as a father, see my *England's First Family of Writers: Mary
Wollstonecraft, William Godwin, Mary Shelley* (Baltimore, MD: Johns Hopkins
University Press, 2007), 257–78.

25 Bruhn, "Shelley's Theory," 402; original emphasis.

26 See Ann Wierda Rowland, *Romanticism and Childhood: The Infantilization of
British Literary Culture* (Cambridge: Cambridge University Press, 2012), 12–16,
67–108.

27 Aranye Fradenburg, "The Goddess of Small Strings," unpublished paper, 5.
28 On the necessity to look away, see Beatrice Beebe, "Co-constructing Mother–Infant Distress: The Microsynchrony of Maternal Impingement and Infant Avoidance in the Face-to-Face Encounter," *Psychoanalytic Inquiry* 20, no. 3 (2000): 421–40.
29 Erik Gray, "Faithful Likenesses: Lists of Similes in Milton, Shelley, and Rossetti," *Texas Studies in Literature and Language* 48, no. 4 (2006): 290–311, 292.
30 Andrew Franta, "Shelley and the Poetics of Political Indirection," *Poetics Today* 22, no. 4 (2001): 765–89; 777; also see Susan Wolfson, *Formal Charges: The Shaping of Poetry in British Romanticism* (Stanford, CA: Stanford University Press, 1997), 195–200.
31 A more explicit linkage is Shelley's poem "Similes, For Two Political Characters of 1819," in *The Poetical Works of Percy Bysshe Shelley*, ed. Harry Buxton Forman, 4 vols. (London: Reeves and Turner, 1882), vol. 4: 6–7.
32 This process enacts via its definitional strategies what a poem like "Ode to Liberty" achieves through its historical narrative. Stanza IV prepares for the rising up of Athens by invoking a series of similes analogous to the yet-veiled condition of "Art's deathless dream" and indicating how "verse" was "yet a speechless child" who only "murmured" (54–9).
33 To Leigh Hunt, *Letters of Percy Bysshe Shelley*, 2 vols. ed. Frederick L. Jones, vol. 2 (Oxford: Clarendon, 1964), 191.
34 On dream as different from sleep, see Firkins, *Power and Elusiveness in Shelley*, 73–81.
35 James Chandler, *England in 1819: The Politics of Literary Culture and the Case of Romantic Historicism* (Chicago: University of Chicago Press, 1998).
36 Ibid., 523; see 515–24.
37 Simon Haines, *Shelley's Poetry: The Divided Self* (New York: St. Martin's Press, 1997); Mellor, *Mary Shelley*.
38 Thomas Pfau, "Figuring the 'Insufficient Void' of Self-Consciousness in Shelley's 'Epipsychidion,'" *Keats–Shelley Journal* 40 (1991): 99–126.
39 Christopher Bollas, "The Aesthetic Moment and the Search for Transformation," *Transitional Objects and Potential Spaces: Literary Uses of D. W. Winnicott*, ed. Peter L. Rudnytsky (New York: Columbia University Press, 1993), 40.
40 Roy R. Male, Jr., "Shelley and the Doctrine of Sympathy," *The University of Texas Studies in English* 29 (1950): 183–203.
41 Gayatri Chakravorty Spivak, "Terror: A Speech after 9–11," *boundary 2* 31, no. 2 (2004): 81–111; 81.
42 *Swellfoot the Tyrant*. See Samuel Lyndon Gladden, "Shelley's Agenda Writ Large: *Oedipus Tyrannus; or, Swellfoot the Tyrant*," online at www.rc.umd.edu/praxis/interventionist/gladden, last accessed 30 August 2013.
43 Lakoff and Johnson, *Metaphors We Live By*, 107–16.
44 Israel, Harding, and Tobin suggest why this classic formulation "gives much too narrow a view of the forms which similes may take" ("On Simile," 125).
45 Ziva Ben-Porat, "Poetics of the Homeric Simile and the Theory of (Poetic) Simile," *Poetics Today* 13, no. 4 (1992): 737–69.

CHAPTER 4

Jane Austen and the persuasion of happiness

Joel Faflak

Everything in life proclaims that earthly happiness is destined to be frustrated, or recognized as an illusion ... There is only one inborn error, and that is the notion that we exist in order to be happy.

Arthur Schopenhauer, *The World as Will and Representation*

Money is human happiness *in abstracto*; and so the man who is no longer capable of enjoying such happiness *in concreto*, sets his whole heart on money.

Arthur Schopenhauer, *Parerga and Paralipomena*

A large income is the best recipe for happiness I ever heard of.

Jane Austen, *Mansfield Park*

I. "However oddly constructed such happiness might seem"

Early in her final novel, *Persuasion* (1817), Jane Austen, after recounting the "little history of sorrowful interest" that is the prequel of Anne Elliot's being persuaded by Lady Russell against marrying the then fortune-less Frederick Wentworth, figures Anne as a kind of happiness *manqué*: "No second attachment, the only thoroughly natural, happy, and sufficient cure, at her time of life, had been possible to the nice tone of her mind, the fastidiousness of her taste, in the small limits of the society around them."[1] Eventually we see that Anne's doom isn't permanent; rather, we're asked to tarry with, to *feel*, her disappointment as a dissatisfaction born of a "nice" or "refined," "fastidious" sense of what should constitute proper happiness. Wentworth persists as the object of her true feeling, the "only thoroughly natural, happy, and sufficient cure" for her melancholy – especially "at her time of life." That he offers a "thorough," as opposed

I dedicate this essay to the students in my fall 2012 graduate seminar, "Romanticism and the Psychopathology of Happiness," from whom I learned a great deal about hope and the prospect of happiness. I thank the Social Sciences and Humanities Council of Canada for supporting the research and writing of this paper.

to less absolute, happiness, however, suggests less the startling revolution or revelation of true affection than degrees of approaching, approximating, and thus simulating "natural" felicity. Put another way, had there been another Frederick Wentworth, a tintype of the man Anne has romanticized him to be, one senses he would have sufficed for the original, for neither figure is the real object of the novel's affection. Rather, by reveling in the dilatory space between tragic prehistory and comic present, the novel works hard to make happiness work as both diagnosis and panacea.

A few chapters on we find one of the novel's central lessons in the cognition of happiness as we catch the narrator catching Anne catching an interaction between her sister Mary and Charles Musgrove. As Anne watches Mary and Charles leave for dinner at Uppercross with Wentworth, now fortuned as captain of the Royal Navy, she observes: "They were gone, she hoped, to be happy, however oddly constructed such happiness might seem" (*P*, 51). The idea of marriage as enterprise is a common trope in Austen's novels, which offer a social laboratory for marital gratification. The subtle acrimony born of compromise between the younger Musgroves is, on one hand, tempered in the novel by the elder Musgroves' less volatile union, and on the other hand finds its anachronism in Sir Walter Elliot's widowhood, a terminally narcissistic example of inbred hereditary connections threatened by Anne's potential union to Wentworth. The brash vitality of this interbreeding with mercantile entrepreneurialism marks the novel's uncertain future but finds one successful precedent in the frank, mature, and enlightened *rapprochement* between Admiral and Mrs. Croft. Their trial of marriage exemplifies how the aborted first meeting between Anne and Frederick might produce a more fruitful union that in turn negates Frederick's explosive attachment to Louisa Musgrove, in which he confuses Anne's persuadability with emotional disability and Louisa's willful nature with entrepreneurial spirit.

As a précis of marital negotiations, Anne's commentary on the Musgroves breaks through the novel's mirror stage of social propriety, suggesting the kind of transformation that attends Romanticism's exploration of feeling, embodied selfhood. But Austen also reads us reading past the Romantic ideology of this embodiment. We know from a few chapters back that Anne's "fastidiousness," compelled by Lady Russell, dictated her rejection of Charles as suitable mate, so that Charles and Mary's "oddly constructed happiness" also projects the fantasy of a dissatisfied future, in which there wouldn't be enough social profit to keep Anne in the style to which she would become emotionally accustomed. Her melancholic insularity makes her compassionate; but her desire for happiness to "seem" as natural as possible also suggests a narcissism that limits sympathy. This isn't a turn back to a neoclassical decorum pressured by domestic content-ment so much as an uncanny glimpse into more avaricious times.

Recent criticism sees Austen's writing more as a response to her time's historical flux than as its timeless exception, though this criticism also asks how and why she came to be de-historicized. This essay takes both tacks to suggest that her final novel sensed the times' dangerous precedent for our current obsession with making happiness a timeless affect. Like Richard Sha's essay in this volume, I read happiness as emotional force at once compelling and evading the period's temperament, what Thomas Pfau would call its mood. Mood shows how feelings constitute a subject's "capacity for agency per se," and thus offers an "affective template for social praxis."[2] Pfau's three moods – (Revolutionary) paranoia, (post-Revolutionary) trauma, and (post-Napoleonic) melancholy – reflect a current critical climate "where," to cite Claudia Johnson, "rupture and privation seem more credible than repose and fulfillment."[3] As an allegory for things as they presently are, this moodiness transforms glad, mad, or sad Romantics into symptoms of their suspicious, shocked, or depressed times. I accede to this symptomatology, but in order to explore rupture/privation and repose/fulfillment as mutually constitutive of one another.

Elsewhere I have argued that, by re-fashioning Enlightenment cognition as a shifting scene of phantasy (anticipated in Hume's theater of the mind), Romanticism tends toward psychoanalysis in advance of Freud and his heirs.[4] Romantic psychoanalysis emerges less from post-Enlightenment science or medicine than from moral philosophy (Hume, Smith), aesthetics (Burke, Kant), and political philosophy (Godwin, Burke again), which offer feeling models of how to overcome adversity in the face of economic, social, and political crisis. Literary print culture works through this melioration's increas-ingly volatile progress via its impact on the individual psyche and feeling. We can trace this unfolding psychomachia from the fictions of Rousseau, Mackenzie, or Goethe, to those of Godwin, Hays, or Wollstonecraft, not to mention through the agon of Romantic poetry. Less concerned with the inscrutabilities of psychic depth than with the emotional or behavioral surface of mannered social interaction, Austen's novels seem immune to psychoanalysis, which only emerges once the idealism of psychiatry, which *does* get invented in Austen's time, confronts its inevitable discontents as the nineteenth century wears on. That is to say, her writing reflects how psychiatry wages happiness against emotional threats to its wellbeing.

Austen's fictions are themselves anything but idealistic, however. From *Sense and Sensibility* to *Mansfield Park*, they increasingly take up how individuals fixate on the apparitions of happiness. This scrutiny, if not patently psychoanalytical, nonetheless reflects the excoriating spirit of Freud's ordinary unhappiness, which comes with recognizing ourselves as the sum of our illusions. By *Persuasion* we see how the social network formed by her characters' awareness of their environments structures the unconscious of their worldview by and as the language of feeling. We thus come to read the otherwise polite surface of social interaction symptomatically – as a volatile terrain overdetermined by the alternate scenes of feeling it displaces, yet by which its civil veneer is constituted.[5] That is to say, Austen's fictions mediate this volatility precisely by thriving upon it; by analyzing the progress of happiness, they promulgate the happiness of progress. In this way her final novel sets a rather danger precedent beyond Freud in our current obsession with happiness: *Persuasion* shows us how *properly* to accept the apparitions of happiness for real. Like Pfau's essay for this volume on the simulation of behavior, I thus explore in Austen the ideological affects and effects of happiness, which disclose and justify the pursuit of one's inner life as a form of social currency. Clifford Siskin has argued that Romanticism gives us the idea of a "self-made mind, full of newly constructed depths"[6] ready to be plumbed. For Andrea Henderson this interiority evokes the "notion of a heart or core in either society or the individual [that] is threatening because such a core becomes ... the center of movement or circulation, a place of dangerous fluidity."[7] The more radically psychoanalytical tendency of Romanticism is to grant the unregenerate or elusive emotion that attends this "dangerous fluidity" an affective and cognitive dignity, as in Percy Shelley's maniac or Mary Shelley's Matilda. Austen can*not* let intractable thoughts or feelings be in this way, so that her writings reflect a broader recuperative, but also managerial, sociopolitical effort.

Early psychiatry, buoyed by the revolutionary spirit of curing madness, also deployed a "latent power ... for enforcing conformity," a tension between revolution and reform that gives the turbulent political climate of Regency Britain its Janus face of personal transformation and social governance.[8] The broader *idea* of psychiatry, disseminated through print culture and a burgeoning asylumdom, binds the self-empowering emotional labor of subjects within an imaginary national classroom in which managing wayward feeling embodies ideals of church and state (Coleridge's Cleric as state psychiatrist becomes the proto-Victorian paradigm here). In Austen the provincial life of family materializes this education as a form of (re) conciliation. For Johnson, *Pride and Prejudice* is Austen's most "profoundly conciliatory work" that "vindicates personal happiness as a liberal category, rescuing it from the suspicion into which it had fallen" by counter-Revolutionary writers, like Burke, afraid of amelioration's excesses.[9] But Johnson also spots the contradiction in Austen's debt to Samuel Johnson, who was intrigued by the desire for happiness, but didn't trust happiness itself. Assessing the desire that drives and complicates the pursuit of an elusive goal, Austen seizes upon the necessity called forth by what is perhaps her era's definitive and overweening affect. Hence her equation between economic fortune and social and moral felicity – between fortune and good fortune – epitomized in the epigraph from *Mansfield Park* above.

By the end of her final novel, we realize what is at stake in this equation:

> Who can be of doubt what followed? When any two young people take it into their heads to marry, they are pretty sure by perseverance to carry their point, be they ever so poor, or ever so imprudent, or ever so likely to be necessary to each other's ultimate comfort. This may be bad morality to conclude with, but I believe it to be truth; and if such parties succeed, how should a Captain Wentworth and an Anne Elliot, with the advantage of maturity of mind, consciousness of right, and one independent fortune between them, fail of bearing down every opposition? (*P*, 199)

Here Austen legitimizes happiness as a future liberalism's social armor and weaponry, for what makes *Persuasion* particularly powerful is how it subtends a global presence hovering beyond domestic spaces. Happiness needed to be in the air as Regency Britain gave way to a second British Empire, which required all the ideological ammunition it could muster. Wentworth is needed to fulfill the civilizing mission of progress, the ideological justification missing from Great Britain's first stab at rapacious global advance that ended with George III losing the Colonies, what Blake figures in *America* as the darkly apocalyptic premonition of an even greater imperial design to come. Wentworth is a properly valuable social alloy: Naval Captain as Captain of Industry galvanizing might and money to create the Empire's perfect emissary.[10] With Anne's inheritance, their marriage deploys the stately measure of hereditary wealth to dignify the implicitly mercenary spirit of a burgeoning capitalist marketplace.

Perhaps most brazen, though, is how the passage's metafiction assumes the reader's complicity – "Who can doubt?" *This* entrepreneurialism, rallying our emotions in the enterprise of happiness, suspends disbelief in the "bad morality" of romance as the dreamwork of liberalism's future in creating, "by perseverance," its own "independent fortune." D. A. Miller argues that Austen's free indirect discourse makes us feel as though we are "*being read* reading" Austen: "Austen's work most fundamentally consists in *dematerializing* the voice that speaks it. From the very start, [the reader's] 'I' has been commuted into a generalized 'you,'" a kind of "universalized utterance" or "foregone personhood" that speaks our subjectivities for us.[11] On one hand, this masterful anonymity, shimmering with the affect of its own accomplishment, encrypts the shameful secret of Austen's lived experience, which was (we imagine) never granted the emotional payoff she imagines for her characters. Yet the otherwise tolerant plasticity of Austen's style exerts a rather more inexorable force. For William Galperin, Deidre Lynch, and others, Austen's fictions are a kind of *tabula rasa* (or better yet, mystic writing pad) upon which culture has traced the overdeterminations of its political unconscious.[12] Austen invites and inscribes our emotional responses because of what her writing doesn't say, or as Lacan would say, for the not-said in the being-said. As Adela Pinch notes, "[t]he subject of Austen's novels . . . is the arduousness of knowing both one's own feelings and the feelings of others – of knowing, as Anne Elliott wonders about Captain Wentworth, 'how were his sentiments to be read?'"[13] But this *project* of knowledge harnesses the inscrutabilities of psychoanalysis toward a broader social amelioration that thrives on the dissatisfaction of the other's lack of self-knowledge by feigning a sympathetic understanding for his plight. Austen's "foregone personhood" is thus also a silent surveillance that interpolates us into its affective regime, which in turn interpellates us as feeling subjects, as subjects *of* feeling whose dominant mood is a happiness that dominates unhappiness.

Confronted by unhappiness, Austen's Romanticism marshals its inner resources toward the *desire* for improvement. As Anne notes, the "Musgroves, like their houses, were in a state of alteration, perhaps of improvement" (*P*, 37–8). Written into the domestic spaces of Romanticism's traumatic encounter with historical change is the potential to turn catastrophe into an ideological force of transformation. Such a deployment creates between unhappiness and happiness an uncanny relationship that finds in the former the latter's constitutive possibility. Wordsworth may be working toward this opportunistic "resolution" in his Preface to *Lyrical Ballads* or his scheme of universal felicity mapped out in the Preface to *The Excursion*, in which the devastated space of Margaret's ruined cottage becomes the sublime (though no less haunted) prospect of a Gothic cathedral in ruins (recall that Wordsworth's verse saved John Stuart Mill from Utilitarianism). *Persuasion* exemplifies this possibility by offering a potent antidote for dissatisfaction and disillusionment. Indeed, that Austen's fiction registers despair or melancholia as discontent or disappointment signals a middling range that, by dampening affect's disruptive nature, implicitly shows us how to achieve, and thus justifies, this diminishment. In Austen's novels, Romanticism's self-examination of feeling trains people how to *get* happy, to acquire happiness, which becomes the novels' at once salient commodity, prized possession, and most elusive affect. And like all training fields, her novels evoke a competitiveness that separates fit from unfit. Finding happiness means encountering others' less felicitous and rehabilitative qualities in order to put both in their place. Happiness in *Persuasion* proves Derrida's *pharmakon*: "there is no such thing as a harmless remedy."[14] This is the novel's darker purpose: addicting us to the right to be happy.

II.   "He is obliged to be benevolent"

Roy Porter writes that the Enlightenment "translated the ultimate question, 'How can I be saved?' into the pragmatic 'How can I be happy?'"[15] Tracing ancient notions of virtue, tempered by Christian training for eternal redemption, to the modern idea of universal felicity in the here and now, Darrin McMahon, as Sara Ahmed notes, shows that the "association of happiness with feeling is a modern one, in circulation from the eighteenth century onward."[16] In Locke's *Essay Concerning Human Understanding* (1690) happiness counts only once "our desire ... makes us uneasy in the want of it,"[17] thus making loss essential to the pursuit of happiness (as in Johnson's *Rasselas*, a key precedent for Austen). Locke's equation is recomputed in Jeremy Bentham's felicific calculus: "it is the greatest happiness of the greater number that is the measure of right and wrong," a kind of Happiness Advisory Alert of a society's secure moral register.[18] Bentham's faith in progressive civil society follows Locke's reformist egalitarianism, stated in the second of his *Two Treatises of Government* (1689), which argued for the right to life, liberty, and property against poverty, injustice, and slavery.[19] That Bentham attaches the superlative "greatest" to happiness but the comparative "greater" to its implementation, however, should be a warning. Guaranteeing the inalienability of rights necessitated the social contract and its legal network, to whose impartial jurisdiction men would cede the right of natural law in order to protect this law from abuse. Protecting rights required naturalizing in individuals the idea that rights *were* natural, which implicitly compromises the pleasure principle of liberal democracy. The progress of industrial, economic, and political relations brought the world's inhabitants inexorably closer, an increasingly complex sociality that required management (this compromise explains how *Caleb Williams* reflects darkly transparent, rational exchange of *Political Justice*). Thus, to justify progress as desirable (i.e., natural) to human evolution meant naturalizing happiness as the driving affect and asset of social advance. Man had to learn to acquire and thus deserve happiness as his natural property, to discern true from illusory forms of happiness, to manage pain in order to foment pleasure.

Here is the preeminent Romantic chemist Humphry Davy in an 1800 notebook entry:

> Life is only estimable in proportion as it is the means of our perceiving pleasurable sensations – A considerable portion of both our happiness & misery depends on our mutual relations. The laws of our existence order us in our connexion with society to search for our individual pleasure & our private pleasure is wisely connected with that of our fellow creatures. Thus man is impelled to be a social being, is impelled to promote the happiness of his fellow creatures on account of its connexion with his own happiness. He is obliged to be benevolent.[20]

Davy connects the aesthetics of feeling to the political economy of social cognition through the pain vs. pleasure rhetoric of the eighteenth century (Burke, Smith, Bentham). The post-Hobbesian "laws of our existence" necessitate that we seek "individual pleasure," but also that we leaven this "private pleasure" by seeking "connexion" with "fellow creatures." One is "impelled to be a social being" and thus "impelled to promote the happiness" of others "on account of its connexion with his own happiness," thus effecting a necessary transfer from private to public. But Davy also touches upon a fundamental paradox: the same "mutual relations" that produce and combine "happiness & misery" are needed to resolve this conflict of faculties. The preeminent Romantic chemist treats happiness as social and ethical alloy, as if to find the alchemical solution to the material dilemma of how bodies relate, at a time when they threatened to react and interact beyond the status quo. There is a sociopolitical urgency to Davy's scientific idealism, which is why the inward impulsion toward happiness becomes an obligation to be benevolent, as if to shape and train an inchoate affective drive toward its properly social emotional purpose.

For David Marshall, in his *Theory of Moral Sentiments* (1759) Adam Smith, unable to see "fellow-feeling [as] automatic or even natural," explores "what it is like to want to believe in the fiction of sympathy."[21] Sympathy's spectacle of witnessing thus presents primarily egoistic concerns in the guise of empathy; that we can only imagine, not experience, an other's suffering frees us of responsibility for others. Vivasvan Soni calls Smith's *Theory* "a conduct manual, teaching those who suffer how to manage their behavior so that the spectator can sustain the fiction of sentimental communion; it is less interested in sentimental concern for suffering than the regulation of sentiments."[22] Aestheticizing sympathy as participation in an other's tragedy, Smith makes us vicarious witnesses who experience self-satisfaction rather than *pathos*. This sentimental veneer of ethical concern masks a sadistic narcissism: "all men for others," as the violent coercions of sympathy demonstrate in *Caleb Williams*, is really "every man for himself." Or as Claudia Johnson notes, Edmund Burke cares only for the simulation of sentiment so long as it "represent[s] the political relations of modern Europe as affectively grounded in benevolizing practices of chivalric heterosexuality." Ideology effects its "affective front" by "registering dominant values in and on the bodies of citizens," which in turn "produces reverent political subjects."[23] This explains Davy's post-Revolutionary opportunism: how one appears to solicit the other's welfare accrues to, and justifies, one's emotional profitability; and this labor of happiness determines the social circulation of one's character. In Marxist terms, happiness becomes a social commodity as elusive, magical fetish.

This exchange value of happiness enables a resourceful transfer between political economy and medicine. For instance, Smith's *The Wealth of Nations* (1776) promotes the feeling subject as yeoman whose self-commanding moral sentiment licenses taking care of business. In Smith's Edinburgh, the epicenter of modern medicine, market leader thus becomes market physician, an at once self-developed, empathic, and self-interested individual disciplined in the efficient deployment of healthy feelings. Good business is healthy business, and keeping bad feelings at bay produces a healthy citizen who ensures a robust marketplace. The eighteenth-century emergence of psychiatry from medical science thus capitalizes happiness as the ideal of civil/civic progress. Coining the term "*Psychiaterie*" in 1808, Johann Christian Reil wrote of psychiatry's promise: "A bold race of men dares to take on this gigantic idea, an idea that dizzies the normal burgher, of wiping from the face of the earth one of the most devastating pestilences."[24] Reil's euphoria had already materialized in 1794 when Philippe Pinel unchained inmates of the Bicêtre asylum in Paris and advocated rehabilitation and reformation over confinement, restraint, and exclusion, what he called *traitement moral*.

But as early psychiatric medicine produced and got lost in as many hidden psychological depths as it revealed (to expand on Siskin's metaphor), psychiatry's moral and ethical "treatment" also meant superintending madness. Indeed, the British coinage for early psychiatry was "moral management." Put another way, as the elusive goal of curing madness

receded, it left in its wake the florid diagnosis, classification, and administration of psychopathology, all of which made the pursuit of happiness
useful in and to the public sphere. In general terms, the demands of clinic
and institution split psychiatry early on: helping minds vs. managing the
body politic, psychology vs. physiology, therapy vs. biology, transformation vs. reformation.[25] A medical psychiatry treated neuropathology as
brain dysfunction, sometimes taking up hereditary factors, whereas a social
psychiatry examined behavioral and environmental factors. The latter
became important as custodianship shifted from family and community
to institution, but also tended to elide the source and cure of madness. By
its very name, William Tuke's York Retreat (founded in 1792) suggested
that the mentally ill needed to be rescued from a frenzied environment; its
social circuitry, rather than their neural circuitry, was the problem. Did
psychiatry rehabilitate the mentally ill to fit back into society or release
them from its normative pressures? This question will become key as we
return to Austen, for as Edward Shorter notes, the "picture of bliss" framed
by an increasingly sentimentalized view of family values left no room or
time for psychopathology.[26]

By the Victorian period psychiatry had "failed most abjectly"; but its
"insidious and worrying capacity to suppress non-conformity in the name
of mental health . . . proved highly efficacious as a repressive instrument for
controlling large numbers of people."[27] Hence, as psychopathology loses
clinical specificity instead to signal a broader dysfunction within the
domestic status quo, madness becomes an empty center around which a
host of issues galvanize themselves. Emerging at the intersection of scientific advance, political idealism, capitalist expansion, and social regulation,
psychiatry mobilized an anxious desire for moral management by getting
society compulsively attuned to its psychopathological life. Given the
Empire's profitable trade in habituates, early psychiatry's aborted excur-
sions became success by another route: the uncanny traffic between
intemperance and sobriety.[28] Via Benjamin Rush, pioneer of American
psychiatry and prison reform, psychiatry's egalitarianism found a ready
home in a country whose Declaration of Independence claimed "life,
liberty & the pursuit of happiness" as its people's "inalienable rights."[29]
But as Soni notes, the "period's revolutionary thinkers balked" on the
question of happiness when it came time "to write their visionary politics
into law" in the Constitution, as if to demonstrate that the "political
project" of "secular happiness" could succeed only as ideology. Happiness
is thus less a "viable political concern" than "the pathological symptom of
an insoluble problem." Soni reminds us of the Solonian judgment of

happiness as a "somber event always colored by the grief that pervades mourning." Political modernity has replaced the cognate melancholy of the ethical and political struggle for wellbeing with a metaphysics of happiness embodied in "family and marriage" and in the "affective conception of happiness." This shift makes happiness "an ordinary concept with no particular privilege" and no history.[30] Austen's *Persuasion* trains its characters – and readers – in a cognition of *this* happiness, although, as we shall see, by simulating the melancholy that attends its labor. The novel thus evokes a psychiatric effort to domesticate the perils of looking inward for the collective payoff of getting people oriented toward the habit of wanting to be better people. Austen re-stages Smith's theater of sympathy to produce a different catharsis: the desire for the desire *for* happiness.

III.   "Will it make you happy?"

Lisa Zunshine argues that literature, in its march toward modernity, reflects increasingly levels of "recursive embedment" that speak to the multifaceted intentionality of character. That "our neural circuits are powerfully attuned to the presence, behavior, and emotional display of other members of our species" means that as the mind processes experience in increasingly complex ways, it acquires training in a multilayered, proto-modernist behavioral logic, of which Austen's fictions are exemplary. Here's how Zunshine encapsulates the Bath scene when Wentworth encounters Elizabeth, in whose face he seeks recognition of his past with Anne: "Anne *realizes* that Wentworth *understands* that Elizabeth *pretends not to recognize* that he *wants* to be acknowledged as an acquaintance." Austen's contribution to this intricate perceptual relay is a sixth level of intentionality: "Anne is *aware* that her keen powers of observation allow her to realize" how the scene unfolds.[31] *This* awareness suggests a feeling observation that entails in turn the recursive mastery that comes with observing feeling.

I use Zunshine's analysis to read between Anne and her cousin William, as they take aim at Bath social pretense, a scene of sympathetic (dis) simulation that reveals William's character, but is more telling for what it says about Anne:

> "My idea of good company, Mr. Elliot, is the company of clever, well-informed people, who have a great deal of conversation; that is what I call good company."
>
> "You are mistaken," said he gently, "that is not good company, that is the best. Good company requires only birth, education and manners, and with

regard to education is not very nice. Birth and good manners are essential; but a little learning is by no means a dangerous thing in good company, on the contrary, it will do very well. My cousin, Anne, shakes her head. She is not satisfied. She is fastidious. My dear cousin (sitting down by her) you have a better right to be fastidious than almost any other woman I know; but will it answer? Will it make you happy? Will it not be wiser to accept the society of these good ladies in Laura-place [Lady Dalrymple and Miss Carteret, distant relatives of the Elliot family], and enjoy all the advantages of the connexion as far as possible?" (*P*, 122)

William has re-surfaced to claim his place as heir to Kellynch Hall. Marriage to Anne would seal the deal, especially via the Elliot family's "connexion" to Viscountess Dalrymple, which William would "accept" in order to accelerate the family's (i.e., his) upward mobility. Hence the need to persuade Anne to slacken her "fastidious" rule of "good company" to include birth and manners if not "education," a "not very nice" indicator of good sense and judgment in the Dalrymples, as Anne would agree, but beside the point for William. Elliot mirrors the generosity of spirit Anne covets by one-upping her discrimination: such company isn't merely "good," it's the "best," a besting that unsettles the decorously effusive equilibrium of social propriety she has so "naturally" voiced.

This gesture signals a false consciousness William continues to reveal: "You may depend upon it, that [the Dalrymples] will move in the first set in Bath this winter, and as rank is rank, your being known to be related to them will have its use in fixing your family (our family let me say) in that degree of consideration which we must all wish for" (*P*, 122). The parenthesis is at once intentional and unconscious, suggesting that wish fulfillment is both magical and arduous. It wishes William into the family, yet by indexing the tenuous social negotiation and behavioral savvy required to make the dream come true, and it does so by further assuming universal complicity in the wishing. The syllogism "rank is rank" likewise insists upon its own authority as blindly as Sir Walter's narcissistic sense of aristocratic precedence, performing a self-canceling redundancy that signals the passing of his world. Also, rank *is* rank, one of Austen's more searing social commentaries. I read both "slips" as what William Reddy calls "emotives," emotional expressions "considered as utterances aimed at briefly characterizing the current state of activated thought material that exceeds the current capacity of attention." They are like performatives "in that they do something to the world,"[32] although unstably so in that their emotional recklessness threatens full comprehension.

But at the same time this affect's potential damage harnesses social cognition toward an ideologically useful end. The passage's moral management is suggested by the phrase "You may depend upon it," in which the impersonal pronoun at once galvanizes and threatens to alter the passage's social order. Grammatically and syntactically, "it" antecedes the stability of rank. Rhetorically, "it" is also anticipatory, staging a promise that the sentence then fulfills, as if to turn Anne's mortifying dependence upon the kindness of the strangers who are her family into the reliability of a rank upon which she has not been able to depend in them. Treated as an emotive, however, "it" also signals the more indeterminate affect of prolepsis. "It" is at once both catalyst and free radical in the process of William's thought. "It" spells the means to the Elliots' potential good fortune through association with social superiors and that goal's ultimate profit, the social fix that will "fix" their "degree of consideration"; but "it" also signifies a more elusive goal set adrift in the sentence to mobilize a labile desire that creates demand precisely by its inability *to be* fixed. "It" sets rank beside the point (hence the redundancy of "rank is rank") to become the ambient, seductive yearning for what "we must all wish." This shimmering hope for felicity seems reckless, which is precisely how "it" functions in the sentence as an enactment of the labor of creating the desire for the desire for happiness.

It is thus telling that money is the passage's absent cause, figured instead through a mobile army of metaphors and metonymies for its acquisition (birth, rank, education, manners, fortune, happiness). If, as Schopenhauer argues, "*Money* is human happiness *in abstracto*,"[33] the compensation for the inevitable failure to make happiness concrete, we might say this passage works to circulate happiness as abstract currency as if to materialize money *in concreto*. This distracts us from the dirtier business of Anne's higher road: the affable social bonds that reward being "clever" and "well informed." Yet "cleverness" rings hollow, for while it signifies the felt sincerity of a cultivated native acumen, it affects intelligence a tad too, well, cleverly. It suggests, in fact, William's stance. However much the scene at once dissimulates and exposes William's social climbing, it also entrenches both Anne and William as actors in and spectators of this unmasquing. William merely reminds Anne, not that she needs to know the advantage of her family's "connexion" to the wealth and rank of a Viscountess, but that it wouldn't kill her to be seen to simulate a passionate attachment to the idea *of* this attachment. The importance of her "being known to be related to them" locates her happiness in the internal satisfaction of desire, but only as this internal revolution is materialized externally through a social exchange fueled by the behavioral efficiency this revolution anticipates. Insofar as the Dalrymples are concerned, Anne happily refuses "being known."

But this refusal signals in other ways. Refusing to "be known" invokes what Khalip calls the novel's "ethical desperation," "a melancholic disinterestedness brought to bear on the worlds of others, one that Anne enacts and induces *in us* as a condition of our own reading."[34] By neither accepting nor disavowing her part in the passage's game, which, Khalip argues, typifies Anne's stance throughout the novel, Anne (which is to say Austen) leaves us to confront our own anonymity. For Anita Sokolsky, this is the situation of the melancholic par excellence, who "is in some sense never recognizably at the heart of his or her own fantasies." The melancholic's "ongoing mortification of feeling . . . necessarily masks the revelation of a true feeling that, *if* revealed, would make the fantasies that sustain it "anachronistic." But her "baroque" and "repetitive psychic configurations," while encrypting the thing they refuse to mourn, are also a vital holding pattern without which the subject might have nothing at all.[35] This refusal, pregnant with the energy of its own disavowal, makes Anne's silence rather explosive for how it elicits William's supererogatory attention to her feelings, gesture, behavior – "My cousin, Anne, shakes her head." Inevitably, William watching Anne watching William trying to parse her affect produces a statement of lack – "She is not satisfied" – which remobilizes the very desire it seeks to quell. At once anticipating and animating her disquiet, he quietly feeds (off) an agitation he, by marking, generates. Anne's "foregone personhood" only agitates William's desire to comprehend her feeling. The result is a prehension of what she will have thought, which seems to leave Anne in a position of mastery, except that her silence leaves neither of them really knowing what the other thinks, which is to put what they might be thinking beside the point. Rather, the scene is telling for how it stages the simulative affect of sympathy we have explored above as liberalism's structuring possibility.

Which is what drives home William's penultimate question: "Will it make you happy?" Unable to persuade Anne of the benefits of social compromise, William instead speaks to a broader impulse within the novel in which happiness is the social capital of a behavioral transaction whose emotional payoff can never come: "Will – it – make – you – happy?" Here "it" registers even more indeterminately as the result of a future possibility that nonetheless promises to materialize in its addressee the very feeling the question prehensively anticipates at the same time it makes of this construction something nearly undesirable for the possibility of its failure *to* materialize. Like William, we sense this to be the point where Anne refuses to cede the very desire she has been denied, but perhaps this doesn't matter. To paraphrase Sokolsky, the novel values Anne's melancholy because it encrypts at once the desire for happiness and an acceptance of its failure, a way of succumbing to but deploying this contingency as a potent weapon of silent disavowal. Such disavowal keeps happiness alive as the afterlife of affect, its spectral hope. This places the emotional stakes in happiness in permanent relation to its potential deprivation. Ultimately, does William's question demand an answer beyond the asking itself?[36] Anne's lack of response makes the asking at once necessary, redundant, and moot.

IV. "A happiness which no description can reach"

To paraphrase Shorter, the melancholy and invisibility that result from the pre-history of Anne's engagement to Wentworth suggest a familial conformity that deforms "true" feeling and natural attachment into a social pathology writ large. Anne's frustration with the narcissism, insipidity, and thoughtless immoderation of Kellynch Hall, Bath, or (to a lesser extent) Uppercross, suggests an ambivalence between forging genuine bonds from the artifice of communal obligation and fleeing the social altogether. The former wish seems part of the novel's gently reformative mission to balance sense and sensibility and ameliorate pride and prejudice. The latter desire capitalizes upon what makes *Mansfield Park* the most difficult of Austen's fictions: the sense that human fallibility and custom are yoked by a hollow yet irrevocable, irredeemable attachment that makes true feeling a moot point. The looming catastrophe of an unregenerate emotional nature dictates the narrator's abrupt turn in the final chapter, which seems to abandon the plot in order to avoid its psychiatric failure: "Let other pens dwell on guilt and misery. I quit such odious subjects as soon as I can, impatient to restore every body ... to tolerable comfort, and to have done with all the rest." The narrator seems to urge the ordinary happiness of marital attachment. Not so for Edmund and Fanny, however. Fanny, like Anne, is elevated above others because of her "mental superiority," "more fearless disposition and happier nerves." Fanny's and Edward's was a "happiness ... which no description can reach," one born "of early hardship and discipline, and the consciousness of being born to struggle and endure." For Sir Thomas, "[s]ick of ambitious and mercenary connections," this means "prizing more and more the sterling good of principle and temper." For Edmund Bertram it adds up to the unrelenting pursuit of happiness: "Having once set out, and felt that he had done so, on this road to happiness, there was nothing on the side of prudence to stop him or make his progress slow."[37]

This sudden exchange of a recurrent disaffection for eternal happiness suggests a rapacious desire to make emotional profit from an otherwise unredeemable human nature. Like William's desire to advance the Elliot cause at any cost, it rather too nakedly exposes the narrative's ideological opportunism, its desperation to make things work out. But *Persuasion*'s narrative alchemy is rather more refined about transforming its dirty emotional compounds, again, a transformation left un-articulated by Anne's lack of response to William's question above, but articulated in other ways. Anne's history morally manages within Fanny Price's frustration an inevitable intolerance and even contempt toward others. For instance, assuming the Musgrove sisters to be, "like thousands of other young ladies, living to be fashionable, happy, and merry," and thus "contemplat[ing] them as some of the happiest creatures of her acquaintance," Anne is nonetheless "saved as we all are by some comfortable feeling of superiority from wishing for the possibility of exchange" and "would not have given up her own more elegant and cultivated mind for all their enjoyments" (*P*, 38). Such baroque melancholy gestures endow Anne with a bitchiness she can unconsciously avoid as the narrator's diagnosis of her character, doubly disavowed as Anne at once envies and denounces the Musgroves' "seemingly perfect good understanding and agreement together, that good-humoured mutual affection, of which she had known so little herself with either of her sisters" (*P*, 38). Such disavowals and projections suggest a narrative passive-aggressiveness that suspends Anne between oppressive domestic obligation, repressive social training, and hopeful marital "release," creating in turn a rather more calculated impression of the potential of and for true feeling. As Anne tells Captain Harville in a penultimate speech overheard by Wentworth and spurring him to express his true feelings, her "feelings prey upon" her (*P*, 187). Such pursuit evokes the passionate detachment of Regency women: the self-cannibalization of feeling creates a sense of objectless dread in which, awakened to their emotions, women find themselves adrift in drifting times. They succeed only by "loving longest, when existence or when hope is gone." Harville need not "covet" such a pyrrhic victory (*P*, 189), she warrants. But saying so allows Anne to disavow her feeling on behalf of others, which also means refusing to cede it *to* others.

On one hand, the novel expresses a narrative bitterness at being persuaded to endorse the sentiment and sensibility that makes Regency fiction possible – a compulsion toward feeling that Austen first parodies in *North-anger Abbey*; on the other hand, it legitimates such feeling as a *fait accompli*. Yet it is on the ambivalence between these positions that the novel thrives by orchestrating an uncanny relationship between the social amelioration of fellow feeling and the narcissistic prize of imagining one's thoughts are one's own, as in the above scene with Harville. Emotion proves a visceral and elusive mode of human negotiation; yet its discipline and management can be *commodified* as social currency. The scene's conflagration of emotional volatilities – Captain Benwick's grief over Harville's dead sister; Anne's aloneness; her missed encounter with Wentworth via the letter he writes while "enduring" listening to her exchange with Harville – creates a matrix of loss that in turn demands behavioral correction. This comes with Wentworth's effusion of feeling: "I can listen no longer in silence" (*P*, 191). This penultimate outburst, like Elinor Dashwood's in *Sense and Sensibility* or the sudden turn at the end of *Mansfield Park*, seems rather desperately contrived. The letter writes passionate intensities as contraband sentiment that, if spoken, would revolutionize the novel's symbolic order. Yet it also preserves social propriety by displacing these attachments into a detached epistolary negotiation. By the time of *Persuasion* this is no innovation, yet it highlights the traumatic fragility of a truncated interpersonal history whose rewriting and recuperation can only be accomplished by the expression of real feeling.[38]

By parlaying true feeling as something that must be written into history as a scene of reading and its dangerous contingency, Austen automatically compromises the feeling she means to express by turning affect into an ideological effect. One might say she gives us the affect of ideology by capitalizing upon the threat of its mystification as the frisson of how emotion at once names and traps our desire. So, Wentworth's true feelings are beside the point; to the point is the fact that he can dramatize them effectively enough so as to convince – persuade – that they are genuine: "I must speak to you by such means as are within my reach. You pierce my soul. I am half agony, half hope. Tell me not that I am too late, that such precious feelings are gone forever" (*P*, 191). Characters are shown to have true feelings by showing us how they show themselves to have – to express, but also to display – such sentiment. That the Musgrove "girls were wild for dancing" and the "young people were all wild to see Lyme" posits a frank but undisciplined enthusiasm that the novel must then be shown to curb, as it does when Louisa Musgrove, "too precipitate by half a second," bashes her head on the Cobb in Lyme right after her "burst" of "raptures of admiration and delight" about the Royal Navy's "friendliness," "brotherliness," "openness," and "uprightness" (*P*, 43, 79, 91, 83). But Louisa's outburst is unconscious, unpremeditated. Whereas she does not gauge the effect of her happiness upon others, Frederick's is a proper contrivance. Put another way, he is far more subtle about how he 'asks' William's earlier question. And so the letter does have the desired effect of knocking Anne off balance with its "overpowering happiness" and destroying the tranquillizing or "tranquility" of emotion that is the novel's defense against such dangerously overweening hope. And now Anne can respond: "Such a letter was not to be recovered from" (*P*, 191). The language of shock and awe point to the novel's tension, as Nina Auerbach and others have examined, between revolution and evolution, especially in relation to Anne's inner life.[39] This is the novel's response to the times' mood swing between an overturning that presages a possible catastrophe and a more calibrated forward movement in which a Malthusian inevitability of disaster is part of society's evolutionary vitality.

Happiness is thus less the novel's tantalizing "cure" than its full-blown pathology, a viral affective attack from which Anne has no immunity. And yet we know from the final chapter's statement of where all characters remain on the pleasure thermometer of Austen's social milieu that Anne has, at some level, been inoculating herself against the disease precisely in order to accept its invasion when it comes. Anne's happiness has a threefold effect on others. It gladly infects those who deserve to be: the disadvantaged Mrs. Smith and the re-persuadable Lady Russell. The narcissism of Anne's immediate family keeps them immune: Sir Walter has his own "vanity . . . to make him really happy" (*P*, 200). The third effect is more catastrophic: "Anne's engagement . . . deranged [William Elliot's] best plan of domestic happiness" (*P*, 201). The Elliot heir having shown himself unworthy of Anne does *not* deserve to share in her good fortune (and thus in her fortune). But to "derange" his plans for happiness, as if foiling them isn't enough, seems extreme. Here the infection is toxic, as if to counteract the further madness against which Anne will have to steel herself: "She gloried in being a sailor's wife, but she must pay the tax of quick alarm for belonging to that profession which is, if possible, more distinguished in its domestic virtues than in its national importance" (*P*, 203). Happiness manages the nervous economy of couples' internal strife as domestic solidarity and immunity against the inevitable violence of outside attack. Unlike the scene between Anne and William, in which he would victimize Anne with happiness, she is now happy to *be* victimized. The previous scene thus becomes a primal scene of how happiness truly works, which the final restages precisely in order to avoid (i.e., overcome) its traumatic effects.

To paraphrase Auerbach, in the novel revolution and evolution sustain one another. When Mrs. Croft "cooly giv[es] the reins a better direction" (*P*, 78) than Admiral Croft and thus averts the disaster of hitting "the post," a potential catastrophe similar to De Quincey's "Vision of Sudden Death" in *The English Mail-Coach*, the scene's quiet revolution in gender and class works by a breathtaking economy in which disaster patiently constitutes feeling. As Khalip argues, "the traumatic everydayness of Austen's world ... registers the unavowable features of a violent, past knowledge,"[40] just as the Musgroves' "game" is something at once "to guard, and to destroy" (*P*, 39). Admiral Croft says that Wentworth's finding a wife will come from his "luck to live to another war," which violence will "make [Wentworth] very thankful to any body that will bring him his wife," perhaps even one of the privateering ships with which the Empire was doing clandestine business (*P*, 60). Like Ricardo's ruin or Malthus's natural disaster, catastrophe is the compost for progress. Wentworth's account of the haphazard way he attained his first Royal Navy commission, as an allegory for how the Empire conducts its business, produces a vicarious frisson in his audience that Croft seems compelled to leaven: "Lucky fellow to get her!" (*P*, 57). Wentworth replies, "I felt my luck admiral, I assure you," as if feeling the contingency of happiness makes it productive.

Sara Ahmed notes how the "hap of happiness then gets translated into something good" in order to make happiness an "*anticipatory causality*" that "something good" *will* happen.[41] Happiness elicits an "ambient attention"[42] to one's surroundings, something at once deeply felt, interpersonal, and anonymous. One's habituation to happiness generates an unspoken but dizzying prospect in the contraband relationship between violence and civility that structures how subjects feel and feel about their environment as it structures and is structured through their experience of others. Like Reil's "dizzying" euphoria, such potentially catastrophic giddiness, one enduring legacy of a heady and headstrong Romantic temperament that the Victorians sought to correct, is symptomatic of the time's sociopolitical volatility. This sense of imminent threat attunes individuals to an imminent crisis for which psychiatry became one of the polestars of social amelioration. *Persuasion* takes back this lead in order to show precisely how "right thinking" might solve psychiatry's dilemma, thinking well past Victorian anxieties about (their own) Romantic excess to a future horizon in which a society of spectacle trained to feed on its own avarice does so by addicting itself to its own sobering impulses.[43]

V. "The War on Unhappiness"

A recent *Harper's Magazine* cover story addresses how therapeutic practices such as Cognitive Behavioral Therapy have eclipsed psychoanalysis. Even when post-World War II America called upon psychoanalysis to deal with specters haunting its triumphant psyche, it did so by rallying the self's defenses against internal and external threats, an ego psychology that Lacan despised. Enduring patriotic optimism and faith in Manifest Destiny, not to mention a post-9/11 world of global entanglements, political uncertainty, and economic volatility, explain this avoidance of inscrutability. Like Arnold criticizing the Romantics, our times demand decisive action rather than painful introspection, which produces delays, detours, and evasions that might terrorize the psyche's healthy borders. So, one outgrowth of CBT is positive psychology, whose founder Martin Seligman coined the phrase "learned helplessness" to indicate how people can reprogram their neural circuitry behaviorally in order to combat bad feelings and lead more productive lives: "Identify and repair the glitches in our operating system – *dysfunctional thoughts* that arise automatically from our unduly negative *core beliefs* – and we will find no adversity we cannot meet with resilience." CBT or positive psychology takes sympathy's illusions for real in order to program people for success, unlike psychoanalysis, whose theater of sympathy plays out unavoidable complexities of human nature that expose the illusions that attend the desire for success. Which is why the American military deploys positive psychology among its therapists "to create an Army that is just as psychologically fit as it is physically fit," in the words of an American defense official. Or as the article says, "soldiers who learn optimism will heal faster when they are wounded on the battlefield," thus minimizing the costly after-effects of dealing with post-traumatic stress.[44] A happy soldier – one who might have to kill for his country's cause – is a soldier who won't think about either the cause's veracity or its chance for success.

Such mobilizations invert the orientalist stereotype of the threat posed to Christian civilization by insensate Muslim hordes steeled by opium. An army made invincible by happiness, like Anne and Wentworth steeled against unforeseeable traumas, welcomes defensiveness as proof of an impervious felicity. Connecting happiness to torture, Slavoj Žižek writes that happiness has become our "supreme duty," our "new *biomorality* – the true counterpart to today's biopolitics." "This is not true of psychoanaly-sis," Žižek hastens to add.[45] In *Studies in Hysteria* (1895) Freud told a patient only "fate" could answer mental illness: "But you will be able to convince yourself that much has been gained if we succeed in transforming your hysterical misery into common unhappiness. With a mental life that has been restored to health you will be better armed against that unhappi-ness."[46] By the time of *Civilization and Its Discontents* (1930), Freud was "convinced" that such disarming arming against common unhappiness was culture's defense against its own illusions. Confronted by psychiatry's scientific confidence, Freud could only promise survival on the ruins of a traumatic suffering psychoanalysis knew it couldn't heal. But psychoanalysis now labors against a psychotherapeutic industry whose economics of happiness gets populations in the habit of wanting to be happy, its success supplemented by psychiatric pharmacology and its neurochemical alchemy. Like early psychiatry, this economics pursues non-materialistic and altruistic solutions to complex global crises. But its "obligation to be benevolent" becomes ideological fuel for the later devel-opment of capitalism, whose global economy increasingly appears to thrive on debt, addiction, and ruin. Such an economy is stirring at more than the margins of *Persuasion*, whose social imagination predicts how to make people happy about impending catastrophe.

Threatened by the real unhappiness of natural disasters, economic volatility, or political instability re-shaping our geopolitical terrain, happiness becomes our default mode, what Žižek calls "interpassivity."[47] Like prayer wheels that do the work of faith for us, the pursuit of happiness in contemporary society substitutes for the real work of living, for the ethical and political struggle necessary to ensure our survival on the planet. Like Smithean sympathy, accepting happiness as our "supreme duty" allows us to be actively passive/passively active toward others, to maintain a civility that avoids confronting the essentially perverse nature of the desire that makes this civility possible. The anticipatory felicity of Austen's last fiction makes this avoidance pos-sible. By creating the demand for feelings to be read, *Persuasion* suggests a desire, less to parse their darker motivation, than to externalize this motivation for public consumption. This labor reverses Freud's oxida-tion of civil and social illusions by polishing the social veneer that sustains these illusions as illusion. Austen's characters do not confess their internal lives free of social or moral restraint; rather free indirect discourse is free association that understands its own illusion of liberty. If Freud came to see that the transferences produced by free association produce an interminable speculation essentially at odds with any cure for psychopathology, which makes psychoanalysis the *pharmakon* of enlightenment, Austen responds with the *pharmakon* of happiness.

In *The World as Will and Representation* (1818), published a year after *Persuasion*, Schopenhauer, godfather to Freud's ordinary unhappiness, states: "Everything in life proclaims that earthly happiness is destined to be frustrated, or recognized as an illusion ... There is only one inborn error, and that is the notion that we exist in order to be happy."[48] Surely Jane Austen never read Schopenhauer, and only with the second volume of *The World as Will* in 1844 did his pessimism resonate with the time's burgeoning *ressentiment*. But in a passage in *Parerga and Paralipomena* (1851), from which I take one of my epigraphs, Schopenhauer writes: "Money alone is the absolutely good thing because it meets not merely one need *in concreto*, but needs generally *in abstracto*."[49] This idea of money as abstract social currency magically circulating the feeling of happiness cynically exploits unhappiness to suggest psychiatry's own eventual end-run around psychoanalysis. Austen's response, in the manner of moral management, is to imagine on behalf of her characters an emotional fullness indicative of a social subject properly attuned to others. Such fullness is especially crucial in cases where its willful excesses or passionate determinations, as in the case of Louisa Musgrove, threatened social propriety precisely in order to summon – at least in those protagonists fit to undergo and accept the ameliorative behavioral correction – the regulative inner resources of civil organization. But this fullness knows itself to simulate emotion from the real of affect, what Lauren Berlant calls "cruel optimism," in which happiness proceeds toward its objects knowing they will fail us and thriving on the failure precisely for this reason.[50] The complex narrative negotiations we have analyzed above demonstrate that training people in this mode of cognition is for Austen a rather subtle labor that, one might argue, is almost undone by its own complexity, thus exposing to failure the very ideological maneuvers it seeks to deploy. Yet that it risks such exposure so nakedly is, I would argue, precisely the sign of a success adumbrated by Austen's enduring hold on our imaginations. Again, it is as if Austen is immersing us in the affect of ideology itself as the place where ideology holds its most seductive, constitutive sway as a network from which happiness itself offers transcendence precisely by way of helping us to disavow the fact that the transcendence comes with our immersion within and emergence out of the network – without which enmeshment we could not exist. Put another way, happiness makes the enmeshment palatable.

Like early psychiatry, happiness encrypts success *and* failure, melancholically protecting its fantasy from the same amelioration that sustains it but
would, if fulfilled, destroy the fantasy that sustains it in turn. Austen's
novels push a proto-Victorian agenda of personal-cum-social regulation
and progress, but this agenda obeys the "baroque but repetitive psychic
configurations" of a pursuit of happiness without which subjects would
disappear. Happiness at once sustains, obliterates, and transcends the
subjects who register its feeling. It exerts the prehensive force of emotion
itself: emoting a subject who will have been by the end of the novel, which
is also to say a figure determined by a prehensive future projected at the
novel's end in an always potential catastrophe. It allows Anne to wish
Wentworth back into love with her so that she can send them both off to
battle: him to Napoleon's defeat on the cusp of a new European world
order, she in the domestic trenches. In *Northanger Abbey* Austen makes a
straw man of the kind of literature that in her day figured behavior as social
pretense, as simulated emotion. Perhaps she spent the rest of her career
refashioning and revivifying this character's motives as behavior taken for
real feelings. Hers is a fictional project not unlike Mary Shelley's sutured
social body kept alive by literary afterlife support. If Shelley's emotional
monstrosity looks like *Matilda*'s unmitigated unhappiness, Austen's happiness can seem equally monstrous.

NOTES

1 Jane Austen, *Persuasion*, ed. James Kingley, intro. Deidre Shauna Lynch (New
   York: Oxford World Classics, 2004), 28. All subsequent references to *Persuasion*
   will be cited parenthetically as *P* followed by page number.
2 Pfau, *Romantic Moods*, 35.
3 Johnson, *Equivocal Beings*, 18.
4 See Joel Faflak, *Romantic Psychoanalysis: The Burden of the Mystery* (Albany:
   State University of New York Press, 2007).
5 On the perils of how consciousness knows itself via feeling, see Damasio, *The
   Feeling of What Happens*.
6 Clifford Siskin, *The Historicity of Romantic Discourse* (New York: Oxford
   University Press, 1988), 13.
7 Andrea Henderson, *Romantic Identities: Varieties of Subjectivity, 1774–1830*
   (Cambridge: Cambridge University Press, 1996), 9.
8 Andrew Scull, "Psychiatry and Social Control in the Nineteenth and Twentieth
   Centuries," *History of Psychiatry* 2 (1991): 154. I examine psychiatry's Regency
   context in "The Difficult Education of Shelley's *The Triumph of Life*."
9 Johnson, *Equivocal Beings*, 73, 78.

10 For Johnson *Pride and Prejudice* "gratifies a conservative yearning for a strong, attentive, loving, and paradoxically perhaps, at times even submissive authority" (*Equivocal Beings*, 73). Daniela Garofalo argues that Austen's fictions "reconcile a liberal appreciation for the individual and a hierarchical desire for submission" (*Manly Leaders in Nineteenth-Century British Literature* [Albany: State University of New York Press, 2008], 113) through the self-cultivated, meretricious, and benevolent but resolved leader whose character naturalizes his superiority to, and thus submission of, his inferiors. See Garofalo, *Manly Leaders*, 113–36; and Johnson, *Equivocal Beings*, 193–203.

11 D. A. Miller, *Jane Austen, or: The Secret of Style* (Princeton, NJ: Princeton University Press, 2003), 3, 6–7, 92. See also Khalip, *Anonymous Life*, 133–71; and Pinch, *Strange Fits of Passion*, 137–63.

12 See William Galperin, *The Historical Austen* (Philadelphia: University of Pennsylvania Press, 2003) and Deidre Shauna Lynch (ed.), *Janeites: Austen's Disciples and Devotees* (Princeton, NJ: Princeton University Press, 2000). Mary Favret argues that Austen's writing easily emigrated as a model for liberal self-definition because, by turning "a dispassionate eye on ... British society," it produces a "new world of free agents ... that looks vaguely American" ("Free and Happy: Jane Austen in America," *Janeites: Austen's Disciples and Devotees*, 176). But demonizing the English encrypts a secret not unlike that explored by Johnson and Garofalo above: submission to the illusion of the other's authority in order to disavow one's own destructive illusions: "[m]aking Austen free and happy in America ... encouraged the nation to 'forget' race, slavery, and unhappiness" (182).

13 Pinch, *Strange Fits*, 142.

14 Jacques Derrida, *Dissemination*, trans. Barbara Johnson (Chicago: University of Chicago Press, 1981), 97.

15 Roy Porter, *Enlightenment: Britain and the Creation of the Modern World* (London: Allen Lane, 2001), 22.

16 Sara Ahmed, "Happy Objects," in *The Affect Theory Reader*, ed. Gregory J. Seigworth and Melissa Gregg (Durham, NC: Duke University Press, 2010), 30.

17 Humphry Davy, *1800 Notebook*, London: Royal Institution MS HD/13d/1800. I am much indebted to Richard Sha for sharing his transcription from Davy's notebooks.

18 Cited in Darrin McMahon, *Happiness: A History* (New York: Atlantic Monthly Press, 2006), 217, 234. That Locke takes up the issue in the *Essay* rather than *Two Treatises of Government*, McMahon notes, shows how cognition and desire drive the politics of happiness.

19 McMahon, *Happiness*, 213; Jeremy Bentham, *A Fragment on Government* (1776), ed. J. H. Burns and H. L. A. Hart (Cambridge: Cambridge University Press, 1988), 3.

20 See John Locke, *Two Treatises of Government*, ed. Peter Laslett (Cambridge: Cambridge University Press, 1988), 269.

122 Joel Faflak

21 David Marshall, *The Surprising Effects of Sympathy: Marivaux, Diderot, Rousseau, and Mary Shelley* (Chicago: University of Chicago Press, 1988), 180, 181.

22 Soni, *Mourning Happiness*, 310.

23 Johnson, *Equivocal Beings*, 6.

24 Cited in Edward Shorter, *A History of Psychiatry: From the Era of the Asylum to the Age of Prozac* (New York: Wiley, 1997), 8.

25 For Michel Foucault, of course, early psychiatry offers the "calculated management of life" whose "will to knowledge" mobilizes the "technology of power" (*The History of Sexuality*, vol. 1, trans. Robert Hurley [New York: Vintage Books, 1990], 140, 12).

26 Shorter, *A History of Psychiatry*, 50.

27 Andrew Scull, "Psychiatry and Social Control in the Nineteenth and Twentieth Centuries," *History of Psychiatry* 2 (1991): 155–6.

28 Texts like Thomas Trotter's 1807 *A View of the Nervous Temperament* (Trotter wrote one of the first tracts on drunkenness) sounded the call for sobriety: man's "habits," "if not restrained soon, must inevitably sap our physical strength of constitution; make us an easy conquest to our invaders; and ultimately convert us into a nation of slaves and ideots [sic]" ([New York: Arno, 1976], 137, xi).

29 Garry Wills, *Inventing America: Jefferson's Declaration of Independence* (Garden City, NY: Doubleday, 1978), 374.

30 Soni, *Mourning Happiness*, 2, 1, 4, 83, 21, 19, 22.

31 Lisa Zunshine, "Why Jane Austen Was Different, and Why We May Need Cognitive Science to See It," *Style* 41, no. 3 (2007): 277, 283. For Zunshine, literature trains minds beyond the brain functioning thus far tracked by cognitive neuroscientists or mind philosophers. Austen and especially Virginia Woolf demonstrate how (the reading of) literature *produces* cognitive abilities the mind doesn't know it has or yet has. Literature thus becomes a laboratory for testing, exercising, and recombinatively generating our neural apparatus.

32 Reddy, *The Navigation of Feeling*, 111. "Emotion," Reddy continues, "can thus be defined as an array of loosely linked thought material that tends to be activated simultaneously (which takes the form of a schema), and that is too large to be translated into action or utterance over a brief time horizon."

33 Arthur Schopenhauer, *Parerga and Paralipomena*, 2 vols., trans. E. F. J. Payne, vol. 1 (Oxford: Clarendon, 1974), 348.

34 Khalip, *Anonymous Life*, 170.

35 Anita Sokolsky, "The Melancholy Persuasion," *Psychoanalytic Literary Criticism*, ed. Maud Ellman (New York: Longman, 1994), 131, 130. Sir Walter's parochialism reflects an "unregenerate anachronism" that "operates as a melancholy shield" (138); even Wentworth's "meritocratic mercantile power," sustained by a privateering trade with an enemy it must disavow, constitutes an internalized melancholy that mirrors both his desire for and disavowal of the happiness he imagines to be lost in Anne.

36 For Sokolsky the condemnation of William Elliot is a "narrative violence" that "exposes the novel's dissimulation of the intransigence and anachronism of its

melancholy structure" (140), its desire to meliorate the status quo of the fantasies that sustain the status quo.

37 Jane Austen, *Mansfield Park*, ed. Kathryn Sutherland (New York: Oxford World Classics, 2003), 428, 438–9.

38 As Sokolsky writes, the scene is exemplary of how "the narrative's denial of [such moment's] necessity and significance disciplines the luxury of [Anne's] fantasies, lest their vengeful character emerge too clearly" ("The Melancholy Persuasion," 141).

39 Nina Auerbach, "O Brave New World: Evolution and Revolution in *Persuasion*," in *Jane Austen: Critical Assessments*, ed. Ian Littlewood, vol. 4 (Mountfield, UK: Helm Information, 1998), 482–96.

40 Khalip, *Anonymous Life*, 165. Khalip is citing Favret's *War at a Distance*.

41 Ahmed, "Happy Objects," 30, 40.

42 Khalip, *Anonymous Life*, 165.

43 I take up the uncanny relation between Romantic excess and sobriety in "Romanticism and the Pornography of Talking," *Nineteenth-Century Contexts* 27, no. 1 (2005): 77–97. This and the current essay owe a debt to Orrin C. Wang, *Romantic Sobriety: Sensation, Revolution, Commodification, History* (Baltimore, MD: Johns Hopkins University Press, 2010), 17–35.

44 Gary Greenberg, "The War on Unhappiness: Goodbye Freud, Hello Positive Thinking," *Harper's Magazine* 321, no. 1924 (2010): 29, 31, 34–5.

45 Slavoj Žižek, *In Defence of Lost Causes* (New York: Verso, 2008), 44, 45.

46 Josef Breuer and Sigmund Freud, *Studies in Hysteria*, trans. James Strachey (New York: Basic Books, 2000), 305.

47 Slavoj Žižek, *How to Read Lacan* (New York: Norton, 2007), 22–7.

48 Arthur Schopenhauer, *The World as Will and Representation*, 2 vols., trans. E. F. J. Payne, vol. 2 (New York: Dover, 1958), 573, 634.

49 Schopenhauer, *Parerga and Paralipomena*, 1: 348.

50 Berlant, *Cruel Optimism*. See also Sara Ahmed, *The Promise of Happiness* (Durham, NC: Duke University Press, 2010).

CHAPTER 5

The General Fast and Humiliation
Tracking feeling in wartime

Mary A. Favret

> In this world, only those people who have fallen to the lowest degree
> of humiliation, far below beggary . . . – only those people, in fact, are
> capable of telling the truth. All the others lie.
>
> Simone Weil[1]

> It is the earth itself that is humanity.
>
> Wallace Stevens[2]

Beginning with the reign of Elizabeth I, the Protestant monarch of Great
Britain did occasionally proclaim a General Fast and Humiliation for the
kingdom. The wording varied little over the centuries. Here is typical
language, from 1795:

> [A] Proclamation for a General FAST and Humiliation before Almighty
> God, to be observed in the most Devout and Solemn Manner, by sending
> up our Prayers and Supplications to the Divine Majesty: For obtaining
> Pardon of our Sins, and for averting those heavy Judgments which our
> manifold Provocations have most justly deserved, and imploring His Bless-
> ing and Assistance on the Arms of His Majesty by Sea and Land, and for
> restoring and perpetuating Peace, Safety, and Prosperity to Himself, and to
> His Kingdom.

Royal subjects were required "reverently and devoutly" to observe the
public fast on a specified day to avoid the "wrath and punishments" of
His Divine Majesty, and to do so "upon pain of such punishment as [His
British Majesty] may justly inflict on all such as contemn and neglect the
performance of so religious and necessary a duty."[3]

A General Fast could be called in the wake of a great disaster, as when a
terrible hurricane flooded half of London, destroying thousands of homes
and buildings during the reign of Queen Anne. The most common
catalyst for the proclamation of fast and humiliation however was war,
and especially military defeat (also called "humiliation") on the battlefield
or at sea. Such proclamations appeared sporadically in the seventeenth

century, every several decades or so. Their frequency increased in the eighteenth century, as the wars in North America especially entailed bruising defeats. The last decade of that and the first fifteen years of the next century, however, brought an unprecedented acceleration. For every single year of the Revolutionary and Napoleonic wars, sometimes even twice a year, the crown called for a day of fasting and humiliation. In 1811, for instance, the new Regent's very first public action was to issue "A General Fast on account of the War." On the appointed day, shops, banks, courts, and the stock market all closed; no mail was delivered. "The whole nation, in the midst of its business, its pleasures, and its pursuits," Anna Barbauld explained, "makes a sudden stop and wears the semblance, at least, of seriousness and concern."[4] Collections were taken up: sometimes for local charities, sometimes for British soldiers and sailors imprisoned in France. As ordained by the proclamation, the Church of England devised a special liturgy for the day, with selected readings from scripture and prayers that were published and distributed throughout the kingdom. Thousands of subjects assembled in their local churches to participate in that liturgy and hear Fast Day sermons preached. Prominent churchmen then published their sermons, which subsequently glutted the marketplace (titles such as "Food for a Fast-Day" [1795] or "Food for National Penitence" [1793] were not uncommon). The day of fasting and humiliation was proclaimed, sustained, extended, and preserved through the medium of print; a flood of words swirled into the void produced – or at least imagined by – collective abstinence and humiliation.

This recurrent practice poses a set of questions, not least of which is the question of its significance: how seriously should we take this "semblance at least of seriousness and concern" and its special intensity in the Romantic period? It might easily be dismissed as the tool of cynical politicians and "hypocritical zeal," as dissenting preacher John Aikin proposed. Yet it might nevertheless prove substantial and instructive, bearing a truth – to borrow from my epigraph by Simone Weil – about the wartime culture of Romantic Britain.[5] My interest here tends towards the second option, guided not only by Barbauld and her contemporaries but also by more recent writers on affect, especially the psychologist and theorist Silvan Tomkins. This paper proposes, then, that the General Fast and Humiliation in time of war generates what Tomkins calls an "affect theory."[6]

By "theory" Tomkins means something quite specific, similar to strategy or protocol. In this light, an "affect theory" offers a procedure for channeling powerful affective force. Extrapolating from Tomkins's thought, we can investigate this protocol, this theory, which the British state proclaimed in response to the unsorted, felt stimuli of ongoing war. By such proclamations king, parliament, and church sought to organize disparate, immediate, as well as more archaic feelings into a "conscious report" which they called General Humiliation. Humiliation served in this instance as "a simplified and powerful" interpretation of an otherwise overwhelming set of forces.[7] The theory generated by these proclamations aimed to foresee, evaluate, and control the affective impact of a distant war: to foresee that we could suffer humiliation (thus narrowing our fears to this particular threat); to evaluate the force and extent of such humiliation; and to control its impact by, in a sense, absorbing the emotional force before it hit. With Tomkins, we might understand an affect theory as "affect acting at a distance," so that "the affect need never be [immediately] activated or experienced."[8] Yet Tomkins also argues that in the case of a negative affect such as humiliation, the theory can be remarkably potent and self-reflexive, so that even as it works to ward off it may sometimes activate and amplify. Distance may disappear; feeling may be actualized. The emotional impact of distant war may thus be structured and routed through narrow channels, but nevertheless – or all the more – brought home.

As an affect theory governing wartime, humiliation proves complex and curious for at least two reasons: first because of its peculiar semantic fluidity in the Romantic period; and second because even before it presents itself as a generalizing theory, humiliation is constitutively implicated in questions of the individual and the general. I have borrowed from Tomkins a model designed for individual psychological experience and applied it to a "general" and indeed official practice. And yet the dynamics of humiliation warrant and indeed promote this translation. As a theory (in Tomkins's sense) of wartime affect, General Humiliation in the Romantic period allows precisely for movement or translation among general states – indeed sovereign states – and individual feelings and, as various Romantic writers demonstrate, between the state of war and everyday emotions. This essay will consider along its way works by Coleridge, Wordsworth, Austen, and Byron, and will end by devoting some attention to Kant's essay *Toward Perpetual Peace* and Anna Barbauld's extraordinary pamphlet, *Sins of the Nation, Sins of Government, or a Discourse for the Fast Appointed April 19, 1793*, where translation between individual and general states produces one of the period's greatest pieces of anti-war writing. Before thinking through humiliation and engaging Barbauld's or Kant's interpretation, though, I will lay out some of the quandaries encountered in thinking seriously about the notion and practice of General Humiliation.

I. General questions

To begin perhaps with the most obvious difficulty: A Day of General Fast
and Humiliation was to be observed *generally* by all subjects of the throne.
Those who "contemned or neglected" the practice would "suffer severe
punishment."[9] That is, if one did not submit to the General Humiliation,
one could suffer otherwise and individually. The demand that all participate in a state religious practice and, in most instances, offer up prayers for
military victory, threatened certain subjects more than others. Members of
Dissenting churches, not to mention non-Christians, understandably
found this condition of the proclamation hard to bear. Yet as Joseph
Priestley points out in the preface to his 1793 Fast Day sermon, the
proclamation was not deemed to carry "the force of law," so that "Quakers
and many Dissenters [were] known to disobey the requisition with impun-
ity."[10] With each new proclamation, Dissenters would debate their obligation to participate and their preachers – like Aikin and Priestley, and in her
own way, Barbauld – would publish their own Fast Day sermons, marking
the event as a matter of public debate. Evidence shows that the lower
classes were not necessarily expected to participate in the proclaimed
abstinence and prostration. Given extra alms, the poor were in fact
thought to feast on fast days.[11] Occasionally, in latter years, factory owners
paid their employees to attend church services on a Day of Fasting and
Humiliation.

How general then were the fasting and the feeling, and who really
participated? A scholar might scroll through databases of diaries and
journals, hoping to find accounts of individual fasting Britons: I have done
this and found only scant mention of General Fast Days, and even fewer
details of actual abstinence or humiliation. Anna Seward in her letters
snipes at those who blandly apologize for "lying abed the morning,
drinking creamed tea on a fast-day"; Miss Mary Berry, obviously a very
well connected young woman, joked in her diary in 1811 that "Lord
Hartington begged me to give him a little party on Wednesday next, the
fast day."[12] Other than these indications that the Fast was casually
breached and the breaches casually noted, references to Fast Days in letters
and journals surface rarely. Among women of an evangelical bent, they
appear as prompts to reflection on the local minister's sermon; elsewhere,
they serve simply as a mode of dating. It is difficult to know by these
accounts what counted as fasting, let alone humiliation. The Countess of
Hardwicke explains that her household turned off the kitchen fires for the
fast day and she set the tone by eating only bread and water. "Many no

doubt will abstain from all food," she adds, "but I know that would make me ill, and unfit me for the duties of the day."[13] There was no uniformity. Total abstinence from food and drink, a diet of bread and water, no meat (or cream), simply meager servings or no eating before sunset: whether the reigning rationale was to abstain from the pleasures of this world or simply to limit what the body took in, these were all possible options for the body that fasted, if it fasted.[14] Perhaps, though, this desire for individual testimony is misguided: the phenomenon of the General Fast and Humiliation may not have lived in individual practices or indeed private feeling. Such individualism runs exactly counter to the proclaimed theory or strategy. Here *ascesis* operates less as self-denial (with all the signs of spiritual distinction such denial might allow) than as collective withholding, where the individual surrenders to the general and the general itself is formed in and by surrender.

The archive of references to the General Fast and Humiliation, then, assembles itself not in diaries and letters but elsewhere: in the posted proclamations and liturgies; in Fast Day sermons, of course, and periodical reviews of those sermons; in newspaper reports; and, to a surprising degree, in poetry published in the period. Cowper, Coleridge, and Wordsworth all invoke fasting and public humiliation in works of a decidedly prophetic strain. Though he does not name the Fast and Humiliation specifically, the outcry of the generic "humble man" in Coleridge's "Fears in Solitude" (1798) mimics the rhetorical structure of many Fast Day sermons:

> We have offended, Oh! my countrymen!
> We have offended very grievously.
>
> (ll. 41–2)

The poem proceeds to give a long list of "our" sins, culminating in a condemnation of the general lust for war:

> We, this whole people, have been clamorous
> For war and bloodshed.
>
> (ll. 93–4)

Though a lyric "I" does emerge in the last section of the poem, it depends upon and claims communion with the "we" that dominates the first 175 lines. That "I" folds back finally into "thoughts that yearn for human kind," the feelingly impersonal words that close the poem (l. 232).[15]

Another interpretive problem arises concerning fasting itself. The General Fast and Humiliation was not precisely an act of self-discipline, but a performance ordained by and for the state. This type of fasting does

not immediately fit our given scholarly models: state-sponsored fasting
does not lead to the individual mystical experience so vividly explored in
the work of Caroline Walker Bynum and others; nor does it conjure the
contemporary anorexic who "starves at large, deliriously," "pursuing
hunger for its own sake."[16] Nor does such fasting evoke the hunger strikes
of political prisoners, suffragettes and other desperate protesters against the
State. The General Fast stands perhaps as the direct opposite of such
protests. The proper analogue seems closer to examples in the Hebrew
Scriptures, notably the passage in the book of Joel where the prophet,
envisioning an army swarming upon the Israelites, calls for communal
fasting in "solemn assembly," with public weeping and repentance by "the
people" – all this understood as a powerful alternative to military
response.[17] Bynum tells of a slightly different practice in the early Christian
Church, where "corporate practices" of fasting functioned in part to restore
the economy of the whole congregation.[18] Members of means would fast
and distribute to the very poor the food they would have consumed, the
alimentary benefits circulating not simply within individuals but now
between bodies in the community. All members would pray for healing.
Though the British fasts were understood to be similarly communal and
included an element of alms-giving by the well-to-do, they emphasized the
work of humiliation and repentance rather than a redistribution of goods.
If these wartime Fast Days aimed to restore or repair the corporate body,
they had to compass not only the living bodies of those in need at home,
but those injured, imprisoned, starving, diseased and dead members of the
community elsewhere: those bodies brought low by war.[19]

That last image introduces the possibility of coordinating the devastation of war with the state of being-brought-low that characterizes General
Humiliation. Our current accounts of humiliation tend to identify it
as a remarkably inward and idiosyncratic, even individuating emotion.
Tomkins – perhaps the most-cited writer on the topic – begins by pairing
humiliation with shame. He identifies an affect he calls "shame-
humiliation" and offers a vivid portrait of its internal, private workings:
"While terror and distress hurt, they are wounds inflicted from the outside
which penetrate the smooth surface of the ego; but shame is felt as an inner
torment, a sickness of the soul . . . [T]he humiliated one . . . feels himself
naked, defeated, alienated, lacking in dignity or worth."[20] Could such
a feeling be experienced generally, as the sickness of a collective soul? The
proclaimed form of humiliation is not individual – something uniquely
familiar to each of us – but general, suffered commonly and in common. It
confesses what the king's proclamation names as "our manifold sins and

provocations," with some ambivalence sounding in that possessive pronoun. The more democratically inclined Barbauld would translate this phrase into "sins of the nation." In either case, these were faults and failings held in common. It seems important even in this communal register to recognize the nearly existential depth plumbed by humiliation, separating it, as Tomkins suggests, from the more punctual feelings of terror or distress. Unlike Tomkins's shame-humiliation, though, General Humiliation is curiously announced from outside and on high (that is, by royal decree) and yet, like all humiliation, generated from within ("judgments which our manifold Provocations have most justly deserved"). The origins of humiliation only multiply when we recognize that his majesty's authority to dictate this emotional reckoning is itself subject to Divine Majesty, "the Arbiter of All."[21] General Humiliation admits that "we" – sovereign and subjects – have all already been brought low by "our" failings and wrong-doings. Both anterior to and resultant from the king's words, humiliation hovers outside any one person. Its temporal vectors are similarly unstable. Announced for its curative effects, the General Humiliation seems designed at once to explain the present situation and ward off future humiliations. It organizes the world in a simple, impersonal, and eternal structure of domination and submission.

This simple power structure may well radiate with magical thinking. Certainly the intensification of proclamations for a General Fast and Humiliation during the Romantic period strike twenty-first-century readers as regressive, decidedly irrational, and resistant to concurrent secularizing impulses. Yet the matter is hardly that one-sided. The practice does align with a reactionary sacralization of the British monarchy in a time of war with republican France, a nation that had initially severed its ties to Christianity. Early in the Revolution, the French Convention debated the idea of a national fast but rejected it, deciding it smacked too much of superstition and tyranny (both fasting and humiliation were strongly associated in France with Roman Catholicism). Perhaps too, in a revolution sparked in part by the shortage of bread, fasting would look... impolitic. This sort of practical calculation was not yet afloat in Britain, though it would surface later, notably in 1832.[22] So on the one hand we find, in the 1790s and onward, this curious holdover from the threatened Protestantism of Elizabethan times, professing a sacred, cosmic understanding of the collective body and moral feeling. On the other hand, however, as the newspapers all indicated (the newspaper hardly a sacralizing medium) the practice was thoroughly routine. With the exception of 1803, when hostilities with France were resumed after a brief period of peace, by the second decade of the war most newspapers reported on the General Fast and Humiliation with a canned sentence or two. The same obligatory adjectives parade in the press – "suitable," "appropriate," "fitting," "solemn" – each betraying not simply the formalization of the practice, but also its apparent lack of a transcendent aim, of anything beyond the proper social order. The General Fast and Humiliation operated, in other words, as both a sacred, searching duty in response to global warfare and as a thoroughly socialized and customary practice in a modern, media culture.

We might then discount the proclamation of Fast Days as acts of historical desperation, all the more intense in the face of their obsolescence. By the mid nineteenth century the practice did indeed wither away. Why it withered is as complicated a question as why it flourished in Romantic wartime. One might assume that a sense of its inefficacy grew: it was no longer perceived to have actual power. Yet the Fast and Humiliation had been deployed several times during the war with the American colonies with no military benefit, and that result did not deter its use during the wars with France (where, in fact, the outcome was arguably beneficial). More to the point perhaps, its non-military benefits became harder to discern. One might assume, similarly, that charges of hypocrisy in 1832 rendered Fast Days rhetorically and politically implausible – though such charges had circulated in the discourse of the 1790s without slowing the proclamations. Coleridge's "Fears in Solitude" is again a good example, for it condemns the hypocrisy of the Fast Day's solemn bellicosity without abandoning the call for general humiliation:

> (Stuffed out[23] with big preamble, holy names,
> And adjurations of the God in Heaven,)
> We send our mandates for the certain death
> Of thousands and ten thousands!
>
> (ll. 101–4)[24]

The authority of the practice was certainly compromised by constitutional restrictions on the Anglican Church and repeal of the Corporation and Test Acts in the 1820s. The onset in the 1830s and 1840s of a bio-political regime organized not by warfare but by epidemics and famine probably made rituals of withholding and prostration unconscionable (though again, famines tore at the 1790s as well). The call in 1832 for a General Fast and Humiliation on behalf of the cholera epidemic and again in 1847 for the Irish Famine met resistance so vociferous it nearly annihilated the practice. The last official Fast and Humiliation in Britain came in response to the Indian Rebellion in 1857.[25]

We could spend even more time teasing out these knotted problems. In what follows I want rather to accept these difficulties as the necessary backdrop to this question: how might the intensive and extensive practice of a General Fast and Humiliation in the Romantic period have been suited to and indeed revelatory of the modern experience of warfare? Even while recognizing the oppressiveness that takes concentrated form whenever state decrees mix with religious observance, can we find a conceptual apparatus that nevertheless reckons the nearly existential and still pressing force of general fasting and general humiliation?

To suggest that we are not merely investigating a distant and archaic cultural phenomenon, let me drag in the example of Texas Governor Rick Perry's recent declaration that 6 August 2011 be a "Day of Prayer and Fasting for Our Nation in Texas," with its accompanying event, known simply as "The Response," where citizens were invited to gather in solemn assembly in Houston's enormous Reliant Park, "the world's first retractable roof, air-conditioned, natural grass football stadium," to have their prayer and abstinence from worldly pleasures shared and televised.[26] Perry's call to "Americans of faith to pray on that day for the healing of our country, the rebuilding of our communities and the restoration of enduring values as our guiding force" cites as precedent President Abraham Lincoln's 1861 Fast Day Proclamation. It ignores, however, Lincoln's pained plea for "public humiliation." Lincoln hoped the nation would "bow in humble submission to [God's] chastisements; to confess and deplore their sins and transgressions . . .; and to pray, with all fervency and contrition, for the pardon of their past offences."[27] Perry's call rejects as well the penitential weight of George III's proclamations: "those heavy judgments which our manifold sins and provocations have most justly deserved." Perry fails, in other words, to give the event its gravity: the lowering gestures customarily required before praying for blessing or assistance. That the Governor's Day of Prayer and Fasting for a Nation in Crisis was a highly scripted media event makes it no more modern than the Fast Days of the Romantic period. Its distance from, if not negation of, those earlier days lies precisely in its failure to engage fully the emotional – and indeed political – weight of humiliation, general or otherwise.[28]

II. Humiliation theories

The political operations of humiliation elude us because the meaning and value of the word shifted during the eighteenth century from an impersonal state or activity to an intimate feeling. From its earliest appearance in

English, humiliation was paired semantically with virtuous humility and attached itself especially to redemptive acts of religious devotion. For Christians, acts of humiliation had special warrant: Jesus Christ himself had chosen humiliation, that is, the lowering of his divine nature into mortal flesh.[29] Humiliation thus designated an action or condition rather than a feeling. It had a physical, nearly gravitational force. As condition, it functioned not subjectively but quite objectively: to humiliate was to bring low, down to earth, down to the very ground (as the root word, *humus*, reveals). Prior to the mid eighteenth century, the usual sense of humiliation referred to "the physical act of bowing, of prostrating oneself."[30] In this sense, humiliation was a grave and frequently ritualized gesture of submission to a higher authority. It simultaneously testified to the common ground of human (also from *humus*) mortality, the "human kind" that concludes Coleridge's "Fears in Solitude." Thus Robert Bloomfield, contemplating a tombstone in his poem, "The Banks of Wye," could point out the contrastive logic of humiliation: "Humiliation," Bloomfield writes,

> bids you sigh,
> And think of Immortality.[31]

In spring, during the season of Lent, Christians repeatedly heard this reminder of the ground of their being: "Remember Man that you are dust and unto dust you shall return." Not coincidentally, most Fast Days were called during Lent. In a later, secular moment, Wallace Stevens would reflect similarly on the "poverty of dirt" and explain, "It is the earth itself that is humanity. . ."[32] Humiliation designated the pull of that earth on all human kind.

When Wordsworth in an 1832 sonnet defended the proclamation of a General Fast and Humiliation during the cholera epidemic, he invoked this older conception of humiliation. Lashing out at critics of the Fast, the poet claimed they had

> doffed
> The last of their humanity

– as if their resistance to collective humiliation served as denial and betrayal of the human condition.

> Upon the Late General Fast, March 1832
> Reluctant call it was; the rite delayed;
> And in the Senate some there were who doffed
> The last of their humanity, and scoffed

> At providential judgments, undismayed
> By their own daring. But the People prayed
> As with one voice; their flinty heart grew soft
> With penitential sorrow, and aloft
> Their spirit mounted, crying, "God us aid!"
> Oh that with aspirations more intense,
> Chastised by self-abasement more profound,
> This People, once so happy, so renowned
> For liberty, would seek from God defence
> Against far heavier ill, the pestilence
> Of revolution, impiously unbound![33]

Wordsworth complicates his case, however, making the General Humiliation less an avowal of shared humanity (and its shared vulnerability, in this instance, to disease) than a tool against political reform, using the practice of general submission to block the general will. "Chastised by self-abasement" (in his words), "the People" in the reform year of 1832 ought to ask God to ward off not only cholera but also, Wordsworth prays, the "pestilence of revolution" (ll. 9, 14). But this is only to admit that revolution, like cholera, could remind "the People" – if not "us" or "me" – of their common humanity.

The royal proclamations were more hotly contested in 1832 than in prior years, in part because while the political rhetoric on both sides took humiliation as a lowering of "the People," the valence of such lowering was now under stress. In 1832 Wordsworth's sonnet displays the fraying of the concept of humiliation as a virtuous, collective submission; we tend to read it here as class-based and, as its critics were quick to point out, selectively degrading. This had not always been the obvious reading of the politics of General Humiliation. In religious custom, humiliation could wield a leveling force, marking out and demonstrating a general, that is to say human, condition shared by sovereign and subjects, allies and enemies alike. It was essential that the king and his ministers participated in the public rituals associated with the Fast Day. This understanding of humiliation performed humility, yet there was nothing necessarily humiliating about it. Indeed the adjective "humiliating," in its role of carrying the emotional cost of humiliation, was scarcely in use even in the early decades of the nineteenth century.[34] Rather the general, leveling, and impersonal aspect of humiliation still governed meaning.

This latter aspect of humiliation fascinated Byron more than any of the other major poets of the period, and he extracted its political value in ways quite different from Wordsworth's sonnet. Byron enlists the term in Act 2 scene 4 of *Manfred*, when Manfred is advised to bow down to Arimanes, "Sovereign of sovereigns." Manfred refuses, in these words:

> ... – many a night on the earth,
> On the bare ground, have I bowed down my face,
> And strewed my head with ashes; I have known
> The fulness of humiliation – for
> I sunk before my vain despair, and knelt
> To my own desolation.
>
> (II.iv: 24, 37–42)[35]

Manfred will not bow to Arimanes because he knows himself to be already fully, positively humiliated. Which is to say that Manfred has already encountered and acknowledged the limits of his mortal condition. In a move that outrages the king's spirit servants, Manfred invites the "Sovereign of sovereigns" to share this humiliation:

> Bid *him* bow down to that which is above him,
> The overruling Infinite.
>
> (II.iv: 46–7)[36]

The political meaning turns sharper in Canto IV of *Childe Harold's Pilgrimage*, where the poet records the humiliation of specific nations and emperors. A long historical note details with admiration the "ceremony of humiliation" performed twice by Fredric Barbarossa to Pope Alexander III: after publicly prostrating himself at the pope's feet, the emperor withdrew his armies from Italy.[37] A subsequent long note on the political demise of Venice takes up the new word "humiliating," as Byron imagines the "humiliating spectacle of a whole nation loaded with chains." He has not left behind humiliation's physical ground: more present participle than adjective, "humiliating" charts the nearly gravitational decline of the "degraded capital" and its republican virtues: Venice "must fall to pieces ... and sink more rapidly than it rose," lowering "into the slime of her choked canals." Venice, according to the poet, "may be said ... 'to die daily'." For Byron, humiliation reveals the mortal – and ethical – limits of the political and economic systems of Venice. "The present race cannot be thought to regret the loss of their aristocratical forms, and too despotic government; they think only on their vanished independence." The "general decay" and lowering suffered by Venice may be inevitable "in the due course of mortality," Byron explains, but he cannot talk of its humiliation without layering it with the degradation of its nobility and the crushing effects of a wealth dependent upon slavery.[38]

As the example of Venice reminds us, humiliation in its general form moved not just in the religious but also the geopolitical sphere. There humiliation indicated not a *feeling* of abasement so much as actual military defeat and subjugation: historians might analyze the humiliation of Carthage by the Romans, as Venice had suffered humiliation before the Turks. The humiliations of the Seven Years War were known to have crippled France. Tom Paine, in *The Crisis*, could imagine Britain reducing its American colonies "to a state of perfect humiliation" through taxation; later the British themselves suffered humiliation in North America. In all these instances, humiliation designated a political and often economic state of affairs, felt – though *felt* hardly seems the right word for such systemic overpowering – let's say *borne* quite generally by a population.

All this suggests that in its earlier dispensation, and indeed lasting into the early nineteenth century, humiliation was inherently general. It referred either to the common condition of being human, and therefore a fallen nature shared with other members of a species; or it referred to a political and economic order, where one set of humans fell beneath the power of another. Either way, as a *condition* humiliation was suffered by humans by virtue of their humanity; it rehearsed their limitations and vulnerabilities and imagined a world organized according to a single vertical distinction: up or down. Regarded as an *action*, humiliation dramatized that preexistent or structural condition, giving it concrete form either as literal prostration, prayers, and supplications, imposed taxes or tribute, or, in the case of war, the fallen bodies that measured defeat.

Yet only part of the story resides here, since we know humiliation underwent a transformation in the latter decades of the eighteenth century from an action or condition to its modern dispensation as an "an experience of the self by the self," to borrow Tomkins's words.[39] Humiliation once required a full body display, a falling to the ground. In the migration of humiliation toward shame and embarrassment, its modern companions, such display declines now to a dropping of the eyes, a bowing of the head. Its verbal form now is less repentance and supplication than apology, "the most frequent ritual of humiliation" we currently practice.[40] Working hard to distinguish humiliation from shame and embarrassment, William Ian Miller pares it down to a linked action and feeling: humiliation is "a piercing of vanity and deflating of pretensions" together with the felt experience of such deflation.[41] He calls upon Jane Austen to ferry humiliation to its more modern usage: "'How despicably I have acted,' [Elizabeth Bennett] cried. 'I who have prided myself on my discernment! I who have valued myself on my abilities! ... How humiliating is this discovery!

Yet how just a humiliation.'"[42] For Miller as for Austen, humiliation in its modern manifestation plays a fundamentally comic role: it serves to "puncture pretensions" and thereby regulate identity (Elizabeth says, "Till this moment I did not know myself!").[43] Its force derives from a finely calibrated social order. Miller proposes that the feeling of humiliation affects those who dread being found to have violated *not* "serious moral and legal norms" but only social norms, such as "norms of bodily control or decorousness."[44] Social norms and one's acquiescence to those norms secure this understanding of humiliation.

As Elizabeth Bennett understands, humiliation now allows us to recognize our individual situation in a social ecology. Modern humiliation, Eve Sedgwick and Adam Frank suggest, serves as "a switch point for ... an individuation [process] that decides not necessarily an identity but a figuration, distinction or mark of punctuation" – punctuation here both puncturing and differentiating (as if Elizabeth's repeated "I" and "myself" are the products of humiliation). Humiliation is one of the ways "quantitative differences become qualitative ones" in this system, and it operates primarily by noting social failure or error.[45] Central to producing and organizing a self – indeed in binding together the self's emotional world – individual humiliation nevertheless requires the background of an abstracted, impersonal world.

In an ethically charged extension of this analysis, Frances Ferguson also situates humiliation in a distinctly modern social order, organized now not vertically but horizontally. She treats humiliation alongside envy; both emotions, she claims,

> accompany democracy and identify the possibilities and the limits of political justice. As the emotions that register the injustices of social regard and the inequalities in the distribution of public endorsement of individuals, envy and humiliation are almost by definition the emotions that would interest political theorists who debate the advantages and disadvantages of democracy ... [;] they are emotions that are resolutely extra-individual emotions.[46]

A democratic emotion, this humiliation is not quite Byron's leveling form of lowering. Ferguson has something less direct in mind: by democratic and extra-individual, she means primarily two things. First, this pair of emotions depends upon a certain abstracting principle that allows comparisons between individuals of the same kind or species (replacing the cosmological difference between god and man). Without this recognition of comparable others, and without a system of coordinating norms or expectations, the modern feeling of envy or humiliation would not work. The common ground of an older humiliation, which is to say the earth-bound ground of the human, has been translated and abstracted into a system of comparisons and finely articulated gradations, such that Fergu-son discerns the emergence of a "fully rationalized and rational emotion."[47] No longer a shared mortality vertically contrasted to the "overruling Infinite," now an elaborate set of mundane distinctions governs humili-ation, comically or not. Second, and as an extension of the first, these extra-individual emotions are "detached from [direct] objects that would enable us to explain them" (as in, say, the case of covetousness or greed). They are tethered not to ground and grave but rather to a horizontal and rationalized "social relation."[48] When we imagine ourselves as democratic equals, "members," as Ferguson explains, "of the same general political species," we feel distinctions intensely.[49] Honing our sense of justice requires us to register acutely inequalities and deviations.

Though her essay goes on to analyze envy exclusively, Ferguson invites a reconsideration of humiliation that chimes with the political and economic upheaval of the decades in Britain between 1790 and 1832 – and beyond. "Envy," she proposes in her reading of Coleridge, Bentham and Dickens, "becomes an attitude towards the structures of [society] rather than an attitude towards a specific person"; more pointedly, it functions as "protest . . . against a state of affairs."[50] Is humiliation then envy's compli-ant twin, surrendering to a dense and unmasterable state of affairs? Not necessarily: already in Byron's "humiliating spectacle" of Venice we glimpse another possibility, where humiliation marks out or punctuates a failed state of affairs that critically highlights an alternative republican ideal. Byron's point is less that Venice has surrendered to the Turks than that it now recognizes its political and ethical failures. Applied to one state among other states, humiliation in Byron's hands exhibits a melding of old and new meanings: sunk low, the Venetians learn to value neither wealth nor power but "only their [lost] independence." In the prophetic tones adopted by the poet in this section of *Childe Harold's Pilgrimage*, general humiliation becomes the condition for a future freedom.

Taken together, Byron's ruminations on Venice, Wordsworth's sonnet, and Elizabeth Bennett's outburst remind us that the meaning of humili-ation was in agitation during this period. The term moved between external condition and inner feeling, between political and emotional states, and between impersonal and personal perspectives. For this very reason, it was precisely suited to express both the condition of a nation at war and the response to that condition. The frequent, even annual call for a General Fast and Humiliation, an organized response to distant war, sounded amidst this agitation, with its swirl of residual theological and political as well as emergent sociological and psychological meanings. Its very mobility allowed humiliation to translate and coordinate several levels of wartime experience: condition, action and, newly, inner feeling in response to an abstracted state of affairs. Bodies – simply human bodies – were indeed falling to the ground, displaying their mortality. Human failure, error, and wrong-doing pushed their way insistently to public notice. This humiliation could be read both as the reminder of common humanity before heaven *and* as the mark that distinguishes losers from winners; it could be read too as the historical failure that upholds a larger political ideal. It could signal both the unique fall of individuals *and* the collective "sins of the nation." It was the occasion for general abasement *and* a reason to lower one's head and avert one's eyes. Humiliation pulsed with meaning and, charged with such vitality, nearly surrendered its effectiveness as a strategy for streamlining and buffering emotion.

III.   Romantic humiliation

If for Ferguson the exemplary site for envy is the classroom, the site for humiliation may well be the battlefield. In current psychological accounts of the emotion there persists an older understanding of humiliation as suffered by armies and nations. Tomkins, for instance, in his presentation of shame-humiliation, sends the term back again in time, so that his humiliated individual is theorized according to the general form of military defeat. The word "defeat" or "defeated" appears so often in Tomkins's analysis of humiliation that its metaphoric quality dissolves into commonplace. Recall the portrait he draws: "the humiliated one ... feels himself naked, defeated, alienated, lacking in dignity or worth."[51] At least four times in a twenty-page stretch, military defeat serves additionally as his clinching analogy, culminating in this passage: "humiliation and defeat ... can be in the life of a child what the loss of a great war can be for a nation – the beginning of an unceasing preoccupation with an intolerable threat."[52] Tomkins's use of "defeat" bears the traces of Romantic humiliation: the translation humiliation performs between individual and general also works between person and nation: as if since childhood we might all have been living in the shadow of military defeat. In such a way humiliation continues to mediate between the battlefield and the everyday. Tomkins's analysis, which dates from the Cold War, brings humiliation more or less into its current accepted form, in which we take on defeat and humiliation unceremoniously, as part of the usual, everyday course of individual development. Such humiliation comes trailing a cloudy romanticism, its politics and protest obscured.

It seems to me at this moment, while acknowledging the fluidity that permits modern humiliation to migrate from the general to the individual, or from the political state of things to the emotions that flare up and mark its edges, that we might want to hold on to the ceremonial, impersonal form of General Humiliation. For this more communal version of humiliation, I have shown, not only bears the weight of actual bodies fallen in war; it licenses a profound acknowledgment of shared responsibility for the fallen state of things. This balance, supporting the weight both of fallen bodies and collective failure, is what some Romantic writers found and exploited when they contemplated the practice of the General Fast and Humiliation. Humiliation was not yet humiliating for them; it could still reach common ground.

Anna Barbauld's "Sins of Government, Sins of the Nation" like other dissenting Fast Day sermons, exploits the critical political potential and weight of General Humiliation. Like her brother John Aikin and her mentor, Joseph Priestley, Barbauld in 1793 bows to the king's proclamation, fully accepting the call to fasting and humiliation as a national examination of conscience. At the heart of this excoriating anti-war sermon she emphasizes the two-way translation between individual and national that humiliation allows. "Every individual, my brethren, who has a sense of religion and a desire of conforming his conduct to his precepts, will frequently retire into himself to discover his faults..." she offers. "Nations have likewise *their* faults to repent of, *their* conduct to examine ..., they should engage in the same duty."[53] This moral equation then opens a political vision where responsibility for the nation's sinful acts – but also sovereignty itself – rests not in the monarch but his subjects. Built into the proclamation of General Humiliation Barbauld finds a logic that makes each individual responsible for those national sins and offenses: why else, she insists, would king and parliament ask us to repent? It would be "presumption" or "absurd mockery" to repent of sins that were not of our own making. "By thus calling us together on every public emergency, [government powers] remind us that these [sins and crimes] are all our *own* acts; and that for every violation of integrity, justice or humanity in public affairs, it is incumbent on every one of us to humble himself personally before the tribunal of Almighty God."[54] By shifting from the discourse of power to that of penitence and humiliation, Barbauld enacts a political shift as well, building her democratic vision.[55] From the egalitarian vantage underwritten by humiliation, she unleashes her searing critique of war.

> War ... is a state in which it becomes our business to hurt and annoy our neighbor by every possible means; instead of cultivating, to destroy; instead of building to pull down; instead of peopling, to depopulate; a state in which we drink the tears and feed upon the misery of our fellow-creatures.[56]

If, as Barbauld sets it up, the very structure of fasting and humiliation depends upon the moral code of persons and shores up our common humanity (as "fellow-creatures"), then war makes a "total and strange inversion" of that structure. War itself is the state of affairs Barbauld most pointedly condemns – "it ought to make a large part of our humiliation this day" – and that condemnation rises in crescendo from the searching collective humiliation ordained, paradoxically, by the crown.[57]

In a different context, but only two years later, Immanuel Kant also calls upon this critical force. Looking with disquiet at the triumphal celebrations of the Prussians after the Treaty of Basle in 1795, Kant offers a critical response to the recent (if temporary) end of warfare. Refusing partisanship, his analysis of the situation insists, even more than Barbauld's, upon placing war on the level of the human race.

> At the end of a war, when peace is concluded, it would not be unfitting for a nation to proclaim, after the festival of thanksgiving, a day of atonement [*Busstag*], calling upon heaven, in the name of the state, to forgive the great sin of which the human race continues to be guilty, that of being unwilling to acquiesce in any lawful constitution in relation to other nations but, proud of its independence, preferring instead to use the barbarous means of war ... Festivals of thanksgiving during war for a *victory* won ... introduce a joy [*Freude*] at having annihilated a great many human beings or their happiness [*Glück*].[58]

The sin is general (it belongs to the human race) and ongoing (Kant will not place it in the past tense). The response to sin, moreover, is tracked via emotional states: Kant's Day of Atonement, his equivalent to the British General Humiliation, folds a massive loss of life together with a massive loss of happiness. (Humiliation, Sedgwick, and Frank suggest, "is characterized by its failure to renounce ... its relation to the desire for pleasure as well as the need to avoid pain.")[59] As David Clark notes in his superb analysis of Kant's essay, this passage is "one of several sober reminders" in *Perpetual Peace* that the defeated in general "are not mere abstractions but precious, singular creatures." Clark goes on to suggest that "the [Prussian] 'festivals of thanksgiving' ... [may] seem consolatory, pacific, and felicitous but in Kant's hands they are described as harbouring an aggression and a murderous nonchalance about lost lives."[60] In other words, Kant suggests, without general humiliation and atonement, without recognition of and responsibility for fallen lives, the violence of war lives on.

We might think of the General Fast and Humiliation of Romantic wartime, then, as a procedure for producing something more than bankrupt feeling or political consensus. We might consider the way it unearths strategies and language for, as well as responsiveness to, a diffuse and overwhelming experience: the distant slaughter of Coleridge's "thousands and ten thousands" of fellow humans. It provides, in however compromised a fashion, a flexible instance of an "affect theory" for wartime. In the history of its usage, humiliation has undergone translation from general to personal, from an overarching condition to an individuating feeling that nonetheless rebounds against the backboard of an abstracted norm. But the striking force of humiliation's ancient, common, physical ground – the body fallen to earth – continues to echo, and echo insistently in wartime.

NOTES

1 Simone Weil, *Waiting for God*, trans. Emma Graufurd and intro. Leslie Fiedler (New York: Harper Collins, 2009), 18.
2 Wallace Stevens, *The Auroras of Autumn* (New York: Alfred A. Knopf, 1950), 398.
3 Great Britain, Sovereign, *By the King: A Proclamation, for a General Fast* (London, 1793), 1; *Eighteenth Century Collections Online*, Gale, Indiana University Libraries, Bloomington, 19 November 2012.
4 Anna Letitia Barbauld, "Sins of Government, Sins of the Nation," *Selected Poetry and Prose*, ed. William McCarthy and Elizabeth Kraft (Peterborough, ON: Broadview, 2002), 298.
5 John Aikin, *Food for National Penitence; or, a Discourse Intended for the Approaching Fast Day* (London: Joseph Johnson, 1793), 14; *Eighteenth Century Collections Online*, Gale, Indiana University Libraries, Bloomington, 19 November 2012.
6 Tomkins, *Shame and Its Sisters*, 164. In their introduction, Sedgwick and Frank adopt the term "everyday theories" to emphasize the heterogeneity, adaptability, and contingency of this notion. Too strong, that is to say too universalizing a theory, risks solidifying into Theory, which is "expensive" and often damaging to those who hold it (23).
7 Tomkins, *Shame and Its Sisters*, 165.
8 Ibid., 167.
9 Great Britain, *A Proclamation*, 1.
10 Joseph Priestley, *A Sermon Preached at the Gravel Pit Meeting, in Hackney, April 19th, 1793, Being the Day Appointed for a General Fast* (London, 1793), iv;

Eighteenth Century Collections Online, Gale, Indiana University Libraries, Bloomington, 19 November 2012.

11 See Mary Berry, *Extracts of the Journals and Correspondence of Miss Berry from the Year 1783–1852*, ed. Lady Maria Theresa Villiers Lister Lewis (London: Longmans, Green, & Co., 1866), 2: 412.

12 Anna Seward, *Letters of Anna Seward: Written Between the Years 1784 and 1807* (Edinburgh: Archibald Constable, 1811), 1: 399; Berry, *Extracts*, 2: 457.

13 Susan Liddell York, Countess of Hardwicke, *Extracts of Letters from Maria, Marchioness of Normandy, et al.*, ed. Georgiana Liddell Bloomfield, Baroness (Hertfordshire: Simpson & Co., 1892), 234.

14 William Combe's poem, *The Fast-Day* ([London: J. Bow 1780], p. 20, fn. 2; *English Poetry Database*, Chadwyck-Healey, 1992, Indiana University Libraries, Bloomington, 22 July 2011) has this illuminating footnote: "It is, I believe, a general matter of faith among devout Christians, that, on days of public fasting and humiliation, no one should eat meat till after the services of the day, which are generally completed at four in the afternoon. In this particular, all persons of Fashion give a very striking example of attention to the duties of such public solemnities."

15 Samuel Taylor Coleridge, "Fears in Solitude," *Samuel Taylor Coleridge*, ed. H. J. Jackson (Oxford and New York: Oxford University Press, 1985), 100–1. Like the Fast Day discourses of Aikin or Barbauld, Coleridge's poem wrests the general "we" away from the established church's Fast Day toward a more general criticism of the war.

16 Caroline Bynum, *Holy Feast and Holy Fast: The Religious Significance of Food to Medieval Women* (Berkeley: University of California Press, 1988). See also Maud Ellman, *The Hunger Artists: Starving, Writing and Imprisonment* (Cambridge, MA: Harvard University Press, 1993), 7. Ellman cites historians who argue that religious abstinence and "a civil practice of fasting with a hostile purpose against an enemy" were once conjoined, then later separated. In this conjunction, God would be considered the enemy and fasting the form of violence most effective in subduing him. "What appears to the modern Christian as sacrifice and humiliation may once have been in some of its aspects, a way of taking the kingdom of heaven by storm" (12–13).

17 See Joel 2: 15–17: "Blow the trumpet in Zion, sanctify a fast, call a solemn assembly: Gather the people, sanctify the congregation, assemble the elders, gather the children, and those that suck the breasts: let the bridegroom go forth of his chamber, and the bride out of her closet. Let the priests, the ministers of the LORD, weep between the porch and the altar, and let them say, Spare thy people, O LORD, and give not thine heritage to reproach, that the heathen should rule over them" (*King James Bible, 1611: a Machine-Readable Transcript*, Joel 2: 15–17, n.p.; *The Bible in English*, Chadwyck-Healey 1997, Indiana University Libraries, Bloomington, 19 November 2012).

18 Bynum, *Holy Feast*, 38–9.

19 A different link might be found between the General Fast and Humiliation and the practice of twentieth-century philosopher Simone Weil who, living in

England during World War II, "limited her food intake to what she believed residents of the parts of France occupied by the Germans ate." She most likely ate even less, as she refused food on most occasions. The coroner's report at her death assumed she "did kill and slay herself" by refusing to eat. Quoted in David McLellan, *Utopian Pessimist: The Life and Thought of Simone Weil* (New York: Simon and Schuster, 1990), 266.

20 Tomkins, *Shame and Its Sisters*, 133.

21 Great Britain, *A Proclamation*, 1.

22 For example see this screed: "The General Fast: An Ode to the Right Honourable, the Ultra-Tory Saints by M," *The Metropolitan* 3, no. 11 (March 1832): 318–19. The 1832 Fast was called in response to the cholera epidemic.

23 Coleridge's backhand mention of the Fast.

24 William Cowper is even more vociferous in his "Expostulation," nailing both the inefficacy and hypocrisy of the Fast:

> Thy fastings, when calamity at last
> Suggests the expedient of a yearly fast,
> What mean they? Canst thou dream there is a power
> In lighter diet at a later hour,
> To charm to sleep the threatenings of the skies,
> And hide past folly from all-seeing eyes?
> The fast that wins deliverance, and suspends
> The stroke that a vindictive God intends,
> Is to renounce hypocrisy.
>
> (ll. 400–8)

William Cowper, *The Poems of William Cowper, Esq. of the Inner Temple* (New York: Charles Wells, 1840), 298; *Google Books*, 19 November 2012.

25 Philip Williamson, "State Prayers, Fasts and Thanksgivings: Public Worship in Britain 1830–1897," *Past and Present* 200, no. 1 (2008): 121–74.

26 A copy of Perry's proclamation is available at http://governor.state.tx.us/news/press-release/16246, last accessed 10 September 2013. A compilation of subsequent media responses can be found at https://docs.google.com/document/d/1At7seEiuBE6WR1_W3L18Xw95lgnNjdUoeRHyzh4MEn8/preview?pli=1, last accessed 10 September 2013. Perry's proclamation was subsequently echoed by Paul LePage, Republican Governor of Maine. On the 71,000-seat Reliant Stadium, see www.reliantpark.com/about, last accessed 10 September 2013.

27 Lincoln's proclamation, the constitutionality of which is still debated, can be found here: www.presidency.ucsb.edu/ws/index.php?pid=69891#axzz1T9bspNi2, last accessed 10 September 2013.

28 Less than a week after "The Response," Perry announced his candidacy in the Republican primary for President of the United States. Perry's proclamation does admit that "even those who have been granted power by the people must turn to God in humility," and it recognizes the language of humiliation in earlier proclamations, but his does not pick up or promote that "affect theory."

29 See for example this short poem by John Wesley, *The Poetical Works of John and Charles Wesley*, ed. George Osborn (London: Wesleyan-Methodist Conference Office, 1868), 33; *Google Books*, 20 November 2012.

> *In His humiliation His judgment was taken, &c. – viii. 33.*
> Justice He could not obtain
> In His humble state beneath,
> No humanity from man,
> No relief – but pain and death.
> Took from earth, He of our sins
> Doth the chastisement receive,
> Endless life's immortal Prince
> Dies, that all mankind may live.

30 William Ian Miller, *Humiliation: And Other Essays on Honor, Social Discomfort and Violence* (Ithaca, NY: Cornell University Press, 1995), 175.
31 Robert Bloomfield, *The Banks of Wye: A Poem in Four Books* (New York: Richard Scott, 1812), 22.
32 Stevens, *The Auroras of Autumn*, 388.
33 William Wordsworth, *Poetical Works*, ed. Thomas Hutchinson, rev. edn. Ernest de Selincourt (Oxford: Oxford University Press, 1981), 402.
34 Miller (*Humiliation*, 176) cites the *OED*'s use of "humiliating" taken from Adam Smith's *Wealth of Nations* (1776) where Smith refers to bankruptcy as a "humiliating calamity." A search of the Chadwyck-Healey English Poetry Database shows only eight uses of the term in poetry published between 1780 and 1835.
35 George Gordon, Lord Byron, *Manfred: A Dramatic Poem* (London: John Murray, 1819), 175–6.
36 Ibid., 176.
37 George Gordon, Lord Byron, *Childe Harold's Pilgrimage, Canto IV* (London: John Murray, 1818), 771, n. 4; *Google Books*, 19 November 2012.
38 Ibid., 772–3, n. 7.
39 Tomkins, *Shame and Its Sisters*, 136.
40 Miller, *Humiliation*, 163.
41 Ibid., 40, n. 4; see also 137.
42 Jane Austen, *Pride and Prejudice*, ed. R. W. Chapman (Oxford: Oxford University Press, 1988), 202.
43 Ibid. See also Mark Schorer, "The Humiliation of Emma Woodhouse," *Jane Austen: A Collection of Critical Essays*, ed. Ian Watt (Upper Saddle River, NJ: Prentice-Hall, 1963), 98–111. Discussion of the heroine's humiliation in Austen's novels has a long history. For a helpful review, see Eve Kosofsky Sedgwick, "Jane Austen and the Masturbating Girl," *Critical Inquiry* 17, no. 4 (1991): 818–37.
44 Miller, *Humiliation*, 138.
45 Sedgwick and Frank, "Introduction," 22, 13.
46 Frances Ferguson, "Envy Rising," *English Literary History* 69, no. 4 (2002): 889–905, 899.

47 Ibid., 903. In a comparable statement, Tomkins insists that all emotions be considered as "important characteristics of an active, searching, and thinking human being" (*Shame and Its Sisters*, 19).

48 Ibid., 889. In this way, Ferguson argues, humiliation and envy mimic Hume's definition of aesthetic judgment: less dependent on objective description than on a sense that some people – the tasteful or the humiliated – are "walking embodiments of the deviations from some unarticulated norm" (890).

49 Ibid., 899.

50 Ibid., 903.

51 Tomkins, *Shame and Its Sisters*, 133; for other examples see 137, 138, 150, and 172.

52 Ibid., 177; see also 157, 161, 175.

53 Barbauld, "Sins of Government," 299.

54 Ibid., 300 and 299.

55 In a remarkable passage, Barbauld offers her "translation" of the Proclamation, ventriloquizing the "governors" who issued it. At the end of this revised proclamation, 'the "governors" (cynically?) offer this: "the guilt be upon your [the people's] heads; we disclaim the awful responsibility" (300–1).

56 Barbauld, "Sins of Government," 312.

57 Ibid., 311, 312.

58 Immanuel Kant, *Toward Perpetual Peace: A Philosophical Project, Cambridge Edition of the Works of Immanuel Kant: Practical Philosophy*, vol. 8, trans. and ed. Mary Gregor (Cambridge: Cambridge University Press, 1996), 357, 328.

59 Sedgwick and Frank, "Introduction," *Shame and Its Sisters*, 23.

60 David Clark, "Unsocial Kant: The Philosopher and the Un-regarded War Dead," *The Wordsworth Circle* 41, no. 1 (2010): 62. Clark's essay allowed me to find the correspondence between Kant's and Barbauld's thought.

CHAPTER 6

A peculiar community
Mary Shelley, Godwin, and the abyss of emotion

Tilottama Rajan

In 1837, on the cusp of the Victorian period, Mary Shelley published her last novel *Falkner*, renewing her stubborn attachment to a Romanticism that had fascinated her throughout her career. As I shall argue, this is not the ineffectual idealism of Percy, figured as Woodville in her second novel *Mathilda*, but the often perverse Romanticism of Godwin and Byron. For the title character of *Falkner* is a confusion of Godwin and Byron, in which Byron figures, extends and is inextricably linked to Godwin. And indeed Godwin had already invented Byron in the misanthropic, brooding personalities of Falkland and Fleetwood. *Falkner* is notable for resisting the nineteenth century's "master-narrative of transition," in which an "immature" and emotional "Byronic phase" gives way to "a sober, adult 'Victorian' phase":[1] a narrative Shelley herself had adopted in her outward transition from woman writer into proper lady, and in her previous novel *Lodore* (1835). Hegel also follows this narrative of sobriety, in Orrin Wang's phrase, when he distinguishes youthful from adult friendships in terms of the supercession of volatile, emotional bonds by more socially mediated relationships. In youth, Hegel writes, individuals live in "community" (*Gemeinschaft*), in relationships "which are indefinite on both sides" (*in gemeinsamer Unbestimmtheit*); they are thus "closely," even obsessively, " bound into one disposition, will, and activity." In friendship between men (*Männerfreundschaft*) this "is no longer the case": "every man fends for himself" and thus becomes "competent to take his place in the world"; "Men find others and separate themselves from them again; their interests and occupations drift apart and are united again."[2] But in its very dismissal, Hegel's account of such youthful friendships raises the question of a "community" – including a community of readers – that transgresses the norms of "society," a community grounded in and ungrounded by unassimilated emotion.

The author acknowledges the support of the Canada Research Chairs Programme in the preparation of this article.

In what follows I approach a constellation of texts by the Godwin circle not only in terms of the "potencies" concealed in their unresolved emotions, but also in terms of the "community" that Shelley tries to establish in revisiting these earlier texts. Standing between what Arnold calls an epoch of criticism and an epoch of creation that in Romanticism was "premature," *Falkner* occupies a unique position as an archival text, and is framed as a retrospective that revisits a gallery of Romantic characters and *topoi* so as to think about the thing at the center of Shelley's writing: the trauma and legacy of Romanticism. If these earlier texts, including Shelley's own *Mathilda*, are stubbornly resistant and separate, *Falkner* is an attempt to put them in community with each other, in Jean-Luc Nancy's sense of community, to which I will return. In the *Aesthetics*, where Hegel makes his comments, a resistance to society and cleaving to community are associated with Romanticism. For in the *Roman*, which serves as an etymological synecdoche for Romanticism, young people "force their way through the course of the world which realizes itself instead of their ideals," and resist the "substantive relations" of "family, civil society, state, laws."[3] Elaborating on the transition from the "excitability" and impressionability of youth, Hegel sees Romanticism as giving way to the "prose of actuality," epitomized in Dutch genre painting and the realist novel as sites of what Hannah Arendt will critique as the social.[4] Although in the spirit of modernity Hegel embraces this transition, it marks the end not only of Romanticism but of art itself: what Georg Simmel, in the aftermath of Hegel's turn to "objective Spirit," calls the tragedy of culture.[5] Hegel's acceptance of the prose of actuality thus masks a profound melancholia. And the symptom of this melancholia, despite a critique of Romantic irony that will later be taken up by Carl Schmitt, is the *typological* category of Romanticism as a restlessness of the negative that cannot find adequate expression in the art produced in the *chronological* period we now call Romanticism. Yet Hegel's account of Romanticism is in the end a missed encounter with this phenomenon, the unsettling materiality of which he stops short of probing. For Hegel stays at the level either of romance (*Roman*), or the inwardness of the beautiful soul: both stereotypes or conventional figures for the more ungraspable "matrix figure" that is Romanticism, to borrow Jean-François Lyotard's term for a figure that is ungraspable, that retreats from visibility or legibility.[6]

Mary Shelley also exhibits a profound ambivalence towards the ascendancy of culture, dismissing the "miss Austen view of domestic life," which itself came to be linked with Dutch painting, yet writing in the mode of the Regency novel in *Lodore*.[7] But in her last novel Shelley wants to make her peace with the inoperative community of Romanticism through her thematizing of its male celebrities: Godwin, Percy, Byron. Constituted by a relationship among three orphans, this community is not so much posited as imagined in separation, passed on to us through the unfinished conversation between texts that Shelley's novel sets in motion. The three orphans are Falkner himself, who is burdened by his guilt over his mysterious crime against Alithea, the woman he loved, who was assumed to have abandoned her family when she disappeared; Elizabeth Raby, coincidentally the daughter of Alithea's best friend, who, as a young child, prevents Falkner from killing himself in remorse when she encounters him near the graves of her parents, and who then becomes his adopted daughter; and Gerard Neville, with whom she falls in love, and who turns out to be the son of Alithea, dedicated to finding his dead mother and restoring her reputation.

At the core of this triangle is the emotionally overdetermined scene in which Falkner tries to free Alithea from the husband she has been compelled to marry during his absence, and from the "substantive relations" of family and civil society. Falkner's love for Alithea, like the Father's love for Diana in *Mathilda*, is intense and "indefinite." Such love necessarily ends in Symbolic disaster because its turbulent grasping of the Real through an imaginary object of love cannot be processed through this object. Thus Falkner impulsively kidnaps Alithea, only for her to drown as she tries to escape during his absence, perhaps because she is too conventional to break with society, or perhaps because of an auto-immune aggression in Falkner's Romantic conception of community as the claustrophobic intimacy of lovers bound into one "will, disposition and activity." Falkner then finds the body and disposes of it, fleeing to the Continent. This scene functions as an index or shortcut to other primal scenes of Romanticism that similarly resist narrativization: Falkland's murder of Tyrrel in Godwin's *Caleb Williams* (1795), Manfred's destruction of Astarte or Cain's murder of Abel in Byron's two plays (1817, 1821); Mathilda's final encounter with her father which precipitates his suicide in Shelley's earlier novella (1819), and the death of Leila as the victim of the mimetic desire that binds Hassan and the Giaour together in Byron's documentary collage of murderous emotion (1813). These scenes bring to the fore some profoundly unreadable emotion, one that combines shame and transgression, in a way that makes the former the deconstruction of what the latter reconstructs. Whether they occur outside the diegesis, or in the case of *Mathilda* and *Cain*, disruptively inside it, the text then becomes the attempt to solve the inaccessible enigma of the negativity that generates it: a negativity that for Shelley is at the core of Romanticism.

These scenes also focus not just on feelings – an innocuous term – but revolve around what Roy Shafer, writing after Melanie Klein, calls "bad feelings," or what Godwin more neutrally describes in *Caleb Williams* as "a total revolution" of the "animal system," wherein "passions," as Mary Hays says, emerge as "powers," but powers or potencies that remain profoundly blocked.[8] For Kant the French "revolution," with the emotions it unleashed, was something that could not be assimilated to an existing model of history, and was thus also the unfinished occasion of a revolution in understanding.[9] As something that cannot be economized in a history – be it personal or cultural – emotion in these scenes asks to be understood not just culturally or psychoanalytically, but also phenomenologically. For emotion, as Sartre suggests, presents itself as a "phenomenon," where "phenomenon" is not the thing in itself, but rather "'that which announces itself,' that of which the reality precisely is the appearance."[10] Following this account of emotion as the insistent showing of a missed encounter, phenomenology itself, as Žižek says, can be "redefined," beyond Husserl's analytic version of it, "as the description of the ways in which the breakdown (failure) of symbolization, which cannot be signified, *shows itself.*"[11] That the scenes mentioned above foreground a breakdown of symbolization suggests that one of Romanticism's contributions to a history of affect is to raise the issue of emotion as a crisis of judgment. For emotion, as Levinas says, "overwhelms"; it registers an experience of "shock" that more conventional phenomenologies of affectivity miss, insofar as they "keep something of the character of comprehension." As a "disruption of equilibrium" impressed with a materiality not conveyed by terms such as "feeling" or "sentiment," emotion "puts into question not the existence, but the subjectivity of the subject"; "it prevents the subject from gathering itself up, reacting, being someone."[12] It thus prevents the subject from constituting itself as the subject of a judgment, in the Kantian sense of judgment, where judgments are the condition of possibility of the cogito. Breaking open the closure of the subject, emotion correspondingly also interrupts the ability of the reader to make a character the object of judgment, ungrounding the structures of moral and social judgment.

We can approach the bad feelings that drive these texts through Sartre's sense of emotion as a behavior of "disadaptation" (*STE*, 35), a term he borrows from the psychologist or "alienist" Pierre Janet,[13] and which suggests the quality of emotion as a missed encounter. For Sartre emotion is a "special type of response adapted to an external situation," and thus an "organized" if "non-reflective" form of "human existence" that is not "unconscious" (which would absolve the emotional subject of responsibility), but is "non-thetically conscious" or conscious of itself only in a "non-positional mode" (*STE*, 55, 28, 56, 61). When the "paths before us become too difficult" and "we can no longer put up with such a difficult and exacting world," we try to "change the world ... to live it as though the relations between things and their potentialities were not governed by deterministic processes but by magic" (63). Falkner's kidnapping of Alithea is an instance of the way emotion "tries to seize [the world] otherwise" or to "transform itself in order to transform the object," to "negate" something in the external world with the force of "one's whole body" (63, 67). Yet this delusional short-circuiting of the world, which "annihilates" something "by means of magical behaviour" is not just a "behaviour of *escape*" and thus "defeat" (35, 66). It is also unsuccessfully transformative, hence the sense that something "announces itself" in emotion (25).

Sartre does not fully develop what seems to be the difference from Janet's understanding of disadaptation implicit in his own use of words such as "transform" and "potentiality." Indeed he does not want to describe his *Sketch* as a "phenomenology" concerned with "affectivity as an existential mode of the human reality" in which man "*assumes* his emotion," and he prefers to limit himself to a more neutral "phenomeno-logical psychology" (*STE*, 28–31). Instead we can turn to Shelley's approxi-mate contemporary, Friedrich Schelling, for a sense of how in the negative "something not yet made good pushes its essence forward."[14] In his *Philosophical Investigations into the Essence of Human Freedom* (1809) Schelling links "evil" or the deviation of the part from the whole to disease, but also sees disease as a potentiality, when he writes that "an individual body part, like the eye, is only possible within the whole of an organism," yet "has its own life for itself, indeed its own kind of freedom," which it "proves through the disease of which it is capable."[15] Continuing to reflect in *Ages of the World* (1815) on why what deviates from the norm is labeled evil – which Blake called "the active springing from energy" – Schelling says that humans show "a predilection for the affirmative just as much as they turn away from the negative." "Everything that is outpouring [is] clear" to us, but we "cannot grasp that which closes itself off" and "denies itself," the "obliquity that resists the straight," "the left that resists the right," as in the brooding depression of Godwin's and Byron's heroes (*AW*, 6).

For Schelling this force of "inhibition" (*Hemmung*)[16] that is the very core of what he calls "selfhood" and "personality," is knotted into a "rotary motion" between what is expansive and affirmative on the one hand, and a restricting, contracting force on the other hand: "something inhibiting

[and] conflicting" that "imposes itself" (*AW*, 6, 20). In the very ground of nature that is also "human" nature (46), the constructive drives are not so much opposed to as interimbricated with what is resistant and recalcitrant. For the positive, the easy solution, needs to be resisted if Idealism is to be grounded in the Real, but the negative in its very withdrawal seeks to expand into its hidden positivity. Hence Schelling's sense of the negating drive as a power or potentiality, something to which Mary Hays's protagonist in *Memoirs of Emma Courtney* also points when she describes her "passions" as "but another name for powers."[17] The positive and negative "potencies," Schelling says, "are infinitely far from each other and infinitely near. Far, because what is affirmed ... in one of them, is posited in the other as negated and in the dark. Near, because it only requires an inversion, a turning out of what was concealed" to "transform, the one into the other" (*AW*, 18)

Novalis calls this turning out "romanticization": a process in which we elevate the lower into the higher by discerning its occluded potential,[18] or in Schelling's words "return [the lower] to its potency" (*AW*, 69). But that turning out is not a sublation of the "lower" within the "higher" (*AW*, 69), since the very sublimation of the negative into the positive conceals a further repression. This repression is evident, for instance, in the revised ending of *Caleb Williams*, where Caleb and Falkland (im)possibly forgive each other, at the cost of disavowing the complex and contradictory emotions that drive Caleb's juridically correct yet violent curiosity and Falkland's shameful concealment of his attempt to magically transform things as they are in his murder of Tyrrel. Hence Schelling's sense of a *rotary* motion between expansive and contracting drives that makes the abyss of emotion at once traumatic and promissory, but in a way that blocks any clear path to the future. For emotion for the Romantics is essentially what Derrida calls an auto-immune process, in which the organism destroys in "more than suicidal fashion, one or other of its organs,"[19] making the crisis of emotion also auto-critical, but in an unreflective, non-thetic way.

Returning to the primal scene of Romantic emotion as a revolutionary but auto-immune structure, *Falkner* is the last episode in an archiviological project that Shelley's own death passes on to us, and that drives her fiction as well as her editing of Percy's poems and her unfinished life of Godwin. For Shelley's fiction from *Frankenstein* to *Falkner* is a continuous auto-metaphoric record of her conflicted relation to Romanticism and the survival of its unfinished legacies into the Regency and Victorian periods. In her mapping of real onto fictitious characters, Shelley divides and redistributes traits belonging to "real" persons between her characters, so as to re-think Percy, Byron, and Godwin. She projects figures from her life as part-subjects or part-objects and puts them in different narratological positions. In the process she plays with these positions, not in Schiller's sense of art as play, but more in D. W. Winnicott's psychoanalytic sense of play as a fantasy that opens up an in-between, or potential, transitional space. Importantly for Winnicott, play is not innocent but involves "aggression and destructiveness." In play, which is best observed in childhood but not confined thereto, an object (or character) can be "destroyed and restored," "hurt and mended": "given away" as unsatisfactory yet also "kept" in reserve, or "killed and brought alive."[20]

Thus Shelley experiments with giving away Percy as the ineffectually angelic Woodville in *Mathilda*, but then condenses him into her own self-representation as Euthanasia in *Valperga*, and brings him back as Adrian in *The Last Man*. This process of aggression and reparation, as Melanie Klein calls it,[21] further extends into the unavowable community between Shelley's texts and Godwin's that connects his *Fleetwood* (1805), her *Mathilda* (1819), his *Deloraine* (1833), and finally *Falkner* (1837). For just as *Deloraine* responds fourteen years later to *Mathilda*, which Godwin withheld from publication when Shelley sent it to him, *Falkner* responds to Godwin's last novel, which was written when Shelley and her father were in daily contact. Like Deloraine, Falkner is an exile and wanderer, driven from England by a crime that is deeply perverse: at once transgressive and shameful. But in a gesture of reparation for her own killing off of the father in her earlier *Mathilda* – an act of violence intensified when Shelley sent Godwin the novel to publish as a way of paying his debts – Shelley also tries to make Falkner everything the Father in *Mathilda* was not, and that Godwin's novel of confessional atonement cannot make Deloraine be. Deloraine flees England with his devoted daughter, the child of his first marriage, having precipitated – by murdering her childhood love – the death of his second wife, who is just four years older than his daughter. More obscurely, the Father's exile and wandering in *Mathilda* after his wife's death in childbirth also bears the trace of a crime: a crime which in this case he has not committed, but which is inscribed in the very fabric of existence as self-consciousness. This crime that exists only as a trace must then be posited, brought out into the open as the crime of incest against his daughter. Yet the Father never commits incest, which is a catachresis for some unspecifiable guilt. For Byronic crime is always more or less than its accounting: it unfolds as a missed encounter with its cause, not warranting the blame assigned to it, yet also surviving any possible exoneration.

Godwin, as we have said, had already imagined something like the Byronic hero *avant la lettre*. But if Godwin makes Byron possible, it was Shelley who reinvented her father more glamorously *as* Byron, so as to keep alive, after the Regency period and Godwin's retreat into middle-class propriety, the scandal of Romanticism as a profound dis-ordering and unfinished revolution of the socio-metaphysical family. For it is Shelley's texts, from her novella *Mathilda* through her short story "The Mourner" (1829) to *Falkner*, that knit together Godwin and Byron by linking the Godwinian tropes of crime and misanthropy to the further Byronic figures of incest and exile: *topoi* that never quite get at the matrix or kernel of which they are simply the shell. Thus in *Mathilda* Shelley casts her father, who resisted her own elopement to the Continent, as a Byronic wanderer who goes from Germany to Hungary and even Turkey: the "unhappy, wandering father" who is the "idol of my imagination."[22] This romanticization is underwritten by the fact that when Mathilda says these words, on the threshold of being reunited with her lost father, she is sixteen, close to Shelley's own age when she eloped with Percy, while Mathilda's father is still young: thirty-seven, and not fifty-eight, as Godwin was at the time of the elopement.[23] Similarly in *Falkner*, the eponymous hero is no more than twenty-seven when Elizabeth saves him from suicide, and is thus barely forty when her relationship with Gerard Neville, the son of the woman whose death Falkner has caused, begins to germinate.[24] Indeed Shelley makes the connection between the lover and the father when Mathilda writes disingenuously of Woodville, the poet who tries to woo her back to society and life: "He was younger, less worn, more passionless than my father and in no degree reminded me of him."[25]

These connections between "real" people and their fantasized transpositions into texts that are neither wholly inside nor classically outside their autopoiesis in their lifeworld are, of course, traces. For Shelley makes the connection between Woodville and the Father only to withdraw it immediately. Indeed her titular evocation of Godwin's play *Faulkener* (1807), whose hero's mission is to vindicate his mother and who thus resembles not Falkner but Neville, points to the auto-bio-graphological work of these texts as a missed encounter in which the letter – the name, motif, or stereotype – never quite finds the matrix it seeks.

In the same vein *Falkner* also revisits Falkland, the anti-hero of *Caleb Williams*. As in *Caleb Williams* there is a trunk containing Falkner's narrative and confession, and like Godwin's first novel, *Falkner* culminates in a trial that raises issues of judgment and of the relation between morality and justice. But Falkner is also linked to Byron, as Shelley's hero tries to expiate his guilt by dying in battle in Greece, yet unlike the Byronic Raymond in *The Last Man*, is forced to live on beyond the end of Romanticism into the Victorian period. The power, and one could say the queerness, of Godwin's novels lies in what I have elsewhere called the perverse identification we experience with characters who represent the obscenity of power, yet also the aporia and enigma of "being what [they are] not" and "not being what [they are]."[26] Fleetwood and Deloraine are hardly admirable: the first marries a woman young enough to be his daughter, who is driven to her death by his insane jealousy; the second does in effect replace his young wife with his daughter, the wife being little more than a conduit to the daughter. Yet because these narratives are written in the first person, we are forced at some level to suspend judgment on their protagonists. Discussing the perverse in its etymological sense of a "turning aside from what is true or right," Richard Sha sees a homology between the aesthetic and sexual perversion, which is itself a form of "stylistics." Both involve what Sha calls a resistance to "function," to the useful or productive, which constitutes in its own way a powerful "critique of society."[27] Yet the involuted quality of this critique, as I shall argue, draws back from investing itself in any kind of identity politics, keeping the work of resistance at the level of figure. For perversion and inversion are deeply tropological, where trope means a "turning," the use of something in a sense other than what is proper to it. Shelley's eroticization of Godwin as Byron, symptomatic in *Mathilda* but deliberate in *Falkner*, responds to this perverse and tropological identification with what is improper: an identification embedded in Godwin's narrative strategy, which calls for an "inversion" or "turning out of what was concealed" that will discern the higher in the lower. Her (con)fusion of Godwin with Byron marks her refusal to see the misanthropy of the Godwinian hero as merely sordid. Shelley, in other words, does what Godwin himself did not: she "romanticizes" the Godwinian hero, in Novalis's sense of the word as "a qualitative raising to the powers (*Potenzirung*)," wherein the "lower self is identified with a better self."[28]

Shelley's previous novel *Lodore* (1835) also has its Byronic father, complete with curling lip, but is significant for a path not taken. Lord Lodore has fled to America because of a guilty secret – a guilt that, typically, is not explained by its cause – and finds his most perfect companion in the daughter he has removed from her socialite mother. Rather than abjecting this relationship as incestuous, as Shelley had done in *Mathilda*, the novel flirts with the perfect communion between father and daughter that Mathilda had fantasized before her father's return from his wanderings: it seems perversely to repeat Godwin's *Deloraine*, which dispenses with the wife to get to the daughter. To be sure we are disturbed when told that "Lord Lodore had formed his ideal . . . of what he had wished to find in his wife, and moulded his daughter accordingly." Yet the narrator also writes, "There is a peculiarity in the education of a daughter, brought up by a father only, which tends to develop early a thousand of those portions of mind, which are folded up, and often destroyed, under mere feminine tuition."[29] Nevertheless, though *Lodore* revisits the incestuous primal scene of Romantic self-constitution at the outset, Lord Lodore is killed off early in the novel. The narrative then takes a more conventional direction, as the daughter Ethel marries and the text rehabilitates the mother, allowing the contested scene of family relations to be reformed along safer, and one could say functional, lines.

Not so *Falkner*, whose Byronic hero is the text's central problem, even if he is wounded and wasted like Godwin's Falkland. That Falkner cannot die, either in the graveyard where he meets Elizabeth or in the war in Greece, marks the novel as concerned with survival: the survival of a Romanticism that had seemed exhausted in the unexpected, violent deaths of Lodore and of Raymond in *The Last Man*. Falkland, the Giaour, the Father and Falkner are all caught within a stubborn involution that seals in the past the "thing" at the core of their being that is manifested in an unreadable emotion. But Shelley insists that these characters survive within a community that, this time, is built around something other than Caleb's curiosity or Mathilda's prying open of the Father's "secret." Survival – *sur-vivre* or living on – as described by Jacques Derrida is not legacy but a kind of haunting, or in Sara Guyer's words, "a state of non-closure, division": a "position of disturbance, torsion" and "the endurance of that which cannot exist."[30] What lives on in Falkner, as a figure for Byron or Godwin, is the space for a "peculiar" thinking of the relation to society: one whose strength lies in having "no future," as Lee Edelman puts it in questioning a culture constituted by the family. For Edelman the heteronormative family configured around the child "shapes the logic within which the political itself must be thought" in terms of "reproductive futurism" or function. No future, by contrast, would not be the exhaustion of Romanticism, but its survival as a "negativity" that is not invested in a "form of social viability."[31] In *Mathilda*, her most radical text, Shelley contracts inward to a desire that has no future in a romantic relationship with the Shelleyan Woodville, and is a transference of the father's desire, which had also failed to find either a future or past in a love that restlessly survives his dead wife. As I argue elsewhere, incest is Shelley's lurid figure for this desire, yet it is never clear whose desire this figure names.[32] In their twisting onto each other, Mathilda's desire and that of her father become the improper, that is to say the tropological, space for an (im)possible thinking of something else: her desire for her father's desire as a desire for herself, his desire in turn being a desire not so much for her as for himself through her.

Falkner, to be sure, is more composed, more superficially proper than *Mathilda*, its sensibility mediated through a kind of sense that tries to repair the madness of *Mathilda*. Yet its move from creation to criticism can be understood only in an asymmetrical dialogue with the earlier text. If *Mathilda* eroticizes the Father as Byron, causing him to survive after being killed off, *Falkner* sanitizes Byron as the imaginary father Godwin could not create so as to revisit *Mathilda* more safely.[33] With Falkner, Elizabeth travels over the world as Mathilda did not. He has her educated in needlework but also in more "masculine studies."[34] In *Falkner* the more disturbing aspects of the bond between father and daughter in *Mathilda* are mitigated by the fact that Falkner is not Elizabeth's father; nor does he seek to possess her; it is she who devotes herself unconditionally to him. In *Falkner*, moreover, the bringing back of Woodville as Neville sanitizes and in Klein's sense "repairs" the idolatrous relationship with the Father. Interestingly in "The Mourner" the role of Woodville in *Mathilda* is played by a character called Horace Neville, who is also unable to woo the heroine Clarice back to society. Whereas in *Mathilda* Woodville is a disappointment because he does not resemble the Father, in *Falkner* Neville as Woodville is a conduit to the father, in a mirror image of Deloraine's use of his wife as a conduit to the daughter. But as Shelley cleverly manages the psychotropology of the relationship there is no accusation of incest, since after all Gerard Neville "in no degree remind[s]" us of Falkner, reminding us only of the *name* Horace Neville, which in turn reminds us that Woodville fails to remind Mathilda of her father.[35]

Yet if *Falkner* is more proper than *Mathilda*, in *Mathilda*, unlike *The Cenci*, incest was also never literally enacted. Rather incest in Shelley's novella is a trope for the dangerous obscurity of a relation, including a relation to the self, which cannot be coded within available social and familial models. As it also is in Byron, incest is the narcissistic transference of the desire for the other onto the desire for oneself: a self that is not oneself but profoundly other. That incestuous relation, albeit idealized, survives in *Falkner* as the trace underlying Elizabeth's excessive devotion to her father. For her devotion, even at the cost of giving up Neville, is in no sense submissive or timid; it is rather what Slavoj Žižek, drawing on Lacan, calls a refusal to cede the Real of her desire.[36] The further scandal of *Mathilda*, which recurs in *Falkner*, lies in the transference onto the Father of a desire that, feminism tells us, should be reserved for the mother. For apart from *Lodore*, mothers are absent from Shelley's corpus, killed off at the inception of her stories, and surviving only as daughters. These daughters, then, form a community with their fathers, like Shelley and Godwin themselves in the 1830s. A "peculiar" community, in that the daughter's bond with the Byronic father is the closet within which her own transgression of normative femininity is generated as a radical but ground-less autonomy.

It is Bataille who most compellingly theorizes this autonomy, or "sover-eignty," in terms of a transgression that cannot be recuperated into an emancipatory politics. For Bataille, who thinks transgression after "the death of God" and thus also outside any secular absolutes, the word must be "liberated" from anything so simple as opposition to the law. Trans-gression is "an action which involves the limit," but it is "not related to the limit as black to white, the prohibited to the lawful." For it is in the same moment the crossing and the experience of the limit.[37] Not the limit which has been crossed and reimposed as law, but the internal limit of a finitude that Bataille calls "inner experience," the "limit-experience" (in Blanchot's words) "that man encounters when he has decided to put himself radically in question."[38]

Mathilda approaches this limit when she insists on knowing the "secret" of her father's melancholy: a secret that is not its content but the very shape of secrecy as a difference at the core of our being. Her desire is transgressive not because what it discloses is scandalous, but because it opens up what the Father has shut up in himself, thus also breaching the closure of her own self. Her transgression creates a peculiar community between her and the Father that survives his death, and which can occur only after he has been put to death in his Symbolic identity so that he can be reimagined. But this community is not the intimacy Mathilda craves on first being reunited with her father. It is not the adolescent communion Hegel criticizes in the *Aesthetics*, in which those who should maturely separate are instead bound "into one will, disposition, and activity."[39] Rather it is a kind of extimacy, an exposure to interiority as radically outside, for which this adolescent communion as a transgression of society is disastrously necessary in the first instance. Thereafter Mathilda survives in a state of exception, in an anonymous landscape that has no clear geographical markers, an inner experience that cannot be communicated. Correspondingly, the novella itself is without issue. For in a gesture as violent as Mathilda asking Woodville to join her in taking hemlock, Shelley sent her text to Godwin to publish, knowing that he could not publish it, seeking the understanding she knew he would not and could not provide.

Following Bataille, Nancy describes a community without the comfort of intimacy as an "inoperative community" (*communauté désœuvrée*), or as Blanchot puts it in his book of that name, an "unavowable community." For Nancy community is not a "*common being*" or "fusion into a body" such as society, which integrates the individual into the whole in the way valorized by Hegel. But neither is it the "lost" organic community (*Gemeinschaft*) that precedes society (*Gesellschaft*) as a "dissociating association of forces, needs, and signs"; nor is it the community of beautiful souls or lovers mystically united in death that we stereotypically associate with Romanticism.[40] These fictions, including the Romantic *Liebestod* that Mathilda proposes to Woodville, are image figures that never quite capture the matrix of community, which must always be endurance rather than any fusional experience. For community – as "partage," or a sharing of differences that is constituted on a parting – is "existence inasmuch as it is *in* common, but without letting itself be absorbed into a common substance."[41] Thus Nancy writes: "Sharing comes down to this: what community reveals to me ... is my existence outside myself. Which does not mean my existence reinvested in or by community, as if community were another subject that would sublate me, in a dialectical or communal mode."[42]

But this is not to say that there is any sharing in *Mathilda* itself. Indeed after her father's death Mathilda opposes herself to any sharing just as much as the Father and Falkland do, living in a sanctuary of depression which, in Keats's words, is "shut against the sunrise ever more."[43] She survives, but only in writing, and at the cost of bearing with her the secret of her father's death. Encrypting this secret in Mathilda's melancholia, Shelley revisits it in her later story, "The Mourner." For "The Mourner" is the other side of *Mathilda*, a secret penance for its ancestor. Haunted by her father's death during a shipwreck, for which she bears the blame, Clarice changes her name and disappears as who she was. Like Mathilda, but more passively, her life becomes a life with no future: a being-towards-death, from which Horace Neville cannot woo her back. Of course Clarice is not the occasion of her father's death, except in the sense of knowing the cruel equation that also underlies *Mathilda*: that "if she were saved, he would remain and die."[44] In their secret sharing, *Mathilda* and "The Mourner" confront the inner experience of transgression. Their avowal of guilt, or rather of what Blanchot calls "faute," discloses the traumatic core of autonomy, of survival on one's own terms, that fantasies of emancipatory politics neglect. This fault, of which crime is a hypostasis, is also the psychoanalytic secret of *Caleb Williams*, whose narrator is guilty of no crime but comes to share with Falkland a symmetrical, and thus structural, guilt. For in Godwin's novel politics is a shell around the kernel we approach through Caleb's excessive curiosity. Politics is almost an accident of this curiosity, which is transgressive not just in disturbing things as they are but also in violating, in transgressing, the very core of each character's being.

In *Falkner*, then, Shelley revisits this troubled scene of a self constituted by its transgression of itself. She returns to it as her own debt to, and implication within, the Romanticism that she acknowledges through the transgressive bond between the surviving daughter and the past that survives within her. The transgressiveness of the bond is marked by the excessive, emotional nature of Elizabeth's relation to the man sanitized as her "father": a relation in which what is "expansive and outpouring" meets "something inhibiting, something conflicting" that it can never truly grasp except within a community of differences (*AW*, 6). To be sure, the novel ends with a restoration of a heteronormative future, as Elizabeth marries Neville and is reconciled with her biological family. Yet the family, as we have said, is made up of three biologically unrelated orphans. And its lines of filiation twist and turn back on themselves to create a community bound by impossible differences and constituted by adoption, as Neville goes back into the past to find that the father of the woman he loves is his mother's destroyer, while Elizabeth gives him the power to destroy her father at the cost of ending their relationship. The sacrifices around which this family is constituted recall the sacrifice Woodville would not make to Matilda, and privately gesture towards the unavowable community described by Blanchot and Nancy. Yet in this novel written a year after the death of Godwin, Shelley seems to close off the restless negativity of Byronic crime. The trunk is opened, the narrative read, and unlike Falkland, Falkner is exonerated. Incredibly he himself insists on his innocence, which he must mean in a narrowly legal sense, given that his mad seizure of Alithea has precipitated her drowning and that like Falkland he has buried his involvement in her death, along with all the issues cathected with it. The last part of the novel wants to pardon Godwin, Byron, and the scandal of such texts as *Cain*, *Caleb Williams*, and *The Giaour*, which is also haunted by an unreadable *crime passionel* as the phantasmatic symptom of something else.

In pardoning these texts, Shelley also wants to pardon herself for her own crime in killing off her father in *Mathilda*. But this pardon does not so much replace guilt with innocence, as close off the enigma of not being one with oneself that these texts disclose. Reparation, which Klein analyzes as the displacement of something unresolved into a new set of relationships that provides a second chance, always occurs at the cost of a repression.[45] In *Caleb Williams*, and almost until the end in *Falkner*, the crime is not legally established even though we know it to have occurred; and this is because in a more fundamental sense the crime does not consist in what it seems to be. In *Mathilda* too the Father's desire materializes, almost crudely, a guilt that cannot speak its name, and which significantly bears the name of "love," not incest.[46] As suggested, this desire is transgressive not just in denying the prohibition of the law, but in transgressing the borders of the self, even to the point that we do not know whose transgression is at issue: whose guilt the text unfolds, the Father's or Mathilda's. Guilt, crime, and their attribution exist in an elliptical relationship that cannot be grasped, enclosed. This in turn is why Byronic crime and the guilt associated with it are so often "secret." For the secret, as Abraham and Torok argue, "designates an internal psychic splitting," something unknown even to oneself and "consigned to internal silence," something that cannot be unlocked.[47] The particular structure of this secret is figured in *Caleb Williams* through the trunk whose contents are never divulged, but whose secret is shared by Caleb and Falkland. That the trunk is never unlocked, even though we "know" that it contains Falkland's confession, means that what we think we know will not tell us what we want to know. As disturbing is that what we do not know is shared with another, for "all secrets are shared at the start,"[48] otherwise they would not be secrets. This is what makes the secret, and the relationship constituted around it, so transgressive: that one shares oneself, and what one does not know about oneself, with someone other than oneself.

But in *Falkner* pardon marks the end of the secret, and the disturbing mixture of strangeness and intimacy associated with it, reconstituting the daughter who pardons as a full ethical subject. To forgive, as Sara Guyer says, "is to render an injury knowable and contained, to turn an incalculable violence into an event whose effects can be catalogued, accounted for, brought to light."[49] And indeed, in bringing this violence to light in the public trial that concludes her text, Shelley does domesticate guilt, attributing it to a single finite action that can be accounted for socially rather than ontologically. But this is not to say, with Mellor, that she "kills off the Byronic hero, whose history of passionate crime [and] remorse" we have been reading. For Mellor *Falkner*, rather like Brontë's *Jane Eyre* ten years later, leaves us with a "humbled old man" who has been symbolically and justly "destroyed" by his daughter, even if the dutiful daughter has not met the standards of a more enlightened twentieth-century feminism.[50] By contrast, I suggest that Shelley departs both from emancipatory models of feminism, and from the narratives of transition in other Victorian texts, in wanting to retrieve the potential of Romanticism for the future. These narratives move on to the next generation, even when they are doubled back on their past through the repetition of characters, as in Emily Brontë's *Wuthering Heights* (1847) or Arnold's *Tristan and Iseult* (1852). But in Shelley's novel, Falkner is not replaced by Neville, nor does Neville represent the "future" like his namesake in "The Mourner" or Woodville in *Mathilda*. Instead the community between Elizabeth and Neville occurs purely by way of the bond – transgressive and abnormal – that they share with a parent who signifies an unfinished relation with the past. It is unfinished because the relation between the daughter and her Byronic father is unfinished. But it is also unfinished because of the still incomplete project of feminism that has not yet come to expression in the mother who does not survive: Alithea, the woman too tied to a family founded on sense rather than sensibility.

Shelley, then, wants to think the presence of the past that is Romanticism, not to leave it behind as she did in *Lodore*. So why then does this unconventional novel end so conventionally? Or does it really do so? Perhaps Shelley can think Romanticism only in the form of a repression: not a rejection or correction but a (self-)protection that allows her to revisit the past without revisiting the trauma that necessitated its burial. Or perhaps, as with her editing of Percy Shelley's poems for a Victorian audience, Mary Shelley's utopianism of the family, consciously interlaced with loose ends, is the heuristic fiction necessary to push Romanticism forward on the threshold of the Victorian period. Shelley does after all concede that not every reader will be convinced that a "position full of difficulty" could be resolved so happily, adding "but so it was."[51] *Falkner* is a novel of "reparation," but in Melanie Klein's attempt to construct a dialectic of aggression, depression, and reparation, the conclusive status of reparation always rings false, as Godwin knew when he avoided such sentimentalism in *Fleetwood* and *Mandeville*, both of which have profoundly unreconciled endings. For community cannot come to rest in reparation: community as Nancy says, "is made of what retreats from it"

and must withdraw from any "hypostasis of the 'common' and its work."[52]
Falkner seems to posit a community, but we should perhaps treat its
reparative relationship to the past as gestural, so as to understand the
community it projects not as achieved in the ending, but as standing in
place of the peculiar community with a family of texts that the novel's
archiviological status makes possible.

But in folding the novel back into this more troubling family, we should
also not too quickly gloss over its difference from these other texts.
Fleetwood, The Giaour, and *Cain* all end with a catastrophic action after
which there is no future, only a past sealed in a disastrous negativity. In
Caleb Williams Godwin tells the equally disastrous story of an attempt to
unseal that past through Caleb's transgressive curiosity. Projecting a reconciliation between Falkland and Caleb in the revised ending, Godwin is
aware of this community as a hysterical and deeply troubled phantasm.
But *Falkner* is all about the future, even if the family it projects is one of
three orphans. Ending as it does in marriage, it cuts against a number of
Romantic texts from the extended Godwin circle. As I argue elsewhere,
these texts are fascinated with single protagonists, often aborting or killing
off the children who transit their space, so as to interrupt the reproduction
of culture at the site of biological reproduction.[53] Thus Mary Hays's
protagonist in *The Victim of Prejudice* (1799) defies the expediency of an
offer of marriage from her Richardsonian persecutor Sir Peter Osborne
that would restore her social position, while *Memoirs of Emma Courtney*
(1796) kills off Emma's mandatory husband. Shelley's Mathilda ends her
life sealed in solitude, and even in *Valperga* none of the three major
characters marry. Many of these texts also disfigure biological reproduction. *Emma Courtney* gets rid of Emma's child, ritually shedding tears over
her death, so as to "move on" by moving back to the past; Sibella's child in
Eliza Fenwick's *Secrecy* (1795) is still-born; and the daughter in
Wollstonecraft's *The Wrongs of Woman* (1798) never appears in the
diegesis.

We could approach this dejection of the family in so many Godwinian
texts through Sha's discussion of perversity, since the closing off of the
future redirects attention to often perverse relationships in the past. Yet
Sha's view that perversity frees "pleasure . . . from reproduction"[54] does not
quite get at the nature of the blocked attachments, or in the case of Hays's
Victim dis-attachment, in the texts we have been discussing. None of
Emma Courtney's desire for Augustus, the Father's passion for his wife
Diana, Mathilda's and her father's mutual obsession, or Falkner's passion
for Alithea have as their goal pleasure: the aleatory eighteenth-century

dissipation of the restlessness of the negative in libertinism. Rather they aim at something more single-minded. Sometimes this is love, one could even say a Platonic love, except that in the case of the Father it is physically consummated, but in that literalization misses its object. For love, or perhaps "desire," has as its goal an Idea which, as Kant puts it, does not "admit ... of an object given by experience corresponding" to it, or as Percy Shelley says in the *Preface* to *Alastor*, it imagines a "prototype" that cannot be realized.[55] The Father is particularly interesting because his, on the surface, is the most normal kind of love: a heterosexual love that leads to marriage and a child. Yet his passion for Diana is excessive and abnormal, and is not directed to settling down and having a family: in Hegel's terms it craves the adolescence of community rather than the adulthood of society. We could even say, in the light of the subsequent narrative, that the Father's love for Diana is "incestuous." But what this really means is that his love is narcissistic, a love of himself, but of something in himself that does not yet exist. Indeed Kristeva makes the connection between narcissism and love, although less disturbingly, when she writes that "love reigns between the two borders of narcissism and idealization"; love is an "*aufhebung* of narcissism" in that the lover "is simply a narcissist with an *object*," but in love it is really oneself that one seeks as an other.[56] Seeking himself as what he is not, the Father does not really find his desire fulfilled in Diana, hence the aptness of transferring this desire to the daughter, as the site of its impossibility. In short, it is more appropriate to speak of detaching "love" or "desire" rather than pleasure from the closure of reproduction, and also not to confine relational perversity within homosexuality, or even physical sexuality.

For as we have seen, heterosexual relationships in these texts are also perverse. Perverse: because in turning aside from what is true or right, these instances of desire turn towards something else that is also "not right." The perverse, as distinct from the more straightforward category of subversion, involves a double twisting that registers an unease both with what is true and right, and with the transgression it substitutes for the good, this being the very ethics of transgression in Bataille's sense. Equally perverse is the single-mindedness of Mary Randolph's singleness in Hays's *Victim*. Here the protagonist's adherence to her violated chastity manifests a kind of "irritability": a term from the contemporary physiology of the nervous body involving a muscular contraction, but which Hegel in his analysis of illness in *The Philosophy of Nature* theorizes more philosophically in terms of negativity. In what Hegel's psychopathology of disease casts as the second stage of illness, the organism, in reacting against an external stimulus, "repel[s]" what is "other," and in the process is "irritated" into conflict with its "being."[57] Given Hegel's analogy between the constitution of the organism and the social body, irritability is a turning of the sick member against the larger social body through a turning in of this member on itself (*PN*, 433, 429). It is an "active maintenance of self" against the outside, but as the negative of itself, through an involution in which the self turns "against its structure," so that "the negative thing" *becomes* "the structure itself" (359, 429). Turning away from what is considered right, namely marriage, because it is *not* right, because it is a continued rape, Hays's protagonist contracts into a deeply resistant chastity that is not so much "right" or "good," as it is an inversion of her mother's life of forced prostitution, and a maintenance of her self as the negative of itself. The self in this novel becomes an "isolated, independent activity" outside society and community, is "shut off from the outer world . . . [and] lives on its own resources" (429–30).

But Elizabeth's devotion to Falkner is not presented as perverse. In recuperating what she had presented as incestuous in *Mathilda* and *Lodore*, Mary Shelley expands what has been contracted and inhibited in her family of texts: "something not yet made good" which "pushes its essence forward," as Habermas puts it in describing the utopianism of Ernst Bloch.[58] For contrary to Edelman's absolute negation of reproductive futurism, Romantic texts are not without issue, though in a textual rather than biological sense. On the one hand, the child who results from the Father's passionate involvement with Diana is only a byproduct that does not bind him into a family, since after his wife's death he leaves Mathilda and enters a sixteen-year period of wandering. Significantly, the real Godwin did not allow himself this abandonment of family, marrying Mary Jane Claremont to create a social cover for what was really a family of three orphans. In so doing he betrayed a restlessness of the negative that he closeted in his fiction, and the exploration of which, through the fictional fathers of Shelley's three novels, constitutes a peculiar community between her and Godwin. Arguably it is this community that is the matrix-figure for which the family of three orphans is no more than a schema.

This is to say, on the other hand, that though the daughter Mathilda seems born only to die, the text *Mathilda* is by no means just a byproduct of its parent-texts. Romantic texts often do include biological children, whose existence points to a future, even as the killing off or abortion of these children (dis)figures biological reproduction and conventional community as sites of this future. In Mathilda's case too, the text is not without issue, sterile though it may remain in its non-publication: a suspension of community that is already thematized in the novella as Mathilda's failure to find anyone to whom she can pass on her story. For this child that is the text *Mathilda*, the child of Godwin's *Fleetwood*, is the site of a survival, a living on of the unfinished work of emotion into some future generation, which in the case of *Mathilda* had to wait for a century. Children, and they are always only children, and often orphans, single and singular entities, are the vehicles not of reproduction but of a living on that distinguishes Romantic perversity from Edelman's absolute negation of reproductive futurism. Hence Romantic parents as often as not *do* have children, but just one child, two parents reduced to just one, as if to concentrate and discontinue rather than reproduce the past. In *Falkner* Alithea has a child, not by Falkner, but by her husband: one child only, who is not the spiritual child of his father, who is disjoined from his biological family and one of the three orphans, and who is yet of a further generation. And Falkner too, even though he embraces singleness after the death of Alithea, is drawn despite himself into having a child who insists that he live on, but a child who is not his own and will always in some way betray him. Indeed Mary Shelley and Godwin also betrayed each other; yet the secret of each could have no future without the other. This is also to say that Romantic literature, although it does not go in the direction of the novel as the institution of family and the social, also cannot be without issue.

NOTES

1 Andrew Elfenbein, *Byron and the Victorians* (Cambridge: Cambridge University Press, 1995), 89.
2 G. W. F. Hegel, *Aesthetics: Lectures on Fine Art*, trans. T. M. Knox, 2 vols. (Oxford: Clarendon, 1975), 1: 568–9. See Orrin Wang, *Romantic Sobriety: Sensation, Revolution, Commodification, History* (Baltimore, MD: Johns Hopkins University Press, 2011).
3 Hegel, *Aesthetics*, 1: 593.
4 Hannah Arendt, *The Human Condition*, 2nd edn. (Chicago: University of Chicago Press, 1998), 36–49.
5 Opposing "figure" to "discourse," Lyotard describes three levels of figuration that are more and more removed from any kind of clear formulation: the image-figure, which is visible but already blurred; the form-figure, which can be "perceived" but not "seen" and is a schema that underlies the visible; and finally the matrix figure, which is neither "visible" nor "readable," and which is "difference itself" (Jean-François Lyotard, *Discours, figure* [Paris: Klinksieck, 1971/2002], 277–8). As David Carroll explains, all three kinds of figure are a "complication of the visible nature of the figure ... The matrix underlies the other categories of figures as a radical alterity of which they are the visible

transformations ... [It] never appears in itself because it is never itself; it appears only in its disappearance, as lost, repressed, already other" (David Carroll, *Paraesthetics: Foucault, Lyotard, Derrida* [New York and London: Methuen, 1987], 39–40).

6 George Simmel, "The Concept and Tragedy of Culture," in *Simmel on Culture*, ed. David Frisby and Mike Featherstone (London: Sage, 1997), 55–74.

7 Mary Shelley, "Modern Italian Romances," in *Mary Shelley's Literary Lives and Other Writings*, vol. 4, ed. Pamela Clemit (London: Pickering and Chatto, 2002), 245. See Ruth Bernard Yeazall, *Art of the Everyday: Dutch Painting and the Realist Novel* (Princeton, NJ: Princeton University Press, 2008), 1–17.

8 Roy Schafer, *Bad Feelings: Selected Psychoanalytic Essays* (New York: Other Press, 2005), xii–xiii; William Godwin, *Caleb Williams* (1794), ed. Gary Handwerk and A. A. Markley (Peterborough, ON: Broadview, 2000), 207; Mary Hays, *Memoirs of Emma Courtney* (1796), ed. Marilyn L. Brooks (Peterborough, ON: Broadview, 2000), 116. Although Schafer's book is part of a Kleinian tradition that finds value (or at least a certain normality) in the paranoid/schizoid and depressive positions, and although this partially aligns the Kleinians with existential psychoanalysis, Schafer (and even in the end Klein) see bad feelings as something to be overcome, perhaps too quickly. Joan Riviere comes closer to recognizing emotions as having value ("Hate, Greed, and Aggression," Melanie Klein and Joan Riviere, *Love, Hate and Reparation* [New York: Norton, 1964], 6–16).

9 Immanuel Kant, *The Conflict of the Faculties*, trans. Mary J. Gregor (Lincoln: University of Nebraska Press, 1992), 153.

10 Jean-Paul Sartre, *Sketch for a Theory of the Emotions*, trans. Philip Mairet (London: Methuen, 1962), 25. Hereafter cited parenthetically as *STE*.

11 Slavoj Žižek, *The Plague of Fantasies* (London: Verso, 2007), 279.

12 Emmanuel Levinas, *Existence and Existents*, trans. Alphonso Lingis (The Hague: Martinus Nijhoff, 1978), 70.

13 Although some consider Janet rather than Freud the founder of psychoanalysis, I keep the earlier term "alienist" used by Sartre here, to mark Sartre's dissociation of himself from psychoanalysis on the grounds that the concept of the unconscious shields the subject from being responsible for his or her behavior.

14 Jürgen Habermas, "Ernst Bloch: A Marxist Schelling," in *Philosophical-Political Profiles* (1971), trans. Frederick G. Lawrence (Cambridge, MA: MIT Press, 1985), 71.

15 F. W. J. Schelling, *Ages of the World* (1815), trans. Jason M. Wirth (Albany: State University of New York Press, 2000), 18. Hereafter cited parenthetically as *AW*.

16 F. W. J. Schelling, *Philosophical Investigations into the Essence of Human Freedom*, trans. Jeff Love and Johannes Schmidt (Albany: State University of New York Press, 2006), 33.

17 Hays, *Memoirs*, 116.

18 See David Farrell Krell, *Contagion: Sexuality, Disease and Death in German Idealism and Romanticism* (Bloomington: Indiana University Press, 1998), 49.

19 Jacques Derrida, *Rogues: Two Essays on Reason*, trans. Pascale-Anne Brault and Michael Naas (Stanford, CA: Stanford University Press, 2005), 124.

20 D. W. Winnicott, *Playing and Reality* (London: Tavistock Publications, 1971), 5, 9, 41; *Psychoanalytical Explorations*, ed. Clare Winnicott, Ray Shepherd, and Madeleine Davis (Cambridge, MA: Harvard University Press, 1989), 57, 60–1.

21 Melanie Klein, "Love, Guilt, and Reparation," in Melanie Klein and Joan Riviere, *Love, Hate and Reparation* (New York: Norton, 1964), 57, 68.

22 Mary Shelley, *Mathilda* (1819), in *The Mary Shelley Reader*, ed. Betty T. Bennett and Charles E. Robinson (New York: Oxford University Press, 1990), 181, 185.

23 The Father loses his mother and falls passionately in love with Diana when he is nineteen, marrying her "by the time he had attained his twentieth birthday." "Fifteen months after their marriage" Mathilda is born, and her mother dies a few days later, which would make him thirty-seven when he and his daughter are reunited (*Mathilda*, 179–80). Godwin was thirty-five when he met Wollstonecraft for the first time, and forty when they met again and fell in love. Thus when Mathilda and her father are reunited, he is about the same age as Godwin was during his relationship with Wollstonecraft. In effect, in the text's emotional tropology, "Godwin" is substituted for "Percy."

24 Elizabeth is ten when she and Falkner arrive in Odessa (Mary Shelley, *Falkner: A Novel* [1837] [Doylestown, PA: Wildside, n.d.], 45), and thus thirteen when she first meets Gerard Neville in Baden: a meeting that is of more significance at the time to Falkner than to her (52). Falkner's resulting decision to seek death in battle in Greece is three years later (66), and it is shortly after this, as Elizabeth is nursing him back to health, that she again meets Neville in Marseilles (85), gets to know his half-sister Lady Cecil, and hears his story.

25 Shelley, *Mathilda*, 228.

26 Jean-Paul Sartre, *Being and Nothingness: An Essay in Phenomenological Ontology*, trans. Hazel E. Barnes (New York: Washington Square Press, 1956), 105–8. On perverse identification see my "The Dis-Figuration of Enlightenment: War, Trauma, and the Historical Novel in Godwin's *Mandeville*," in *Godwinian Moments: From Enlightenment to Romanticism*, ed. Robert Maniquis and Victoria Myers (Toronto: University of Toronto Press, 2011), 180; and Tilottama Rajan, *Romantic Narrative: Shelley, Hays, Godwin, Wollstonecraft* (Baltimore, MD: Johns Hopkins University Press, 2010), 138–9.

27 Richard C. Sha, *Perverse Romanticism: Aesthetics and Sexuality in Britain, 1750–1832* (Baltimore, MD: Johns Hopkins University Press, 2010), 3–5.

28 Quoted in Krell, *Contagion*, 47.

29 Mary Shelley, *Lodore* (1835), ed. Lisa Vargo (Peterborough, ON: Broadview, 1997), 82, 62–4.

30 Sara Guyer, "The Rhetoric of Survival and the Possibility of Romanticism," *Studies in Romanticism* 46, no. 2 (2007): 251–2.

31 Lee Edelman, *No Future: Queer Theory and the Death Drive* (Durham, NC: Duke University Press, 2004), 2, 9.

32 Tilottama Rajan, "Mary Shelley's *Mathilda*: Melancholy and the Political Economy of Romanticism," *Studies in the Novel* 26, no. 2 (1994): 43–68.

33 I borrow this term from Julia Kristeva, who defines the "Imaginary Father" as an "archaic unity" or conglomeration of the two parents, the "father in individual prehistory" (*Tales of Love*, trans. Leon S. Roudiez [New York: Columbia University Press, 1987], 26, 41, 222).

34 Mary Shelley, *Falkner*, 50.

35 Shelley, *Mathilda*, 228.

36 Slavoj Žižek, *Looking Awry: An Introduction to Jacques Lacan through Popular Culture* (Cambridge, MA: MIT Press, 1991), 62–3. By contrast, Jane Blumberg claims that Shelley's women "are praised for their timidity, docility . . . [and] fidelity to a man. They are . . . completely in thrall – by choice – to the men who control their lives" (*Mary Shelley's Early Novels: "This Child of Imagination and Misery"* [Iowa City: University of Iowa Press, 1993], 222). Anne Mellor also complains that Shelley's women have an "identity constructed entirely in relational terms" and do not achieve autonomy (*Mary Shelley: Her Life, Her Fiction, Her Monsters* [New York: Methuen, 1988], 205). Hence Mellor sees Shelley as idealizing the bourgeois family, which "only reproduces the patriarchal structure of bourgeois capitalism." Her novels "uncomfortably suggest that the female raised within the bourgeois family may never be able to escape the father's seduction," even though they "support a feminist position" to the limited extent that they see female culture as "superior to male culture" (217–18). A different reading of the family in *Falkner* is provided by Kate Ferguson Ellis ("Subversive Surfaces: The Limits of Domestic Affection in Mary Shelley's Later Fiction," in *The Other Mary Shelley: Beyond Frankenstein*, ed. Audrey A. Fisch, Anne Mellor, and Esther Schor [New York: Oxford University Press, 1993], 231–2).

37 Michel Foucault, "A Preface to Transgression" (1963), in *Language, Counter-Memory, Practice*, ed. Donald F. Bouchard, trans. Donald F. Bouchard and Sherry Simon (Ithaca, NY: Cornell University Press, 1977), 35.

38 Maurice Blanchot, *The Infinite Conversation* (1969), trans. Susan Hanson (Minneapolis: University of Minnesota Press, 1993), 203.

39 Hegel, *Aesthetics*, 1: 568.

40 Maurice Blanchot, *La Communauté inavouable* (Paris: Editions de Minuit, 1983); Jean-Luc Nancy, "The Inoperative Community," in *The Inoperative Community*, ed. Peter Connor, trans. Peter Connor *et al.* (Minneapolis: University of Minnesota Press, 1991), xxxviii, 9–11, 26.

41 Ibid., xxxviii.

42 Ibid., 26.

43 John Keats, *The Fall of Hyperion: A Dream*, in *The Poems of John Keats*, ed. Jack Stillinger (Cambridge, MA: Harvard University Press, 1978).

44 Mary Shelley, "The Mourner" (1829), in *Collected Tales and Stories*, ed. Charles E. Robinson (Baltimore, MD: Johns Hopkins University Press, 1976), 93.

45 Klein, "Love," 95.

46 Shelley, *Mathilda*, 201.

47 Nicholas Rand, "Editor's Note" to "New Perspectives in Metapsychology: Cryptic Mourning and Secret Love," in Nicholas Abraham and Maria Torok, *The Shell and the Kernel*: vol. 1, ed. and trans. Nicholas Rand (Chicago: University of Chicago Press, 1994), 99–100.

48 Nicholas Abraham and Maria Torok, *The Shell and the Kernel*, vol. 1, ed. and trans. Nicholas Rand (Chicago: University of Chicago Press, 1994), 158.

49 Sara Guyer, "The Pardon of the Disaster," *SubStance* 35, no. 1 (2006): 91.

50 Mellor, *Mary Shelley*, 204.

51 Shelley, *Falkner*, 330.

52 Nancy, "The Inoperative Community," xxxix.

53 Tilottama Rajan, "Dis-Figuring Reproduction: Natural History, Community, and the 1790s Novel," *CR: The New Centennial Review* 2, no. 3 (2002): 211–52.

54 Sha, *Perverse Romanticism*, 12.

55 Immanuel Kant, *Critique of Pure Reason*, 2nd edn. (1787), trans. J. M. D. Meiklejohn (London: J. M. Dent, 1934/1991), 219–20; Percy Shelley, "Preface" to *Alastor*, in *Shelley's Poetry and Prose*, ed. Reiman and Fraistat, 73.

56 Kristeva, *Tales*, 6, 33.

57 G. W. F. Hegel, *The Philosophy of Nature* (1816), trans. A. V. Miller (Oxford: Clarendon, 1970), 358–9. Hereafter cited as *PN*.

58 Habermas, "Ernst Bloch," 71.

CHAPTER 7

Emotion without content
Primary affect and pure potentiality in Wordsworth

David Collings

In his recent, pivotal book, *Romantic Moods*, Thomas Pfau provides a subtle, capacious account of mood as it underlies Romantic literary texts as well as modern philosophical and theoretical formulations of concerns familiar in those texts. Drawing on the work of Martha Nussbaum, in his introductory chapter he argues that while mood is prior to thought itself, and indeed to conscious emotion *per se*, it nevertheless is "quasi-cognitive" – that is, cognitive without becoming fully conscious – and through it "communities establish a sustained, quasi-intentional and tacitly evaluative relation to their experiential world."[1] For Pfau, as for Heidegger, mood is "the horizon wherein all conscious practice . . . is being transacted, a horizon that therefore can never come into view as such," much less be fixed in "representational form." Accordingly, following Heidegger's suggestion that mood should be awakened, rather than represented, Pfau argues that this "desired awakening can only ever be realized in the figural, virtual domain of the aesthetic."[2] In his account, this understanding of affect is already broached in Kant as well as Novalis, Hölderlin, and Hegel, who "progressively conceived 'mood' as an aesthetic phenomenon," something best captured "in the modality of virtual, figural constructions."[3]

Over the course of the ensuing chapters, which treat of the moods paranoia, trauma, and melancholy, Pfau's argument exemplifies a rigorously nonreductive mode of reading, one that displaces its focus from the empirical abundance of history to a certain historicity, a "perilous historical situatedness" endlessly thematized and falsified by history's actual events.[4] Yet, as I have argued elsewhere, Pfau's focus on the properties of each mood as distinct from others does not address the interplay between them, the possibility that

I presented earlier versions of this paper at Western University on the invitation of Tilottama Rajan, and at the Center for the Humanities, CUNY Graduate Center, on the invitation of Nancy Yousef. I wish to thank them for these invitations, their thoughts on my work, and to all those who responded during my visits with their thoughtful comments, especially Steven Bruhm, Elizabeth Effinger, Joel Faflak, Ruth Leys, Nicola Masciandaro, Jan Plug, Alexander Schlutz, and Rasmus Simonsen.

one mood might modulate into another or encrypt another within itself. Differentiating between moods allows Pfau to interweave literary, critical, and philosophical articulations of a given mood across many periods from Romanticism to the present and thereby to demonstrate how in each case modernity perpetually reworks a continuing problematic in its recursive elaborations; in effect, this approach permits a fuller exploration of the characteristic moods of modernity over the past two centuries than would otherwise be possible. Nevertheless, his own readings of key texts in the period of central concern, especially those written in the mid 1790s by Wordsworth, Blake, and Godwin, suggest that the formulation of paranoia at times transforms into that of trauma and thus that a given mood can modulate into another.[5] These works suggest that a given mood, occupying as it does a space prior not only to explicit cognition but also to conscious differentiation, can never quite be defined in contrast to others. But in that case, the study of mood requires that we attend to a further problematic, a certain affective and discursive mobility that demands careful attention in its own right.[6]

I would like to extend that discussion here to suggest that Wordsworth, writing at about the same time that the Jena Romantics formulated their approach to mood, sought in his own way to trace literature's capacity to reflect on affective mobility. His focus on these matters is particularly evident in his writing from the mid to late 1790s. Furthermore, the attention he gives to that mobility, and to the quasi-tropological relation between various moods, eventually inspires him to attend as well to the question of feeling as such, to the affective capacity evident in particular moods but distinct from them and logically prior to them. This attention to feeling as such eventually leads him to conceive of an affective state without emotional content, a state of pure receptivity and affective aspiration, of primary affect, which arises in response to mere being. Wordsworth's interest in this dimension of affective life indicates that he was increasingly drawn to reflect on the most basic levels of experience, a reflection that takes him through the mobility of mood and the problem of embodied and gendered subjectivity, both of central concern over a century later to psychoanalysis, the fundamental state of exposed life, or what Heidegger called *Dasein*, and the origins of personhood in a mode of relation, toward a barely articulable condition at the threshold of existence itself. Although Wordsworth locates that state almost entirely outside ordinary experience, he evokes it as available to that experience, creating a domain of affect related to yet unanticipated in phenomenological reflection. In a handful of supremely difficult, marvelously evocative passages, the poet anticipates certain categories now familiar to us and stretches them beyond their limits, challenging us to reconceive the boundaries not only of mood but of subjectivity and the human as well.

***

To begin this discussion, I will take up the shift Wordsworth carries out in the mid 1790s between the moods that, following Pfau, I will here call paranoia and trauma, a shift I discussed in slightly different terms in chapter 1 of *Wordsworthian Errancies*.[7] In the early 1790s, the poet wrote texts marked by a revolutionary passion, one that readily accepted the polarizing terms we could well align with a certain paranoia. This mood is quite visible in the poem *Salisbury Plain*, which depicts how a total violence overtakes the world, deprives the wanderers on the plain of refuge, drowns them in darkness and tempest, and subjects them to the return of the dead and of Druidic human sacrifice. The poem underlines its sharp resistance to this violence in its concluding stanzas, where it celebrates Enlightenment at the expense of ancient superstition. In the revision to that poem, *Adventures on Salisbury Plain*, written roughly between 1795 and 1797, the polarizing scenario of the initial draft has changed remarkably: the wanderer on the plain, once a victim of dismembering violence, has now become an involuntary participant in it, for on his return from war he murders a man on the threshold of his own home, an act that reveals how greatly the experience of slaughter has estranged him from the idea of homecoming. The violence that inundates the plain also arises from within him, suggesting that he now embodies the very thing that he loathes and cannot escape. In these and other ways the poem outlines with exemplary force the dense affect of what we might now call trauma, in which one becomes implicated in horror or violence against one's will and involuntarily suffers or replicates on the most intimate level the very thing one most intensely resists.

This revision thus makes visible how a poem, in the process of revision, might shift from the attribution of violence to one's opponent, in an exemplary version an either/or logic, to an awareness that one's own stance along with the other's is profoundly violent, leading to the logic of both/ neither, in which one is at once opposed to, yet indistinguishable from, the other. We could pause to reflect here on how to account for this shift: does it primarily register how historical events might alter the collective mood inspired by such events? In that case, does it speak of a change in the tone of historicity itself, in the mood whereby the common exposure to history is felt? Or does the revision arise from the poet's critique of his own prior poetics, his sense that the figurative logic of either/or insists on a polarization that is no longer tenable? Or, what is most likely, does it point to a blend of these possibilities, whereby the collective mood quasi-cognitively critiques itself to enter another mood, thereby embedding a prior state within its new, more complex condition? If literature can awaken mood through its virtual articulation, as Pfau and others suggest, and if it can reflect as well on the limitations of a given figural logic that underlies such a virtual articulation, then it follows that it can also ponder the limitations of the quasi-cognitive dimensions of the underlying mood as well. Thus the revision of this poem may demonstrate how the transformation in literary figuration registers the collective's process of reconsidering its mood and finding its way toward an affect more attuned to its historical exposure, especially as that exposure alters over time. The collective sense of historicity moves; literature's task in part is to articulate this shift, doing so in this case through an unusually clear instance of autocritique.

But the value of these poems goes further. Insofar as both of them feature a solitary figure setting forth in a barren landscape, abandoned to the elements and much more, they depict the situation of *Dasein*, that figure of abandonment familiar in Heidegger's *Being and Time*. Indeed, with very rare exceptions, it is difficult to find so clear a poetic exemplar of *Dasein* before these poems, a possibility that confirms Pfau's argument that the sense of radical exposure to historicity so familiar in the past two centuries first becomes paramount in this period.[8] Yet insofar as it does emerge in the way Pfau suggests, it is for the Jena Romantics, Wordsworth, and other authors of that moment a novel problematic calling out for sustained treatment. As I have just suggested, in Wordsworth's case that treatment takes the form of a careful exploration of scenarios surprisingly akin to those that appear in Heidegger. Yet the varying renditions of *Dasein* in the Salisbury Plain poems suggest that the bare, lost anguish of *Dasein* can be evoked variously as the situation of being exposed to an alien force or of bearing the guilt of having violated the world, or both; abandonment, as it were, does not speak for itself, for it seems to imply a broader scenario and an attendant figural logic.

Within these poems, the exact significance of *Dasein*'s implication in such scenarios remains unclear. While one could propose that these scenarios are not intrinsic to the fundamental situation of *Dasein*, arising instead as elaborations of it, one could also suggest that without such renderings we cannot evoke that situation at all, that these are not elaborations but attempts to awaken what is primary, what preexists articulation. The originality of Pfau's treatment of mood comes to the fore here, for it keeps in focus the question not of figuration *per se*, which could lead to a de Manian analysis of rhetorical tropes, nor of representation *per se*, which could lead to the familiar question of how to grasp the real within the field of signification, but of awakening what must remain quasi-cognitive. From this perspective, attempts to evoke that fundamental exposure of *Dasein* are at once necessary and inadequate. But in that case, we must conclude that no figural logic can articulate that situation with much authority, simply because the historicity of *Dasein* has no proper form, no objective existence. As a result, even Heidegger's own terms must be taken as evocative rather than definitive: they insistently rely on a spatial rhetoric (being-there, thrownness, fallenness, being "not-at-home"), even though the dilemma they depict is not fundamentally spatial, but existential. Given the difficulty of capturing that exposed condition in language, one could argue that its evocation now in one figural logic and now in another takes the measure of its elusive status, conveying the latter precisely through the movement from one tonality to another. The very movement of trope, in this view, may be the most adequate language for evoking *Dasein*'s perilous, ultimately unknowable situation.

Although the Salisbury Plain poems broach these questions, shifting from one articulation of mood to another, they do not yet meditate on the implications of what they have just carried out. Wordsworth takes this further step soon thereafter in a series of revisionary texts written in 1797 and 1798, which I have discussed at length in chapters 3 and 4 of *Wordsworthian Errancies*.[9] In one sequence of poems, he muses on the transformation of the anguished sailor into the untroubled old men of "Animal Tranquillity and Decay," "The Discharged Soldier," "The Old Cumberland Beggar," and the biography of the Pedlar. These poems explore how pain, endured long enough, may undergo a figurative transformation by turning into an insensitivity to pain and accordingly how exposure to existence can take on the tone of a numbed peacefulness. The initial mood, pursued to its extreme, modulates into another, or perhaps into its own encrypted variant, into a more muted, but still palpable, evocation of pain.

Wordsworth pursues these explorations further in his juxtaposition of *The Ruined Cottage* and "The Thorn," in the contrast between Margaret, who for the Pedlar is eventually transfigured in death, and Martha Ray, who remains rooted to the grave of her child forever chanting her misery. Here the poet takes figuration in the opposite direction, from apparent calm to sensationalized distress, from a privileged narrator to one who clearly invents his tale in the telling, as if to undercut the reassurances of the prior poem and indeed the reliability of narrative depiction overall. He does so not to pass to a more powerful evocation of a collective mood but to underline the starkly figurative and reversible element of all virtual evocations of affect, to expose the rhetorical and fictive dimensions of articulation. To pursue the poet's intuition further, one can delve into the manuscript history of these texts and read them as elaborations of the situation evoked in "Incipient Madness," a short draft that preceded them, in which a solitary traveller, once again lost on barren ground, finds his impropriety figured in a "speck of glass" he sees in a ruined hut and sustains a "mood" explicitly compared to that of a "sucking babe" who "Create[s] [food] where it is not."[10] The themes of the abandoned child, obsessive desire, and the ruined hut are already present in this fragment, a prospect that implies that one could evoke the themes of *The Ruined Cottage* and "The Thorn" and cut through their elaborations by melting them down into a handful of stark, almost pre-literary terms. In that case, the relationship between these three texts is highly instructive: the two longer poems ramify the fundamental situation in mutually implicated but contrasting scenarios by elaborating on the potential narratives embedded in the original assemblage of bare figures. But given how the poet casts doubt on the rhetorical, fictive nature of those elaborations, one might value in retrospect the relatively minimal articulation he gives his themes in that initial fragment.

These three poems, taken together, emphasize the psychoanalytic, rather than strictly phenomenological, rendition of *Dasein*'s exposure, for they evoke a babe's search for the mother's breast, and as I argue elsewhere, borrowing somewhat anachronistically on Freud's account of the *fort/da* game, enlarge upon infantile fantasies of revenge against the abandoning mother.[11] For Wordsworth, the abandoned child is clearly embodied, caught in a world defined by gender, riven with desire, and pierced by a range of competing fantasies whereby to address the sense of abandonment. But the elaboration of these fantasies, in turn, is interwoven with the evocation of a certain historicity, a radical impoverishment registered in the themes of unemployment, material distress, and the ruin of things without being reducible to the latter. By thus swerving from a purely existential scenario, these three poems implicitly address a concern of interest to reflection since 1900: whether it is more rigorous to sustain a focus on the bare situation of existential thrownness, as in the work of Heidegger; to emphasize by contrast the implications of embodiment, as in Merleau-Ponty; to highlight the logic of fantasy that elaborates on the dilemmas of such embodiment, as in Freud; or to foreground the dimension of materiality and historicity, as in a range of recent interventions, including that of Pfau himself.[12]

Wordsworth's strategy in this regard over 1797 and 1798 is to expand further on a proto-Freudian scenario, for as the manuscript history of *The Ruined Cottage* suggests, he begins to weave together his work on the solitary male wanderers with that on the abandoned woman and child, and both with the themes of a fundamental impoverishment, particularly as he matches up the Pedlar, who is an apparently non-traumatized wanderer, with Margaret, who in the Pedlar's telling achieves a peace in death. By this means, he begins to stitch together his figural speculations on male and female abandonment, mapping out a fairly capacious poetics of gendered fantasy. The increasing focus on the Pedlar's manner of addressing his listener also foregrounds the problematic of narrating and receiving tales about such abandonment, making explicit the problem of how to encounter the basic existential dilemma through the dynamics of interpretive exchange, in this regard again anticipating the concerns of psychoanalysis.[13]

Although mapping out this broader intersection between various ways of capturing the experience of abandonment continues to interest the poet for much of his career, sustaining his work through *The Excursion*, his critique of narrative elaboration in "The Thorn" inspires him to pursue yet another strategy of evoking mood more directly. In the First Part of the 1798–9 *Prelude* he once again brings together solitary wandering, the experience of being out of place, the orientation to spots linked to abandonment, murder, and guilt, erotic fantasies circulating around signifiers of gender, and the retrospective feeding upon these charged scenes. But in this poem he invokes a broadly defined autobiographical framework to justify leaving these scenes virtually in their melted-down state, and before long, in the spots of time sequence, writes openly about the limitations of his resources for interpreting them. Although he continues to articulate the core themes in terms of gendered embodiment, he allows the organizing tropes of his concern to emerge more nakedly; he attempts to do little more than present the pivotal, archaic elements of his mind alongside the affect he associates with them. Stripping away narrative and figurative elaborations, he evokes the underlying mood with as few mediations as possible, even if in consequence it becomes ever more elusive.

In several episodes, then, he suggests that a given scene's ability to exceed his interpretive capacity is a sign of its privilege, its proximity to an affect too early and dense for him to decipher. Accordingly, he eventually leaves that affect undefined, writing of the second spot of time that a scene inspires "the workings of [his] spirit" (I. 374) without clarifying where those workings might lead or why they might be satisfying.[14] What is more, insofar as he narrates these episodes directly to his reader, without staging the scene of storytelling as he does in *The Ruined Cottage* or "The Thorn," he suspends the interpretive dynamic, tacitly repudiating the endeavor to decipher whatever those episodes convey. The further he goes in this direction, the more he redirects his narrative impulse into assembling these episodes into what one might call a history of his affective education. Such an education, he suggests, is more crucial to him than his learning how to analyze his experience, for he regards the affect of those moments as more layered and resonant than a more formally narrative or interpretive figuration could possibly capture. Yet because he leaves the import of that resonance unclear, his strategy in Part One threatens to founder, to run aground on pure reminiscence. If one effaces narrative or figural elaboration, how can one make a case for the significance of these episodes? What exactly might this rehearsal of experience allow him to claim?

***

Wordsworth's awareness of this difficulty soon inspires him to make a new departure in his evocation of mood. The recitation of the leading episodes does indeed founder well into the second portion of the two-part *Prelude* when he sets out to "tell / How nature, intervenient till this time / And secondary, now at length was sought / For her own sake" (2.239–42). Here the poet indicates that in his view the recounting of his affective education should eventually lead to a larger poetic argument about the contours of his adult emotional capacity, the disposition of mind that underlies his poetic vocation. Yet this very step beyond the earlier problematic forces him to encounter a set of new questions about the relation of affect and its discursive elaboration, especially the problem of whether to seize and map the mind's affective capacities philosophically.

From the start, the poet revolts against the prospect of attempting to capture the mind's overall affective disposition in any speciously elaborate scenario of knowledge, indicating that he will require a different approach – one that will eventually lead him to attempt evoking the mood of mood itself. The poet's initial approach to the task of imagining how one might trace the shift from a series of local attachments to a general love of nature provokes him to attack any attempt to "parcel out / His intellect by geometric rules" or to propose interpretive "distinctions" while believing they are "things / Which we perceive and not which we have made" (2.242–3; 253–4). This passage voices a core resistance to deriving any account of the whole from its parts; the attempt to "analyse" the soul, it seems, can only misconstrue its fundamental character (2.262). This attack is inspired not by a repudiation of reason but by the view that each dimension of the "soul" – its "general habits and desires" and "each most obvious and particular thought" – "in the words of reason deeply weighed / Hath no beginning" (2.262, 263–5). What does have a beginning, he proposes in the Blest Babe passage that immediately follows, is the individual's affective life *per se*, a life that arises in the infant's capacity to "gather passion from the Mother's eye" (2.273) and to "combine / In one appearance all the elements / And parts of the same object" (2.277–9). This explicitly figural capacity to render parts into a whole, Wordsworth suggests, makes the mother available to the child, founds relationship, and thus makes possible the infant's orientation to "All objects through all intercourse of sense" (2.290).

In these lines, the poem responds to the initial question driving this new sequence: the love of nature for its own sake, it argues, arises from the infant's initial response to the mother and thereafter to the world. But this argument carries with it a crucial implication; in the following line, "No outcast he, bewildered and depressed" (2.291), the poem invokes the scenario of abandonment evident in earlier poems and sets it aside, proposing in effect that the solitary exposure of *Dasein* is *not* fundamental to affective experience, that the infant enters the world on the contrary in a richly affective interplay that shapes human life to the core. As it turns out, then, the question regarding what can generate the love of nature for its own sake not only carries the poem beyond the framework of autobiography, memory, and the lineaments of an individual life into the question of human affective origins in general, but also opens the way toward conceiving of originary experience in non-Heideggerian terms. To answer a question about his own life, the poet ends up shifting into the first-person plural, considering "the progress of our being" (2.269) in general, and as a result has recourse to a mode of fundamental, poetic speculation – and what is more, a mode of speculation that contests the poetry of abandonment he explored over the previous five years or so. In these lines, the poem broaches a philosophy not of exposure but of relationship.

Yet even this apparently definitive movement is not conclusive. The poet soon returns to an autobiographical mode as he offers up what many have read as an encrypted discussion of the consequences for him of enduring his mother's death at the age of eight. Suddenly it seems as if the speculations in the Blest Babe passage serve as the foreground to a more crucial drama, the poet's reflections on how his mother's death intruded into that mode of responsiveness and transformed it into another. The passage that inaugurates this new movement returns to the problem of abandonment, but with an urgency and rigor not anticipated by any of his previous poems:

> For now a trouble came into my mind
> From obscure causes. I was left alone
> Seeking this visible world, nor knowing why.
> (2.321–3)

If we pursue the familiar reading, here the poem evokes a child's inability to understand the mother's death *as* a death, and indeed in any terms at all: the mother's disappearance has causes he cannot understand. More radically, the passage even seems to suggest that for the child, this event is not understood with reference to the mother, a mode of understanding that assumes a prior capacity to treat her as a separate person, for instead it is rendered as an inexplicable trouble in the operations of the child's own mind – a construction thoroughly consistent with the theory sketched a few lines before in the Blest Babe passage.[15] It is as if the child, having derived passion, love, perception, world, and even his sense of himself from his mother's presence, in her absence loses his access to them all, loses even his secure sense of his own mind. In yet another move, it suggests that the child, now facing "this visible world," does not understand why he should do so, for the world may have no significance outside the presence of the mother; the mere demand to deal with the world at all is felt as an imposition. Furthermore, when it describes the child "seeking" without knowing why, it raises the prospect of a seeking without desire, a yearning that seems not to be intrinsic to the subject but purely structural. Derived from an orientation to a presence that is now absent, such a seeking seems to be pointless, yet it endures, revealing the persistence of a seeking intrinsic to affective life as such.

But the passage bears another, perhaps more crucial reading as well. Because the poem here does not explicitly refer to the mother's death, even though it does so elsewhere, one might rightly object that it refers not to that event but to another, perhaps more general condition. After all, every child raised by a mother must at some point discover that she is absent and thus confront an existence in which she is missing. The mother's loss and her death are on some level structurally similar, for both events would lead the child to ponder how to sustain a mode of being despite that loss. One could thus surmise that even if the poem here refers to the mother's death, it treats that event as an instance of a general pattern, folding an autobiographical into a nearly universal experience. In doing so, it complicates the earlier account of relational phenomenology, suggesting that the lines on the Blest Babe tell only a part of the story, which necessarily includes a much more difficult episode. By treating of that episode here, Wordsworth pushes well beyond the problematic of his earlier poems, for in these lines he conceives of abandonment not through the figural logic familiar from 1795 through 1798, but radically *without* figuration, as if the absence of the mother is precisely the *loss* of all figure – of reality, world, and motive, and indeed of mood itself. The passage thus figures a prospect scarcely conceived in Heidegger; one might surmise that it evokes what Emmanuel Levinas calls "existence without a world," except that in contrast to Levinas, who describes that experience in a nocturnal insomnia that oscillates with the daytime security of a world, Wordsworth depicts a crisis that puts even the latter in danger.[16] No wonder the poem introduces these lines with the dire warning, "Yet is a path / More difficult before me, and I fear / That in its broken windings we shall need / The Chamois' sinews, and the Eagle's wing" (2.317–20). This domain without figure, it seems, is like an Alpine peak where the chamois roams and the eagle soars: it represents the very pinnacle of difficulty.

The poet's marking of this difficulty rightly indicates that his project carries him into a zone that skirts along the very edges of what will later become phenomenological and psychoanalytic discourse, indeed along the edges of language itself. With the loss of all figure, with the loss of reality itself, the child finds himself in a domain almost inaccessible to virtual evocation. Yet just as the poet describes the child's dilemma, he hints at its narrative resolution:

> The props of my affections were removed
> And yet the building stood as if sustained
> By its own spirit.
>
> (2.324–6)

At first these lines suggest that the child endures as an existent without a world, sustained through pure spiritual persistence in the absence of all props, all figures. Yet the sliding of one metaphor into another, the absorption of those props into the timbers of the child's building, suggest instead that the figural capacity that oriented the child to the mother in the first place sustains him again, having become the very form of his spirit. "All that I beheld / Was dear to me," he continues, "and from this cause it came / That now to Nature's finer influxes / My mind lay open" (2.326–9). Thanks to his relation to the mother, the world is dear to him, and accordingly he can treat the world as a single figure, as "Nature," in a mode of intense receptivity; the mother's loss makes more evident what her presence made possible for him, a relation to the world of sense. As Geoffrey Hartman writes of this passage, "The fixated or literally animistic mind feels that if nature remains alive when what gave it life (the mother) is dead [or, we might prefer, simply absent], then the mother is not dead but invisibly contained in nature."[17] Clearly, the child relies on an instance of figuration, whereby one vivid psychic reality stands in for another. But insofar as the substitution of reality for the mother makes a relationship to reality possible, this figure constitutes a primordial event that conserves the possibility of world as such. For the poet, at least, it is a kind of *ur*-figure, a prefigural figure, without which the building's entire superstructure would collapse.

By designating this initial, enabling figure, the poem tacitly enters Kantian terrain, sketching out the preconditions of response without which the child could never experience the world of sense. In effect, it proposes an answer to a question Kant never pauses to consider, how any given child enters the space of cognition or posits those a priori categories experientially. In Wordsworth's account, the child does so by extending the terms of relationship with a person to the world, orienting himself to it precisely through an "intercourse of sense." One might object that by transferring the figural dynamics of relationship to the world, the child treats the world as other than it is. But it seems on the contrary that this primordial conception of the world as a counterpart in relationship brings it into existence for the child; no domain of literal objects preexists this gesture, for only through the latter does that domain become available to the child in the first place. Relationship founds the world, rather than vice versa. This portion of the poem, from the Blest Babe through the lines on loss and recovery, offers a remarkable alternative to the Kantian analytic, forcefully challenging what Nancy Yousef has called the "isolated cases" of Enlightenment epistemological speculation, those figures of consciousness that seem to emerge in utter solitude, as well as proleptically the isolated case of *Dasein*, in favor of a far more cogent account of embodied affect and relational epistemology.[18] In effect, here Wordsworth provides, as does Coleridge some decades later in his *Opus Maximum*, a theory of the person as an alternative to the modern subject, a person who initially emerges in relation, and specifically in relation to the mother.[19] By depicting how a child may enter the mother–infant bond, suffer its loss, and restore it in a new key, the poem suggests that the child may discover a capacity to apply the dynamism of relationship to a domain where no person is explicitly evident, and thus respond to an apparently faceless world in affective and potentially ethical terms.[20]

Several lines later in the same verse paragraph, the poem elaborates on this child's unusually problematic relation to the world of sense in a passage on the power of sound. This passage does not flow directly from the lines that precede it and has no introduction; it intrudes upon its context, suggesting that it bears upon those questions about the child's recuperation that the poem has not yet fully addressed and delves into

them in an even more rigorous fashion, and for that reason deserves
unusually close scrutiny:[21]

> [F]or I would walk alone
> In storm and tempest or in starlight nights
> Beneath the quiet heavens, and at that time
> Would feel whate'er there is of power in sound
> To breathe an elevated mood by form
> Or image unprofaned: and I would stand
> Beneath some rock listening to sounds that are
> The ghostly language of the ancient earth
> Or make their dim abode in distant winds.
> Thence did I drink the visionary power.
> I deem not profitless these fleeting moods
> Of shadowy exultation, not for this,
> That they are kindred to our purer mind
> And intellectual life, but that the soul
> Remembering how she felt, but what she felt
> Remembering not, retains an obscure sense
> Of possible sublimity to which
> With growing faculties she doth aspire,
> With faculties still growing, feeling still
> That whatsoever point they gain, they still
> Have something to pursue.
>
> (2.351–71)

This passage's references to elevated places and dim sounds imply that here
at last the poet is attempting to trace some length of those broken windings
he mentioned earlier. Indeed, it is no easy matter to construe these lines.
Given its phrasing regarding the soul's "Remembering how she felt, but
what she felt / Remembering not," one could read this passage as depicting
the adult's difficulty in reconstructing what the child felt in this scene. But
the passage overall disallows this reading, for it tacitly equates the "elevated
mood" the child experiences with the "fleeting moods / Of shadowy
exultation" one feels in the mode of such an odd remembering and thus
suggests that the suspension of all form and image in that sound suspends
any particular emotion as well.[22] The child himself, it seems, does not
know *what* he feels: he feels with great intensity no specific emotion. This
passage is thus a meditation on what I will call primary affect, that is, on an
affect that arises in the utter loss of a world, in the erasure of any *specific*
form, image, motive, thought, or feeling. *This* is what it is like, the passage
seems to say, to find oneself in a space logically prior to any particular

affective scenario, certainly before emotion can be rendered in the figure of exposure or abandonment.

While the passage in context seems to be provided as an illustration of how the child felt after finding a positive orientation to the world, since it follows on lines that explore that theme, one must conclude instead that it evokes an emotion that transpired not after that event but in its midst, in the transitional moment when the child discovers that the world and feeling are still possible. In effect, the passage describes the moment when the child, left alone and seeking the visible world, discovers a relation to that world in its blank entirety by regarding it as a domain with which he might maintain an "intimate communion" and thereby sustain affect at all (2.330). Crucially, the child discovers primary affect when he is awakened by "the power of sound," by the capacity of aesthetic experience broadly conceived to bring forth that mood. Earlier, in the Blest Babe passage, the infant discovered feeling from the apprehension of something outside himself, "gather[ing] passion from his Mother's eye" (2.273), from "one appearance" in which he combines the "parts of the same object"; here, however, the child absorbs emotion from what is *without* form or image, coalescing appearances around an absent presence, a ghostly power that "breathe[s] an elevated mood." Here again, and more starkly, Wordsworth conceives of mood quite differently from Heidegger: where the latter argues that mood can be awakened after the fact through its virtual articulations, Wordsworth suggests that primary affect arises through a response to a pure virtuality in the world of sense. For the poet, the mood of a solitary, motherless child is not intrinsic, as if awaiting in his depths, but is brought forth by his attending to an expressive capacity outside himself. The passage is thus much closer to a possibility outlined by Jean-François Lyotard, who suggests that there is a "mindless state of mind" required not to grasp matter but *so that there be* some something," a "presence in the absence of the active mind" which "is never other than timbre, tone, nuance in one or other of the dispositions of sensibility" – in this case, in the sound of the wind – "a singular, incomparable quality – unforgettable and immediately forgotten," of which the mind "conserves only the feeling – anguish and jubilation – of an obscure debt."[23] What the mind encounters in such an instant, Lyotard speculates, is a matter that "has no need" of the mind, insisting "'before' questioning and answer, 'outside' them," in a zone, Wordsworth would add, that is dim, ancient, ghostly, that preexists the child's apprehension.[24] But in that case, the child comes into being this time not through "mute dialogues," as in the Blest Babe passage, but through a radical receptivity, through listening to and drinking from the sound of the *there is*, through attending to something "not answerable to human life or logic."[25]

At first one might conclude from the passage's final lines that this primary affect is a mode of yearning, a struggle to find a specific mood and thereby a figurable world. But the thought of a specific affect does not appear, even in the distance; the sound breathes a mood that has virtually no reference to any particular feeling, much as it speaks a "ghostly language" without form or figure. Because the mood evoked in the distance is so formless, the pursuit of it is equally without content, obeying an entirely intransitive aspiration. It is another version of what the earlier passage marked out as a seeking without motive, a seeking embedded in the situation itself, prior to subjectivity – a pure potentiality of the "soul" to feel emotion as such, to exist in and as a pure affect of growing intensity. One might attempt to read this formless aspiration as an instance of the sublime. But the parallel with the instant described by Lyotard suggests that he might place it instead in a zone "after the sublime," for it arises in response to matter without finality or destination – or, in Wordsworth's terms, in a zone before the sublime, before the thought of destination has arisen.[26] Indeed, the passage suggests that the mind's faculties aspire only to an "obscure sense / Of possible sublimity," for they are oriented not to any formal structure of aesthetic response but to the possibility of responsiveness itself.

The passage suspends familiar determinations in yet another respect. It is virtually unique in *The Prelude* for not locating a moment of affective education in a single time or place, perhaps because it speaks of an emotion free of form and image. As a result, the opening lines of the passage retain a certain equivocation: the child experienced this moodless mood at times "in storm or tempest" and at other times "in starlight nights / Beneath the quiet heavens." This contrast between storm and calm evokes a similar contrast between distressed and peaceful wanderers, between the misery of Martha Ray and the peace of the dead Margaret; in effect, it points to the divergence between two ways this poet evokes the experience of *Dasein*. One would think that the mood of exultation would take place in the midst of calm rather than storm, for it seems to register the crossing from anxiety to reassurance. Yet the equivocation indicates on the contrary that this shadowy mood blends features of *both* possibilities, calm *and* storm. It does so not because the passage reduces these two modes to the same content, but rather because it reads both as instances of mood as such, whatever its features may be. The child's experiencing primary affect indifferently on stormy or calm nights speaks to his capacity to feel what it is like to have feeling, to reduplicate mood on a second level. But in that case, Wordsworth suggests, primary affect is more fundamental than anything he explored in the earlier poems of storm or calm, than *Dasein* itself; by invoking both of those latter modes he makes clear that he now wishes to surpass his earlier work, to locate a mode of feeling and a conception of poetic figure not anticipated there and to outline an understanding of affect more absolute than any single location or episode can evoke.

Only on this basis can the poet return to his initial question yet again and now explain for good how he came to love nature as a whole for its own sake. In the verse paragraph following this passage, he insists on the continuing power of his affective apprehension of the world, suggesting that in certain moments "what I saw / Appeared like something in myself — a dream, / A prospect in my mind" (2.399–401) or, conversely, that his mind was "Subservient strictly to the external things / With which it communed" (2.416–17), as if to suggest simultaneously that the world was in his mind and his mind in the world. Such confusion, perhaps, follows inevitably from his manner of discovering his capacity for primary affect through responding to nature's breathing. Because the key passage on the power of sound comes to rest on no stabilizing figure, such as internalization, identification, or explicit personification, the exact import of the enabling moment remains imprecise, leaving the way open for the poem to depict his response to the affective charge of nature in a variety of ways. Nevertheless, the upshot of this entire sequence is the claim that at age seventeen, he was only "Contented when with bliss ineffable / [He] felt the sentiment of being spread / O'er all that moves, and all that seemeth still," for "in all things / [He] saw one life, and felt that it was joy" (2.449–51; 459–60). In effect, the poem argues, because he gained access to primary mood in response to a pure, formless sound, he can experience being itself affectively, indeed primarily as a blissful sentiment. The equivocation here between mood and world suggests that the phrase "sentiment of being" must be taken in its full grammatical complexity as a sentiment that being feels and a sentiment that he feels in the presence of being:[27] both are saturated in a mood that brings the child into the world and the world to the child. Since this mood must underlie all other moods and this apprehension of being subtend the experience of all specific phenomena, it follows that this primary affect at least potentially accompanies his experience of any aspect of the natural world (see 2.448–60). The utter disappearance of the world with the death of his mother, in short, makes possible a stunningly affirmative response to the world when it reappears and potentially an ethical disposition to the life of things.[28] But if this is so, the poem once again proleptically revises Heidegger, linking speculations that the philosopher never definitively conjoined, suggesting that only through the experience of absolute deprivation can one attain what Heidegger elsewhere describes as the astonishment of being, the pathos in response to the fact that the world exists at all, for only if the world seems to be entirely lost can one experience a "bliss ineffable" in the prospect that it endures.[29] In that case, primary affect sustains an intimate link with bliss or joy, a mood that paradoxically is no specific mood but a bliss in the possibility of having affect in the first place.

Although this overall poetic sequence culminates in apparent triumph, its import is not entirely soothing; after all, the child's capacity to respond to the power of sound does not ground nature in anything secure, for it derives the world's reality from the child's capacity to rediscover relationship after its disappearance. In effect, the child survives by orienting himself to the world of things as if to a person, thus soliciting the regard of something or someone neither fully responsive nor utterly absent. The difficult implications of these gestures are evident in "A Slumber Did My Spirit Seal," written in late 1798, roughly contemporaneously to the two-part *Prelude*. This poem, too familiar to quote in full, similarly blends storm and calm in response to the posthumous endurance of a female figure in nature. She now has "[n]o motion" and "no force," yet she is nevertheless "Rolled round in earth's diurnal course / With rocks and stones and trees": her motion dissolves into the revolution of the earth, into a repetitive energy at once agitated and calm.[30] What she evokes, in short, is closely akin to primary affect, the mood of mood. But the tonality of that affect here receives a slightly different accent. This poem's speaker has awakened, it seems, to the knowledge that she *could* feel the "touch of earthly years" (4), those revolutions in which she is now "rolled round." If so, then this speaker, too, can feel those years: he has now been tutored in affect, in such things as "human fears" (2), or perhaps in human calm. But how human are these fears, or this fearful calm, if she feels those years in her being "rolled round" with the earth? The speaker seems to discover affect not by discerning a human state but by finding it in the mood of the posthumous or nonhuman; though to him she once seemed to be a "thing that could not feel" (3), she is now for him apparently a "thing" that paradoxically *can* feel what it is like to be "rolled round ... / With rocks and stones and trees." Sensing her, the poem's speaker may thus participate in a certain ghostly affect of the ancient earth, not in distant winds but in the cycling of the planet itself, in its endless, restless peace. In that case, primary affect arises from an orientation to the nonhuman, or what Lyotard would designate as the inhuman – to the "life of things," as the poet puts it in another moment of posthumous apprehension – that is, from a responsiveness to what finds its life in a resonant, empty turning.

The poetry of primary affect thus brings about something altogether more eerie than a poetics of transcendence. That eerie quality evoked in "A Slumber" emerges cryptically in several further lyrics written in ensuing years that suggest how a poetic persona who can see into the life of things might also come to share in that life, to participate in inanimate affect. "These chairs they have no words to utter," for example, contemplates the possibility that one might lie in bed as "Happy as they who are dead" while yet drawing breath (12), and "Personal Talk" (initially titled "I am not One who much or oft delight") celebrates the ability to "sit without emotion, hope, or aim" by the fireside (11). In these instances, primary affect arises in a state of absolute rest, without emotion or apparent life, in which one can share in the bare mood of the world.

The poet eventually gives this dimension of his work a singular urgency, embedding it in the "Intimations Ode," completed in 1804, which he thereafter regards as the most significant poem of his career. The turning point of that poem, stanza 9, reworks the initial bewilderment of "seeking the visible world, nor knowing why" into the "obstinate questionings / Of sense and outward things, / Fallings from us, vanishings" (144–6), transforming a motiveless seeking into interrogation, a sign of the mind's independent strength over against a world that has dared to disappear and of its foundation in a state that precedes and supersedes mere phenomena, or what it regards as "worlds not realized" (148). These high claims bear a strong affinity with those earlier lines, eventually deleted under pressure from Coleridge, on how for the child "the grave / Is but a lonely bed without the sense or sight / Of day or the warm light, / A place of thought where we in waiting lie" (120–3): the child can question the phenomenal world, I would argue, only because he can imagine a posthumous state of mind, of thought without thoughts, a counterpart of the Levinasian night in which one apprehends a bare "there is" – a state of mind, the poem suggests, in which the child already participates (perhaps because he resembles the child of the power of sound passage, who listens to the motions of being from "[b]eneath some rock," as if beneath a gravestone, in a posthumous state of his own).[31] On this same basis, it seems, the poet can claim that those "first affections" still endure in him as the "fountain light of all our day" (151, 154), that primary affect – which he nearly names as such here – underlies all of an adult's seeing in this life.

This intimation at the poem's turning point suggests that in the poet's view, nonhuman, anonymous, primary affect *is* what he calls immortality, for as a state logically prior to all specific experience it can never be cancelled by that experience nor by the birth, life, or death of any individual consciousness, any persona that operates in the world.

Rei Terada has outlined for us the shape of emotion after the death of the subject, opening up a space, we can now see, that Wordsworth was already exploring in these texts – though he describes an affect at the origins of the person instead.[32] Having outlined the alternative to the modern subject in a poetics of relation in the Blest Babe passage and beyond, before long he conceives of something more strange, an anonymous figure who arises in a mode of responsiveness to mere being. This figure, it turns out, does not disappear when it becomes the precondition for the human person; accordingly, the poet suggests, one can thus half-remember, or at times re-experience, that figure's primary affect and can sense that affect as it underlies one's mode of consciousness and indeed makes possible one's entire affective life. While that initial figure is not yet human, neither is it antagonistic to the human; perhaps one can say that it designates the pre-human dimension of the human person, the non-mortal aspect of mortality. In the poet's view, it may also make possible the apprehension of the non-thing dimension of things, the existence of existents. By providing an alternative to an array of familiar notions (the subject, the person, and *Dasein*), Wordsworth thus opens up even further the range of paths by which we may experience that most elusive of states, "the sentiment of being."

NOTES

1 I follow Pfau in using the designation "quasi-cognitive" not to indicate any reservation about interpreting mood as cognitive, only to be precise about what region of cognition it occupies – that is, a zone prior to and underlying conscious articulation.

2 Pfau, *Romantic Moods*, 10.

3 Ibid., 12.

4 Ibid., 11, 25. Pfau's emphasis on historicity, rather than the events of history *per se*, makes possible his powerfully non-reductive mode of reading. However, because he argues that this experience of history arises in the late eighteenth century, thereby historicizing a certain "perilous historical situatedness" and thus *Dasein* itself, a situatedness that he extends into writing up through the present, he ultimately finds himself treating modernity both as a contingent formation and as the overall horizon of experience. This strategy opens up a possibility he does not explore: an examination of modernity from a stance not

already implied in its premises. For my discussion of these aspects of his work, see my "Troping Mood: Pfau, Wordsworth, and Hegel," *Literature Compass* 6 (2009): 373–83.

5 Although the terms "paranoia" and "trauma" arise much later, Pfau attends closely to their specific import, analyzing the logic whereby the articulations of these moods in Romantic texts reappear in later interpretive or critical discourses. A strict fidelity to historical differentiation might thus betray the recursive temporalities to which Pfau draws attention. Although I will draw upon his overall stance here, hoping to delve further into the problematic he has mapped out, elsewhere I have commented on how this overall strategy of interweaving texts from the late eighteenth and early nineteenth centuries with critical reflection of the twentieth century ultimately encloses the writing of both periods within a self-confirming ensemble; see Collings, "Troping Mood."

6 For a further discussion of this point, see Collings, "Troping Mood."

7 David Collings, *Wordsworthian Errancies: The Poetics of Cultural Dismemberment* (Baltimore, MD: Johns Hopkins University Press, 1994), 18–49. Because I wish to focus on the shift between moods, my argument here leaves out of view the place of melancholy in the tropological relations between moods. In principle, however, it must be possible to decipher melancholy's position within those relations.

8 Martin Heidegger, *Being and Time*, trans. John Macquarrie and Edward Robinson (London: SCM Press, 1962); Pfau, *Romantic Moods*, 2; 4–7.

9 Collings, *Wordsworthian Errancies*, 69–99; 70–117.

10 William Wordsworth, *The Ruined Cottage* and *The Pedlar*, ed. James Butler (Ithaca, NY: Cornell University Press, 1979), ll. 23, 7, 10–11.

11 Collings, *Wordsworthian Errancies*, 69–99.

12 Merleau-Ponty, *Phenomenology of Perception*.

13 Compare Faflak, *Romantic Psychoanalysis*, 79–91.

14 William Wordsworth, *The Prelude, 1798–1799*, ed. Stephen Parrish (Ithaca, NY: Cornell University Press, 1977), 1. 374. All references to *The Prelude* are to this edition, cited hereafter in the essay by part and line numbers.

15 Here I pursue the possibility, broached by Nancy Yousef, that one cannot read these lines as referring simply to the death of the mother; see *Isolated Cases: The Anxieties of Autonomy in Enlightenment Philosophy and Romantic Literature* (Ithaca, NY: Cornell University Press, 2004), 124.

16 Levinas, *Existence and Existents*, 45–60.

17 Geoffrey H. Hartman, *The Unremarkable Wordsworth* (Minneapolis: University of Minnesota Press, 1987), 22.

18 Yousef, *Isolated Cases*.

19 Samuel Taylor Coleridge, *Opus Maximum*, ed. Thomas McFarland and Nicholas Halmi (Princeton, NJ: Princeton University Press, 2002), 119–33; see Pfau, "Community as Metaphysics: Coleridge on Person and Conscience," Talk given at Colloquium Romanticism and the Question of Community, Brown University, Providence, Rhode Island, 13 November 2010.

20 For relevant discussions of the ethical dimension of this level of phenomeno-logical experience, see Emmanuel Levinas, *Totality and Infinity: An Essay on Exteriority*, trans. Alphonso Lingis (Pittsburgh, PA: Duquesne University Press, 1969), and *Otherwise than Being: Or Beyond Essence*, trans. Alphonso Lingis (Pittsburgh, PA: Duquesne University Press, 1998).

21 The passage may not be fully integrated into the rhetoric of its context because Wordsworth wrote it originally as a separate manuscript draft emerging out of work for the Pedlar. Never incorporating it into a draft of *The Ruined Cottage*, he eventually revised it and brought it into *The Prelude* in the present context: see *The Ruined Cottage* and *The Pedlar*, ed. Butler, 371.

22 The passage may be related to a portion of the opening of MS JJ, the earliest draft toward the two-part *Prelude*, which reads: "what there is / Of subtler feeling of remembered joy / Of soul & spirit in departed sound / That can not be remembered" (13–16; see *The Prelude*, ed. Parrish, 123). These lines depict a remembered joy in response to a sound that cannot be remembered, whereas the passage eventually included in the two-part *Prelude* depicts a remembered emotion whose content cannot be remembered – in response to a sound without content. In each case, something crucial to the memory disappears, but the later version is more subtle than the earlier, retaining both mood and occasion for memory but removing anything specific from either, ultimately describing a nameless affect in response to a formless sound.

23 Jean-François Lyotard, "After the Sublime, the State of Aesthetics," *The Inhuman: Reflections on Time*, trans. Geoffrey Bennington and Rachel Bowlby (Stanford, CA: Stanford University Press, 1991), 140–1.

24 Ibid., 142. I thank Rasmus Simonsen for drawing my attention to the relevance of these passages in Lyotard for this reading of Wordsworth.

25 Adam Potkay, "Wordsworth and the Ethics of Things," *PMLA* 123, no. 2 (2008), 400.

26 Lyotard, "After the Sublime," 141.

27 Compare Potkay, "Wordsworth," 397.

28 Ibid.

29 Martin Heidegger, *What Is Philosophy?*, trans. Hugh Tomlinson and Graham Burchell (London: Vision, 1963), 51–3, 79–85.

30 William Wordsworth, *The Major Works*, ed. Stephen Gill (Oxford: Oxford University Press, 1984), ll. 5, 7–8. All references to Wordsworth's poetry, besides *The Prelude*, are from this edition, cited hereafter in the essay by line number.

31 Levinas, *Existence*, 51–60.

32 Terada, *Feeling in Theory*.

CHAPTER 8

Kant's peace, Wordsworth's slumber

Jacques Khalip

> . . . I breathe again!
> Trances of thought and mountings of the mind
> Come fast upon me: it is shaken off,
> That burthen of my own unnatural self,
> The heavy weight of many a weary day
> Not mine, and such as were not made for me.
> Long months of peace (if such bold word accord
> With any promises of human life),
> Long months of ease and undisturbed delight
> Are mine in prospect. Whither shall I turn,
> By road or pathway, or through open field,
> Or shall a twig or any floating thing
> Upon the river point me out my course?[1]

In these opening lines from the first book of the 1850 version of *The Prelude*, that famously posthumous work of retrospection, recovery, and failed imaginings, Wordsworth reckons with the mixed welcome of things seemingly not too far off. Although lightened of the weight of days, he remains caught up in the consequences of further surmises that do little to clarify the unknowable future course of life. "Trances of thought and mountings of the mind" appear as swiftly as they are "shaken off," while the sense of "many a weary day / Not mine, and such as were not made for me" confesses an experience that is just as easily ignored as it is committed to memory. When Wordsworth summons the murky figure of peace, it is with a mood somewhere between apprehension and non-knowing. Indeed, in the 1850 *Prelude*, Wordsworth shuts away that "bold word" into the space of the parenthetical where it is silently acknowledged as a vanishing that haunts thought, an aside only the poem itself could avow in its own inner voice.

A much different version of this essay first appeared as "The Melancholy of Peace," *CR: New Centennial Review* 11, no. 1 (2011): 243–75.

Whatever Wordsworth takes the "still waters" of peace to be, they turn us as much away from as toward the yet-to-come. Appropriately, questions concerning "Whither shall I turn, / By road or pathway, or through open field, / Or shall a twig or any floating thing, / Upon the river point me out my course?" are about the kinds of orientations that peace prescribes and loses sight of altogether. In times of ease and delight, the open road, pathway, or field are prospective figures of movement that seem as untrustworthy as twigs or "floating things" which direct one to forget the future even as they suggest other means of discovery. The recoil that peace provokes also hints at a poetics of idealism and possibility, albeit simultaneously encrusted in a theory of mourning: to appreciate the boldness of the declaration of peace is to feel for an opportunity that has palpably gone missing. It is for these reasons that Wordsworth's own "sweet dream of perpetual peace" (to cite Kant's words) is both welcomed and elegized as an almost charmingly ineffectual anachronism – a floating thing one greets as if it had already disappeared.[2]

Like much Romantic writing, *The Prelude* was written amidst the sobering realities of eighteenth- and early-nineteenth-century warfare when feelings of peace were never quite distinguishable from the ever-growing chance of more wars on the horizon. As Mary Favret has forcefully argued, the innocuous "everyday" peace of Romanticism is full of the sounds, stammerings, and silences of battles fought at a distance but also never far from the despairs of the quotidian. Such an everyday is characterized by a shell-shocked consciousness that attempts to hear and repair "a history not entirely possessed," and for Favret, the everyday is never at peace with itself; rather, it is permeated by a structure of feeling that resembles the abstruse and ephemeral temporality of trauma through and through. The everyday circulates between past, present, and future, and peacetime in this schema is dim at best – it can never be accounted for, either epistemologically or affectively, because it is a byproduct or "mark of a literature saturated by the awareness, however unconscious, of a world lost to war ... the pained effort to bind what is present and familiar with another reality, absent and destructive."[3] Similarly emphasizing the privative dimensions of historical feeling in his *Romantic Moods: Paranoia, Trauma, and Melancholy, 1790–1840*, Thomas Pfau has theorized melancholy as an index of post-Waterloo wartime, looming less as a pathology than a distinct Heideggerian "mood" (*Stimmung*) or "latent principle" that discloses "the deep-structural situatedness of individuals within history as something never actually intelligible to them in fully coherent, timely, and

definitive form." Melancholy's conceptual consistency derives from its
fitful encryption of an opaque knowledge:

> melancholy bespeaks the deep structural fatigue of a culture that has grown
> oppressively familiar with itself and hence begins to despair over the
> apparent inefficacy of its generic and rhetorical means. Born of an excess
> of knowledge and, it would seem, terminally mired in the lucid inertia of
> the saturnine individual ... melancholy is distinguished from the earlier
> paradigms of emotion (paranoia, trauma) by its apparent proximity to what
> Hegel calls self-consciousness.[4]

Melancholy, for Pfau, is the affective correlate of historical conditions
whose difficulties we have yet to fully glimpse because we have exhausted
the means for coinciding with their evacuated meanings. Broadly speaking,
one might say that for these reasons, melancholy's emphases on dissociation and out-of-placeness permeate our contemporary theoretical landscape, where loss is often deployed as the affect par excellence of ethical
thought and cultural politics.

For both Favret and Pfau, melancholy, trauma, or loss *tout court* lend
shape to the devastations and absences of historical knowledge even as the
terms themselves infuse the emotional substance of such vacancies with
critical force. Thus the implicit recalcitrance that Pfau discovers in melancholic thought becomes a way for thinking the disabling of the limits of
possibility *as a historical condition*. Indeed, in a larger stroke, Stanley Cavell
has suggested that fatigue, melancholy, or boredom are circumstances of
philosophy, charged as it is to contemplate justice in the face of the
depletion of possibilities in the world: "Naming a historical phenomenon,
this names not an isolated matter of an individual sense of pointlessness in
saying anything, but a more general sense of lacking, or failing, the
language in which to express what has to be said, as if calling philosophical
as well as political attention to a shared aphasia." For Cavell, philosophy's
need to overcome melancholy depends upon a sense that "thinking has
come to a dead end, or say, has become exhausted. We may express this as
philosophy's coming to conceive of itself as taking place in, or as, an
aftermath, an aftermath of thought, sometimes now called a closure of
philosophy or of history."[5] Exhaustion, then, isn't so much opposed to but
dialectically coupled with the very critical movement of thought it appears
to extinguish; in this way, the end of the world becomes a necessary
function of skepticism: it entrusts the work of philosophy with imagining
forms of ethical engagement that counteract the world's annihilation. For
Hegel, consciousness

is something that goes beyond limits, and since these limits are its own, it is something that goes beyond itself . . . Thus consciousness suffers violence at its own hands: it spoils its own limited satisfaction . . . it can find no peace. If it wishes to remain in a state of unthinking inertia, then thought troubles its thoughtlessness, and its own unrest disturbs its inertia.[6]

Hegel's reproductive judgment colors Cavell's skepticism, which concentrates on the possible as a concept linked to future survival or "aftermath" – something that can happen and thus may count as the most minimal requirement of progress.

In the pages that follow, I want to suggest that whatever Romantic peace might be, it is quite often a matter of affect, richly suggestive of atmospheric changes, disruptions, and movements that are irreducible to the vagaries of the subject; and while peace's affective shape emerges out of these dominant philosophical contexts, it also strikingly differs from them. Bound to a reality constructed as "absent and destructive," peace often evinces residual modes of starkly attenuated, inhuman perseverance, or forms of being and thinking that live through and *on* absence in different ways. While Favret and Pfau point to traumatisms that shatter late Romantic literature and culture, I want to explore alternate sites of coping, where the resources available for approaching crisis are reorganized by Romantic writers struggling to absorb (without necessarily intervening in) the conditions of liveability in a world tragically disposed to ruin. If peace is too often linked to destitution and hopelessness in some of the texts I read, it is because its form remains latent, affectless, grey-on-grey, at once workless and flexible in its vagueness even if its gradations of change seem minimal if not utterly imperceptible.

I shall interweave two strands of argument: on the one hand, I explore how and why deployments of peace in Enlightenment and post-Enlightenment literature and culture often turn to the affective rhetoric of loss – why peace figures for lost objects, lost histories, and lost causes that haunt liberal narratives of progressive modernity. *Haunt*, after all, is an operative word here: if peace comes back as a critical concept in Romantic thought, its time often figures as future past: in contrast with its bellicose opposite, peace configures what David Scott has described as an opening onto the ways in which "expectation of – or longing for – particular futures helps to shape the kind of problem the past is constructed as for the present."[7] As a diminished expectation, peace signals a horizon of alteration that might never arrive. But on the other hand, peace's moody failure to translate into some kind of reality – its seemingly melancholic attachment to that which might never be – gestures toward an inert presentness that is not about nostalgia, melancholy, trauma, or false expectation *per se*, but rather an immanent, underperformed experience of processing that occurs while at rest. To be sure, for some writers touched upon in this essay, peace is the lost thing within certain narratives that gloomily envision worlds permanently annulled by warfare; for others, like Wordsworth and Kant (my main exhibits), a confrontation ensues with the borders of sheer exhaustion and despair, and awakens new potentials for thinking and feeling peace from within boredom, helplessness, and inertia. Kant traces, for example, an attrition of peace to the point where its exhaustion is replaced by a sense of the now, but a now that can be nonacquisitively felt in the absence of any object. And similarly, though in a less speculative manner, Wordsworth, in poems such as "A Slumber Did My Spirit Seal" and "Old Man Travelling," reflects on how a peace or restfulness within the present, in its sheer transience, gives way to a cluster of energies that achieve a zero-degree affect that is nevertheless sensed in its abstinence. Of course, to say that Wordsworth is really speaking of peace in these two poems might be a counterintuitive (if not wholly exaggerated) claim, especially given that he is explicitly describing situations or characters that are profoundly *not* at peace. But I do think that Wordsworth's abiding interest in movements of rest or putting-at-rest sketches out a far more complex kind of Romantic habitus that tries to respond to and endure the intolerability of a situation in ways that are not explained with reference to either melancholy or trauma, even as the poetic responses remain on the level of hypothesis.

I.   "Difficult to bear"

Describing the psycho-historical period in Europe (chiefly Britain) after the Battle of Waterloo, Jerome Christensen states that peace is an

> aftermath, a time of demobilization ... Peace, the future presupposed by wartime, itself presupposes no future of its own. If the discourse of Waterloo is marked by the medicalization of the past as a time of diseased thought and action, then peace, as Coleridge and Scott would identify it, is a time of extended convalescence, which anticipates no return of robust, belligerent health.[8]

Peace's temporality invokes postwar survival as a continuation of wartime, a conservative mode of exhausted living which "presupposes no future of its own," and generates no capacity for progress. Such peace convalesces – it hopes for the return of a time that was, a time of "robust, belligerent

Fig. 1.   James Gillray, POLITICAL-DREAMINGS! – VISIONS OF PEACE! – PERSPECTIVE HORRORS! 1801.
Courtesy of the Anne S. K. Brown Military Collection, Brown University Library.

health." In effect, it is nothing more than the false future of a war that rages on because of a desire to rehabilitate an irrecoverable (and inconsolable) past. In this way, peace invokes a retrospective melancholy whose cure is worse than the disease.

In James Gillray's mordantly satiric print, "Political Dreamings! ... Visions of Peace! ... Perspective Horrors!" (Fig. 1, see previous page) Christensen's insight finds stunning proof: Britain's Secretary of War, William Windham, who was opposed to the Peace of Amiens of 1801, experiences a sleepless night over nightmares of a French invasion crowding his bedroom. Napoleon Bonaparte stands amidst the fires alongside a dejected Britannia and a guillotine, while Prime Minister William Pitt is seen to the left of the French leader signing the nation's death warrant as a French skeleton overlooks the scene. The truce of peace, held in the vulture's beak, occurs *in medias res*: figured in the middle of the nightmarish print, it appears as an afterthought to an already destructive encounter with the French other. The hallucination, however, brings forth one more effect: it foregrounds Windham's body as the displaced participant in an authorless world pressing around him, and it imagines other counterfactual lives occurring while he sleeps. In this case, sleep is a conflicted state of persistent vigilance, at once bringing things near *and* relegating them beyond control: Windham's notions are invisible both to him and to us. But the print represents them as effects of a troubled mind that thinks it can relate its dreams as if they were our own. In doing so, the print exposes the nightmare of peace as a symptom of Windham's dream of the other. Windham's dream of survival transforms into a sleepy, suspended attentiveness oriented at something one can neither know nor expect.

On the one hand, the missed opportunity of endorsing peace as a substantive change of affairs remains lost in Gillray's print where peace only breeds specters of warmongering; but on the other, it also persists as the gloomy manifestation of an attrition of living, an immobilization of Windham's body by geopolitical forces in the service of a torpid normalcy – what Lauren Berlant has described as the "slow death" or exhaustion of "practical sovereignty" by means of rendering agency incoherent and temporally lagging. In such a condition, one is resigned to perpetually reattaching oneself to the "convalescent" time of an innocuous future past (read "peace"), itself a fantasy produced by the very deflated consciousness that is indentured to the exhaustion of the everyday.[9] After all, although Windham dreams of the Peace of Amiens as literally signed, sealed, and delivered, the pact is represented as the Pandora's Box of wartime affect – the open possibility that unleashes these images of political apocalypse only to keep Windham indolently in bed.

As the "as if" that is never taken and never to be, peace in part resembles a state strangely akin to the haunted process of living-on or survival in disaster. For Derrida, survival affirms a form of attention to that which has passed by – an attentiveness, however, that is not preservational but residual. Survival is a structure of non-relational relationality, a vigilance about something that is impossible to convey because its opportunity has been missed or left unaccounted for. Survival emerges out of what Derrida calls in one of his final interviews a "war against myself," a contradictory experience of internal disruption that doesn't simply collapse peace and war, but rather testifies to a terror that is infinitely self-differential – a form of wartime ontology:

> I am at war with myself, it's true, you couldn't possibly know to what extent, beyond what you can guess, and I say contradictory things that are, we might say, in real tension; they are what construct me, make me live, and will make me die. I sometimes see this war as terrifying and difficult to bear, but at the same time I know that it is life. I will find peace only in eternal rest. I thus cannot really say that I assume this contradiction, but I know that it is what keeps me alive, and makes me ask precisely the question you recalled earlier, "how does one to learn how to live?"[10]

Survival prompts an ethical injunction to respect the singularity of the event as something welcomed only after it has been deposited – an acknowledgment made in the absence of any capacity to fully possess or know the event.

For Derrida, this barest sense of survival – a life that is led as a living-on or dogged depletion of affective resources – stubbornly resists the kinds of neoliberal projects of sovereignty, nationalism, and community that depend on surviving intact into the future. "Life," or the variant of it he calls survival, is an affirmation of something that is not simply beyond living, but rather the merest, most evanescent form of the capacity to affirm for the sake of affirming – an oddly material emotionality without an object, an example *without* an example. As Sara Guyer has reminded us, this affirmation is also at times linked by Derrida to a "state of suffering," evoking at once "the violent metaphorics of survival – war, torture, tearing – but also passivity, patience, and everything that in French is related to the *pas*, or the "no", the "non"- that also plays on the other sense of the word as "step." Guyer notes that in other instances (especially in the version of the interview that appeared in *Le Monde*), Derrida specifically aims to separate survival from "the very morbidity that the discussion of torture and war would seem to introduce" and specifies it as "marked by the structure of the trace, the testament."[11] Thus survival's iterability – the paradoxical capacity to continue bearing witness for that which no act of witnessing is ever adequate – invokes a far more impersonal affective drive that is decidedly resistant to violence even as it confesses its own contamination by a violence it cannot ever dismiss. But Derrida's earlier avowal, that to feel the war within himself is "terrifying … difficult to bear, but at the same time [knowing] that it is life," imagines the capacity to endure life as if it were underwritten by sublime forbearance and a patient staying power organized by survival's futural commitments. Indeed, peace for Derrida still remains a limit case of survival insofar as its inertness renders it impossible to feel: final peace would seem to be the unbearability of the "difficult to bear," or the radical passivity that is felt *only as* something one can only know in the moment of one's annulment: "I *will* find peace *only* in eternal rest." Peace's posterity is annihilating – it is the aftermath of a war against oneself. Gillray exactly helps us to see this ominous temporal shadow cast by peace: in the print, it figures as a paranoid convalescence and "slow death" that bloats all confrontations with pasts and futures, yet simultaneously, it also cannot bear to process and weigh the heaviness of the present.

II.   "A peace of extermination"

The strange temporality of such peace is freighted with a powerful historical background. To begin looking for it, I propose that we turn back even further to Thomas Hobbes's equation of war with weather:

> For War consisteth not in battle only, or the act of fighting, but in a tract of time wherein the will to contend by battle is sufficiently known. And therefore, the notion of time is to be considered in the nature of war, as it is in the nature of weather. For as the nature of foul weather lieth not in a shower or two of rain, but in an inclination thereto of many days together, so the nature of war consisteth not in actual fighting, but in the known disposition thereto during all the time there is no assurance to the contrary. All other time is PEACE.[12]

For Hobbes, peace is another name for that period when one comes to know that the disposition to fight has been given up for another day. What is at issue is how knowing functions at all in relation to battles and their ends. Hobbes suspends the prediction of any sufficient knowledge of peace: like the weather, we cannot know peacetime except as the opposite of the "will to contend by battle." Because of this, one cannot ever know peace's volition because it is entirely implicated in (and thus indistinguishable from) the will of war. Hobbes formulates war and peace as tropological: they compel a temporal disruption between act and identity, and they render the action or "will" of the other an infinitely unknowable concept. Peace is *negative peace* for Hobbes, a time of endless preparation for an event one cannot ever fully possess:

> Paix, ou trêve de Dieu, étoit une cessation d'armes, depuis le soir du mercredi de chaque semaine, jusqu'au lundi matin, que les ecclésiastiques & les princes religieux firent observer dans le tems où il étoit permis aux particuliers de tuer le meurtrier de leur parent, ou de se venger par leurs mains en tel autre cas que ce fait. [Peace, or truce of God, was a suspension of arms, from Wednesday night of each week until Monday morning, which the clergymen and religious sovereigns observed as the time when it was permitted to kill the murderers of their parent, or to avenge themselves.][13]

In this passage from Diderot's *Encyclopédie*, peace is the time between the suspension of violence and its eventual execution – it is the delay or deferral of bloodshed yet to come. In flattening out peace's conceptual richness, Hobbes anticipates the *Encyclopédie*'s definition by inscribing peace with a temporal lack: if peace is the absence of a sustained duration of battle, then what time properly belongs to it? Is it an infinite patience, a calm before the carnage? Or is it the loss of preparation? For Hobbes, peace "happens" within the durée of war, and thus its time is never its own.

Hobbes's remarks on the temporal contraction and climactic disappearance of peace are subtended by a skepticism regarding free will. Hannah Arendt points out in *The Origins of Totalitarianism* that there is "hardly a single bourgeois moral standard which has not been anticipated by the unequaled magnificence of Hobbes's logic. He gives an almost complete picture, not of Man but of the bourgeois man ... 'reason is nothing but Reckoning'; 'a free Subject, a free Will' ... [are] words ... without meaning; that is to say, Absurd."[14] The Hobbesian state of war provides a fable about individuals' will-lessness: possessed by private interests, individuals are enslaved to the flickering economy of their own motives and desires. Peace's strange non-time is related to the impossible performativity of personal will. Hobbes's words anticipate Enlightenment instances of peace unraveling the self-confirming positions of free-willing, liberal citizens whose sense of improvement and cultural participation are exposed as desires propped up by the violent machinery of war. If peace in the eighteenth century is often imagined as the idealized future of the state, such wishes are obtained on the understanding that peace should be endlessly secured and represented through the will's repetitive, traumatizing violence – a point that bears out Kant's thought that peace is a "pleonasm" that secures *logos* and *polemos* through a false relation. In a remarkably Hobbesian mood, Kant states that the "state of nature (*status naturalis*) is not a state of peace among human beings who live next to one another but a state of war, that is, if not always an outbreak of hostilities, then at least the constant threat of such hostilities."[15] Such a state is evidence of a rampant will for representation. "War is the motor behind institutions and order," remarks Michel Foucault in his lectures from the Collège de France:

> In the smallest of its cogs, peace is waging a secret war. To put it another way, we have to interpret the war that is going on beneath peace; peace itself is a coded war. We are therefore at war with one another; a battlefront runs through the whole of society, continuously and permanently, and it is this battlefront that puts us all on one side or the other. There is no such thing as a neutral subject. We are all inevitably someone's adversary.

The Hobbesian flavor of Foucault's pronouncements bespeaks a melancholic stance vis-à-vis the image of a blood-soaked modernity: "Who saw war just beneath the surface of peace," Foucault asks; "who sought in the noise and confusion of war, in the mud of battles, the principle that allows us to understand order, the State, its institutions, its history?" Deep in this question, war emerges as the founding loss of knowledge, the noise that makes audible the violent phenomena of life: "No matter how far back it goes, historical knowledge never finds nature, right, order, or peace. However far back it goes, historical knowledge discovers only an unending war, or in other words, forces that relate to one another and come into conflict with one another."[16] Historical knowledge at once disfigures and shapes the very history whose future horizons it would seek to subjugate. The compulsion that drives historical knowing to brood over the effects of war reveals a need to install war as the object and origin of consciousness. By such a design, there can be no peace because it has never been thinkable outside of war's temporal framework. Peace isn't lost entirely – it remains bound to what Hobbes calls "all other time."

If Foucault's sobering words amount to a promise of some kind, it is that society as we know it promises war everywhere and forever. Underneath peace, coded within it, being waged through it, war is the all too conspicuous wolf in sheep's clothing, and for Foucault, wartime operates as the organizing figure of domination as well as the prevailing discourse that has buoyed social relations since the sixteenth century. Both Clausewitz's declaration that war is merely the continuation of politics and

Foucault's subsequent inversion that politics is the continuation of war (and Foucault's further insistence that Clausewitz had in fact made that inversion in the first place), bear this point out. It is for this reason that Enlightenment attempts (by Fontenelle, Abbé Saint-Pierre, Rousseau, Bentham, amongst others) to envision peace as a term for alternative possibilities are frequently limited or foreclosed by blockages permeated by the violent, totalizing aspirations of philosophical self-consciousness, "spoil[ing] its own limited satisfaction," as Hegel reminds us. David Bates has argued that Enlightenment struggles to theorize a "limit" to war (a struggle which managed, with relative success, to isolate warfare in ways that starkly contrasted with the all-destroying wars of earlier centuries) seemed to near a radical turn in the revolutionary wars which exploded in the "wake of 1789" and marked "the beginning of a new form of warfare, characterized by a deadly intensity that would only be exacerbated by new technologies of destruction in the industrial age."[17] Peace, as the endpoint of war, provokes an anxious need to secure limits through an excessive devastation of future possibilities – something that resonates in Edmund Burke's *Letters on the Regicide Peace*:

> We are in a war of a peculiar nature. It is not with an ordinary community, which is hostile or friendly as passion or as interest may veer about; not with a State which makes war through wantonness, and abandons it through lassitude. We are at war with a system, which, by its essence, is inimical to all other Governments, and which makes peace or war, as peace and war may best contribute to their subversion. It is with an armed doctrine, that we are at war.

The perceived irrationality of the French "system" figures for a war that is literally against a species of thought that is otherwise: neither wanton nor given to "lassitude" in its warfare, such a state is organized precisely by the seriousness of its unknowable aims. This is war waged against the bastard-izing (the regicide) of a narrative of "peace" that has been abandoned in the time of the revolution, and become ghoulishly drafted into a new time of war: "There is always an augury to be taken of what a peace is likely to be, from the preliminary steps that are made to bring it about … The regicides were the first to declare war. We are the first to sue for peace."[18] Burke's petition for more war against France thus responds against sus-penseful "augury" of a peace that is as "likely to be" as it is likely not to be. His language is tinged with a nostalgic melancholy that strains to find solace in a proper object of grief – a true peace – that might return England to stability, but such melancholy has no actual object; indeed, the rage that fuels Burke's melancholy is stimulated by a search for a non-existent thing. In his 1814 essay, "On the Late War," William Hazlitt states that, because Britain's war with France was "a war of extermination, so the peace ... must be a peace of extermination" for the reason that the government's presumptive attitudes towards the so-called enemy are the result of a hypercathexis onto the enemy, one which in turn renders war indistinct from peace.[19] In Hazlitt's summary of war melancholy, peace further amplifies war's repressiveness by phantasmatically representing the supposed object of a conservative nostalgia that can never be recuperated, but is nevertheless posited as the beckoning source of a desire that endlessly greases the motors of a relentless war machine. Hazlitt's terrifying statements expose a self-preserving battle undertaken against the other, one which turns into a war with our own being. In such a fantasy, one negatively feels peace *as* nothing; at the origins of our misery lies a violent fiction that is necessary to the declaration of war itself.

III.   "After agitation"

The idea of peace emerging out of melancholic fatigue is approached in Kant's *Toward Perpetual Peace*, a text begun in 1795 in the immediate wake of the Peace of Basel between Prussia and France. The truce came during a period at the end of the eighteenth century that saw the culmination of centuries of bloody battle on the continent, and marked an extraordinary apogee in the history of German warfare. Kant's prescriptions for peace disclose a far more conflicted reception of the term: his "sketch" presses toward a mode of philosophizing that appears implicitly exhausted by the kind of war discourse Foucault envisions – a discourse, moreover, Kant figures and refigures in the "slow death" image of the inn which mordantly begins his sketch. Rather than read Kant's text as an atemporal wish for messianic triumph over history or a reflection on peace as an aporetic event within language, I follow David L. Clark's argument that *Toward Perpetual Peace* marks a decisive shift in Kant's writing toward a form of philosophy bereft of any immediate guarantees of peace – a work "directly symptomatic of war, and of the melancholically difficult experience of critiquing militarism, including an internalized militarism, in a time of perpetual war."[20]

Of course, in other instances in Kant's writings, like *The Critique of Judgment*, peace is displaced by a taste for the sublimity of war and the veneration of the soldier. And even in *Toward Perpetual Peace*, he will argue in an utterly bizarre section of the treatise that the ecology of war has contributed to the growing sociality of the world by forcibly displacing persons around the globe: "populat[ing] all regions of the earth . . . [war is] embedded in human nature, and [counts] as something noble."[21] Although I by no means wish to apologize for these passages, I do think that they testify to the deep-rooted political and critical contradictions that are brought upon all projects that seek to conceptualize peace both within and without a framework of systemic violence. By implication, then, the darkly symbiotic relationship between war and peace turns philosophizing into a work of mourning: peace's uneasy residual status might signal a movement of "unusable negativity" that Tilottama Rajan has located in melancholy's challenge to the Symbolic order.[22] To be sure, peace for Kant should ideally emerge as more than a mere truce amidst the carnage of wartime; and yet, his repeated statements that peace is a concept rather than an objective reality – that "the state of peace must be established," that we share a "duty to work toward it" – imply that the word can also evoke a calcifying status quo – a nostalgic desire for peace-as-return-to-self or peace-as-self-origination.[23]

For Kant, peace has yet to happen because it never happened or has never happened at all. It is a deflated registry of a feeling not yet experienced or never to be felt. If we look to one of Jaucourt's entries for peace in the *Encyclopédie*, the differences between "paix," "tranquillité" and "calme" are outlined as follows: "On a la tranquillité en soi-même, la paix avec les autres, & le calme après l'agitation. Les gens inquiets n'ont point de tranquillité dans leur domestique. Les querelleurs ne sont guere en paix avec leurs voisins. Plus la passion a été orageuse, plus on goûte le calme." "Tranquillity is within us, peace is with others, and calm comes after agitation": all three words, Jaucourt notes, equally share an exemption from "trouble and agitation." Peace, like calm, is felt only in relation to another, and thus its experience depends on the external: peace "looks at the situation in relation to the outside, and to those enemies who might cause conflict," meaning that peace is always experienced as the expectation of another.[24] But what ultimately collapses Jaucourt's language is the pervasive sense that all feeling might well be at its core a form of waiting or *acedia*, or what Giorgio Agamben describes as "a flight from, but also a flight toward, which communicates with its object in the form of negation and lack," the desire for a desire in total absence of any will.[25] The feeling for and of peace would seem to be no feeling at all, a purely formal or figurative straining. In this way, peace is more than a mode of Derridean survival: it is the mood that is so affectively present that it need not (cannot) be either affirmed or expected – a here and now that dissolves the anxious, instrumentalizing prospects cast on the time to come.

IV.   "Settled quiet"

In order to develop the thought that peace suggests passive experiences of self-absenting, impotent value that remain oblivious to the future, I want to pull back and focus on two of Wordsworth's most frequently discussed poems, "Old Man Travelling (Animal Tranquillity and Decay, A Sketch)" and "A Slumber Did My Spirit Seal," in order to consider how this insistence on a peaceful "nowness" resonates as an event that suffuses and sustains the tolerability of the present tense even in its apparent ungraspability. What emerges in the poems, I argue, is something resembling a powerlessness that strives towards rest: in outlining these helpless counterlives, Wordsworth reflects on how peace is neither elegiac nor traumatic, and thus its affective "time" is unchanging. It does not bear the burdens of an encrypted retrospection, nor has any disabling purchase on futurity:

> The little hedge-row birds,
> That peck along the road, regard him not.
> He travels on, and in his face, his step,
> His gait, is one expression; every limb,
> His look and bending figure, all bespeak
> A man who does not move with pain, but moves
> With thought – He is insensibly subdued
> To settled quiet: he is one by whom
> All effort seems forgotten, one to whom
> Long patience has such mild composure given,
> That patience now doth seem a thing, of which
> He hath no need. He is by nature led
> To peace so perfect, that the young behold
> With envy, what the old man hardly feels.
> – I asked him whither he was bound, and what
> The object of his journey; he replied
> "Sir! I am going many miles to take
> "A last leave of my son, a mariner,
> "Who, from a sea-fight has been brought to Falmouth,
> "And there is dying in an hospital."[26]

The sibilance heard in "insensibly subdued / To settled quiet" layers on the pressures of subjection implicitly experienced by the old man. Indeed, the logic of the commodity, as David Simpson has brilliantly argued, permeates his figuration – mechanized and automatic, the man's movement "with thought" rather than "with pain" isn't simply a pathic overcoming of suffering through motion, but a psychic exercise that continues in excess of or separate from the man's intentions.[27] But the differentiation here is critical: rather than evoke a full mortification of the body in the wake of industrialized control, Wordsworth suggests that a condition of thought remains in the style of the old man's characterization, one that is responsive to the numbness and matter-of-factness of the poem. On the one hand, one could construe the old man's bare liveliness as the spectral animation of a death-in-life, unwillingly regulated by quasi-biopolitical forces that are harnessed by the lyric's aestheticizing lull which, in turn, affectively compels insensibility and routinization:

> He travels on, and in his face, his step,
> His gait, is one expression.

Terry Eagleton has identified this particular power as part and parcel of Enlightenment aesthetic ideology: "The ultimate binding force of the bourgeois social order, in contrast to the coercive apparatus of absolutism, will be habits, pieties, sentiments and affections. And this is equivalent to saying that power in such an order has been aestheticized. It is at one with the body's spontaneous impulses, entwined with sensibility and the affections, lived out in unreflective custom."[28] Indeed, we might be tempted to read the old man's gait as a coerced habitus produced by the lyric's drive toward unreflection, itself a symptom of a bourgeois order founded upon transposing the trappings of power into the sentimentalized figure of the "body."

But on the other hand, the old man's "one expression" also hints at a certain minimal affectivity, a "settled quiet" that is more than just a condition of his being, but a place to which the old man is curbed as he travels to see his dying son during wartime. "Settled" here is a key word: etymologically referring to a place to sit, the word as adjective also evokes arranged order, fixing or defining, emplacement or establishment. Thus "settled quiet" at once means quiet that occurs through resolution, but also a normalized repose. Peace (like the patience that the old man now no longer needs) occurs in the moment it floods into resolution or reconciliation. Indeed, this normalization of the man intimates a low-grade form of extra-individual singularity that is neither subject to discipline, nor freed into surplus motion. On-the-go while set in space/place, the man's bare singularity evokes a contented non-power, something immanent and decidedly plain in its beatitude. Bare affect here is in many ways the numbing response to war, to the son's impending death empathetically felt on the body; but like war itself, that death is unseen, elsewhere, an event to arrive at, and yet, like all else in the old man's life, it is something for which the man has neither expectation nor anxiety for – a patience for which he "has no need" because whatever will happen has already occurred and suffused his *now*. In his simplicity, the man's habitus signals a kind of self-refitting (or outfitting), a habituation or acclimatization to sentiments that are experienced before they take hold:

> All effort seems forgotten, one to whom
> Long patience has such mild composure given,
> That patience now doth seem a thing, of which
> He hath no need.

The man's apparent non-existence, then, is not quite Agamben's bare life (even if he does embody one of Wordsworth's countless poetic specters of homeless wartime refugees) because *his* life is not at all lived through death, potentiality, process, or vitality. The man feels the almost technical (re) inscription of minimal affect upon which his subsistence depends. To forget the effort to live means to decline the ascription of value to life itself once the body no longer must feel in order to be productive. In this way, it paradoxically feels in order to forget itself through the very practices – patience, for example – once required to bring it to this point.

Wordsworth suggests that the man is guided by a thinking without thought, one that unleashes responses around a series of events that work to bring him to a "peace so perfect" to which he is already led by his "nature," and this circuit becomes less the symptom of a forced codification that adjusts the man according to what he must be, than it is a wish for a perfection that one "hardly feels" – the mere notation of an affective extravagance that is freed of value and reciprocity by virtue of its sheer minimalism. Or put differently, the old man comes to dwell or be put at peace with a "settled quiet" that would be otherwise read as constraining him. Turning now to "A Slumber Did My Spirit Seal," this movement of putting-at-peace discloses a similar concern for affects that reverberate in spite of seeming to be the opposite of anything contributing to human life:

> A slumber did my spirit seal;
>   I had no human fears:
> She seemed a thing that could not feel
>   The touch of earthly years.
>
> No motion has she now, no force;
>   She neither hears nor sees;
> Rolled round in earth's diurnal course,
>   With rocks, and stones, and trees.[29]

Wordsworth wrote "A Slumber" in 1798 during a period in Germany spent with his sister, and notwithstanding the historical frame of its composition, the lyric is not immediately assimilable to the kinds of wartime traumas that haunt much of his poetry from the late eighteenth to early nineteenth centuries. Indeed, in comparison to other titles in the 1800 *Lyrical Ballads* where "A Slumber" eventually appeared, particularly "The Female Vagrant" or "Tintern Abbey," this brief poem ostensibly works like an affective palliative that softens the blow that otherwise buries the unknown "she" into a world of rocks and stones and trees. Geoffrey Hartman has noted that one of the elements of the poem is to effect transferences that unlink the economy of self and other: "human," for example, becomes a "transferred epithet" that might go from poet to girl or vice versa. Transference here is part of a logic of euphemism that Wordsworth deploys (according to Hartman) to mitigate the catastrophe of death.[30] But rather than read this as an attempt to deflect the traumas associated with the lyrical subject, "A Slumber" also uncannily "feels" an event that occurs with little endorsement: it embeds the reader in a process of intuitive adjudication that provides no respite, no consequential gains or enlightenments; it insists on staying with a crisis in a way that disempowers subjectivity of any capacity to claim that crisis in the first place. To think of "A Slumber" along these lines would be to read the slowly obliterated difference between the speaker and the "she" as the smallest turn of a poem that shifts from questions around subjectivity to those that suspend the very quality of human experiences to begin with. In its inability to fully describe either the crisis or the resolution of that crisis itself, "A slumber" is less about trauma than a trace of a peacefulness that is fleeting and transitory in its circumstantial scarcity, and by virtue of this scarcity, it exists, as it were, through an (en)durable series of inhuman affects. Marjorie Perloff, building on Paul de Man's insights on the poem's temporal and epistemological differentiations, has remarked how the "now" is a present sedimented by retrospection: "it is only 'now' that the poet faces the reality of her death, but, literally speaking, 'No motion has she now, no force' refers to a moment prior the poem's opening line, with its retrospective account of her death."[31] And yet, the line "No motion has she now, no force," has the grammatical effect of disengaging the recognition of "no motion" as a state of affairs that has transpired *to* Lucy; in turn, it quickens the pressure of the line onto the word "now," which visually comes in the middle, as if to hit home the realization that whatever "she" is or feels does not exist or may have never existed at all, and for this reason, what we are reading is the inhuman feeling of that very non-existence, that voiding of an ontological horizon. Rather than suffuse the present with an accumulated affective meaning of an event that had already occurred in the past as something lost, the poem focuses on what transpires from another, less knowable angle of vision, one where the lure of the affect lies in its evanescent yet no less searching mode of adaptation to a present that is not at home with itself, a present that appears decidedly unliveable and *unlived*.

In this way, "A Slumber" tends toward a different kind of reparative reading from the sort that follows Eve Sedgwick's definition: "The desire of a reparative impulse, on the other hand, is additive and accretive. Its fear, a realistic one, is that the culture surrounding it is the inadequate or inimical to its nurture; it wants to assemble and confer plenitude on an object that will then have resources to offer to an inchoate self."[32] "A Slumber," however, vies for no "self," no nurturing desires and reparations; rather, it *underperforms* its capacity for change by endlessly subduing and putting to rest an experience whose sightline of change is its own solvent. As a "thing," after all, Lucy distinctly rolls "with rocks, and stones, and trees," and the commas typographically draw attention to what is also felt as a material muteness and heaviness within the lines themselves, which posit Lucy's thingly rolling in a series of gaps or spacings that blank out utterance. This is a thingliness whose material sanction will not resolve into affective plenitude. If Wordsworth's "slumber" thematizes in part a peaceful hush in the poem, it does so in order to equate the spirit's sealing off as a gesture of proximation to the inhumanness it discovers in the encounter with Lucy.

In her work on neoliberal affects, Lauren Berlant has suggested that we might differently reorient our powers around the inert relationalities that characterize our contemporary cultural and socio-political projects, and subsequently reflect on the compromised conditions of dullness, inactivity, or apathy that reveal attachments to other modes of affective experimentation. For Berlant, the present, rather than the past or the future, is the space where affect "works" as praxis – it is a time measured, undertaken, and undergone. In this way, affect is always experienced even if it isn't expressive, particularly when it confronts a forestalled presentness or "historical situatedness" that qualifies that situation in the first place. Berlant's insights powerfully develop what she calls "genres of crisis," but as she also goes on to suggest, impasse might be the stronger term that defines a particular kind of subjectivity that is all too adjusted to the terrors of crises, and has no place to go: "the impasse is a space of time lived without narrative genre . . . [it] is a *cul-de-sac*" for which one develops other kinds of coping skills.[33] In "Old Man Travelling" and "A Slumber Did My Spirit Seal," Wordsworth produces two such "genres of crisis" that recalibrate the incessant (or "chronic") impacts of the everyday by rearranging its contents in such a way as to change nothing at all. But unlike Berlant's proprioceptive attention to the subject of impasse, Wordsworth's rearrangements ceaselessly wither lyrical affect of all stuff of subjectivity, as if to conjure impasses felt in their *unliveliness*, in their unlived dormancy. As Agamben has noted in *The Idea of Prose*, fatigue is deeply inscribed in peace's significance: remarking that the word originally referred to a pact, he writes that

> the state that derived from the pact was not pax, but otium ... A gesture of peace might thus be only a pure gesture, without meaning, showing the inactivity and emptiness of the hand ... there is not, nor can there be, a sign of peace, since true peace would only be there where all the signs were fulfilled and exhausted.[34]

Peace, like the empty handshake, is a sign or gesture that expends as it stretches affective presence – a de-posited possibility that occurs once all other gestures are laid to waste and rendered inactive. Put differently, the "emptiness of the hand" is the formalization of the very (im)possibility of feeling that peace itself – a gesture without reciprocity or recognition that is nevertheless felt as a gestic thing. And in "A Slumber," peace is gestured in the thingliness of Lucy's inhuman rolling to no end – a flattening movement that adapts to and accepts the present at hand as something that takes one out of life, eroding feeling into thingly materiality.

V. "That peace / Which passeth understanding"

In Kant's *Toward Perpetual Peace*, the place where a similar process of erosion and exhaustion occurs, albeit satirically, is in the image of the Dutch innkeeper's sign, ghoulishly depicting a graveyard over which hovers the caption, "To Perpetual Peace." Kant's hotel sign neither opens nor closes like a door, but rather swings: it outlines (like Lucy's rolling or the old man's shuffling) a pathic movement that is neither life nor death. The sign's force is iterative: it allusively repeats an image that also appears in Leibniz and Fontenelle; and by virtue of its iterability, it transmits something erosive through the error of its inscription. After all, the sign depicts, in Peter Fenves's words, the absence of any direction: it is "an image of irreparable loss: the gravestones through which a graveyard is recognizable are themselves signs by which the end of life's road is

marked ... the sign says 'no passage,' or in Greek, aporia: there is no path
to peace, this, the gravestone, marks the end of the road."[35] What Kant also
seems especially alert to is the fact that the melancholy of the sign also
produces an impasse: it collapses forward movement into indefiniteness
and indeterminacy. Of course, the innkeeper's sign terribly links rest to
death – a grim irony heard in the German, *Zum ewigen Frieden*, which
alludes to the "großen Kirchhofe der Menschengattung" or "great graveyard of humanity" where "perpetual peace" truly dwells.[36] But there might
be another kind of link here: according to the Duden dictionary, *Frieden*
(peace) etymologically derives in part from the Middle High German *vride*
and the Old High German *fridu*, which means *Schonnung* or care, protec-
tion, sparing; it is also genealogically related to friendship or kinship
(*Freund*). Tracing the word's complexity in "Building Dwelling Thinking," Heidegger remarks that the Gothic word *wunian* evokes

> to be at peace, to be brought to peace, to remain in peace ... To free really
> means to spare ... To dwell, to be set at peace, means to remain at peace
> within the free, the preserve, the free sphere that safeguards each thing in its
> nature. *The fundamental character of dwelling is this sparing and preserving.* It
> pervades dwelling in its whole range. That range reveals itself to us as soon
> as we reflect that human being consists in dwelling and, indeed, dwelling in
> the sense of the stay of mortals on the earth.[37]

The inn's hospitality is a dwelling, both in the sense of a shelter and a
preserving or gathering that defines our finitude. It performs a guarding of
place in the absence of any intent; put differently, it is dwelling as *inaction*.
Peace is the emptiness, the *something* always already here – but for Kant, it
is not always available to mortals who confuse it with death. We might
find a point of comparison with Wordsworth's remark in the Fourteenth
Book of the 1850 *Prelude*:

> Hence, amid ills that vex and wrongs that crush
> Our hearts – if here the words of Holy Writ
> May with fit reverence be applied – that peace
> Which passeth understanding, that repose
> In moral judgments which from this pure source
> Must come, or will by man be sought in vain.[38]

The lines allude to Philippians (4: 6–7): "Be careful for nothing; but in
every thing by prayer and supplication with thanksgiving let your requests
be made known unto God. And the peace of God, which passeth all
understanding, shall keep your hearts and minds through Christ Jesus."
"The peace / Which passeth all understanding" reads as transcendent

divine knowing, and it can signal a form of predestination that releases one from the charge to perform in the absence of any need of assertion. But it can also evoke a peace which passes by or passes on reason, or even more, a peace that isn't so much acquired as it is unknowingly taken in as nothing at all. Wordsworth helps us see that insofar as peace presents the sense of an anticipated experience rather than the experience itself, it is something affectively felt in the nearness of things, experiences, and possibilities that escape human sentiment altogether.

NOTES

1 William Wordsworth, *The Prelude: 1799, 1805, 1850*, ed. Jonathan Wordsworth, M. H. Abrams, and Stephen Gill (New York: Norton, 1979), 1.18–30.
2 Kant, *Toward Perpetual Peace*, ed. Kleingeld, 67.
3 Favret, *War at a Distance*, 146, 158, 159.
4 Pfau, *Romantic Moods*, 7, 23.
5 Stanley Cavell, "The Future of Possibility," in *Philosophical Romanticism*, ed. Nikolas Kompridis (New York: Routledge, 2002), 27, 26.
6 Hegel, *Phenomenology of Spirit*, trans. Miller, 51.
7 David Scott, *Conscripts of Modernity: The Tragedy of Colonial Enlightenment* (Durham, NC: Duke University Press, 2004), 31.
8 Jerome Christensen, *Romanticism at the End of History* (Baltimore, MD: Johns Hopkins University Press, 2004), 7.
9 Berlant, *Cruel Optimism*, 95–120.
10 Jacques Derrida, *Learning to Live Finally: An Interview with Jean Birnbaum*, trans. Pascale-Anne Brault and Michael Naas (Hoboken, NJ: Melville House, 2007), 46.
11 Sara Guyer, "The Rhetoric of Survival and the Possibility of Romanticism," *Studies in Romanticism* 46, no. 2 (2007): 252.
12 Thomas Hobbes, *Leviathan*, ed. Edwin Curley (Indianapolis: Hackett, 1994), 76.
13 Denis Diderot and Jean Le Rond D'Alembert, eds. *Encyclopédie, ou dictionnaire raisonné des sciences, des arts et des métiers*, ARTFL Encyclopédie Projet, ed. Robert Morrissey, http://encyclopedie.uchicago.edu/, 2008; my translation.
14 Hannah Arendt, *The Origins of Totalitarianism* (New York: Harcourt Brace, 1979), 139.
15 Kant, *Toward Perpetual Peace*, 72.
16 Michel Foucault, *"Society Must Be Defended": Lectures at the Collège de France, 1975–1976*, ed. Mauro Bertani and Alessandro Fontana, trans. David Macey (New York: Picador, 2003), 50–1, 47, 72.
17 David Bates, "Constitutional Violence," *Journal of Law and Society* 34, no. 1 (2007): 15.
18 Edmund Burke, "Three Letters Addressed to a Member of the Present Parliament, on the Proposals for Peace with the Regicide Directory of France,"

in *The Works of the Right Honorable Edmund Burke*, vol. 8 (London: F. and C. Rivington, 1801), 24, 26, 27.

19 William Hazlitt, *Collected Works of William Hazlitt*, vol. 3 (London: J. M. Dent & Co., 1902), 96.

20 David L. Clark, *Bodies and Pleasures in Late Kant* (Stanford, CA: Stanford University Press, forthcoming).

21 Kant, *Toward Perpetual Peace*, 87.

22 Rajan, "Mary Shelley's *Mathilda*," 44.

23 Kant, *Toward Perpetual Peace*, 73, 87.

24 Jaucourt, "Tranquillité, Paix, Calme," in *Encyclopédie*.

25 Giorgio Agamben, *Stanzas: Word and Phantasm in Western Culture* (Minneapolis: University of Minnesota Press, 1993), 7.

26 William Wordsworth, *The Major Works*, ed. Stephen Gill (Oxford: Oxford University Press, 1984), 29.

27 David Simpson, *Wordsworth, Commodification, and Social Concern* (Cambridge: Cambridge University Press, 2009).

28 Terry Eagleton, *The Ideology of the Aesthetic* (Oxford: Blackwell, 1990), 20.

29 Wordsworth, *The Major Works*, 147.

30 Geoffrey Hartman and Daniel T. O'Hara, eds., *The Geoffrey Hartman Reader* (New York: Fordham University Press, 2004), 392.

31 Marjorie Perloff, "Emily Dickinson and the Theory Canon," http://epc.buffalo.edu/authors/perloff/articles/dickinson.html, last accessed 29 August 2013.

32 Eve Kosofsky Sedgwick, "Paranoid Reading and Reparative Reading; or, You're So Paranoid, You Probably Think This Introduction Is About You," in *Novel Gazing: Queer Readings in Fiction* (Durham, NC: Duke University Press, 1997), 28.

33 Berlant, *Cruel Optimism*, 199.

34 Giorgio Agamben, *The Idea of Prose*, trans. Michael Sullivan and Sam Whitsitt (Albany: State University of New York Press, 1995), 81.

35 Peter Fenves, *Late Kant: Toward Another Law of the Earth* (New York: Routledge, 2003), 94.

36 Kant, *Toward Perpetual Peace*, 71.

37 Martin Heidegger, "Building Dwelling Thinking," in *Poetry, Language, Thought*, trans. Albert Hofstadter (New York: Perennial, 1971), 149. Italics in the original.

38 Wordsworth, *The Prelude*, 14.124–9.

CHAPTER 9

Living a ruined life
De Quincey's damage

Rei Terada

I. Understanding ruin

Suspiria de Profundis professes to be written from a condition in which "the ruin is understood to be absolute."[1] Ruin, however, is not synonymous with the end. Rather, it calls attention to a temporal tension, indicating both irrevocable damage and submersion in an ongoing process. De Quincey describes the resources that can be drawn from a condition that bears witness to an irreversible catastrophe, yet has continuing effects on experience. Attention to the permanence of psychic damage, in De Quincey's case, brings him a subsidiary skepticism toward conditions that make competing claims of inexorability. Ruin shifts him, especially, from the forms of gender and species he had previously known, generating a monstrous and productive novelty without ceasing to appear as ruin. Although De Quincey's framework is psychological, his sense of deviance relies on and returns to the social, and resonates especially with the concerns of readers in "dark times." Such readers may be interested in De Quincey's description of what happens after hope of recovery has been foregone.

The challenge is to take both of De Quincey's terms straightforwardly: "ruin" and "understood." For recent trauma theory, if not always Freud's own, can sometimes make it sound as though ruin were by definition what cannot be understood, at least at the time of its occurrence (thus trauma's primary feature of delayed response). Freud's emphasis on traumatic memory originates in his use of scenes of childhood sexuality as paradigms of trauma and his sense that the young child cannot understand sexual experience well enough to be traumatized by it at the time.[2] In Cathy Caruth's lastingly compelling account, trauma is the symptom of a catastrophic contact with reality and history that "arise[s] where *immediate understanding* may not." Caruth's claim is qualified by her carefully chosen

Thanks to Rebecca Schuman for her assistance with this chapter.

adjective "immediate": I take "immediate understanding" to mean understanding that coincides with the time of the disaster – the disaster "is not
fully perceived as it occurs" – as well as understanding that is transparent
or unmediated.[3] If the mind semi-automatically defends against the worst
catastrophes – where "the worst" is meant strongly, not just as something
very bad but as that which destroys one's very organization – then when
De Quincey explains that he understands ruin in the death of his best-
loved sister Elizabeth, the ruin is either not as absolute as he thinks it is, or
he does not really understand it. De Quincey's invocation of ruin will
appear in these terms to be a hyperbole that defends against mixed feelings,
perhaps disguising his guilt and disappointment at being able actually to
detach himself from his sister.

   Described in this way, De Quincey's condition might then be better
accounted for by theories of melancholy than of trauma. A way of
negotiating with loss which neither blots it out nor confronts it head on,
melancholy pertains to disasters that are not absolute: to objects that can
be identified as dead, in a certain way, and yet retained within one's given
psychic structure. In trauma, in contrast, the capacities of the given psyche,
including those of consciousness, are acknowledged to be overwhelmed.
Yet the ambiguity between disastrous external impact and unproductive
defense – which is more important? – that appears in the tension between
trauma and melancholy is also present within the theory of trauma, in
which initial trauma, understood as lack of defense, modulates into
defense.[4] In addition, it seems easier to theorize the overwhelming of the
system than the *filling* of capacity that must precede its overflow, and that
sometimes must stop just before the point of overflow. Often, an impact
assumed to have occurred is deduced only from an unconscious defense
that is supposed to be the result of too little defense.

   More than melancholy, then, trauma recognizes the limits of the given
psyche and damage to the ego, yet does not involve realizing this damage:
the possibility of realizing serious damage remains outside the boundary of
Freud's theory, while recent trauma theory reflects on damage through
reflection on the limits of understanding damage.[5] Philosophically, negative understanding is no small matter, and not even separable from positive
understanding. My point is not to minimize the value of coming to grips
with the limits of knowledge and experience, which seems eminently
therapeutic; in a different way, I will be emphasizing the same value. Still,
I'd like to explore co-existing possibilities that De Quincey suggests, on the
assumption that trauma, melancholy, mourning, and working through do
not exhaust the varieties of response to catastrophe.

The narratives of melancholy and trauma alike rely on Freud's theory of working through (*Durcharbeitung*), the normative model of psychic change from which they depart. Working through, in turn, is an incompletely explained phenomenon in Freud's oeuvre. "Remembering, Repeating, and Working Through" (1914), which I will come to in the last section of this essay, offers in place of a causal account of working through a patchwork of suggestions whose only active ingredient is temporary hypercathexis to the lost object. As I will review momentarily, Freud's connection elsewhere of "cathexis [*Besetzung*]" to "binding [*Bindung*]" helps to fill in some missing steps, but the theory of healthy response to loss remains indefinite. Freud's reader can only guess at the mechanisms of healthy mourning by bringing his entire thought on the removal of resistances to bear on pathological obstacles to mourning, and imagining the moderate flow of energy in the healthy state. But this still leaves a question at the center of Freud's work: how does the healthy psyche deal with very serious injury, such as that which must occur when the system fills to capacity with damaging stimuli, but does not overflow? What is the normal condition to which the pathological one of trauma corresponds?

If we set the familiar terms aside to explore the face value of De Quincey's contention that a catastrophe can be "understood to be absolute," other possibilities emerge, including those of change more radical and states of being queerer than may be allowed by the normative dynamics of trauma, melancholy, and working through. One thing we can notice already is that the healthy condition of realization seems to be worse than the pathological one of trauma and forgetting: does this condition lie outside Freud's theory because, by virtue of not being pathological, it suggests a kind of *objective* ruin, one that is beyond help? Instead of the normative claim that the healthy self recovers from its losses, De Quincey's account of ruin offers transformation without recovery – that is in fact the opposite of recovery: transformation that consists in damage, and in activity around damage, that is understood to be irredeemable. Now, according to Freud, working through inherently implies resistance: where one needs to work through, an obstacle to normal progress has already arisen. In light of De Quincey's account, it begins to look as though Freud struggles to explain how working through is possible because in certain situations, perhaps many situations, working through is neither possible nor called for. When the obstacle is not the displacement typical in melancholy – for instance, the desire to avoid feeling some relief that the love object is dead – but the as it were rational recognition of massive destruction, working through is not an option: one does not work through the ruination of one's world. Trauma is the defensive response; the healthy response, De Quincey's narrative suggests, is to undergo the damage in awareness that one is doing so, without a sense that there is an end to it.[6]

In what follows, I'll first make the case for De Quincey's commitment to ruin that is understood, treating De Quincey as a theorist of disaster who can illuminate the general problem. I'll then suggest that the invariance of this understanding in *Suspiria* is connected causally to his belief in the relative mutability of other aspects of natural order such as gender and species. As we will see, De Quincey does not work through his grief, but works around it.

II.   Depths of awareness

Exploring the obverse of trauma as the not fully known, *Suspiria de Profundis* describes the absorption of catastrophe against which trauma defends, that "worst" that survivors of trauma are surprised to have evaded. De Quincey declares that he completely understands at the time the enormity and finality of the loss of his sister Elizabeth when he is seven and she is eight (or in some accounts, nine). De Quincey's thought and writing is not and couldn't possibly be free of defense; he notes the "new strategem[s] of grief" (*S*, 120) that spring up in response to his very conviction that the worst *has* occurred and the impossibility of a zero degree of hope. What is possible is not that De Quincey's perception could be transparent, but that his insistence on understanding ruin is not itself one of these "strategem[s] of grief" – not primarily defensive – but a valid attempt to define catastrophe by its unusual ability to penetrate. De Quincey furnishes a paradigm at the beginning of the text when, expecting to overcome opium addiction for a third time, he instead "became profoundly aware that this was impossible" (90). De Quincey evokes here a panorama of consciousness, a sense of impossibility as far as his awareness extends. The problem is not that there is more to the disaster than he can know; it is that it's all he does know. What all the figures of depth, including the title figure, are doing in *Suspiria de Profundis* is rather claiming a totalization of awareness that characterizes catastrophe – positing that profundity is a feature of ruin.[7]

For De Quincey, profundity figures the interpenetration of mind and body. The dualism is set up only so that it may be overcome, so that seeming layers of the self may measure absorption and differentiate superficial from thorough diffusion. A conclusion is understood *deeply* when it is registered even by the involuntary body; yet it cannot be deep *understanding* unless it is also cognized consciously. Deep understanding is something like an undisplaced hysteria, perspicuous and based on a justifiable assessment of the state of affairs, which suffuses consciousness instead of taking its place.

In *Suspiria*, the possibility of a catastrophe understood both consciously and in the body is evidenced when De Quincey experiences physical manifestations of conscious understanding – signs of the "depth" of his understanding. These manifestations are less symptoms – since they are not displacements – than expressive gestures. De Quincey gives two examples: his visceral recoil from his sister's corpse in the crucial scene in which he steals into the bedroom where her body lies, and the "sigh from the depths" itself. In the bedroom scene, what he calls "the parting which should have lasted forever" (*S*, 107) fails to take place because he recognizes that Elizabeth is already too far gone – too dead to want to kiss.[8] So he had imagined it, he writes of his interlude with her corpse, but "so it was *not*" (105). De Quincey italicizes the negative here and again later, when he "languishe[s] for things 'which' (a voice from heaven seemed to answer through my own heart) '*can*not be granted'; and which, when again I languished, again the voice repeated, '*can*not be granted'" (121). As in the theodicies of Leibniz and the early Kant, his dialogue with the internalized wish-granter seems to find the edge of an omnipotence that is constrained by physical laws. The collapse of omnipotence under the pressure of reality, consciously registered by the emphatic *not*, informs De Quincey's hesitation to kiss.

In *Studies in Hysteria* (1895) and *Beyond the Pleasure Principle* (1920), Freud links traumatic repetition to conditions that suppress affect where it wants to be expressed. It seems at first as though we see such conditions here, where unanticipated repulsion truncates De Quincey's farewell performance. What happens in the bedroom may leave De Quincey with damage, as he believes, and with unspoken emotions. But De Quincey's reaction to the sight of Elizabeth and the knowledge it implies is neither evasive nor excessive. It is both the involuntary reflex of the living body before the dead one and an eloquent manifestation of the conscious realization: *I am alive; it is dead.* The deadness of his sister is disastrous – more than simply sorrowful – since it overturns De Quincey's entire self-organization, which has evolved in dialogue with his sister and assumed her continued presence. What he plans to put in place through the ritual in Elizabeth's bedroom is an internal object he can go on living with, a "parting which should have lasted forever" (*S*, 107). The difficulty, however, is *that* De Quincey understands that his sister is dead, and the "depth" to which he understands it, reflected not in the gestures he does not have the opportunity to complete, which anticipate a delicious defense, but in the *adequate* gesture in which he hesitates and knows why, unconsciously acknowledges his understanding by hesitating, and realizes consciously, to his horror, that he has done so.

The ruling figure of the sigh from the depths, like De Quincey's flinch before his sister's corpse, also registers an intake of perception, a "gather [ing] up." It happens just when the "sentiment which attends the sudden revelation that *all is lost*[,] silently is gathered up into the heart" (*S*, 91), and acknowledges intake (inhalation) with exhalation. The agreement of external and internal awareness is figured again in the "voice from heaven" that "answer[s] through [his] own heart" (121). The *suspiria* is telling in the way that the sound of an artery giving way would be if we could hear it – the sound of a heart breaking, not just the sentence "My heart is breaking" – yet accompanied by consciousness and even verbal consciousness. This circuit of recognition scorches the path that it travels, as though by the logic of pedagogies that hope that a realization learned will settle permanently in the body. De Quincey pays homage to such a logic in his peroration on Levana, a goddess of "human education": "not [of] the poor machinery that moves by spelling-books and grammars, but by that mighty system of central forces . . . which by passion, by strife, by temptation, by the energies of resistance, works forever upon children, – resting not day or night" (147).

III.   De Quincey unbound

One of Freud's main ways of discussing trauma is to remark that excitations that are brought on by catastrophe and may cause trauma are "unbound." Since *Suspiria* suggests an unconceptualized space between binding and trauma, it's helpful to revisit this part of Freud's theory. The theory of binding (*Bindung*) goes all the way back to *Studies in Hysteria* and the *Project for a Scientific Psychology* (1895), in which Freud describes energy as "free" or "bound" (*SE*, 1: 368).[9] That Freud's discussion of binding is important to the *Project*'s elaboration of "quantitative," material aspects of psychic function is already relevant to De Quincey's account of the sigh as the corporeal indication of realization. Both try to grasp the material basis of thought, in Freud's case in the dynamics of neuronal connections. In the *Project*, psychic investment results from the quantity and connectedness of thoughts: depth of commitment, and ultimately ego identity itself, is our name for a kind of mental strength in numbers. A cluster of thoughts and affects becomes an egoic "mass" with gravitational force to attract others, while an unbound, "*untamed [ungebändigt] mnemic* image" is one not yet attached to a mass (*SE*, 1: 381).[10] De Quincey famously develops the notion of the "involute," a ganglion of powerful associations, and like the early Freud, presents the concept in spatial terms.[11] The competing idea that psychic recovery is helped along by the construction of a narrative straightens out the involute, representing it sequentially; for both De Quincey and the early Freud, identity consists less in the order of thoughts than in their density. Since reified cathexes are also problematic, the implicit ideal of cathectic dynamics is an ego that is neither straitjacketed by its own bindings nor overwhelmed by stimuli inconveniently coming unbound.[12]

In *Beyond the Pleasure Principle*, Freud reverts to binding to explain how the excitations brought on by catastrophe destabilize one's energy system. In his description of the challenge of binding, stimulus threatens the sensitive core of the system. When something "provoke[s] a disturbance on a large scale of the functioning of the organism's energy,"

> there is no longer any possibility of preventing the mental apparatus from being flooded with large amounts of stimulus, and another problem arises instead – the problem of mastering the amounts of stimulus which have broken in and of binding them, in the psychical sense, so that they can then be disposed of.[13] (*SE*, 18: 29–30)

> [Die Überschwemmung des seelischen Apparats mit großen Reizmengen ist nicht mehr hintanzuhalten; es ergibt sich vielmehr eine andere Aufgabe, den Reiz zu bewältigen, die hereingebrochenen Reizmengen psychisch zu binden, um sie dann der Erledigung zuzuführen. (*GW*, 13: 29)]

In suggesting that the unwanted excitation is *unbound*, Freud does not state that it is *unconscious*. In fact, breaching the hardened outer layer of the organism, its "protective shield [*Reizschutz*]," requires interaction with the sensitive cortical core that "is later to become the system *cs.*" (*SE*, 18: 28; *GW*, 13: 26). Freud's invented term "Reizschutz," which straightforwardly enough denotes "stimulus shield," indexes the sexual overtone of the stimulation involved, since "*schutz*" connotes a prophylactic device. Freud's future tense – the cortex "is later to become" consciousness ["das spätere System Bw"] – reflects a certain blurriness of the entity he imagines, a blurriness that we also see in his frequent reluctance to draw a boundary between consciousness and the preconsciousness that mediates between consciousness and unconsciousness.[14] This passage, however, is blurry because its target is in motion. It narrates how the development of the protective shield, by its hardening through "the ceaseless impact [*unausgesetztem Anprall*] of external stimuli on the surface" (*SE*, 18: 26; *GW*, 13: 25), creates the conditions for an also developing consciousness that could not evolve without the shield. The more the shield is "baked through [*durchgebrannt*]" (*SE*, 18: 26; *GW*, 13: 25), the more conscious the inner cortex can afford to be: "by its death, the outer layer has saved all the deeper ones from a similar fate – unless, that is to say, stimuli reach it which are so strong that they break through the protective shield" (*SE*, 18: 27; *GW*, 13: 27). The core that forms in tandem with the self-sacrificing shield *is* the ever-evolving "system *cs*."; when disastrous stimuli breach the shield and suffuse the "deeper layers [*eine gewisse Tiefe*]" of the mind, then, those which are responsible for "reception [*Reizaufnahme*]" (*SE*, 18: 27; *GW*, 13: 25), it can only be the system *cs*. that is flooded. Until overflow and trauma, the problem is neither unconsciousness nor uneven consciousness, but the difficulty of binding that of which the mind is unwillingly aware.

In the discussion that follows, the system's reaction to the breach of the shield assumes that diffusion of energy throughout *cs*. – "being flooded" – is the worst of possibilities:

> And how shall we expect the mind to react to this invasion? Cathectic energy is summoned from all sides to provide sufficiently high cathexes of energy in the environs of the breach. An "anticathexis" on a grand scale is set up, for whose benefit all the other psychical systems are impoverished, so that the remaining psychical systems are extensively paralysed or reduced. We must endeavor to draw a lesson from examples such as this and use them as a basis for our metapsychological speculations. From the present case, then, we infer that a system which is itself highly cathected is capable of taking up an additional stream of fresh inflowing energy and of converting it into quiescent cathexis, that is of binding it psychically. The higher the system's own quiescent cathexis, the greater seems to be its binding force; conversely, therefore, the lower its cathexis, the less capacity it will have for taking up inflowing energy and the more violent must be the consequences of such a breach in the protective shield against stimuli. (*SE*, 18: 30)

> [Und was können wir als die Reaktion des Seelenlebens auf diesen Einbruch erwarten? Von allen Seiten her wird die Besetzungsenergie aufgeboten, um in der Umgebung der Einbruchstelle entsprechend hohe Energiebesetzungen zu schaffen. Es wird eine großartige "Gegenbesetzung" hergestellt, zu deren Gunsten alle anderen psychischen Systeme verarmen, so daß eine ausgedehnte Lähmung oder Herabsetzung der sonstigen

psychischen Leistung erfolgt. Wir suchen aus solchen Beispielen zu lernen, unsere metapsychologischen Vermutungen an solche Vorbilder anzulehnen. Wir ziehen also aus diesem Verhalten den Schluß, daß ein selbst hochbesetztes System imstande ist, neu hinzukommende strömende Energie aufzunehmen, sie in ruhende Besetzung umzuwandeln, also sie psychisch zu "binden." Je höher die eigene ruhende Besetzung ist, desto größer wäre auch ihre bindende Kraft; umgekehrt also, je niedriger seine Besetzung ist, desto weniger wird das System für die Aufnahme zuströmender Energie befähigt sein, desto gewaltsamer müssen dann die Folgen eines solchen Durchbruches des Reizschutzes sein. (*GW*, 13: 30)]

As binding anchors and contains energy, energy is unbound if nothing catches it before it seeps through and through the system. To put it another way, unbound energy metastasizes, restructuring the system by affecting each part of it. Metastasization – the suffusion of something harmful – would seem to be the counterpart of psychoanalysis's common use of the figure of metabolization, the suffusion of a nutrient,[15] and so calls attention to the permeability implied by the latter as well. Freud's accounts of "working out" or "working off" energies, too, suggest that certain energies may be so "worked in" as to transform the organism altogether.

The idea of worked-in energies is consistent with Freud's account of trauma as a break-in. But while Freud's theory of trauma concentrates on unwanted excitation's subsequent career in the unconscious, from where it makes itself known indirectly by deforming consciousness or appearing in disguises of compromise,[16] the logic of binding insinuates that the unconscious or conscious status of an experience or memory may be less important than the control of its mobility, and that its mobility is greatest when it is conscious.

The sometimes unfortunately free, unfortunately complete nature of conscious thoughts is emphasized by Breuer in *Studies in Hysteria* and carried forward by Freud. Although there may not be a single place where Breuer establishes the distinction between primary and secondary processes,[17] his psychic topography in these pages is sensitive. Breuer discusses what Freud terms the breach of the shield, using the figure of "damage done to the system itself through a break-down of its insulation" (*SE*, 2: 199; *Studien*, 177). But what is most interesting for my purposes is his speculation that *conscious* thoughts and affects are frighteningly free. The power and danger of conscious ideas, he writes, is their aptitude for association, which can bring the brain "into a state of higher facilitation [*Zustand höherer Bahnung*]" (*SE*, 2: 196; *Studien*, 173). In contrast, in sleep "ideas that emerge do not, as in waking life, activate all the ideas which are connected with them"; the deeper the sleep, the more "association is defective and incomplete" (*SE*, 2: 193; *Studien*, 168). In sleep we are as a rule not likely to act physically on our thoughts. But "when we are fully awake every act of will initiates the corresponding movement; sense-impressions become conscious perceptions; and ideas are associated with the whole store present in potential consciousness," reflecting the fact that the conscious brain is "completely ... traversable [*gangbar*]" by whatever psychic energy it holds (*SE*, 2: 193; *Studien*, 168).[18]

The other, advantageous side of conscious thought's mobility is that "complete" thought, by trending toward motor action, is also likely to lead to discharge. Freud draws on Breuer's material for his conclusion in *Beyond the Pleasure Principle* that "resistance ... to passage [*Übergangswiderstand*] from one element to another would no longer exist" in the system *cs*. (*SE*, 18: 26; *GW*, 13: 26), as though consciousness were the Canada of thoughts on the lam. Only unconsciousness, Freud hypothesizes, is scarred by mnemic traces; mnemic traces and conscious thoughts cannot simultaneously exist. As De Quincey's account reminds us, however, there are times when conscious thoughts are worse than scars: when damaging, they are active damage.

These worries about the liabilities of consciousness underpin the theory of trauma, replacing the problem of mnemic scarring with a new problem. If conscious thoughts are so easy to release, why panic when the system *cs*. gets taken by surprise? The concerted action of the system, rushing from "all sides" to contain awareness, implies that it regards comprehensive realization as both a plausible possibility and as the most damaging of outcomes. It is not hard to see why that might be. While the symptoms of unconscious conflict – displacements, resistances, blanks in memory – are auto-immune effects in which one's defenses do more than is convenient, but are at least doing something to protect the ego, the ill effects of conscious ruin are more invidious to the extent that they are not defensive at all. On the other hand, in *The Interpretation of Dreams*, Freud stresses more the embattled quality of consciousness itself. It is here that he assigns to preconsciousness the role of exploring thoughts before either releasing them to consciousness or cathecting them in a way that would "avoid releasing the unpleasure [*Unlustentbindung*]" (*SE*, 5: 601; *GW*, 2: 606). Noting that a secondary process that takes place in preconsciousness raises the possibility of "thought seeking to convey itself into the preconscious so as to be able then to force its way through into consciousness" (*SE*, 5: 610; *GW*, 2: 615),[19] he goes on to observe that the distinctness of consciousness is by no means pure, and that in fact consciousness is not necessarily an achievement to write home about. In that case, damage done by the breach of the protective shield would be less likely to be compensated by the benefits of consciousness's access to discharge, and so ameliorated by later actions.

The theory of trauma radicalizes the threat posed by consciousness by focusing on the more-than-maximal moment when overstimulation whites out. By doing so, it proposes that trauma is the residue of too much, not too little consciousness, yet skips over the entire arena of conscious injury, as though the breach were *instantly* traumatic. Between melancholy defense and traumatic excess, both mainly unconscious, there is little theoretical articulation of what happens after consciousness is stimulated and before its capacity is overrun – even though this territory would seem to be the area that corresponds to suffering.

If we stop reading Freud here (for there seems to be nothing left to read) and begin to extrapolate, we can imagine several possibilities that might occupy this space. Part of the consciousness of damage, however great, would presumably belong to that healthy reaction to what would otherwise be trauma on which Freud is relatively silent. A conscious awareness of what would otherwise be trauma would mean awareness of the effect of the breach of the system *cs.*, namely, "permanent disturbances of the manner in which the energy operates" (*Introductory Lectures on Psychoanalysis* [1916–17], *SE*, 16: 275; *GW*, 11: 284). Technically, permanence is not something you can "see" – but De Quincey's indicative gestures, as we read above, are as close to the sudden apprehension of permanent ruin as one can get. Such awareness arises where a working-in too large-scale and well-grounded to be corrected for precludes working through and defense alike. While one might still want to call De Quincey's suffering traumatic since we have preserved the features of the broken barrier, systemic crisis, and lasting effects, other features of what counts as trauma would need to be changed: it would consist not in missing the catastrophe but in getting it, getting it to an extent compared to which traumatic forgetting *and* successful binding are both obfuscatory. If the catastrophe involved is instead characterized as automatically exceeding the capacities of the organism to register it, the problem is not that we experience ruin and cannot recover from it, but that we cannot experience it and cannot recover from a non-experience. What De Quincey claims to undergo, instead, is excessive *to binding*, yet not to consciousness, nor to a combination of conscious and unconscious understanding.

In *Studies in Hysteria*, Breuer and Freud leave open the possibility of something that is not abreacted because of its very nature. Classifying the circumstances under which patients' emotional responses seem to fail, they notice a "first group" of "cases in which the patients have not reacted to a psychical trauma *because the nature of the trauma excluded a reaction, as in the case of the apparently irreparable loss of a loved person*" (*SE*, 2: 10, my italics; *GW*, 1: 89). When this category disappears, we are left with a self that in theory can bind any excitation that the body survives. This hypothetically adept self works in concert with recent trauma theory's ultimately comforting idea that the worst has been evaded: it posits as its limit a worst-case outside consciousness instead of ruin inside consciousness. Seen from this angle, Freud's middle-period theories of pathological mourning resist the possibility of damage one may have to undergo and understand comprehensively. Breuer and Freud hint at this defensive impulse already in *Studies in Hysteria* by adding the qualifier "apparently" to their formulation: "the apparently irreparable loss of a loved person." "Apparently [*erscheinend*]" suggests that the patient doesn't wish to understand that the loss may in some way be repaired (for instance, by finding a new object), and in fact the passage goes on to conflate patients with "apparently irreparable" losses with those who merely "wished to forget ... distressing things" associated to their losses (*SE*, 2: 10).[20] But the hypothesis of the wishful patient may itself be wishful in comparison to psychoanalysis's own mourning over cases that are irreparable, and not pathological: over the existence of that to which pathology is a defense.

In this way we return to De Quincey's idea that the effect of understanding a catastrophe, suffusing mind and body alike, resembles a hysteria well-grounded in reality – a nonpathological condition of which pathological hysteria would be the imitation. Breuer envisions such a condition when he writes that excitement can spread from the brain "to the peripheral organs" and notes that "such phenomena cannot be described as hysterical" if their affect "has an objective basis" (*SE*, 2: 204, 205; *Studien*, 182, 183). If we take up the neglected idea that ruin may come through and as understanding, the task then becomes to conceive of a nonpathological response to ruin that is not working through. One can see why such a response could be mistaken for melancholy, but some other notion is needed – perhaps that of Adorno's "damaged life" – to name the project of living with ruin: living a ruined life nonpathologically. This project begins when De Quincey hears the door of recovery close. As we'll see, the motive to imagine a life the possibility of which is not acknowledged socially, and therefore seems "against nature," makes the ruined life a queer project.

III. Working around

De Quincey is a mutant both in substance and in attitude, in his view, because of events "of a nature to alter the whole economy of [his] mind" (*S*, 91) and to leave a physiological weakness (to which he discreetly refers as "a weakness in one organ" [89]).[21] Now, these changes, precisely because De Quincey regards them as exempt from being worked through, generate other mutations, since everything must work around them. That is to say that they have the power to revoke orders: their resistance passively bends forces that otherwise would seem insuperable. So, reflecting on change in the form of damage to himself, and at the same time understanding that damage to be the permanent condition of his life, De Quincey begins to discover effects of Elizabeth's death different from those offered by redemptive or ameliorative schemes that would seek to repair or soften its impact. Instead, he goes with the damage, in spite or because of the likelihood that the damaged self will be seen as deviant.

De Quincey's comparison between permanent change wrought by catastrophe – change that cannot be changed, as it were – and other forms of possible change is reflected in two contrasting passages. The first is his famous rejection of Paul's version of transfiguration in First Corinthians, "We shall be *changed*":

> when I heard those dreadful words of St. Paul applied to my sister, namely, that she should be raised a spiritual body, nobody can suppose that selfishness, or any other feeling than that of agonizing love, caused the rebellion of my heart against them. I knew already that she was to come again in beauty and power. I did not now learn this for the first time. And that thought, doubtless, made my sorrow sublimer; but also it made it deeper. For here lay the sting of it, namely, in the fatal words – "We shall be *changed*" ... if a mother were robbed of her child at two years old, by gypsies, and the same child were restored to her at twenty, a fine young man, but divided by a sleep as it were of death from all remembrances that could restore the broken links of their once tender connection, – would she not feel her grief unhealed, and her heart defrauded? Undoubtedly she would ... It is true that the sorrowing person will also be changed eventually, but that must be by death. And a prospect so remote as that, and so alien from our present nature, cannot console us in an affliction which is not remote, but present – which is not spiritual, but human. (*S*, 109)

De Quincey rejects the promise of change for his sister because her transfiguration is desirable only relative to a degradation that should never have occurred, and because he and Elizabeth would have had eternity anyway but had only one chance for a mortal life together. Even if Elizabeth were resurrected, their ruined earthly lives would remain uncompensated. The passage is not so much a rejection of the plausibility of immortality as of its ability to obviate living.

First Corinthians continues,

> So when this corruptible shall have put on incorruption, and this mortal shall have put on immortality, then shall be brought to pass the saying that is written, Death is swallowed up in victory. O death, where is thy sting? O grave, where is thy victory? The sting of death is sin; and the strength of sin is the law.[22]

De Quincey answers these words in another passage, only two pages later, that details the permanent effect of Elizabeth's death on himself. This second passage marks the revolution of the kingdom of ruin on earth:

> Now, however, all was changed; and for anything which regarded my sister's memory, in one hour I received a new heart. Once in Westmoreland I saw a case resembling it. I saw a ewe suddenly put off and abjure her own nature, in a service of love, – yes, slough it as completely as ever serpent sloughed his skin. Her lamb had fallen into a deep trench, from which all escape was hopeless, without the aid of man. And to a man she advanced boldly, bleating clamorously, until he followed her and rescued her beloved. Not less was the change in myself ... And when I was told insultingly to cease "my girlish tears," that word "*girlish*" had no sting for me. (*S*, 110–11)

Given the contrast with the former passage, we might read De Quincey's emphasis, "*now*, however, all *was* changed." Paul's promised transfiguration is "fatal" – a continuation of the logic of death, as Donne stresses in his own allusion to Paul's rhetoric: "Death, thou shalt dye."[23] For Paul, the "sting of death" is its finality, but this sting can be activated only by sin in the context of the true finality of the law. Its effects are complementarily able to be suspended by the law of redemption at the cost of the transformation of the sinful. For De Quincey, that very sting of sin that Paul would remove cannot be removed for the duration of life, and becomes a force for change around itself for the very reason that it is fixed.

The trope of the sting first appears in *Suspiria* before the citation of First Corinthians, when De Quincey observes that through his sister he was "stung, by the necessity of being loved" (*S*, 101). The Greek etymology of "trauma," we may recall, connotes a wound that breaks the skin;[24] De

Quincey's reflection that "necessity" is the wounding agent repeats again the idea that only an inarguable piece of reality punctures the defenses in this way. Hélène Cixous observes that a sting "leaves behind and takes away, annoys and excites at the same time," and that "stigmata are traces of a sting" that inscribe the body with the traits of the sacred outlaw: "one can be stung by the bug of (*se piquer de*) literature or philosophy as others can shoot (*se piquer de*) drugs."[25]

Being stung thus inaugurates the ruined way of life – already contains it, in a way – that De Quincey depicts in *Confessions* and *Suspiria*. Like the energy that eludes capture, the physical residue of past drug use compels its own renewal. Addiction's sting lies in its power to institute a new physical reality beyond dispute as fact, however undesirable it may be as value. It is the mode of living in which energies that cannot be bound reorganize one's economy, overturning previous commitments in their path. Its accompanying physiological and psychological changes are "objective," like the mirror image of hysteria Breuer imagines.

At stake in the changes wrought in De Quincey's body is deformation of the natural order,[26] expressed in terms of innovation in gender and species. The ewe of Westmoreland resembles a serpent because she changes her given nature – although, on another level, this ability to change one's nature must also be a heretofore unknown, given possibility. The association between the serpent that sloughs its skin, the sting that breaks the skin, and the trauma that breaches the protective barrier suggests that for De Quincey a nonpathological response to catastrophe is to shed the skin and continue in an unheard-of state that nonetheless was an unforeseen possibility of the organism, like Schreber who realizes that he must become female in the service of a heretofore unknown ontological order. So the ewe exceeds the traditional abilities of sheep to address a man; De Quincey returns the gesture, treating the ewe's appeal as just another in a series of psychological anecdotes which remind him of himself (a relation of "I and ewe"?). A new and in a broad sense queer era has begun, in which boys may legitimately be called girlish, the personal experiences of sheep are resources for human self-understanding, and prose is deformed beyond genre in ways that have come to be thought of as De Quincey's invention. While De Quincey's flirtation with exception may seem fantastic – he claims to believe that in his case "the whole economy of the dreaming faculty had been convulsed beyond all precedents on record" (*S*, 137) – his abjuration of nature's laws is not fantastic to the extent that it is truly unclear where natural laws end and social ones begin.

De Quincey's considerations of gender and species often occur simultaneously or in close proximity. His unapologetic tears at the death of a
kitten in *Suspiria* and at Kate Wordsworth's death in the account left by
Henry Crabb Robinson indicate his willingness to occupy illegible territory. Crabb Robinson writes that De Quincey's "no doubt" genuine grief
was "in danger of being mistaken for a puling and womanly weakness,"[27]
but this is exactly the insult by which De Quincey refuses to be offended.
He makes a practice of using "seals from young ladies, when closing [his]
letters" (*S*, 147); and, as Catherine Robson points out, appropriates from
Wordsworth his "account of heavenly infancy and all its feminized accre-
tions [but, unlike Wordsworth] . . . applies this model to his own life, even
though the move necessarily entails a gender crossing."[28]

Critics have noted that De Quincey's project is a broadly queer textual
development of what he calls "a power not contented with reproduction"
(*S*, 157). Sarah Dillon, for example, has argued that De Quincey's palimp-
sestic psychological model is a "queer structure in which are intertwined
multiple and varying inscriptions" of "'masculinity' and 'femininity,' 'heterosexuality' and 'homosexuality.'"[29] De Quincey's reflections on social
and natural constraints on animals extend the same interest in the question
of natural order. De Quincey recalls that "it was in vain to tell me that all
people, who had property out of doors to protect, chained up dogs in the
same way" as in his guardian's household (*S*, 123) and is upset to learn that
saving the life of a spider hurts the chances of flies: "it troubled my musing
mind to perceive that the welfare of one creature might stand upon the
ruin of another" (126). His solicitude for insects indicates not just his
propensity for sentimentality, but his attention to the entire order and its
principles of economy and reproduction. In this De Quincey claims that
he resembles the slave who takes a distance from nature because "the earth,
our general mother," is "for *him* a step-mother" (151). As a measure for the
perception of social phenomena, De Quincey's awareness of "things
'which . . . *can*not be granted'" (*S*, 121) thus sets a high standard for
inevitability; it is "in vain to tell [him] that all people" do something
(123), for example chain others.[30] De Quincey's conviction is therefore
stronger than the idea that things *must be made* different: it is that one
thing in nature – his own being – has already been made different,
although this meant the physical alteration of the brain to an extent that
had once seemed impossible.[31] The damage to De Quincey cannot be
greater to him, in the sense that if it were any greater, he would traumat-
ically cease to feel it; and it can't be less, in that it involves an apprehension
of reality too well-grounded to evade and a stimulus too massive to work

through. The damage of which he is aware violates the order of his world, and its gravity pulls at anything that can be moved – at all ideas that prove to be connected by convention and do not, like real necessities, belong among those things that "*can*not be granted."[32] As Freud points out, one may mourn not only for a person or a love but for a cause, a community, a civilization. If binding obfuscates catastrophes in comparison to comprehension that cannot be bound, from a social perspective trauma on the one hand and binding and working through on the other begin to look like defenses of the social body against the mutation that would be effected by the unbound understanding of its ruin.

De Quincey's narrative thus leads to the nineteenth- and early twentieth-century culture of decadence, where ruin as an ongoing process – even a "lifestyle" – is reviled and dignified as perverse and creative. Nietzsche registers both reactions when he reflects that "nihilism" can signal both creativity and despair.[33] In *An Outline of Psychoanalysis* (1940) Freud, for his part, places the unbinding of energy on the side of the destructive instincts on the reasoning that "to undo connections" is "to destroy things" (*SE*, 23: 148; *GW*, 17: 71) – a formulation that conveys anxiety that whatever is not actively preserved eventually falls apart. His calling this unbinding "destruction" registers his strong protest against what might otherwise be viewed as a natural phenomenon, neither good nor bad, like the expansion of the universe. Many of the attitudes and styles called decadent, most of all queer ones, are of course not really destructive or decay-haunted in any way.[34] Yet, as De Quincey helps to explain, by starting from the consciousness of a ruined life one may arrive at unintelligible ideas and experiences which are likely to be perceived as queer and which cannot be assimilated to recovery or, in any simple way, to growth. The appeal of such a life is its ability to bear witness to the impact of certain events and to make conceptual room for the notion of *things that should not have happened*. The permanence of the damage and its symmetrical relation to disaster form a memorial that, unlike an encrypted object, does not purport to keep a version of Elizabeth alive or to become her. Instead, De Quincey becomes different.

IV. Damage

"Remembering, Repeating, and Working-Through" movingly traces Freud's own struggle to integrate his experiences as an analyst with limit and failure, to the point at which these seem to be what the essay works through. Freud begins by reminding his readers of the itinerary of psychoanalytic theory. He characterizes each phase by what it learns to give up: "when hypnosis had been *given up*, the task became one of discovering from the patient's free associations what he failed to remember." Direct abreaction is then "replaced by the expenditure of work" upon resistances. "Finally, there was evolved the consistent technique used today, in which *the analyst gives up* the attempt to bring a particular moment or problem into focus. *He contents himself* with studying whatever is present for the time being on the surface of the patient's mind" (*SE*, 12: 147, my italics; *GW*, 10: 126). Once in dialogue with the patient's resistance, Freud writes, the sensitive analyst "has nothing else to do than to wait and let things take their course, a course which cannot be avoided nor always hastened." The analyst's "waiting" "allow[s] the patient time to become more conversant with this resistance with which he has now become acquainted," and it is now this "becom[ing] more conversant," more familiar with something already known, scarcely distinguishable from awareness of being over time, that Freud identifies with working through: "one must allow the patient time to become more conversant with this resistance . . . to *work through* it, to overcome it, by continuing, in defiance of it, the analytic work" (*SE*, 12: 155; *GW*, 10: 135). Paralleling the patient's struggle against resistance over time, the analyst gradually gives up on catalytic techniques that manifest his own fantasy of omnipotence.

"Remembering, Repeating, and Working Through" stages (indeed, symptomatically repeats) in professional terms Freud's core thesis of living beings' unwilling encounter with reality. There is nothing wrong with this unwillingness. As a therapist, Freud certainly ought to be reluctant to forego techniques that might shorten patients' suffering. If the story sounds familiar, it is because narratives of this kind have been written over and over by analysts to the present day, each of whom learns for herself to give up more and do less.[35] In a completely non-ironic sense, such givings-up are the very location of analytic success.

This entirely understandable reluctance to give up, I suggest, also shapes trauma theory. The conceptual vacancy I noted – the absence of a healthy counterpart to damage, an other of pathological trauma – reads like an attempt to avoid what must be the most painful of human experiences: the deep awareness of serious and permanent damage. Such an awareness transgresses the binarism of the normal and pathological, combining a nonpathological – i.e., reality-based – perception with an observed path-ology; it is no more impossible logically, however, than watching your leg being sawn off without losing your mind. Short of traumatic blackout, it is possible, if far from inevitable, to be aware of irreparable damage.

To be beyond the reach of psychoanalytic technique in this respect should not mean to be beyond the mention of psychoanalytic theory, whose highest achievements have to do with making room for the non-teleological. But an understanding of ruin is difficult to theorize because the very reluctance to notice unwelcome facts centrally noted by Freud tends to make us take awareness for healing and transformation as progress. When I wrote that as a result of Elizabeth's death, De Quincey "becomes different," I could have said instead that he "becomes damaged." I have written this idea in two different ways to show that we tend to assume that becoming different is a good thing, exchanging growth for change. It is not hard to see even damage – perhaps with the help of Nietzsche or Hegel – as some kind of growth: we are all too willing.

Is damage, then, perhaps neither good nor bad? Adorno, the expert on damaged life, barely theorizes it. The word "damage" [*Schade, Schädigung*] scarcely appears in *Minima Moralia*. Adorno's main discussions of the concept – and they are fleeting – occur in "The Meaning of Working Through [*Aufarbeitung*] the Past" (1959) and in his essay on Stravinsky (implicitly an essay on postwar culture, 1962–3). In the former, he remarks of postwar Germany,

> collective narcissism was severely damaged by the collapse of Hitler's regime, but the damage occurred at the level of mere factuality, without individuals making themselves conscious of it and thereby coping with it. This is the social-psychological relevance of talk about an unmastered past. Also absent is the panic that, according to Freud's theory in *Group Psychology and the Ego*, sets in whenever collective identifications break apart ... Even in the face of the obvious catastrophe the collective Hitler integrated has *held together*.
>
> [Dieser kollektive Narzißmus ist durch den Zusammenbruch des Hitlerregimes aufs schwerste geschädigt worden. Seine Schädigung ereignete sich im Bereich der bloßen Tatsächlichkeit, ohne daß die Einzelnen sie sich bewußt gemacht hätten und dadurch mit ihr fertig geworden wären. Das ist der sozialpsychologisch zutreffende Sinn der Rede von der unbewältigten Vergangenheit. Auch jene Panik blieb aus, die nach Freuds Theorie aus 'Massenpsychologie und Ich-Analyse' dort sich einstellt, wo kollektive Identifikationen zerbrechen ... Noch angesichts der offenbaren Katastrophe hat das durch Hitler integrierte Kollektiv *zusammengehalten*.][36]

Here the value or harm of damage to what libidinal ties hold together depends on the value of the entity binding has created. Damage to the collectivity created by identifications to Hitler is just what is called for; it is up to "individuals" to "[make] themselves conscious of it."[37]

The possible separation between the individual and the collective in "The Meaning of Working Through the Past" deflects discussion of damage to oneself, which is much harder to perceive as neutral. Even in the case of individuals unjustly damaged by modernity, however, Adorno still advocates living one's damage [*Beschädigung*]. The art forms he promotes, rather like De Quincey's ruined prose, show "damage within order," as he writes of Stravinsky:

> The sections he strings together may not be identical and yet may never be anything qualitatively different. This is why there is damage instead of development. The wounds are inflicted by time, something which identity finds offensive and which in truth does not allow identity to persist.
>
> [Seine gereihten Felder dürfen nicht dasselbe und können doch nichts qualitative Verschiedenes sein. Darum tritt ihre Beschädigung anstelle von Entwicklung. Ihre Wundmale werden von der Zeit geschlagen, an der das Identische sich stößt und die in Wahrheit Identität verweigert.][38]

The individual who remains conscious during modernity, for Adorno, need *only* remain conscious during modernity in order to be damaged, and if unconscious is worse than damaged. The notion of such damage captures something additional to, if compatible with, the living on posited by survivorship, as damage constitutes a kind of judgment on the condition that produced it.

Adorno's call for reflection on postwar damage envisions "seriously working upon the past, that is, through a lucid consciousness breaking its power to fascinate."[39] It is interesting that Adorno is optimistic that consciousness "cope[s] with" damage. Yet, inspired by the example of Freud's gradual release of analytic omnipotence and mindful of the blank in the theory of trauma where the nonpathological response to catastrophe might be, I would also want to leave room for consciousness of damage that it is not possible to work through. Adorno comes to a better and, to my mind, more fully analytic conclusion when he writes of Stravinsky's wounded music that "time . . . in truth does not allow identity to persist," as does Freud when he remarks in *Beyond the Pleasure Principle* that the destructive instinct "at last . . . succeeds in killing the individual," and all the sooner if "his libido has been used up or fixated in a disadvantageous way" (*SE*, 18: 150; *GW*, 13: 149). The trace of animism in both of these sentences protests the state of affairs they describe, writing as though time and the death instinct were intentionally malevolent entities, and indeed there is no reason why they should not protest, since their conclusions are necessary without being acceptable. They enhance the available theories of response to catastrophe by being able, like De Quincey, to imagine damage that one does not work through, not because one is insufficiently aware of it but because the best life available to be lived is a ruined life.

NOTES

1 Thomas De Quincey, *Suspiria de Profundis, Confessions of an English Opium-Eater and Other Writings*, ed. Grevel Lindop (Oxford: Oxford University Press, 1985), 91; hereafter cited parenthetically as *S*, followed by page number.
2 Sigmund Freud and Josef Breuer, *Studies in Hysteria* (1895), in *Standard Edition of the Complete Psychological Works of Sigmund Freud*, trans. James Strachey, vol. 2 (London: Hogarth Press, 1955), 7; *Studien über Hysterie* (Leipzig: Franz Deuticke, 1895), 87; hereafter cited parenthetically as *Studien*, by page number. Hereafter all references to Freud's writings are from the *Standard Edition*, cited parenthetically as *SE*, by volume and page number; all references to Freud's original German, except where noted, are from *Gesammelte Werke, Chronologisch Geordnet*, 17 vols. in 16, ed. Anna Freud, E. Bibring, W. Hoffer, E. Kris, and O. Isakower (London: Imago, 1963), cited as *GW*, by volume and page number. Jean Laplanche develops this idea into the theory of implantation, in which sexual parental messages transmitted in early childhood fail to be metabolized because they are too enigmatic. See Jean Laplanche, "Seduction, Persecution, Revelation," in *Essays on Otherness*, trans. Philip Slotkin (New York: Routledge, 1999), 166–96.
3 Cathy Caruth, *Unclaimed Experience: Trauma, Narrative, and History* (Baltimore, MD: Johns Hopkins University Press, 2006), 11, 18. I don't believe in completely transparent understanding, and find the absoluteness of De Quincey's terms unhelpful, even though it is the ruin and not the understanding that he calls "absolute." But I do think that De Quincey challenges both the temporal strictures on occurrences that we now call "traumatic" and the supposed boundaries of the understanding involved in trauma by raising the question of what it would mean if catastrophes were understood deeply at the time of their occurrence. *Suspiria* answers the question by proposing an understanding that pervades the living being consciously, even if some of it is also pre- and unconscious. Such a comprehensive understanding exemplifies the figurative "depth" of *Suspiria*. Caruth notes that a main element of Freud's late theory of traumatic fright is the syncopation of proleptic fear with threat: "the fact that, not being experienced in *time*, it [the threat] has not yet been fully known" (62). For a similar model, see Shoshana Felman and Dori Laub, *Testimony: Crises of Witnessing in Literature Psychoanalysis, and History* (London: Routledge, 1992). The "affect of fright" ("der Schreckaffect") appears in Freud's work on hysteria as well, as in his early "On the Psychical Mechanism of Hysterical Phenomena" (1893): "what produces the result [of traumatic hysteria] is not the mechanical factor but the affect of fright, the *psychical* trauma" (*SE*, 3: 31; *GW*, 1: 84).

4 Laplanche and Pontalis comment that Freud's early "highlighting of the defensive conflict in the genesis of hysteria and, more generally, in that of the 'neuro-psychoses of defense,' does not imply that the function of the trauma is weakened, but it does complicate the theory of the trauma. . . [S]everal texts of the period . . . expose or presuppose a well-defined thesis tending to explain how the traumatic event triggers the setting-up by the ego of a 'pathological defense' (of which repression constituted the model for Freud at this point) operating in accordance with the primary process, instead of the normal defenses generally used against an unpleasurable event (e.g. diversion of attention)" (Jean Laplanche and J.-P. Pontalis, *The Language of Psycho-Analysis*, trans. Donald Nicholson-Smith [New York: Norton, 1973], 467).

5 In some accounts the survivor's first order of business is to deal with the unrepresentability of the trauma and the disorientation of survival – the peculiarity of finding oneself still there after ruin. See Ann Smock's sensitive *What Is There to Say? Blanchot, Melville, Des Forêts, Beckett* (Lincoln: University of Nebraska Press, 2003). Caruth also argues that "the dreams and flashbacks of the traumatized . . . bear witness to a survival that exceeds the very claims and consciousness of the one who endures" (*Unclaimed*, 60). Caruth thus takes the repetition symptomatic of trauma to be an effort to "*claim one's own survival*" (64). Ruth Leys's criticism of recent trauma theory's focus on the unrepresentable singles out what she sees as the consequence, that trauma is considered "a purely external event that befalls a fully constituted subject" (*Trauma: A Genealogy* [Chicago: University of Chicago Press, 2000], 299).

6 Jonathan Lear's *Radical Hope: Ethics in the Face of Cultural Devastation* (Cambridge, MA: Harvard University Press, 2008) explores related issues by tracking what he sees as the healthy response by the Crow chief Plenty Coups to the annihilation of the Crow way of life. Such a situation marks an objective limit of psychoanalysis, not a failing of it. Jacques Derrida explores this structure with regard to the concept of the resistance "of" rather than "to" psychoanalysis. See Jacques Derrida, *Resistances of Psychoanalysis* (1996), trans. Peggy Kamuf, Pascale-Anne Brault, and Michael Naas (Stanford, CA: Stanford University Press, 1998).

7 Of course I mean not that our capacity for awareness is total, but that such as it is, it can be flooded.

8 John Barrell points out that Elizabeth's head would have been deformed by her hydrocephalus, and speculates that De Quincey may, in addition, have seen her after her autopsy (despite his avowals that the scene takes place before it). Either condition would be graphic enough to disrupt De Quincey's orchestrated serenity. See John Barrell, *The Infection of Thomas De Quincey: A Psychopathology of Imperialism* (New Haven, CT: Yale University Press, 1991).

9 Sigmund Freud, "Entwurf einer Psychologie," in *Aus den Anfängen der Psychoanalyse* (London: Imago, 1950), 457. In a note to *Studies in Hysteria* James Strachey attributes to Josef Breuer "the distinction between bound (tonic) and unbound (mobile) psychical energy and the correlated distinction between primary and secondary psychical processes" (*SE*, 2: xxiii). In a note to *The*

Interpretation of Dreams (1900), Strachey explains that Freud himself gives
Breuer the credit even though "there is some difficulty in identifying"
exactly where Breuer makes such a distinction (*SE*, 5: 601 n.1). I'll discuss
Breuer's contribution below.

10 Freud, "Entwurf," 465.

11 On the notion that language becomes most powerful when human beings
connect it to a referent by means of a physical act, see Claudia Brodsky, *In the
Place of Language: Literature and the Architecture of the Referent* (New York:
Fordham University Press, 2009). Freud's notion of the "mnemic trace" may
be one of the most far-reaching of such conceptions of language, beside the
example of Heidegger studied by Brodsky.

12 Leys believes that "in the economic terms associated with Freud's ideas, the
traumatic experience involves a fragmentation or loss of unity of the ego
resulting from the radical unbinding of the death drive, but it also involves a
simultaneous binding (or rebinding) of cathexes" not accounted for by Freud
(*Trauma*, 34). She argues that because the traumatized person's defenses have
been breached, she or he is bound to the external world, "so mimetically
identified with the world's dangers as to be completely impressionable" (35).
I think this interpretation is itself defensive, immediately taking the positive
aspect of a destructive event to be positive in an affective sense. Logically it is
always possible to re-describe something using positive terms, but there is little
symbolic significance to that kind of positivity.

13 "Mourning and Melancholia" (1917) explains that energy is "disposed of" by
being gradually released. Thus the role of "binding" becomes that of making
possible the regulation and timing of unbinding. The pathological mania that
often follows melancholy unleashes "the whole quota of anticathexis" ("der
ganze Betrag von Gegenbesetzungen") that had immobilized the object, while
a normal mourning detaches from the object gradually and in the "work of
severance," slowly expends energy (*SE*, 14: 255; *GW*, 10: 442). In the model
implied by "Mourning and Melancholia" binding and unbinding both shape
the ego, whose homeostasis is served by control of both. By *The Ego and the Id*
(1923) and *An Outline of Psychoanalysis* (1940), binding plays a privileged role
in ego preservation.

14 In "The Unconscious" (1915) Freud remarks on "our oscillations in regard to
the naming of the higher system – which we have hitherto spoken of indifferently, sometimes as the *Pcs.* and sometimes as the *Cs.*" (*SE*, 14: 189; *GW*,
10: 288).

15 See, for example, Jean Laplanche, "Interpretation between Determinism and
Hermeneutics: A Restatement of the Problem," trans. Philip Slotkin, in *Essays
on Otherness*, ed. John Fletcher (New York: Routledge, 1999), 160–8.

16 See *Interpretation of Dreams*, in which Freud considers what happens to ideas
that are "abandoned [*verlassen*] by the preconscious cathexis," and assumes
that when they "are left to themselves" they are unconscious and "striving to
find an outlet [*Abfluß*]" (*SE*, 5: 605; *GW*, 2: 610–11). Or, again, "They are left
to themselves – 'repressed'" (*SE*, 5: 604; *GW*, 2: 609).

17 See n.9.
18 The only brake on ideas in consciousness is their contradiction with other ideas (*SE*, 2: 193). An unresolvable conflict between equally founded ideas is an aporia, not a neurosis.
19 For more on preconsciousness as mediator, see Freud, "The Unconscious" (*SE*, 14: 188–9).
20 We encounter again here Freud's and Breuer's hesitation between external impact and defense.
21 Fantasies about deviant organs recur in the literature of gender anxiety. Nietzsche, for example, writes to Franz Overbeck that he feels as though he has "an extra sense organ and a new, terrible source of suffering" (Friedrich Nietzsche, *Selected Letters of Friedrich Nietzsche*, ed. and trans. Christopher Middleton [Indianapolis: Hackett, 1996], 206). The result of De Quincey's coyness is implicitly to sexualize his brain.
22 Corinthians 1: 15, 53–6, in *The Bible*, King James Version (University of Virginia Etext Library).
23 John Donne, "Death, Be Not Proud," *Variorum Edition of the Poems of John Donne*, ed. Gary A. Stringer (Bloomington: Indiana University Press, 1995), l. 14.
24 See the etymological discussion in Laplanche and Pontalis, *The Language of Psychoanalysis*.
25 Hélène Cixous, *Stigmata*, trans. uncredited (New York and London: Routledge, 1998), xiii.
26 Paul Youngquist considers De Quincey's reflections on bodily decay through De Quincey's translation of Christoph Wasianski's "The Last Days of Immanuel Kant." As De Quincey's writings raise anxieties about plagiarism – the transgression of the self-identity of a literary text – Youngquist's article raises similar anxieties by not making clear, in turn, De Quincey's translation of Wasianski. The debate about scholarly property might be reconsidered in the context of the genre and boundary transgressions of De Quinceyan texts. Margaret Russett provides a beginning for such a conversation by connecting concern about De Quincey's transgression of literary property boundaries to his "minority." See Paul Youngquist, "De Quincey's Crazy Body," *PMLA* 114 (1999): 346–58; Margaret Russett, *De Quincey's Romanticism: Canonical Minority and the Forms of Transmission* (Cambridge: Cambridge University Press, 1997).
27 Quoted in Grevel Lindop, *The Opium-Eater: A Life of Thomas De Quincey* (London: J. M. Dent, 1981), 197–8.
28 See also Russett, *De Quincey's Romanticism*, 252 n.17; Catherine Robson, *Men in Wonderland: The Lost Girlhood of the Victorian Gentleman* (Princeton, NJ: Princeton University Press, 2001), 36.
29 Sarah Dillon, "Reinscribing De Quincey's Palimpsest: The Significance of the Palimpsest in Contemporary Literary and Cultural Studies," *Textual Practice* 19, no. 3 (2005): 257.
30 The propensity to revalue values can be used for any political purpose, as De Quincey's strident defenses of colonial power show. Amplifying De Quincey's

gender identifications allegorically, Cannon Schmitt argues that De Quincey's version of nationalism uses a "rationale for aggression based, paradoxically, in a sense of itself as the beleaguered heroine of Gothic romance." Schmitt's article is especially relevant since it stresses De Quincey's desire to "find an adequate expression for the catastrophic and an adequate explanation of its ubiquity" ("Narrating National Addictions: De Quincey, Opium, and Tea," in *High Anxieties: Cultural Studies in Addiction,* ed. Janet Farrell Brodie and Marc Redfield [Berkeley: University of California Press, 2002], 84, 65).

31 We miss the radical nature of De Quincey's insight if, in following Lacan, we make the ruination of the ego into nothing more than the birth of the subject. We can agree with Lacan that the very construction of the ego is a defense, and yet extend a similar criticism to the Lacanian subjectivity that so instantly replaces it.

32 Although De Quincey's attitude toward the authority of economy is critical, it follows from his respect for invariance that the main subject of his *Logic of Political Economy* (Edinburgh and London: William Blackwood and Sons, 1844) is the vertiginous effect of economics when it meets the exigency of some inarguable subjective need. The subjective complement of that which "*can*not be granted" is that which *must* be had, and the point of greatest pain is when what *must* be had may not be acquired. De Quincey's solution to the unwieldiness of "use value" and "exchange value" is to configure in their place two kinds of exchange value, "affirmative" and "negative" value. Affirmative value ("U") is the maximum the buyer will pay for what the object does for her subjectively; negative value ("D" for "difficulty") results from circumstances such as "difficulty of attainment" (27) or the going rate of labour power. To put it another way, U is "what good it will do to yourself," while D is "what harm it has done to some other man" (60–1). For what we can have at a market price or less, we don't need to pay more, no matter how much we like it; and what we don't value affirmatively to some degree, we won't buy at all, no matter how cheap it is. "It is rare that the whole potential utility value is exhausted by the cost or difficulty value. But the inverse case is monstrous: D can never outrun U by the most fractional increment" (34). The external forces of D are usually operative, so that U doesn't have to reveal itself entirely. But an economic sublime opens under one's feet when the market no longer protects the consumer from naked need: "Instantly, under these circumstances, U springs up to its utmost height. But what *is* the utmost?" (30). *What will you pay?*, De Quincey knows, is a traumatic question for the buyer who takes it literally, not only because the answer might be "Everything" but because no matter what the answer is, on the other side is certain loss. It does not matter that the answer "fluctuates with the feelings or opinions of the individual" (70) – that ten minutes later, you might pay much less; the answer of the moment is what is owed. Bargaining and gambling move through deceptions, false answers, because the true answer is beyond dealing. It stands on the exigency that ends all deals, an exigency all the more painful for depending on another person's arbitrary power. So, De Quincey explains that

Theophrastus describes a "knavish friend" whose knavishness consists in just this, that he answers queries about a commodity's price by returning the question, *What will you pay?* (111). De Quincey comments: "Scamp seems to have the best of it: *their* benefit from the article could not be affected by the terms on which he had acquired it" (112). Price, then, "instead of being founded on [the object's] cost (or the resistance to its reproduction), is founded on its power" to realize a purpose for the buyer even if that purpose is objectively pointless, "pernicious, or even destructive to the user" (103). De Quincey writes as the addict who understands exigency that is so "deeply" subjective that it is also objective and vice versa. Pharmaceuticals, sex, and toys are prominent among his examples.

33 Friedrich Nietzsche, *The Will to Power*, trans. Walter Kaufmann and R. J. Hollingdale, ed. Walter Kaufmann (New York: Vintage, 1968), §111.

34 For an eloquent defense of the queerness of the death drive see Edelman, *No Future*.

35 D. W. Winnicott is especially good at describing his givings-up, especially of interpretation: "I have always felt that an important function of the interpretation is the establishment of the *limits* of the analyst's understanding" ("Communicating and Not Communicating Leading to a Study of Certain Opposites," in *The Maturational Processes and the Facilitating Environment: Studies in the Theory of Emotional Development* [Madison, CT: International Universities Press, 1965], 185). But such statements are literally everywhere in analytic writing.

36 Theodor W. Adorno, "The Meaning of Working Through the Past," in *Critical Models: Interventions and Catchwords*, trans. Henry Pickford (New York: Columbia University Press, 1998), 96, my italics; "Was bedeutet: Aufarbeitung der Vergangenheit?", *Gesammelte Schriften*, vol. 10.2, ed. Rolf Tiedemann, Gretel Adorno, Susan Buck-Morss, and Klaus Schultz (Frankfurt am Main: Suhrkamp, 1978), 563–4.

37 For a more skeptical reading of the aftermath of the group see Mikkel Borch-Jacobsen, "The Primal Band," in *The Emotional Tie: Psychoanalysis, Mimesis, and Affect* (Stanford, CA: Stanford University Press, 1993), 1–14.

38 Theodor W. Adorno, "Stravinsky: A Dialectical Portrait," in *Quasi Una Fantasia: Essays on Modern Music*, trans. Rodney Livingstone (London: Verso, 1998), 153; "Strawinsky. Ein dialektisches Bild," in *Musikalische Schriften I–III. Schriften*, vol. 16 (Frankfurt am Main: Suhrkamp, 1978), 389.

39 Adorno, "Meaning," 89; "Was bedeutet," 555.

Bibliography

Abraham, Nicholas and Maria Torok. *The Shell and the Kernel.* Vol. 1. Ed. and trans. Nicholas Rand. Chicago: University of Chicago Press, 1994.

Adler, Jeremy. "Goethe and Chemical Theory in Elective Affinities." In *Romanticism and the Sciences.* Ed. Andrew Cunningham and Nicholas Jardine. Cambridge: Cambridge University Press, 1990, 263–79.

Adorno, Theodor W. "The Meaning of Working Through the Past." In *Critical Models: Interventions and Catchwords.* Trans. Henry Pickford. New York: Columbia University Press, 1998, 89–104.

"Stravinsky: A Dialectical Portrait." In *Quasi Una Fantasia: Essays on Modern Music.* Trans. Rodney Livingstone. London: Verso, 1998, 145–78.

"Strawinsky. Ein dialektisches Bild." In *Musikalische Schriften I–III. Schriften.* Vol. 16. Frankfurt am Main: Suhrkamp, 1978, 382–412.

"Was bedeutet: Aufarbeitung der Vergangenheit?" *Gesammelte Schriften.* Vol. 10.2. Ed. Rolf Tiedemann, Gretel Adorno, Susan Buck-Morss, and Klaus Schultz. Frankfurt am Main: Suhrkamp, 1978, 555–72.

Adorno, Theodor W. and Max Horkheimer. *Dialectic of Enlightenment.* London: Verso, 1997.

Agamben, Giorgio. *The Idea of Prose.* Trans. Michael Sullivan and Sam Whitsitt. Albany: State University of New York Press, 1995.

Stanzas: Word and Phantasm in Western Culture. Minneapolis: University of Minnesota Press, 1993.

Ahmed, Sara. *The Cultural Politics of Emotion.* New York: Routledge, 2004.

"Happy Objects." In *The Affect Theory Reader.* Ed. Gregory J. Seigworth and Melissa Gregg. Durham, NC: Duke University Press, 2010, 29–51.

The Promise of Happiness. Durham, NC: Duke University Press, 2010.

Aikin, John. *Food for National Penitence; or, a Discourse Intended for the Approaching Fast Day.* London: Joseph Johnson, 1793. *Eighteenth-Century Collections Online.* Gale.

Altieri, Charles. "The Concept of Force as Modernist Response to the Authority of Science." *Modernism/Modernity* 5, no. 2 (1998): 77–93.

Anastopoulos, Charis. *Particle or Wave: The Evolution of the Concept of Matter in Modern Physics.* Princeton, NJ: Princeton University Press, 2008.

Arendt, Hannah. *The Human Condition.* 2nd edn. Chicago: University of Chicago Press, 1998.

The Origins of Totalitarianism. New York: Harcourt Brace Jovanovich, 1979.

Armstrong, Nancy B. *How Novels Think: The Limits of Individualism, 1719–1900.* New York: Columbia University Press, 2005.

Armstrong, Isobel. "Textual Harassment: The Ideology of Close Reading, or How Close is Close?" *Textual Practice* 9, no. 3 (1995): 401–20.

Auerbach, Nina. "O Brave New World: Evolution and Revolution in Persuasion." In *Jane Austen: Critical Assessments.* Vol. 4. Ed. Ian Littlewood. Mountfield, UK: Helm Information, 1998, 482–96.

Augustine of Hippo, St. *The Confessions.* Trans. William Watts. Cambridge, MA: Harvard University Press, 2006.

Austen, Jane. *Mansfield Park.* Ed. Kathryn Sutherland. New York: Oxford World Classics, 2003.

   Persuasion. Ed. James Kingley. Intro. Deirdre Shauna Lynch. New York: Oxford World Classics, 2004.

   Pride and Prejudice. Ed. R. W. Chapman. Oxford: Oxford University Press, 1988.

Barbauld, Anna Letitia. "Sins of Government, Sins of the Nation." *Selected Poetry and Prose.* Ed. William McCarthy and Elizabeth Kraft. Peterborough, ON: Broadview, 2002, 297–320.

Barker-Benfield, G. J. *The Culture of Sensibility: Sex and Society in Eighteenth-Century England.* Chicago: University of Chicago Press, 1992.

Barrell, John. *The Infection of Thomas De Quincey: A Psychopathology of Imperialism.* New Haven, CT: Yale University Press, 1991.

Bates, David. "Constitutional Violence." *Journal of Law and Society* 34, no. 1 (2007): 14–30.

Beebe, Beatrice. "Co-constructing Mother–Infant Distress: The Microsynchrony of Maternal Impingement and Infant Avoidance in the Face-to-Face Encounter." *Psychoanalytic Inquiry* 20, no. 3 (2000): 421–40.

Benjamin, Walter. "Goethe's *Elective Affinities.*" In *Walter Benjamin: Selected Writings.* Vol. 1. *1913–1926.* Ed. Marcus Bullock and Michael W. Jennings. Cambridge, MA: Harvard University Press, 1996, 297–360.

Ben-Porat, Ziva. "Poetics of the Homeric Simile and the Theory of (Poetic) Simile." *Poetics Today* 13, no. 4 (1992): 737–69.

Bentham, Jeremy. *Deontology together with A Table of the Springs of Action and The Article on Utilitarianism.* Ed. Amnon Goldsmith. Oxford: Clarendon Press, 1983.

   A Fragment on Government (1776). Ed. J. H. Burns and H. L. A. Hart. Cambridge: Cambridge University Press, 1988.

   An Introduction to the Principles of Morals and Legislation. Ed. J. H. Burns and H. L. A. Hart. Intro. R. Rosen. Oxford: Clarendon Press, 1996.

Berlant, Lauren. *Cruel Optimism.* Durham, NC: Duke University Press, 2011.

Berry, Mary. *Extracts of the Journals and Correspondence of Miss Berry from the Year 1783–1852.* Ed. Lady Maria Theresa Villiers Lister Lewis. Vol. 2. London: Longmans, Green, & Co., 1866.

The Bible. King James Version. University of Virginia Etext Library.

Blackwell, Adrian. "Love is a force that acts as the productive motor of every emancipatory politics." JMB Gallery. University of Toronto, 2010.

Blake, William. *Jerusalem.* Ed. Morton D. Paley. Princeton, NJ: William Blake Trust and Princeton University Press, 1991.

Blanchot, Maurice. *La Communauté inavouable.* Paris: Editions de Minuit, 1983. *The Infinite Conversation* (1969). Trans. Susan Hanson. Minneapolis: University of Minnesota Press, 1993.

Blank, G. Kim. *Wordsworth and Feeling.* Madison, WI: Fairleigh Dickinson University Press, 1995.

Bloomfield, Robert. *The Banks of Wye: A Poem in Four Books.* New York: Richard Scott, 1812.

Blumberg, Jane. *Mary Shelley's Early Novels: "This Child of Imagination and Misery."* Iowa City: University of Iowa Press, 1993.

Bollas, Christopher. "The Aesthetic Moment and the Search for Transformation." In *Transitional Objects and Potential Spaces: Literary Uses of D. W. Winnicott.* Ed. Peter L. Rudnytsky. New York: Columbia University Press, 1993, 40–9.

Bonca, Tedi Chichester. *Shelley's Mirrors of Love: Narcissism, Sacrifice, and Sorority.* Albany: State University Press of New York, 1999.

Borch-Jacobsen, Mikkel. "The Primal Band." In *The Emotional Tie: Psychoanalysis, Mimesis, and Affect.* Stanford, CA: Stanford University Press, 1993, 1–14.

Bowlby, John. *Attachment and Loss.* 3 vols. New York: Basic Books, 1969.

Breuer, Josef and Sigmund Freud. *Studies in Hysteria (1895).* Trans. James Strachey. New York: Basic Books, 2000.

Brodsky, Claudia. *In the Place of Language: Literature and the Architecture of the Referent.* New York: Fordham University Press, 2009.

Brown, Nathaniel. *Sexuality and Feminism in Shelley.* Cambridge, MA: Harvard University Press, 1979.

Brown, Thomas. *Observations on the Zoonomia of Erasmus Darwin, MD.* Edinburgh, 1798.

Bruhn, Mark J. "Harmonious Madness: The Poetics of Analogy at the Limits of Blending Theory." *Poetics Today* 32, no. 4 (2011): 619–62. "Shelley's Theory of Mind: From Radical Empiricism to Cognitive Romanticism." *Poetics Today* 30, no. 3 (2009): 373–422.

Burke, Edmund. "Three Letters Addressed to a Member of the Present Parliament, on the Proposals for Peace with the Regicide Directory of France." In *The Works of the Right Honorable Edmund Burke.* Vol. 8. London: F. and C. Rivington, 1801.

Bybee, Joan and Paul J. Hopper, eds. *Frequency and the Emergence of Linguistic Structure.* Amsterdam: John Benjamins, 2001.

Bynum, Caroline. *Holy Feast and Holy Fast: The Religious Significance of Food to Medieval Women.* Berkeley: University of California Press, 1988.

Byron, George Gordon. *Byron's Letters and Journals.* 13 vols. Ed. Leslie Marchand. London: John Murray, 1973–94. *Childe Harold's Pilgrimage, Canto IV.* London: John Murray, 1818. *Google Books.*

Manfred: A Dramatic Poem. London: John Murray, 1819.

The Complete Poetical Works of Lord Byron. 7 vols. Ed. Jerome J. McGann and Barry Weller. Vol. 3. Oxford: Oxford University Press, 1980–93.

Carlson, Julie A. *England's First Family of Writers: Mary Wollstonecraft, William Godwin, Mary Shelley*. Baltimore, MD: Johns Hopkins University Press, 2007.

"Romantic Poet Legislators: An End of Torture." In *Speaking about Torture*. Ed. Julie A. Carlson and Elisabeth Weber. New York: Fordham University Press, 2012, 221–46.

Carroll, David. *Paraesthetics: Foucault, Lyotard, Derrida*. New York: Methuen, 1987.

Caruth, Cathy. *Unclaimed Experience: Trauma, Narrative, and History*. Baltimore, MD: Johns Hopkins University Press, 2006.

Cavell, Stanley. "The Future of Possibility." In *Philosophical Romanticism*. Ed. Nikolas Kompridis. New York: Routledge, 2002, 21–31.

Chandler, James K. *England in 1819: The Politics of Literary Culture and the Case of Romantic Historicism*. Chicago: University of Chicago Press, 1998.

Chang, Ku-Ming (Kevin). "Alchemy as Studies of Life and Matter." *Isis* 102, no. 2 (June 2011): 322–9.

Cheah, Pheng. "Non-dialectical Materialism." *Diacritics* 38, nos. 1–2 (2008): 143–57.

Christensen, Jerome. *Romanticism at the End of History*. Baltimore, MD: Johns Hopkins University Press, 2004.

Cixous, Hélène. *Stigmata*. Trans. uncredited. New York: Routledge, 1998.

Clark, David L. *Bodies and Pleasures in Late Kant*. Stanford, CA: Stanford University Press, forthcoming.

"Unsocial Kant: The Philosopher and the Un-regarded War Dead." *The Wordsworth Circle* 41, no. 1 (2010): 60–8.

Clej, Alina. *A Genealogy of the Modern Self: Thomas De Quincey and the Intoxication of Writing*. Stanford, CA: Stanford University Press, 1995.

Clough, Patricia. T. "The Affective Turn: Political Economy, Biomedia, and Bodies." In *The Affect Theory Reader*. Ed. Melissa Gregg and Gregory J. Seigworth. Durham, NC: Duke University Press, 2010, 206–28.

"Introduction." *The Affective Turn: Theorizing the Social*. Ed. Patricia Clough. Durham, NC: Duke University Press, 2007, 1–33.

Coelho, Ricardo Lopes. "On the Concept of Force: How Understanding Its History Can Improve Physics Teaching." *Science and Education* 19 (2010): 91–113.

Coleridge, Samuel Taylor. *Opus Maximum*. Ed. Thomas McFarland and Nicholas Halmi. Princeton, NJ: Princeton University Press, 2002.

Samuel Taylor Coleridge. Ed. H. J. Jackson. Oxford and New York: Oxford University Press, 1985.

Coleridge, Samuel Taylor and Robert Southey. "Love an Act of the will." In *Omniana*. Fontwell: Centaur Press, 1969.

Colley, Linda. *Britons: Forging the Nation, 1707–1837*. New Haven, CT: Yale University Press, 1992.

Collings, David. "Troping Mood: Pfau, Wordsworth, and Hegel." *Literature Compass* 6 (2009): 373–83.

Wordsworthian Errancies: The Poetics of Cultural Dismemberment. Baltimore, MD: Johns Hopkins University Press, 1994.

Combe, William. *The Fast-Day*. London: J. Bow 1780. *English Poetry Database*.

Coole, Diana. "The Inertia of Matter." In *New Materialisms: Ontology, Agency, and Politics*. Ed. Diana Coole and Samantha Frost. Durham, NC: Duke University Press, 2010, 92–115.

Cowper, William. *The Poems of William Cowper, Esq. of the Inner Temple*. New York: Charles Wells, 1840. *Google Books*.

Crighton, Alexander. *An Inquiry into the Nature and Cause of Mental Derangement*. London: T. Cadell, 1798.

Cronin, Richard. *Shelley's Poetic Thoughts*. New York: St. Martin's Press, 1981.

Curran, Stuart. *Shelley's Annus Mirabilis: The Maturing of an Epic Vision*. San Marino, CA: Huntington Library, 1975.

Dalton, John. *A New System of Chemical Philosophy* (1808). New York: Philosophical Library, 1967.

Damasio, Antonio. *The Feeling of What Happens: Body and Emotion in the Making of Consciousness*. New York: Harcourt Brace, 1999.

Looking for Spinoza: Joy, Sorrow, and the Feeling Brain. Orlando: Harcourt, 2003.

Darwin, Erasmus. *Zoonomia*. London: 1794–6.

Davy, Humphry. *1800 Notebook*. London: Royal Institution. HD/3/13d/1800.

Elements of Chemical Philosophy. Part 1. Vol. 1. Philadelphia, 1812.

Dear, Peter. *The Intelligibility of Nature*. Chicago: University of Chicago Press, 2006.

de Man, Paul. "The Rhetoric of Temporality." In *Blindness and Insight*. 2nd rev. edn. Minneapolis: University of Minnesota Press, 1983, 187–228.

De Quincey, Thomas. *The Logic of Political Economy*. Edinburgh and London: William Blackwood and Sons, 1844.

Suspiria de Profundis, Confessions of an English Opium-Eater and Other Writings. Ed. Grevel Lindop. Oxford: Oxford University Press, 1985.

Derrida, Jacques. *Dissemination*. Trans. Barbara Johnson. Chicago: University of Chicago Press, 1981.

Learning To Live Finally: An Interview with Jean Birnbaum. Trans. Pascale-Anne Brault and Michael Naas. Hoboken, NJ: Melville House, 2007.

Resistances of Psychoanalysis (1996). Trans. Peggy Kamuf, Pascale-Anne Brault, and Michael Naas. Stanford, CA: Stanford University Press, 1998.

Rogues: Two Essays on Reason. Trans. Pascale-Anne Brault and Michael Naas. Stanford, CA: Stanford University Press, 2005.

"White Mythology: Metaphor in the Text of Philosophy." *New Literary History* 6, no. 1 (1974): 5–74.

Diderot, Denis and Jean Le Rond D'Alembert, eds. *Encyclopédie, ou Dictionnaire raisonné des sciences, des arts et des métiers*. ARTFL Encyclopédie Projet. Ed. Robert Morrissey. http://encyclopedie.uchicago.edu. 2008.

Dillon, Sarah. "Reinscribing De Quincey's Palimpsest: The Significance of the Palimpsest in Contemporary Literary and Cultural Studies." *Textual Practice* 19 (2005): 243–63.

Dixon, Thomas. *From Passions to Emotions: The Creation of a Secular Psychological Category*. Cambridge: Cambridge University Press, 2003.

Donne, John. *Variorum Edition of the Poems of John Donne*. Ed. Gary A. Stringer. Bloomington: Indiana University Press, 1995.

Eagleman, David. *Incognito*. New York: Pantheon, 2011.

Eagleton, Terry. *The Ideology of the Aesthetic*. Oxford: Blackwell, 1990.

   The Trouble with Strangers: A Study of Ethics. Oxford: Wiley-Blackwell, 2009.

Edelman, Lee. *No Future: Queer Theory and the Death Drive*. Durham, NC: Duke University Press, 2004.

Eilenberg, Susan. *Strange Power of Speech: Wordsworth, Coleridge, and Literary Possession*. New York: Oxford University Press, 1992.

Elfenbein, Andrew. *Byron and the Victorians*. Cambridge: Cambridge University Press, 1995.

Ellis, Kate Ferguson. "Subversive Surfaces: The Limits of Domestic Affection in Mary Shelley's Later Fiction." In *The Other Mary Shelley: Beyond Frankenstein*. Ed. Audrey A. Fisch, Anne Mellor, and Esther Schor. New York: Oxford University Press, 1993, 220–34.

Ellison, Julie. *Cato's Tears: The Making of Anglo-American Emotion*. Chicago: University of Chicago Press, 1999.

Ellman, Maud. *The Hunger Artists: Starving, Writing and Imprisonment*. Cambridge, MA: Harvard University Press, 1993.

Encyclopaedia Britannica. 3 vols. Edinburgh: A. Bell and C. Macfarquhar, 1771.

Faflak, Joel. "The Difficult Education of Shelley's The Triumph of Life." *Keats–Shelley Journal* 58 (2009): 53–78.

   "Romanticism and the Pornography of Talking." *Nineteenth-Century Contexts* 27, no. 1 (2005): 77–97.

   Romantic Psychoanalysis: The Burden of the Mystery. Albany: State University of New York Press, 2007.

Faraday, Michael. *The Forces of Matter*. Mineola, NY: Dover Books, 2010.

   "Observations on the Inertia of the Mind." IET Manuscript SC MSS 002/1/4. London.

Favret, Mary A. "Free and Happy: Jane Austen in America." In *Janeites: Austen's Disciples and Devotees*. Ed. Deidre Shauna Lynch. Princeton, NJ: Princeton University Press, 2000, 166–87.

   "The Study of Affect and Romanticism." *Literature Compass* 6, no. 6 (2009): 1059–66.

   War at a Distance: Romanticism and the Making of Modern Wartime. Princeton, NJ: Princeton University Press, 2010.

Felman, Shoshana, and Dori Laub. *Testimony: Crises of Witnessing in Literature, Psychoanalysis, and History*. London: Routledge, 1992.

Fenves, Peter. *Late Kant: Toward Another Law of the Earth*. New York: Routledge, 2003.

Ferguson, Frances. "Envy Rising." *English Literary History* 69, no. 4 (2002): 889–905.

Firkins, Oscar W. *Power and Elusiveness in Shelley*. Minneapolis: University of Minnesota Press, 1937.

Foucault, Michel. *The History of Sexuality*. Vol. 1 (1978). Trans. Robert Hurley. New York: Vintage Books, 1990.

"A Preface to Transgression" (1963). In *Language, Counter-Memory, Practice*. Ed. Donald F. Bouchard. Trans. Donald F. Bouchard and Sherry Simon. Ithaca, NY: Cornell University Press, 1977, 29–52.

"Society Must Be Defended": Lectures at the Collège de France, 1975–1976. Ed. Mauro Bertani and Alessandro Fontana. Trans. David Macey. New York: Picador, 2003.

Frankfurt, Harry. "Autonomy, Necessity, and Love." In *Necessity, Volition, and Love*. Cambridge: Cambridge University Press, 1999, 129–41.

"Freedom of the Will and the Concept of a Person." In *Free Will*. Ed. Robert Kane. Oxford: Blackwell, 2002, 127–44.

The Reasons of Love. Princeton, NJ: Princeton University Press, 2004.

Franta, Andrew. "Shelley and the Poetics of Political Indirection." *Poetics Today* 22, no. 4 (2001): 765–89.

Frazer, Michael. *The Enlightenment of Sympathy*. Oxford: Oxford University Press, 2010.

Freud, Sigmund. *Abriss der Psychoanalyse. Gesammelte Werke, Chronologisch Geordnet*. 17 vols. in 16. Ed. Anna Freud, E. Bibring, W. Hoffer, E. Kris, and O. Isakower. Vol. 17. London: Imago, 1963, 63–140.

Beyond the Pleasure Principle (1920). *The Standard Edition of the Complete Psychological Works of Sigmund Freud*. 24 vols. Trans. James Strachey. Vol. 18. London: Hogarth Press, 1956–1974, 7–64.

"Entwurf einer Psychologie." *Aus den Anfängen der Psychoanalyse*. London: Imago, 1950, 371–466.

"Erinnern, Wiederholen, Durcharbeiten." *Gesammelte Werke*. Vol. 9, 125–36.

The Interpretation of Dreams (1900). *The Standard Edition*. Vol. 5.

Introductory Lectures on Psychoanalysis (1916–17). *The Standard Edition*. Vol. 16.

Jenseits des Lustprinzips (1920). *Gesammelte Werke*. Vol. 13, 1–70.

"Mourning and Melancholia" (1917), *Standard Edition*. Vol. 14, 243–358.

"On the Psychical Mechanism of Hysterical Phenomena" (1893). *The Standard Edition*. Vol. 3, 25–42.

An Outline of Psychoanalysis (1940). *The Standard Edition*. Vol. 23, 141–207.

Project for a Scientific Psychology (1895). *The Standard Edition*. Vol. 1, 295–398.

"Remembering, Repeating, and Working Through (Further Recommendations on the Technique of Psychoanalysis II)" (1914). *The Standard Edition*. Vol. 12, 145–56.

"Trauer und Melancholie" (1917 [1915]). *Gesammelte Werke*. Vol. 10, 427–46.

Die Traumdeutung (1900). *Gesammelte Werke*. Vols. 2–3.

"Das Unbewußte" (1915). *Gesammelte Werke*. Vol. 10, 263–303.

"The Unconscious" (1915). *The Standard Edition*. Vol. 15, 159–216.

Vorlesungen zur Einführung in die Psychoanalyse (1916–17 [1915–17]). *Gesammelte Werke*. Vol. 9.

"[Vortrag:] Über den psychischen Mechanismus hysterischer Phänomene" (1893). *Gesammelte Werke*. Vol. 1, 81–98.

Freud, Sigmund and Josef Breuer. *Studien über Hysterie.* Leipzig: Franz Deuticke, 1895.
  Studies in Hysteria. The Standard Edition. Vol. 2.
Galperin, William. *The Historical Austen.* Philadelphia: University of Pennsylvania Press, 2003.
Garofalo, Daniela. *Manly Leaders in Nineteenth-Century British Literature.* Albany: State University of New York Press, 2008.
"The General Fast: An Ode to the Right Honourable, the Ultra-Tory Saints by M." *The Metropolitan* 3, no. 11 (1832): 318–19.
Gladden, Samuel Lyndon. "Shelley's Agenda Writ Large: *Oedipus Tyrannus; or, Swellfoot The Tyrant.*" *Romantic Circles.* www.rc.umd.edu/praxis/interventionist/gladden, last accessed 30 August 2013.
  Shelley's Textual Seductions: Plotting Utopia in the Erotic and Political Works. New York: Routledge, 2002.
Godwin, William. *Caleb Williams* (1794). Ed. Gary Handwerk and A. A. Markley. Peterborough, ON: Broadview, 2000.
Goethe, Johann Wolfgang von. *Elective Affinities.* Trans. David Constantine. Oxford: Oxford University Press, 1994.
  Scientific Studies. Trans. Douglas Miller. New York: Suhrkamp Publishers, 1988.
  The Sorrows of Young Werther and Selected Writings. Ed. Marcelle Clements. Trans. Catherine Hutter. New York: Signet Books, 1962.
  Die Wahlverwandtschaften. Stuttgart: Philipp Reclam, 1957.
Goffman, Erving. "Embarrassment and Social Organization." *American Journal of Sociology* 62, no. 3 (1956): 264–71.
Goldsmith, Steven. "William Blake and the Future of Enthusiasm." *Nineteenth-Century Literature* 63, no. 4 (2009): 439–60.
Gooding, David. "Metaphysics versus Measurement: The Conversion and Conservation of Force in Faraday's Physics." *Annals of Science* 37 (1980): 1–29.
Gray, Erik. "Faithful Likenesses: Lists of Similes in Milton, Shelley, and Rossetti." *Texas Studies in Literature and Language* 48, no. 4 (2006): 290–311.
Great Britain. Sovereign. *By the King: A Proclamation, for a General Fast.* London, 1793. *Eighteenth Century Collections Online.*
Greenberg, Gary. "The War on Unhappiness: Goodbye Freud, Hello Positive Thinking." *Harper's Magazine* 321, no. 1924 (2010): 27–35.
Gregg, Melissa and Gregory J. Seigworth. "An Inventory of Shimmers." *The Affect Theory Reader.* Ed. Melissa Gregg and Gregory J. Seigworth. Durham, NC: Duke University Press, 2010, 1–28.
Gregory, Eric. *Politics and the Order of Love: An Augustinian Ethic of Democratic Citizenship.* Chicago: University of Chicago Press, 2008.
Gross, Daniel. *The Secret History of Emotion: From Aristotle's Rhetoric to Modern Brain Science.* Chicago: University of Chicago Press, 2006.
Guyer, Sara. "The Pardon of the Disaster." *SubStance* 35, no. 1 (2006): 85–105.
  "The Rhetoric of Survival and the Possibility of Romanticism." *Studies in Romanticism* 46, no. 2 (2007): 247–63.

Habermas, Jürgen. "Ernst Bloch: A Marxist Schelling." In *Philosophical-Political Profiles* (1971). Trans. Frederick G. Lawrence. Cambridge, MA: MIT Press, 1985, 53–79.

 Structural Transformation of the Public Sphere. Trans. Thomas Burger. Cambridge, MA: MIT Press, 1991.

Haines, Simon. *Shelley's Poetry: The Divided Self.* New York: St. Martin's Press, 1997.

Hankins, Thomas L. "Eighteenth-Century Attempts to Resolve the *Vis Viva* Controversy." *Isis* 56, no. 3 (1965): 281–97.

Hansen, Mark. "The Time of Affect, or Bearing Witness to Life." *Critical Inquiry* 30 (2004): 584–626.

Hardt, Michael. "Foreword: What Affects Are Good For." In *The Affective Turn: Theorizing the Social.* Ed. Patricia Clough with Jean Halley. Durham, NC: Duke University Press, 2007, ix–xiii.

Hartman, Geoffrey. *Easy Pieces.* New York: Columbia University Press, 1985.

 The Unremarkable Wordsworth. Minneapolis: University of Minnesota Press, 1987.

Hartman, Geoffrey and Daniel T. O'Hara, eds. *The Geoffrey Hartman Reader.* New York: Fordham University Press, 2004.

Hays, Mary. *Memoirs of Emma Courtney* (1796). Ed. Marilyn L. Brooks. Peterborough, ON: Broadview, 2000.

Hazlitt, William. *Collected Works of William Hazlitt.* Vol. 3. London: J. M. Dent & Co., 1902.

Hegel, G. W. F., *Aesthetics: Lectures on Fine Art.* 2 vols. Trans. T. M. Knox. Oxford: Clarendon, 1975.

 Phenomenology of Spirit. Trans. A. V. Miller. Oxford: Oxford University Press, 1979.

 The Philosophy of Nature. Trans. A. V. Miller. Oxford: Clarendon, 1970.

Heidegger, Martin. *Being and Time.* Trans. John Macquarrie and Edward Robinson. London: SCM Press, 1962.

 "Building Dwelling Thinking." In *Poetry, Language, Thought.* Trans. Albert Hofstadter. New York: Perennial, 1971, 145–61.

 What Is Philosophy? Trans. Hugh Tomlinson and Graham Burchell. London: Vision, 1963.

Heilbron, J. L. *Electricity in the Seventeenth and Eighteenth Centuries.* Berkeley: University of California Press, 1979.

Henderson, Andrea. *Romantic Identities: Varieties of Subjectivity, 1774–1830.* Cambridge: Cambridge University Press, 1996.

Hirshman, Albert O. *The Passions and the Interests: Political Arguments for Capitalism before Its Triumph.* Princeton, NJ: Princeton University Press, 1977.

Hobbes, Thomas. *Leviathan.* Ed. Edwin Curley. Indianapolis: Hackett, 1994.

Hogle, Jerrold E. *Shelley's Process: Radical Transference and the Development of His Major Works.* New York: Oxford University Press, 1988.

hooks, bell. *All About Love: New Visions.* New York: William Morrow, 2001.

Hume, David. *Essays Moral, Political, and Literary*. Ed. Eugene F. Miller. Indianapolis: Liberty Fund, 1985.

The Letters of David Hume. 2 vols. Ed. John Young Thomson Greig. Oxford: Clarendon, 1932.

Huneman, Philippe. "Montpelier Vitalism and the Emergence of Alienism in France (1750–1850): The Case of the Passions." *Science in Context* 21, no. 4 (2008): 615–47.

Hutcheson, Francis. *An Essay on the Conduct of the Passions and Affections, with Illustrations on the Moral Sense*. Ed. Aaron Garrett. Indianapolis: Liberty Fund, 2002.

Israel, Michael, Jennifer Riddle Harding, and Vera Tobin. "On Simile." In *Language, Culture, and Mind*. Ed. Michel Achard and Suzanne Kemmer. Stanford, CA: CSLI Publications, 2004, 123–35.

Jackson, Noel. *Science and Sensation in Romantic Poetry*. Cambridge: Cambridge University Press, 2008.

Jakobson, Roman. *Language in Literature*. Ed. Krystyna Pomorska. Cambridge, MA: Harvard University Press, 1987.

Jammer, Max. *Concepts of Force*. Cambridge, MA: Harvard University Press, 1957.

Jenkins, Alice, ed. *Michael Faraday's Mental Exercises: An Artisan Essay-Circle in Regency London*. Liverpool: Liverpool University Press, 2008.

Johnson, Claudia L. *Equivocal Beings: Politics, Gender, and Sentimentality in the 1790s, Wollstonecraft, Radcliffe, Burney, Austen*. Chicago: University of Chicago Press, 1995.

Jones, Mark. *The "Lucy Poems": A Case Study in Literary Knowledge*. Toronto: University of Toronto Press, 1995.

Kant, Immanuel. *The Conflict of the Faculties*. Trans. Mary J. Gregor. Lincoln: University of Nebraska Press, 1992.

Critique of Pure Reason (1787). 2nd edn. Trans. J. M. D. Meiklejohn. London: J. M. Dent, 1934/1991.

Philosophy of Material Nature. Trans. James Ellington. Indianapolis: Hackett, 1985.

Toward Perpetual Peace and Other Writings on Politics, Peace, and History. Ed. Pauline Kleingeld. Trans. David L. Colclasure. New Haven, CT: Yale University Press, 2006.

Keach, William. *Shelley's Style*. New York and London: Methuen, 1986.

Keats, John. *John Keats's Anatomical and Physiological Note Book*. Ed. Hyder Rollins. New York: Haskell House, 1970.

The Letters of John Keats. 2 vols. Ed. Hyder Rollins. Cambridge, MA: Harvard University Press, 1958.

The Poems of John Keats. Ed. Jack Stillinger. Cambridge, MA: Harvard University Press, 1978.

Khalip, Jacques. *Anonymous Life: Romanticism and Dispossession*. Stanford, CA: Stanford University Press, 2009.

Kim, Mi-Gyung. *Affinity, That Elusive Dream: A Genealogy of the Chemical Revolution*. Cambridge, MA: MIT Press, 2003.

King James Bible, 1611: A Machine-readable Transcript. The Bible in English. Chadwyck-Healey 1997. Indiana University Libraries Bloomington.

Klein, Melanie. "Love, Guilt, and Reparation." In Melanie Klein and Joan Riviere. *Love, Hate and Reparation*. New York: Norton, 1964, 57–119.

Klein, Ursula and Wolfgang Lefevre. *Materials in Eighteenth-Century Science*. Cambridge, MA: MIT Press, 2007.

Knight, D. M. "The Physical Sciences and the Romantic Movement." *History of Science* 9 (1970): 54–75.

Science and Spirituality: The Volatile Connection. London: Routledge, 2004.

Krell, David Farrell. *Contagion: Sexuality, Disease and Death in German Idealism and Romanticism*. Bloomington: Indiana University Press, 1998.

Kristeva, Julia. *Tales of Love*. Trans. Leon S. Roudiez. New York: Columbia University Press, 1987.

Lacan, Jacques. "Agency of the Letter in the Unconscious." *Ecrits: A Selection*. Trans. Alan Sheridan. New York: Norton, 1977, 146–78.

The Seminar. Book I. Freud's Papers on Technique, 1953–54. Trans. John Forrester. New York: Cambridge University Press, 1988.

Lakoff, George and Mark Johnson. *Metaphors We Live By*. 2nd edn. Chicago: University of Chicago Press, 2003.

Laplanche, Jean. "Interpretation between Determinism and Hermeneutics: A Restatement of the Problem." Trans. Philip Slotkin. In *Essays on Otherness*. New York: Routledge, 1999, 138–65.

"Seduction, Persecution, Revelation." In *Essays on Otherness*, 166–96.

Laplanche, Jean and J.-P. Pontalis. *The Language of Psycho-Analysis*. Trans. Donald Nicholson-Smith. New York: Norton, 1973.

Lear, Jonathan. *Radical Hope: Ethics in the Face of Cultural Devastation*. Cambridge, MA: Harvard University Press, 2008.

Ledoux, Joseph. *The Emotional Brain*. New York: Simon and Schuster, 1996.

Levere, Trevor. *Affinity and Matter: Elements of Chemistry 1800–1865*. Oxford: Clarendon, 1971.

Levinas, Emmanuel. *Existence and Existents*. Trans. Alphonso Lingis. The Hague: Martinus Nijhoff, 1978.

Otherwise than Being: Or Beyond Essence. Trans. Alphonso Lingis. Pittsburgh, PA: Duquesne University Press, 1998.

Totality and Infinity: An Essay on Exteriority. Trans. Alphonso Lingis. Pittsburgh, PA: Duquesne University Press, 1969.

Levinson, Marjorie. "A Motion and a Spirit: Romancing Spinoza." *Studies in Romanticism* 47, no. 4 (2007): 366–408.

Lewis, William. *The Edinburgh New Dispensatory*. London, 1789.

Leys, Ruth. *From Guilt to Shame: Auschwitz and After*. Princeton, NJ: Princeton University Press, 2007.

Trauma: A Genealogy. Chicago: University of Chicago Press, 2000.

"The Turn to Affect: A Critique." *Critical Inquiry* 37, no. 3 (2011): 434–72.

Lincoln, Abraham. "Proclamation 97 Appointing a Day of National Humiliation, Fasting, and Prayer." *The American Presidency Project*.

Lindop, Grevel. *The Opium-Eater: A Life of Thomas De Quincey.* London: J. M. Dent, 1981.

Locke, John. *An Essay Concerning Human Understanding* (1690). Ed. Peter H. Nidditch. Oxford: Clarendon, 1975.

   Two Treatises of Government (1689). Ed. Peter Laslett. Cambridge: Cambridge University Press, 1988.

Lussier, Mark. *Romantic Dynamics: The Poetics of Physicality.* Basingstoke: Macmillan, 2000.

Lynch, Deidre Shauna, ed. *Janeites: Austen's Disciples and Devotees.* Princeton, NJ: Princeton University Press, 2000.

Lyotard, Jean-François. "After the Sublime, the State of Aesthetics." In *The Inhuman: Reflections on Time.* Trans. Geoffrey Bennington and Rachel Bowlby. Stanford, CA: Stanford University Press, 1991, 135–43.

   Discours, figure. Paris: Klinksieck, 1971/2002.

Makdisi, Saree. *William Blake and the Impossible History of the 1790s.* Chicago: University of Chicago Press, 2002.

Male, Roy R., Jr. "Shelley and the Doctrine of Sympathy." *The University of Texas Studies in English* 29 (1950): 183–203.

Marshall, David. *The Figure of Theater: Shaftesbury, Defoe, Adam Smith, and George Eliot.* New York: Columbia University Press, 1986.

   The Surprising Effects of Sympathy: Marivau, Diderot, Rousseau, and Mary Shelley. Chicago: University of Chicago Press, 1988.

Massumi, Brian. "The Future Birth of the Affective Fact: The Political Ontology of Threat." In *The Affect Theory Reader.* Ed. Melissa Gregg and Gregory J. Seigworth. Durham, NC: Duke University Press, 2010, 52–70.

   Parables for the Virtual: Movement, Affect, Sensation. Durham, NC: Duke University Press, 2002.

McGann, Jerome. *The Poetics of Sensibility: A Revolution in Poetic Style.* Oxford: Clarendon, 1996.

McLellan, David. *Utopian Pessimist: The Life and Thought of Simone Weil.* New York: Simon and Schuster, 1990.

McMahon, Darrin. *Happiness: A History.* New York: Atlantic Monthly Press, 2006.

Mee, John. *Dangerous Enthusiasm: William Blake and the Culture of Radicalism in the 1790s.* Oxford: Clarendon, 1992.

Mellor, Anne. *Mary Shelley: Her Life, Her Fictions, Her Monsters.* New York: Routledge, 1989.

Melville Logan, Peter. *Nerves and Narratives: A Cultural History of Hysteria in Nineteenth-Century British Prose.* Berkeley: University of California Press, 1997.

Merleau-Ponty, Maurice. *Phenomenology of Perception.* Trans. Colin Smith. New York: Routledge, 2002.

Miall, David S. "Estimating Changes in Collocations of Key Words across a Large Text: A Case Study of Coleridge's *Notebooks.*" *Computers and the Humanities* 26, no. 1 (1992): 1–12.

Miller, D. A. *Jane Austen, or: The Secret of Style*. Princeton, NJ: Princeton University Press, 2003.

Miller, William Ian. *Humiliation: And Other Essays on Honor, Social Discomfort and Violence*. Ithaca, NY: Cornell University Press, 1995.

Minsky, Marvin. *The Emotional Machine*. New York: Simon and Schuster, 2006.

Mitchell, Robert. "Suspended Animation, Slow Time, and the Poetics of Trance." *PMLA* 126, no. 1 (2011): 107–22.

Sympathy and the State in the Romantic Era. New York: Routledge, 2007.

Mouffe, Chantal. *The Democratic Paradox*. London: Verso, 2000.

Muri, Allison. *The Enlightenment Cyborg*. Toronto: University of Toronto Press, 2007.

Nagle, Christopher. *Sexuality and the Culture of Sensibility in the British Romantic Era*. New York: Palgrave Macmillan, 2007.

Nancy, Jean-Luc. *The Inoperative Community*. Ed. Peter Connor. Trans. Peter Connor, Lisa Garbis, Michael Holland, and Simone Sawhney. Minnesota: University of Minnesota Press, 1991.

Ngai, Sianne. *Ugly Feelings*. Cambridge, MA: Harvard University Press, 2005.

Nietzsche, Friedrich. *Selected Letters of Friedrich Nietzsche*. Ed. and trans. Christopher Middleton. Indianapolis: Hackett, 1996.

The Will to Power. Ed. Walter Kaufmann. Trans. Walter Kaufmann and R. J. Hollingdale. New York: Vintage, 1968.

Nussbaum, Martha. *Political Emotions: Why Love Matters for Justice*. Cambridge, MA: Belknap, forthcoming.

The Therapy of Desire. Princeton, NJ: Princeton University Press, 1996.

Ouziel, Pablo. "Love-Force as Educator." www.pabloouziel.com/academic-essays, last accessed 29 August 2013.

Papoulias, Constantina and Felicity Callard. "Biology's Gift: Interrogating the Turn to Affect." *Body and Society* 16, no. 29 (2010): 29–56.

Penrose, Francis. *Essays, Physiological and Practical; Founded on the Modern Chemistry of Lavoisier*. London: Fourcroy, &c., 1794.

Perloff, Marjorie. "Emily Dickinson and the Theory Canon." http://epc.buffalo.edu/authors/perloff/articles/dickinson.html, last accessed 29 August 2013.

Peterfreund, Stuart. *Shelley among Others: The Play of the Intertext and the Idea of Language*. Baltimore, MD and London: Johns Hopkins University Press, 2002.

Pfau, Thomas. "Community as Metaphysics: Coleridge on Person and Conscience." Talk given at colloquium Romanticism and the Question of Community. Brown University, Providence. 13 November 2010.

"Figuring the 'Insufficient Void' of Self-Consciousness in Shelley's 'Epipsychidion.'" *Keats–Shelley Journal* 40 (1991): 99–126.

Minding the Modern. Notre Dame, IN: Notre Dame University Press, 2013.

Romantic Moods: Paranoia, Trauma, and Melancholy, 1790–1840. Baltimore, MD: Johns Hopkins University Press, 2005.

Pinch, Adela. *Strange Fits of Passion: Epistemologies of Emotion, Hume to Austen*. Stanford, CA: Stanford University Press, 1995.

Plotnitsky, Arkady. "All Shapes of Light: The Quantum Mechanical Shelley." In *Shelley: Poet and Legislator of the World*. Ed. Betty Bennett and Stuart Curran. Baltimore, MD: Johns Hopkins University Press, 1996, 262–73.

Pocock, J. G. A. *The Machiavellian Moment*. Princeton, NJ: Princeton University Press, 1975.

——— *Virtue, Commerce, and History*. New York: Cambridge University Press, 2009.

Polanyi, Karl. *The Great Transformation*. Boston, MA: Beacon, 1957.

Porter, Roy. *English Society in the Eighteenth Century*. Harmondsworth: Penguin, 1982.

——— *Enlightenment: Britain and the Creation of the Modern World*. London: Allen Lane, 2001.

Potkay, Adam. "Wordsworth and the Ethics of Things." *PMLA* 123, no. 2 (2008): 390–404.

Priestley, Joseph. *A Sermon Preached at the Gravel Pit Meeting, in Hackney, April 19th, 1793, Being the Day Appointed for a General Fast*. London, 1793. Eighteenth Century Collections Online.

Rajan, Tilottama. "The Dis-Figuration of Enlightenment: War, Trauma, and the Historical Novel in Godwin's Mandeville." In *Godwinian Moments: From Enlightenment to Romanticism*. Ed. Robert Maniquis and Victoria Myers. Toronto: University of Toronto Press, 2011, 172–93.

——— "Dis-Figuring Reproduction: Natural History, Community, and the 1790s Novel." *CR: The New Centennial Review* 2, no. 3 (2002): 211–52.

——— "Mary Shelley's *Mathilda*: Melancholy and the Political Economy of Romanticism." *Studies in the Novel* 26 (1994): 43–68.

——— *Romantic Narrative: Shelley, Hays, Godwin, Wollstonecraft*. Baltimore, MD: Johns Hopkins University Press, 2010.

Rand, Nicholas. "Editor's Note" to "New Perspectives in Metapsychology: Cryptic Mourning and Secret Love." In Nicholas Abraham and Maria Torok. *The Shell and the Kernel*: Vol. 1. Chicago: University of Chicago Press, 1994, 99–106.

Ratcliffe, Matthew. *Rethinking Commonsense Psychology*. Basingstoke: Palgrave Macmillan, 2007.

Reddy, William. *The Navigation of Feeling: A Framework for the History of Emotions*. Cambridge: Cambridge University Press, 2001.

Redfield, Marc. *The Politics of Aesthetics: Nationalism, Gender, Romanticism*. Stanford, CA: Stanford University Press, 2003.

Richardson, Alan. *British Romanticism and the Science of the Mind*. Cambridge: Cambridge University Press, 2001.

Ricks, Christopher. *Keats and Embarrassment*. Oxford: Clarendon, 1984.

Riskin, Jessica. *Science in the Age of Sensibility*. Chicago: University of Chicago Press, 2002.

Riviere, Joan. "Hate, Greed, and Agression." In Melanie Klein and Joan Riviere. *Love, Hate and Reparation*. New York: Norton, 1964, 3–56.

Robson, Catherine. *Men in Wonderland: The Lost Girlhood of the Victorian Gentleman*. Princeton, NJ: Princeton University Press, 2001.

Rowland, Ann Wierda. *Romanticism and Childhood: The Infantilization of British Literary Culture.* Cambridge: Cambridge University Press, 2012.

Russett, Margaret. *De Quincey's Romanticism: Canonical Minority and the Forms of Transmission.* Cambridge: Cambridge University Press, 1997.

Sartre, Jean-Paul. *Being and Nothingness: An Essay in Phenomenological Ontology.* Trans. Hazel E. Barnes. New York: Washington Square Press, 1956.

Sketch for a Theory of the Emotions. Trans. Philip Mairet. London: Methuen, 1962.

Schafer, Roy. *Bad Feelings: Selected Psychoanalytic Essays.* New York: Other Press, 2005.

Schelling, F. W. J. *Ages of the World* (1815). Trans. Jason M. Wirth. Albany: State University of New York Press, 2000.

Philosophical Investigations into the Essence of Human Freedom. Trans. Jeff Love and Johannes Schmidt. Albany: State University of New York Press, 2006.

Schmitt, Cannon. "Narrating National Addictions: De Quincey, Opium, and Tea." In *High Anxieties: Cultural Studies in Addiction.* Ed. Janet Farrell Brodie and Marc Redfield. Berkeley: University of California Press, 2002, 63–84.

Schmitter, Amy M. "Seventeenth and Eighteenth-Century Theories of Emotions." *Stanford Encyclopedia of Philosophy.* Ed. Edward N. Zalta. Stanford, CA: Stanford University Press, 2010. http://plato.stanford.edu/entries/emotions-17th18th, last accessed 29 August 2013.

Schneewind, Jerome. *The Invention of Autonomy.* Cambridge: Cambridge University Press, 1998.

Schopenhauer, Arthur. *Parerga and Paralipomena.* 2 vols. Trans. E. F. J. Payne. Oxford: Clarendon, 1974.

The World as Will and Representation. 2 vols. Trans. E. F. J. Payne. New York: Dover, 1958.

Schorer, Mark. "The Humiliation of Emma Woodhouse." In *Jane Austen: A Collection of Critical Essays.* Ed. Ian Watt. Upper Saddle River, NJ: Prentice-Hall, 1963, 98–111.

Scott, David. *Conscripts of Modernity: The Tragedy of Colonial Enlightenment.* Durham, NC: Duke University Press, 2004.

Scull, Andrew. "Psychiatry and Social Control in the Nineteenth and Twentieth Centuries." *History of Psychiatry* 2 (1991): 149–69.

Sedgwick, Eve Kosofsky. "Jane Austen and the Masturbating Girl." *Critical Inquiry* 17, no. 4 (1991): 818–37.

"Paranoid Reading and Reparative Reading; or, You're So Paranoid, You Probably Think This Introduction Is About You." In *Novel Gazing: Queer Readings in Fiction.* Durham, NC: Duke University Press, 1997, 1–40.

Touching Feeling: Affect, Pedagogy, Performativity. Durham, NC: Duke University Press, 2003.

Sedgwick, Eve Kosofsky and Adam Frank. "Shame in the Cybernetic Fold: Reading Silvan Tomkins." In *Shame and Its Sisters: A Silvan Tomkins Reader.* Ed. Eve Kosofsky Sedgwick and Adam Frank. Durham, NC: Duke University Press, 1995, 1–28.

Seneca. *De Ira ("On Anger")*. Trans. Jeffrey Henderson. Cambridge, MA: Harvard University Press, 2003.

Seward, Anna. *Letters of Anna Seward: Written between the Years 1784 and 1807.* Vol. 1. Edinburgh: Archibald Constable, 1811.

Sha, Richard C. *Perverse Romanticism: Aesthetics and Sexuality in Britain, 1750–1832.* Baltimore, MD: Johns Hopkins University Press, 2009.

Shelley, Mary. *Falkner: A Novel* (1837). Doylestown, PA: Wildside, n.d.

    Lodore (1835). Ed. Lisa Vargo. Peterborough, ON: Broadview, 1997.

    Mathilda (1819). In *The Mary Shelley Reader*. Ed. Betty T. Bennett and Charles E. Robinson. New York: Oxford University Press, 1990, 173–246.

    "Modern Italian Romances." In *Mary Shelley's Literary Lives and Other Writings*. Vol. 4. Ed. Pamela Clemit. London: Pickering and Chatto, 2002.

    "The Mourner" (1829). In *Collected Tales and Stories*. Ed. Charles E. Robinson. Baltimore, MD: Johns Hopkins University Press, 1976, 81–99.

Shelley, Percy. *The Complete Works of Percy Bysshe Shelley*. 10 vols. Ed. Roger Ingpen and Walter Peck. New York: Gordian Press, 1965.

    Letters of Percy Bysshe Shelley. 2 vols. Ed. Frederick L. Jones. Oxford: Clarendon, 1964.

    The Poetical Works of Percy Bysshe Shelley. 4 vols. Ed. Harry Buxton Forman. London: Reeves and Turner, 1882.

    Shelley's Poetry and Prose. 2nd edn. Ed. Donald Reiman and Neil Fraistat. New York: Norton, 2002.

Shorter, Edward. *A History of Psychiatry: From the Era of the Asylum to the Age of Prozac*. New York: Wiley, 1997.

Simmel, Georg. "The Concept and Tragedy of Culture." In *Simmel on Culture*. Ed. David Frisby and Mike Featherstone. London: Sage, 1997, 55–74.

Simpson, David. *Wordsworth, Commodification, and Social Concern*. Cambridge: Cambridge University Press, 2009.

Siskin, Clifford. *The Historicity of Romantic Discourse*. New York: Oxford University Press, 1988.

Smith, Adam. *The Theory of Moral Sentiments*. Ed. D. D. Raphael and A. L. Macfie. Indianapolis: Liberty Fund, 1984.

    The Wealth of Nations. Ed. James Cannan. Chicago: University of Chicago Press, 1976.

Smock, Ann. *What Is There to Say? Blanchot, Melville, Des Forêts, Beckett*. Lincoln: University of Nebraska Press, 2003.

Sokolsky, Anita. "The Melancholy Persuasion." In *Psychoanalytic Literary Criticism*. Ed. Maud Ellman. New York: Longman, 1994, 128–42.

Soni, Vivasvan. *Mourning Happiness: Narrative and the Politics of Modernity*. Ithaca, NY: Cornell University Press, 2010.

Southey, Robert and Samuel Taylor Coleridge. *Omniana*. Fortwell: Centaur Press, 1969.

Sperry, Stuart. *Keats, the Poet*. Princeton, NJ: Princeton University Press, 1973.

    Shelley's Major Verse: The Narrative and Dramatic Poetry. Cambridge, MA: Harvard University Press, 1988.

Spivak, Gayatri Chakravorty. "Terror: A Speech after 9–11." *boundary* 2 31, no. 2 (2004): 81–111.

Stauffer, Andrew. *Anger, Revolution, and Romanticism*. Cambridge: Cambridge University Press, 2005.

Stengers, Isabelle. *Cosmopolitics I*. Trans. Robert Bononno. Minneapolis: University of Minnesota Press, 2003.

Stevens, Wallace. *The Auroras of Autumn*. New York: Alfred A. Knopf, 1950.

Strauss, Leo. *Natural Right and History*. Chicago: University of Chicago Press, 1953.

Terada, Rei. *Feeling in Theory: Emotion after the "Death of the Subject."* Cambridge, MA: Harvard University Press, 2001.

Thackray, Arnold. *Atoms and Powers: An Essay on Newtonian Matter-Theory and the Development of Chemistry*. Cambridge, MA: Harvard University Press, 1970.

Todd, Janet M. *Death and the Maidens: Fanny Wollstonecraft and the Shelley Circle*. Berkeley, CA: Counterpoint, 2007.

Sensibility: An Introduction. New York: Methuen, 1986.

Tomkins, Silvan. *Shame and Its Sisters*. Ed. Eve Kosofsky Sedgwick and Adam Frank. Durham, NC: Duke University Press, 1995.

Trotter, Thomas. *A View of the Nervous Temperament* (1807). New York: Arno, 1976.

Ulmer, William. *Shelleyan Eros: The Rhetoric of Love*. Princeton, NJ: Princeton University Press, 1990.

Vogl, Joseph. *Kalkül und Leidenschaft: Poetik des ökonomischen Menschen*. Zurich: Diaphanes, 2008.

Wang, Orrin. *Romantic Sobriety: Sensation, Revolution, Commodification, History*. Baltimore, MD: Johns Hopkins University Press, 2011.

Weber, Alan. *Nineteenth-Century Science: A Selection of Original Texts*. Peterborough, ON: Broadview, 2000.

Weil, Simone. *Waiting for God*, trans. Emma Graufard and intro. Leslie Fielder. New York: Harper Collins, 2009.

Weisman, Karen A. *Imageless Truths: Shelley's Poetic Fictions*. Philadelphia: University of Pennsylvania Press, 1994.

Wesley, John. *The Poetical Works of John and Charles Wesley*. Ed. George Osborn. London: Wesleyan-Methodist Conference Office, 1868.

Williamson, Philip. "State Prayers, Fasts and Thanksgivings: Public Worship in Britain, 1830–97." *Past & Present* 200, no. 1 (2008): 121–74.

Wills, Garry. *Inventing America: Jefferson's Declaration of Independence*. Garden City, NY: Doubleday, 1978.

Winnicott, D. W. "Communicating and Not Communicating Leading to a Study of Certain Opposites." In *The Maturational Processes and the Facilitating Environment: Studies in the Theory of Emotional Development*. Madison, CT: International Universities Press, 1965, 179–92.

Playing and Reality. London and New York: Tavistock, 1971.

Psychoanalytical Explorations. Ed. Clare Winnicott, Ray Shepherd, and Madeleine Davis. Cambridge, MA: Harvard University Press, 1989.

Wolfson, Susan. *Formal Charges: The Shaping of Poetry in British Romanticism.* Stanford, CA: Stanford University Press, 1997.

Wordsworth, William. *The Major Works.* Ed. Stephen Gill. Oxford: Oxford University Press, 1984.

Poetical Works. Ed. Thomas Hutchinson. Rev. edn. Ernest de Selincourt. Oxford: Oxford University Press, 1981.

The Prelude: 1799, 1805, 1850. Ed. Jonathan Wordsworth, M. H. Abrams, and Stephen Gill. New York: Norton, 1979.

The Prelude, 1798–1799. Ed. Stephen Parrish. Ithaca, NY: Cornell University Press, 1977.

The Ruined Cottage and The Pedlar. Ed. James Butler. Ithaca, NY: Cornell University Press, 1979.

Shorter Poems, 1807–1820. Ed. Carl H. Ketchum. Ithaca, NY: Cornell University Press, 1989.

Yeazell, Ruth Bernard. *Art of the Everyday: Dutch Painting and the Realist Novel.* Princeton, NJ: Princeton University Press, 2008.

York, Susan Liddell, Countess of Hardwicke. *Extracts of Letters from Maria, Marchioness of Normandy, et al.* Ed. Georgiana Liddell Bloomfield, Baroness. Hertfordshire: Simpson & Co., 1892.

Youngquist, Paul. "De Quincey's Crazy Body." *PMLA* 114 (1999): 346–58.

Yousef, Nancy. *Isolated Cases: The Anxieties of Autonomy in Enlightenment Philosophy and Romantic Literature.* Ithaca, NY: Cornell University Press, 2004.

Žižek, Slavoj. *How to Read Lacan.* New York: Norton, 2007.

In Defence of Lost Causes. New York: Verso, 2008.

Looking Awry: An Introduction to Jacques Lacan through Popular Culture. Cambridge, MA: MIT Press, 1991.

The Plague of Fantasies. London: Verso, 1997.

Zunshine, Lisa. "Why Jane Austen Was Different, and Why We May Need Cognitive Science to See It." *Style* 41, no. 3 (2007): 275–99.

Index

Page numbers in *italics* refer to illustrations.

Lightning Source UK Ltd.
Milton Keynes UK
UKHW01f0836300918
329669UK00021B/591/P